AF711529

Marx, Engels, and Marxisms

Series Editors
Marcello Musto, York University, Toronto, ON, Canada
Terrell Carver, University of Bristol, Bristol, UK

The Marx renaissance is underway on a global scale. Wherever the critique of capitalism re-emerges, there is an intellectual and political demand for new, critical engagements with Marxism. The peer-reviewed series Marx, Engels and Marxisms (edited by Marcello Musto & Terrell Carver, with Babak Amini, Francesca Antonini, Paula Rauhala & Kohei Saito as Assistant Editors) publishes monographs, edited volumes, critical editions, reprints of old texts, as well as translations of books already published in other languages. Our volumes come from a wide range of political perspectives, subject matters, academic disciplines and geographical areas, producing an eclectic and informative collection that appeals to a diverse and international audience. Our main areas of focus include: the oeuvre of Marx and Engels, Marxist authors and traditions of the 19th and 20th centuries, labour and social movements, Marxist analyses of contemporary issues, and reception of Marxism in the world.

More information about this series at
https://link.springer.com/bookseries/14812

Stephen Maher

Corporate Capitalism and the Integral State

General Electric and a Century of American Power

palgrave
macmillan

Stephen Maher
Political Science
Ontario Tech University
Oshawa, ON, Canada

ISSN 2524-7123 ISSN 2524-7131 (electronic)
Marx, Engels, and Marxisms
ISBN 978-3-030-83771-6 ISBN 978-3-030-83772-3 (eBook)
https://doi.org/10.1007/978-3-030-83772-3

© The Editor(s) (if applicable) and The Author(s), under exclusive license to Springer Nature Switzerland AG 2022
This work is subject to copyright. All rights are solely and exclusively licensed by the Publisher, whether the whole or part of the material is concerned, specifically the rights of translation, reprinting, reuse of illustrations, recitation, broadcasting, reproduction on microfilms or in any other physical way, and transmission or information storage and retrieval, electronic adaptation, computer software, or by similar or dissimilar methodology now known or hereafter developed.
The use of general descriptive names, registered names, trademarks, service marks, etc. in this publication does not imply, even in the absence of a specific statement, that such names are exempt from the relevant protective laws and regulations and therefore free for general use.
The publisher, the authors and the editors are safe to assume that the advice and information in this book are believed to be true and accurate at the date of publication. Neither the publisher nor the authors or the editors give a warranty, expressed or implied, with respect to the material contained herein or for any errors or omissions that may have been made. The publisher remains neutral with regard to jurisdictional claims in published maps and institutional affiliations.

Cover illustration: Stocktrek/Stockbyte/Getty Images

This Palgrave Macmillan imprint is published by the registered company Springer Nature Switzerland AG
The registered company address is: Gewerbestrasse 11, 6330 Cham, Switzerland

For Safa

Series Foreword

Titles Published

1. Terrell Carver & Daniel Blank, *A Political History of the Editions of Marx and Engels's "German Ideology" Manuscripts*, 2014.
2. Terrell Carver & Daniel Blank, *Marx and Engels's "German Ideology" Manuscripts: Presentation and Analysis of the "Feuerbach chapter,"* 2014.
3. Alfonso Maurizio Iacono, *The History and Theory of Fetishism*, 2015.
4. Paresh Chattopadhyay, *Marx's Associated Mode of Production: A Critique of Marxism*, 2016.
5. Domenico Losurdo, *Class Struggle: A Political and Philosophical History*, 2016.
6. Frederick Harry Pitts, *Critiquing Capitalism Today: New Ways to Read Marx*, 2017.
7. Ranabir Samaddar, *Karl Marx and the Postcolonial Age*, 2017.
8. George Comninel, *Alienation and Emancipation in the Work of Karl Marx*, 2018.
9. Jean-Numa Ducange & Razmig Keucheyan (Eds.), *The End of the Democratic State: Nicos Poulantzas, a Marxism for the 21st Century*, 2018.
10. Robert X. Ware, *Marx on Emancipation and Socialist Goals: Retrieving Marx for the Future*, 2018.

11. Xavier LaFrance & Charles Post (Eds.), *Case Studies in the Origins of Capitalism*, 2018.
12. John Gregson, *Marxism, Ethics, and Politics: The Work of Alasdair MacIntyre*, 2018.
13. Vladimir Puzone & Luis Felipe Miguel (Eds.), *The Brazilian Left in the 21st Century: Conflict and Conciliation in Peripheral Capitalism*, 2019.
14. James Muldoon & Gaard Kets (Eds.), *The German Revolution and Political Theory*, 2019.
15. Michael Brie, *Rediscovering Lenin: Dialectics of Revolution and Metaphysics of Domination*, 2019.
16. August H. Nimtz, *Marxism versus Liberalism: Comparative Real-Time Political Analysis*, 2019.
17. Gustavo Moura de Cavalcanti Mello and Mauricio de Souza Sabadini (Eds.), *Financial Speculation and Fictitious Profits: A Marxist Analysis*, 2019.
18. Shaibal Gupta, Marcello Musto & Babak Amini (Eds), *Karl Marx's Life, Ideas, and Influences: A Critical Examination on the Bicentenary*, 2019.
19. Igor Shoikhedbrod, *Revisiting Marx's Critique of Liberalism: Rethinking Justice, Legality, and Rights*, 2019.
20. Juan Pablo Rodríguez, *Resisting Neoliberal Capitalism in Chile: The Possibility of Social Critique*, 2019.
21. Kaan Kangal, *Friedrich Engels and the Dialectics of Nature*, 2020.
22. Victor Wallis, *Socialist Practice: Histories and Theories*, 2020.
23. Alfonso Maurizio Iacono, *The Bourgeois and the Savage: A Marxian Critique of the Image of the Isolated Individual in Defoe, Turgot and Smith*, 2020.
24. Terrell Carver, *Engels before Marx*, 2020.
25. Jean-Numa Ducange, *Jules Guesde: The Birth of Socialism and Marxism in France*, 2020.
26. Antonio Oliva, Ivan Novara & Angel Oliva (Eds.), *Marx and Contemporary Critical Theory: The Philosophy of Real Abstraction*, 2020.
27. Francesco Biagi, *Henri Lefebvre's Critical Theory of Space*, 2020.
28. Stefano Petrucciani, *The Ideas of Karl Marx: A Critical Introduction*, 2020.
29. Terrell Carver, *The Life and Thought of Friedrich Engels, 30thAnniversary Edition*, 2020.

30. Giuseppe Vacca, *Alternative Modernities: Antonio Gramsci's Twentieth Century*, 2020.
31. Kevin B. Anderson, Kieran Durkin & Heather Brown (Eds.), *Raya Dunayevskaya's Intersectional Marxism: Race, Gender, and the Dialectics of Liberation*, 2020.
32. Marco Di Maggio, *The Rise and Fall of Communist Parties in France and Italy*, 2020.
33. Ryuji Sasaki, *A New Introduction to Karl Marx: New Materialism, Critique of Political Economy, and the Concept of Metabolism*, 2020.
34. Kohei Saito (Ed.), *Reexamining Engels's Legacy in the 21st Century*, 2021.
35. Paresh Chattopadhyay, *Socialism in Marx's Capital: Towards a Dealienated World*, 2021.
36. Marcello Musto, *Karl Marx's Writings on Alienation*, 2021.
37. Michael Brie & Jörn Schütrumpf, *Rosa Luxemburg: A Revolutionary Marxist at the Limits of Marxism*, 2021.
38. Stefano Petrucciani, *Theodor W. Adorno's Philosophy, Society, and Aesthetics*, 2021.
39. Miguel Vedda, *Siegfried Kracauer, or, The Allegories of Improvisation: Critical Studies*, 2021.
40. Ronaldo Munck, *Rethinking Development: Marxist Perspectives*, 2021.
41. Jean-Numa Ducange & Elisa Marcobelli (Eds.), *Selected Writings of Jean Jaurès: On Socialism, Pacifism and Marxism*, 2021.
42. Elisa Marcobelli, *Internationalism Toward Diplomatic Crisis: The Second International and French, German and Italian Socialists*, 2021.
43. James Steinhoff, *Automation and Autonomy: Labour, Capital and Machines in the Artificial Intelligence Industry*, 2021.
44. Juan Dal Maso, *Hegemony and Class Struggle: Trotsky, Gramsci and Marxism*, 2021.

Titles Forthcoming

Gianfranco Ragona & Monica Quirico, *Frontier Socialism: Self-organisation and Anti-capitalism*

Vesa Oittinen, *Marx's Russian Moment*

Kolja Lindner, *Marx, Marxism and the Question of Eurocentrism*

Adriana Petra, *Intellectuals and Communist Culture: Itineraries, Problems and Debates in Post-war Argentina*
George C. Comninel, *The Feudal Foundations of Modern Europe*
Spencer A. Leonard, *Marx, the India Question, and the Crisis of Cosmopolitanism*
Joe Collins, *Applying Marx's Capital to the 21st century*
Levy del Aguila Marchena, *Communism, Political Power and Personal Freedom in Marx*
Jeong Seongjin, *Korean Capitalism in the 21st Century: Marxist Analysis and Alternatives*
Marcello Mustè, *Marxism and Philosophy of Praxis: An Italian Perspective from Labriola to Gramsci*
Satoshi Matsui, *Normative Theories of Liberalism and Socialism: Marxist Analysis of Values*
Shannon Brincat, *Dialectical Dialogues in Contemporary World Politics: A Meeting of Traditions in Global Comparative Philosophy*
Francesca Antonini, *Reassessing Marx's Eighteenth Brumaire: Dictatorship, State, and Revolution*
Thomas Kemple, *Capital after Classical Sociology: The Faustian Lives of Social Theory*
Tsuyoshi Yuki, *Socialism, Markets and the Critique of Money: The Theory of "Labour Note"*
V Geetha, *Bhimrao Ramji Ambedkar and the Question of Socialism in India*
Xavier Vigna, *A Political History of Factories in France: The Workers' Insubordination of 1968*
Attila Melegh, *Anti-Migrant Populism in Eastern Europe and Hungary: A Marxist Analysis*
Marie-Cecile Bouju, *A Political History of the Publishing Houses of the French Communist Party*
Gustavo Moura de Cavalcanti Mello & Henrique Pereira Braga (Eds.), *Wealth and Poverty in Contemporary Brazilian Capitalism*
Peter McMylor, Graeme Kirkpatrick & Simin Fadaee (Eds.), *Marxism, Religion, and Emancipatory Politics*
Mauro Buccheri, *Radical Humanism for the Left: The Quest for Meaning in Late Capitalism*
Rémy Herrera, *Confronting Mainstream Economics to Overcome Capitalism*
Tamás Krausz, Eszter Bartha (Eds.), *Socialist Experiences in Eastern Europe: A Hungarian Perspective*
Martin Cortés, *Marxism, Time and Politics: On the Autonomy of the Political*
João Antonio de Paula, Huga da Gama Cerqueira, Eduardo da Motta e Albuquer & Leonardo de Deus, *Marxian Economics for the 21st Century: Revaluating Marx's Critique of Political Economy*
Zhi Li, *The Concept of the Individual in the Thought of Karl Marx*
Lelio Demichelis, *Marx, Alienation and Techno-capitalism*

Dong-Min Rieu, *A Mathematical Approach to Marxian Value Theory: Time, Money, and Labor Productivity*
Salvatore Prinzi, *Representation, Expression, and Institution: The Philosophy of Merleau-Ponty and Castoriadis*
Agon Hamza, *Slavoj Žižek and the Reconstruction of Marxism*
Kei Ehara (Ed.), *Japanese Discourse on the Marxian Theory of Finance*
Éric Aunoble, *French Views on the Russian Revolution*
Paolo Favilli, *Historiography and Marxism: Innovations in Mid-Century Italy*
Terrell Carver, Smail Rapic (Eds.), *Friedrich Engels for the 21st Century: Perspectives and Problems*
Patrizia Dogliani, *A Political History of the International Union of Socialist Youth*
Alexandros Chrysis, *The Marx of Communism: Setting Limits in the Realm of Communism*
Paul Raekstad, *Karl Marx's Realist Critique of Capitalism: Freedom, Alienation, and Socialism*
Alexis Cukier, *Democratic Work: Radical Democracy and the Future of Labour*
Christoph Henning, *Theories of Alienation: From Rousseau to the Present*
Daniel Egan, *Capitalism, War, and Revolution: A Marxist Analysis*
Genevieve Ritchie, Sara Carpenter & Shahrzad Mojab (Eds.), *Marxism and Migration*
Emanuela Conversano, *Capital from Afar: Anthropology and Critique of Political Economy in the Late Marx*
Marcello Musto, *Rethinking Alternatives with Marx*
Vincenzo Mele, *City and Modernity in George Simmel and Walter Benjamin: Fragments of Metropolis*
David Norman Smith, *Self-Emancipation: Marx's Unfinished Theory of the Working Class*
José Ricardo Villanueva Lira, *Marxism and the Origins of International Relations*
Bertel Nygaard, *Marxism, Labor Movements, and Historiography*
Fabio Perocco (Ed.), *Racism in and for the Welfare State*
Marcos Del Roio, *Gramsci and the Emancipation of the Subaltern Classes*
Marcelo Badaró, *The Working Class from Marx to Our Times*
Tomonaga Tairako, *A New Perspective on Marx's Philosophy and Political Economy*

Foreword

A solid case study can be illustrative of larger issues. But being only a singular example, it clearly carries limited weight in broader debates. Arguing that General Electric had a particular relationship to the American state is suggestive but does not *prove* this was emblematic of corporate America more generally. Where, on the other hand, the challenge is to confront an "obvious" general truth like the general predominance of free markets in building America, the burden of proof shifts, a single significant *counter-example* can matter a great deal. In this case, by documenting the dependence of GE on state-driven railroads, nuclear power, military research and development, and of course the state-sustained financial system, Maher provides an important political reminder of how central the US state was to the development of the American economy.

But Maher's concern goes far beyond justifying that GE is in fact representative of general trends (though what he does argue in this regard is convincing) or that the GE story is an effective antidote to pervasive untruths. He has far bigger fish to fry. What his excavation of GE brings us is a corporate history that merits attention in its own right—as the best of case studies can do—but primarily as a base for a brilliant, empirically grounded *theoretical* treatise. That ambition leads Maher to stretch the GE case into a series of valuable empirical and theoretical insights ranging across political economy, finance, the theory of the corporation, the understanding of the American state, and the corporate-state nexus.

Among his targets, Maher looks to expose those who see the development of capitalism as a move from competition to monopoly, missing what workers know from experience: the development of capitalism's concentrated administrative, productive and financial resources has radically *intensified* competition. This inclination to populist explanations (competition good, monopoly bad) extends to presumptions about finance (finance parasitic, manufacturing value-creating). It ignores the functionality of finance *within* capitalism, not only in allocating capital and supporting old and new ventures but also in the very structure of manufacturing corporations. He's equally critical of the sharp polarization in the understanding of state, pitting structuralists who overplay structural determinants and so remove agency, against those declaring the full autonomy of states, thereby setting aside the actual limits of concrete institutions.

Some may react negatively to Maher's rejection of "sharper" positions, his nuance allegedly replacing clarity. But Maher can hardly be accused of rejecting the categorical. The state, he directly asserts, is a capitalist state. Neoliberalism is a class project. Finance has added to capitalism's dynamism, not undermined it. But—and this is a repeated investigative emphasis on Maher's part—if we are to put such categorical positions forward so as to give them substantive, not just abstract meaning, we can't avoid confronting all the complex, contingent (and yes, nuanced) questions and politics that follow.

The strength of Maher's work is rooted in his methodological insistence on the development of an "Institutional Marxism" very much inspired by—like his mentor, Leo Panitch—taking the "historical" in historical materialism seriously. History is the real terrain of both study and action and speaks to the contradictions, uncertainties, and especially the socially constructed institutions that are integral to the mechanisms of political economy, the state and their mutual interaction.

The prime application of Institutional Marxism that Maher presents here revolves around an understanding of the "integral state." Having insisted that the state has a degree of autonomy in standing up to business lobbying pressures, Maher probes further, asking how the state then wins business to some accommodation to the state's orientation. His answer isn't based on any theoretical prediction; the answer comes from careful research on what *actually* happened historically. It is only in that light that Maher constructs a credible theoretical framework for grasping the corporate-state interaction.

The dialectic involved can be briefly summarized as follows: Capital, because of its fragmentation, seeks cross-corporate institutions to express common interests to the state. The state not only responds to those concerns in the context of the state's more universal and longer-term concerns but also comes to actually encourage the development of such business lobbying structures. Having a negotiating partner as opposed to a myriad of conflicting demands makes reaching some consensus more manageable and the lobbying organizations can also serve to legitimate the outcomes to their affiliates. All this also affects developments inside the state, which though centralized, has its own divisions and layers of hierarchic agencies and departments.

What this book ultimately offers is the impressive achievement of a GE "case study" being transformed into a methodological "case example" on how to do serious research. That it will be controversial speaks to the current relevancy of its empirical and theoretical conclusions.

Toronto, Canada
April 2021

Sam Gindin

Acknowledgments

It is one of the great conceits of academia, and indeed liberal society, that knowledge is the product of an individual brain rather than embedded within communities and social processes. As such, though this project is the result of years of intensive work on my own part, it also reflects the guidance, care, and intellectual engagement of those who supported and taught me. First and foremost, I must thank my excellent doctoral committee, with each of whom I formed the deepest of intellectual and personal bonds. My supervisor, mentor, and friend Leo Panitch constantly pushed me to think harder and more critically, to question comforting dogmas, to never take the easy way out, and to be the best scholar I could be. Above all, his unwavering commitment to the truth, even when it involves overturning deeply held beliefs, and to soberly facing reality rather than taking solace in wishful thinking or empty posturing, showed me what it means to be a socially engaged intellectual. Sadly, Leo passed away in December 2020, making this book the product of the final Ph.D. dissertation he supervised.

I have been similarly fortunate to know Sam Gindin and to benefit from his personal warmth, patience, and wisdom. In addition to his friendship and constant support over the years, the countless hours we spent talking about the ideas contained in this project were essential to shaping the final product. Sam's generosity of spirit and ability to remain optimistic about the capacities of ordinary people without getting lost in illusions has been a continuous source of inspiration for me. Finally, the influence of Greg

Albo on this project has been as great as that of anyone. The intensity of his commitment to ideas and his unique ability to combine a truly stunning scope of knowledge with charitableness toward a wide range of views and perspectives—seeking to build bridges within critical scholarship rather than walls—is a remarkable example of open-mindedness and open-heartedness.

The origin of this work is research I conducted while completing my Ph.D. in the York University Department of Political Science in Toronto, Ontario, a unique community of engaged and critical scholars. Countless conversations over the years with innumerable scholars have shaped my thinking and contributed to this project—not least through the memorable graduate seminars I attended in my years in the department. I would like to recognize in particular the contributions that Elizabeth Dauphinee, Dennis Pilon, Hannes Lacher, David McNally, Stephen and Judy Hellman, and Sabah Alnasseri have made to my intellectual and personal development during my years at York. I would also like to recognize the staff who did so much to make the York Political Science Department a welcoming and supportive place to complete my doctoral research, including Marlene Quesenberry, Judy Matadial, Angie Schwartz, Carolyn Cross, and Jlenya Sarra-DeMeo.

My fellow graduate students, and the friendships I formed while completing this project, were equally essential to my growth and development. Indeed, some of the friends I have made at York and in Toronto now become family. I would especially like to mention Jordan House, Sarah Ovens, Bob Froese, Janaya Letkeman, Paul Gray, Adam Hilton, Tom Cheney, and Robin Chang, from whose intellectual engagement, knowledge, and support I have gained more than could possibly be recounted here. I would also like to thank the old friends who, though we are now far apart geographically, I carry with me all the time, and who are always there to offer encouragement as we proceed together on our separate journeys—especially Samuel Shepson, Michael Rodriguez, and Chisda Magid.

This project would not have been possible without the support and encouragement of my family. My father and stepmother, Steve and Sheryl, my mother Colleen, my brothers David, Michael, and Chuck, and my sister Catherine all deserve a special thanks for helping me along the way.

I owe the biggest debt to my incredible partner, Safa Ali. The sacrifices she has made, and the love she has offered me, were essential to my ability to complete this dissertation. The life of a graduate student involves a great many hardships and difficulties, and Safa supported my decision to devote myself to this project with kindness and patience. Without her there to celebrate, the victories would not have been so sweet, and without her consolation, the setbacks would have been so much harder. As a small token of thanks for her endless support, I dedicate this book to her.

Praise for *Corporate Capitalism and the Integral State*

"This book offers a ground-breaking interpretation of class, corporate and state power, through the all-important case study of GE and the US state. It shows why and how the class of capitalists can overcome their political fragmentation *only* through the actions of the (capitalist) state. The 'integral state'—or the institutional networks through which corporate power is transformed into class power—is examined in detail in this extraordinarily valuable work of scholarship. This book will transform the field of political economy."

—Alfredo Saad-Filho, *Professor of Political Economy and International Development and Chair of International Development, King's College London, UK*

"Stephen Maher's impressive book draws on political economy, critical state theory, and historical institutionalism to elaborate a theory of the integral state. Maher argues that business associations do not merely express the pre-existing interests of members but are mechanisms used by the state to organize the political power of the capitalist class in pursuing the state's own objectives. It is a major contribution to critical state theory and American political development."

—Clyde W. Barrow, *Professor and Chair of Political Science, University of Texas Rio Grande Valley, USA*

"Stephen Maher's excavation of GE provides a corporate history valuable in its own right, but along the way also delivers an ambitious theoretical treatise offering insights ranging across political economy, finance, the theory of the corporation, the understanding of the American state and the corporate-state nexus."

—Sam Gindin, *Former Research Director of the Canadian Auto Workers*

Contents

Abbreviations

AC	Alternating Current
ACI	Advisory Commission on Information, US Information Agency
AEA	Atomic Energy Act of 1954
AEC	Atomic Energy Commission
AFL	American Federation of Labor
BAC	Business Advisory Council, Department of Commerce
BC	Business Council
BCIU	Business Council for International Understanding
BPC	Board of Patent Control
BR	Business Roundtable
CCS	Corporate Consulting Services, General Electric Company
CEA	Council of Economic Advisors, Executive Office of the President
CED	Committee for Economic Development
CEO	Chief Executive Officer
CFO	Chief Financial Officer
CFR	Council on Foreign Relations
CIA	Central Intelligence Agency
CIEP	Council on International Economic Policy, White House
CIO	Congress of Industrial Organizations
CISC	Construction Industry Stabilization Committee
CMP	Committee for the Marshall Plan to Aid European Recovery
COLC	Cost of Living Council
COWPS	Council on Wage and Price Stability
CUAIR	Construction Users Anti-Inflation Roundtable
DC	Direct Current
DECs	District Export Councils, President's Export Council

DNC	Democratic National Committee
DOC	Department of Commerce
DOD	Department of Defense
DOJ	Department of Justice
EBASCO	Electric Bond and Share Company
EEC	European Economic Community
EEIC-NY	Edison Illuminating Company of New York
EELC	Edison Electric Light Company
EGE	Edison General Electric Company
EITA	Electric Industry Trades Alliance
EPA	Environmental Protection Agency
EPG	Economic Policy Group ("the Quadriad")
ERP	European Reconstruction Program ("the Marshall Plan")
ESA	Economic Stabilization Act of 1970
ESOP	Employee Share Ownership Plan
FDI	Foreign Direct Investment
FTC	Federal Trade Commission
GATT	General Agreement on Tariffs and Trade
GBC	General Business Advisory Committee, US Information Agency
GDP	Gross Domestic Product
GE	General Electric Company
GECC	General Electric Credit Company
GOP	"Grand Old Party" (the Republican Party)
IBEW	International Brotherhood of Electrical Workers
IBRD	International Bank for Reconstruction and Development
ICC	International Chamber of Commerce
IGE	International General Electric Company
IIAC-TN	Inter-Association Advisory Council for Trade Negotiations
IMF	International Monetary Fund
ITO	International Trade Organization
IUE	International Union of Electrical, Radio and Machine Workers
JCAE	United States Congress Joint Commission on Atomic Energy
LLSC	Labor Law Study Committee
MNC	Multinational Corporation
MTN	Multilateral Trade Negotiations
NAM	National Association of Manufacturers
NASA	National Aeronautics and Space Administration
NATO	North Atlantic Treaty Organization
NDAC	National Defense Advisory Commission, Executive Office of the President
NELC	National Electric Lamp Company
NEMA	National Electrical Manufacturers Association
NIRA	National Industrial Recovery Act of 1933

NLRB	National Labor Relations Board
NOAA	National Oceanographic and Aviation Administration
NRA	National Recovery Administration
NSC	National Security Council, White House
NTB	Non-Tariff Barrier
ODM	Office of Defense Mobilization
OMB	Office of Management and Budget, White House
OPEC	Organization of the Petroleum Exporting Countries
OPM	Office of Production Management
PAC	Political Advisory Committee, Department of Commerce
PEC	President's Export Council, Department of Commerce
R&D	Research and Development
R&P	Research and Policy Committee, Committee for Economic Development
SBU	Strategic Business Unit, General Electric Company
SEC	Securities and Exchange Commission
STR	Office of the Special Representative for Trade Negotiations / US Trade Representative
TACs	Technical Advisory Committees, Department of Commerce
TVA	Tennessee Valley Authority
UE	United Electrical Workers
UI	Utah International Company
USCC	United States Chamber of Commerce
USG	United States Government
USIA	United States Information Agency
WFC	War Finance Corporation, Council of National Defense
WIB	War Industries Board, Council of National Defense
WLB	War Labor Board, Council of National Defense
WOC	Without Compensation Employees ("Dollar-a-Year Men")
WPB	War Production Board

CHAPTER 1

The Making of the Integral State

The capitalist state and corporation are the major institutional foundations of political order in contemporary society. In the United States, these twin leviathans emerged together at the end of the nineteenth century and have since coevolved through a dialectical historical process as two heads of a single system of class power. This duality is rooted in the framework of capitalist property relations: that ownership and control of capital remains in private hands means that institutional constraints must be built into the structure of state power itself, delineating the boundary between *public* and *private* authority. The capitalist corporation that is today the primary means for organizing private control over large-scale productive property is itself a creation of the law. The firm is predicated on the separation of ownership (shareholders) and control (managers) of productive assets, and the relationship between these functions, established within a structure of 'corporate governance,' is substantially determined by state regulation. While it shifts along with the development and evolution of the corporation and financial system, the state plays a fundamental role in shaping these economic relations. At the same time, the exercise of political power, and the organization of class hegemony, has required continuous coordination between political and economic institutions. As a fundamental basis of class power, the corporation is not merely an economic, but also a political institution. The economic power it confers

© The Author(s), under exclusive license to Springer Nature Switzerland AG 2022

S. Maher, *Corporate Capitalism and the Integral State*, Marx, Engels, and Marxisms,
https://doi.org/10.1007/978-3-030-83772-3_1

upon owners and managers constitutes the material foundation upon which the state organizes the political hegemony of the capitalist class.

Although Marxists have studied the preeminent role of the corporation in contemporary capitalism, all too often it is seen as part of "the economy," and separable from an analysis of the state. Similarly, while Marxists have long understood that a primary function of the state is to organize a capitalist class internally riven by competitive pressures, they have devoted surprisingly scant attention to historical analysis of the specific institutional mechanisms and political forms through which it does so. This can leave the impression that this simply happens "automatically."

This inattentiveness to the manifold concrete linkages between state and corporate institutions has made it difficult for Marxist scholars to understand the function of "civil society" business associations, which are both "private" and "political," in reproducing the structure of power in contemporary capitalist democracies. On the other hand, even the most critical among the more empirically grounded institutionalist accounts have tended to reduce corporate political power in liberal democracies to a matter of "lobbying," based on a pluralist conception of state power. In this view, the state is *fundamentally* neutral, even if specific well-organized and well-funded interest groups tend to pull it in the direction of capitalist interests. Class power, from this perspective, is largely an effect of business political agency on the terrain of "civil society"—which is defined as existing outside of the state, and even seen as a limit or constraint on state power. We are thus faced with a field of civil society "interest groups"—labor unions, environmental groups, business associations, and others—all vying to influence a *passive* state. "Capturing" or influencing state power is a function of organizational coherence, ideological power, and command of resources. However, the state is in no way "neutral," but is always tainted by the "original sin" of being a *capitalist* state. All of its apparatuses and functions are defined by their immersion within capitalist society, and ultimately serve to reproduce the hegemony of the capitalist class. Furthermore, this pluralist framing conceals the fact that the capitalist state is a dynamic, substantive, and creative social force in its own right.

This book will argue that, far from simply passively responding to interest group pressures, the state is a key agent in forming and reproducing business associations. When contextualized within the specific, historically evolved linkages that traverse and interpenetrate the state bureaucracy, the legislature, the industrial policy apparatus, and corporate institutions, it becomes clear that such civil society organizations do not merely *express* the pre-existing interests of their constituents, but are also mechanisms through which the state organizes the political power of the capitalist class—forming what I refer to as an *integral state*. As opposed to merely advocating for a fixed agenda, business associations facilitate the systematic collaboration between state and corporate institutions that is essential for developing and implementing policy. They also serve as crucial forums for building consensus and support among business for political initiatives. Meanwhile, the capacity of state agencies to mobilize business impacts their position within the hierarchy of state apparatuses. Business associations therefore do not merely influence the state on behalf of corporations; rather, they are also important mechanisms through which the state organizes otherwise fragmented and competitive corporate power into a coherent political bloc, which then reacts back upon the state. Moreover, the networks and relays that constitute the integral state are in no way reducible to business associations, but are fundamental to the organizational structure of both state and corporation. These deeper linkages constitute the basis for the formation of business associations that are integral to the reproduction of state power and class hegemony.

At the core of this project is an attempt to better understand the ways in which state and corporate institutions, particularly in the United States, come to constitute specific forms of class hegemony. It is argued that the development of American capitalism can broadly be broken down into four periods: entrepreneurialism, finance capital, managerialism, and neoliberalism. These "hegemonic regimes" are by no means conceived as discrete, static, functionally integrated, closed systems; rather, this is a rough, general periodization of a continuously evolving historical process. The passage from one phase to another does not consist of a sharp "break," but rather illustrates the systematic operation of integral state mechanisms in changing circumstances. By examining the active role of the state in articulating class power *across* these different periods, I seek to highlight the *continuity* of this function—though the structures of the state complex and of corporate power, as well as the particular business associations affiliated with the integral state, are by no means static over time. In fact, periods of development are differentiated on the basis of distinct patterns of state and corporate organization. Similarly, new policy paradigms and institutional forms are not the result of the imposition of fixed ideological programs by either corporate lobbyists or state officials. Instead, these emerge from the crucible of class struggle, under the relentless discipline of capitalist competition, and amidst tremendous uncertainty.

It would be difficult to find a more compelling case to illustrate the deep relationship between state and corporate power in the United States, and the role of the state in organizing class power, than that of the General Electric Company. One of the first major corporations, GE later became a cornerstone of the integral state—occupying a central point of contact between state and corporate power and playing a pivotal and systematic role in organizing capitalist class power. An important foundation for this was GE's integration within the state industrial policy system, which was fundamental to its basic reproduction. Yet what makes it an especially good case for demonstrating the structure of the integral state is the wide scope of the state-corporate linkages in which it is embedded, and the variety of forms these have taken across time. Formed in the finance capital period of bank control, GE went on to become the paradigmatic managerial corporation—and was at the heart of efforts to build corporate support for the New Deal. From New Deal "corporate liberalism," GE ended its first hundred years as the foremost exponent of "shareholder value" and neoliberal restructuring. Few cases could better illustrate the dynamism of American capitalism as it expanded and restructured over its first century.

Neo-Pluralism and the Capitalist State

The field of political science was for decades caught up in the false opposition between the dominant "pluralist" and the critical "elite theory" paradigms. Pluralists like Robert Dahl and Charles Lindblom argued that political power in capitalist democracies was dispersed among a fragmented array of diverse groups.[1] The sheer range of different interests advanced by these groups meant that it was impossible for any one of

[1] Robert Dahl, *Who Governs?: Democracy and Power in an American City* (New Haven: Yale University Press, 1961); Robert Dahl, *Pluralist Democracy in the United States: Conflict and Consent* (Chicago: Rand McNally, 1967); Robert Dahl, *Polyarchy: Participation and Opposition* (New Haven: Yale University Press, 1971); Robert Dahl and Charles Lindblom, *Politics, Economics, and Welfare: Planning and Politico-Economic Systems* (Chicago: University of Chicago Press, 1976).

them to consistently dominate the "political system." Though pluralists accepted that political and economic power was not evenly distributed, they held that most people had at least some power, and moreover that liberal democratic institutions generally prevent ownership of money from conferring excessive control to any one group. Thus the structure of power in such systems is "polyarchic," dispersed among myriad elite-led groups with little coherence between them. Moreover, conflict over specific policy areas cuts across boundaries of class and status. This fractious nature of power allows any group sufficiently motivated about a specific issue to exert at least some influence on policy. The function of the "political system," then, was to organize coalitions among competing interest groups, of which specific policies are the outcomes.

"Elite theorists" like C. Wright Mills, Floyd Hunter, and E. E. Schattschneider advanced a different view, according to which a coherent, singular elite had emerged through the institutional coalescence of giant corporations, the state bureaucracy, and the military establishment.[2] Despite divisions within the elite, the overriding unity of interest within this group, coupled with its command over resources, allowed it to monopolize control over civil society to an extent that rendered notions of "pluralist democracy" mostly illusory. In the debate between the pluralists and elite theorists, the question of whether or not there is a ruling class in the advanced capitalist democracies was thus dissolved into a question of the degree of elite cohesion. While pluralists emphasized conflict between divergent elite groupings and cross-class political conflicts, elite theorists sought to empirically demonstrate the existence of a unitary elite with coherent political interests, even if this was merely a general consensus around the need to preserve elite control. Just as pluralists emphasized the general acceptance of democratic "rules of the game," elite theorists advanced a version of the "false consciousness" thesis, whereby the masses were unknowingly inculcated with values and ideas imposed through the structures of elite domination.

[2] C. Wright Mills, *The Power Elite* (Oxford, UK: Oxford University Press, 1956); Floyd Hunter, *Community Power Structure: A Study of Decision Makers* (Chapel Hill, NC: University of North Carolina Press, 1953); E. E Schattschneider, *The Semisovereign People: A Realist's View of Democracy in America* (New York: Holt, Rinehart and Winston, 1960).

In many respects, this debate—which preoccupied political science for decades—was a false opposition.[3] What both of these arguments were missing, as Ralph Miliband and Nicos Poulantzas argued in the 1970s, was a theory of the capitalist state.[4] Consequently, though elite theorists certainly made important scholarly contributions in identifying institutional trends in the organization of power and the limits of capitalist democracy, they yielded far too much to their opponents in staking the existence of a ruling class on the presence of a basic political unity among an "elite" achieved *prior to* and *outside of* an encounter with the state. Lacking a theory of the capitalist state—or a conception of the state's systematic role in capital accumulation—both pluralists and elite theorists dissolved the state into an ontologically neutral "political system," which constituted a space for the interaction between variously organized social groups. The difference between pluralism and elite theory can thus be resolved into an empirical question over the extent to which a singular and cohesive "elite" monolithically dominated this *essentially* pluralistic terrain, or whether there were sufficient divisions within the elite to justify seeing this as a polyarchic structure. Either way, elite domination—that is, class power—was understood as a function of its superior resource mobilization and organizational cohesion, which allowed it to trump other, competing forces within the overall pluralist pastiche. Thus elite theory failed to fundamentally challenge the social ontology advanced by the pluralists.

Miliband and Poulantzas sought to critique the pluralist school and to transcend "orthodox Marxist" theories which saw the state as merely epiphenomenal of an economic "base."[5] They argued that political power in capitalist societies does not emerge upon the neutral terrain of a passive and generic "political system," but is actively organized by a capitalist

[3] Mark Mizruchi, *The Structure of Corporate Political Action: Interfirm Relations and Their Consequences* (Cambridge, MA: Harvard University Press, 1992). See especially the Introduction.

[4] Ralph Miliband, *The State in Capitalist Society* (London, UK: Merlin Press, 2009 [1969]); *Marxism and Politics* (London, UK: Merlin Press, 2004 [1977]); *Class Power & State Power* (London, UK: Verso, 1983); Nicos Poulantzas, *Political Power and Social Classes* (London, UK: New Left Books, 1978 [1968]); *Classes in Contemporary Capitalism* (London, UK: New Left Books, 1975 [1973]); *State, Power, Socialism* (London, UK: New Left Books, 1978).

[5] Leo Panitch, "The Impoverishment of State Theory," *Socialism and Democracy* 13, no. 2 (July 1, 1999): 19–35.

state that is necessary to bring about the political cohesion of the capitalist class. Class rule in advanced capitalist democracies does not take the form of political domination by an elite with a self-understood unity of interests, even at the most abstract level of "preserving the overall system of elite dominance." Indeed, this view attributes far too much prescience and political awareness to individual capitalists. Rather, the capitalist class "rules" by virtue of its ownership of society's productive assets, even as this class is itself "ruled" by the imperative to produce profits. Individual capitalists are motivated not by broad class-wide concerns, but rather with the needs of individual firms or industries. As a result, the capitalist class is incapable of directly ruling itself, and requires a "relatively autonomous" state to formulate and implement the general, long-term interests of the system as a whole. State theory thus turns elite theory inside-out: rather than an elite that politically organizes itself to impose its will on a neutral "political system," state theorists see a state which organizes the political hegemony of a capitalist class internally riven by competitive pressures, and which would otherwise be unable to form a stable political unity.[6]

The critique of pluralism mounted by Miliband and Poulantzas was utterly devastating to that paradigm. Over the 1970s, pluralists, especially Charles Lindblom, made huge concessions on the importance of the unequal distribution of wealth and power, to the extent that one could plausibly claim that pluralism had become indistinguishable from elite theory.[7] But the Marxist critique—that understanding power in contemporary capitalism meant situating the state as a distinct social relation of force that reproduces the overall system of capitalist class rule—also undermined elite theory. Substantial conflict within the "elite" certainly imbued capitalist democracies with a "polyarchic" character, as the pluralists emphasized. Yet the Marxists held that the state is not merely the

[6] Leo Panitch, "Elites, Classes and Power in Canada," in Peter H. Russell, Francois Rocher, Debra Thompson, and Linda A. White (eds.), *Essential Readings in Canadian Government and Politics* (Toronto, Canada: Emond Montgomery Publishing, 2010), 453–59.

[7] Charles Lindblom, *Politics and Markets: The World's Political Economic Systems* (New York: Basic Books, 1977); Charles Lindblom, "Another State of Mind," *The American Political Science Review* 76, no. 1 (1982): 9–21; Robert Dahl, *Dilemmas of Pluralist Democracy: Autonomy Vs. Control* (New Haven: Yale University Press, 1982); John F. Manley, "Neo-Pluralism: A Class Analysis of Pluralism I and Pluralism II," *The American Political Science Review* 77, no. 2 (1983): 368–83; Mizruchi, *The Structure of Corporate Political Action*.

passive object of competing interests, even capitalist interests. Rather, it is an active and dynamic social force in its own right. The state's concrete functions and apparatuses are determined by their immersion within capitalist social relations, which ultimately reproduce the hegemony of the capitalist class. The field of action of state apparatuses is defined by the structural limits and crisis points of capital accumulation; their overarching purpose is to make capitalism "work." A relatively unified business grouping with a coherent political program may indeed be able to trump other agendas, but the absence of such unity does not imply the absence of class rule.

It became clear that constructing a credible mainstream paradigm meant incorporating those elements of Miliband's and Poulantzas' critique that were sufficiently palatable, which was precisely the task undertaken by Theda Skocpol and her "new institutionalist" confederates.[8] In the mid-1980s, Skocpol sought to "bring the state back in" as an object of political science analysis—but without its class foundations. The state, she argued, was *fully* autonomous from the broader social structures in which it was embedded. However, as Paul Cammack showed, her critique of the Marxist state theory literature was contradictory: in general statements and broad conclusions, she tended to suggest a *strong* view of the state autonomy thesis (i.e. that the state *always* acts autonomously from "society"), while at other points and in concrete case studies she adopted a *weak* version (i.e. that the state *can* act autonomously in specific circumstances). In the end, it is the weak version of the autonomy thesis that is supported by the case studies she reviews, which can be understood as empirical support for the concept of relative autonomy. Thus, far from challenging Marxist theory, Skocpol inadvertently confirmed the validity of that analysis.[9]

Recently, scholars such as Jacob Hacker and Paul Pierson, Kim Phillips-Fein, Julian Zelizer, and Benjamin Waterhouse, have retreated from Skocpol's strongest statements of state autonomy and acknowledged the

[8] Theda Skocpol, *Bringing the State Back In* (New York and Cambridge: Cambridge University Press, 1985); Peter Hall and Rosemary Taylor, "Political Science and the Three New Institutionalisms," *Political Studies* 44, no. 5 (December 1996): 936–57; Ellen Immergut, "The Theoretical Core of the New Institutionalism," *Politics & Society* 26, no. 1 (March 1998): 5–34; Kathleen Thelen, "Historical Institutionalism in Comparative Politics," *Annual Review of Political Science* 2 (June 1999): 369–404.

[9] Paul Cammack, "Bringing the State Back In?," *British Journal of Political Science* 19, no. 2 (1989): 261–90.

important role played by other actors in shaping policy, especially corporate lobby groups.[10] "Rather than assuming the power of business in politics," Phillips-Fein and Zelizer write, they "seek to show that the role of business in politics and the political effects of economic elites need to be understood as historically specific and distinct." The result "is an image of American politics that is more complex and contested than it often has been thought to be."[11]

In effect, these so-called New Political Historians have resuscitated the pluralist paradigm by introducing the concept of "civil society" to moderate Skocpol's strong theorization of state autonomy. From this perspective, the state is an essentially neutral force that is externally related to a polyarchic field of competing interests—civil society—which oscillates between relatively pluralist and elite-dominated configurations. That is, on the pluralist terrain of "civil society" something resembling a coherent "elite" interest has occasionally self-organized: as Phillips-Fein and Zelizer put it, they aim to "show business actors *organizing themselves* to affect government in myriad different ways."[12] The main task is then to narrate the specific conditions in which this "elite" grouping emerges, and to identify its impact on the state via "lobbying" and other forms of influence peddling. This serves as the basis for Philips-Fein's analysis of the rollback of the New Deal, which she sees as the outcome of a business "crusade."[13] Despite the emphasis on historical contingency and empirical investigation, that the structure of political power basically conforms to the pluralist model is not questioned or examined.

[10] Jacob Hacker and Paul Pierson, *Winner-Take-All Politics: How Washington Made the Rich Richer–and Turned Its Back on the Middle Class* (Simon and Schuster, 2010); Kim Phillips-Fein and Julian E. Zelizer, *What's Good for Business: Business and American Politics Since World War II* (Oxford: Oxford University Press, 2012); Kim Phillips-Fein, *Invisible Hands: The Businessmen's Crusade Against the New Deal* (New York: W. W. Norton, 2009); Benjamin Waterhouse, *Lobbying America: The Politics of Business from Nixon to NAFTA* (Princeton: Princeton University Press, 2013); See also: Mark Mizruchi, *The Fracturing of the American Corporate Elite* (Cambridge: Harvard University Press, 2013); Lee Drutman, *The Business of America Is Lobbying: How Corporations Became Politicized and Politics Became More Corporate* (Oxford, UK: Oxford University Press, 2015).

[11] Phillips-Fein and Zelizer, *What's Good for Business*, 3–4.

[12] Phillips-Fein and Zelizer, 1, emphasis added.

[13] Phillips-Fein, *Invisible Hands*.

Hacker and Pierson's widely influential *Winner-Take-All Politics* faces similar problems.[14] Despite repeatedly emphasizing the contingent role of "organizations" in shaping politics, Hacker and Pierson do not examine the processes whereby specific business organizations were formed, nor their relationships to particular state agencies or firms. In fact, they reduce the rise of "oligarchy" in the United States entirely to an effect of business political agency. Fed up with expanding state regulations and the political power of labor, in the 1970s business became more active in funding campaigns and forming interest groups, thereby "capturing" state power. Like Phillips-Fein and Zelizer, they see civil society as a "pendulum" that swings between pluralist and elitist configurations. In the current oligarchic configuration, it has become "stuck" as a result of a positive feedback loop. The increased "political capacity" of business that resulted from its greater activism led to the enactment of a regulatory and tax regime that increased the concentration of wealth and power at the top, which in turn further reinforced business' political capacity. But the source of business mobilization *itself* is not interrogated or explained, nor is the possibility of an active role for the state considered. The processes through which the policies pushed by business associations were developed are treated as self-evident, while the extent to which the restructuring of state and corporate power was *functional* to restoring capital accumulation and ending the crisis of the 1970s is overlooked.

In seeing "business organization" as the independent cause of state policy, these neo-pluralist accounts obscure the mutual interaction between the two—in particular, the way in which causality moves in the opposite direction, from "state" to "civil society." Indeed, that influence flows democratically from "civil society" to the state is assumed at the outset, and then again "discovered" at the conclusion. This deprives state agencies of any real part in forming policy, despite the fact that this is ostensibly their entire purpose. These writers explicitly claim to seek to highlight the contingency of business influence on politics. Yet they ignore the actual historical and institutional interactions between business and the state that lead to the contingent emergence of the business organizations they purport to examine.[15]

[14] Hacker and Pierson, *Winner-Take-All Politics: How Washington Made the Rich Richer–and Turned Its Back on the Middle Class* (Simon and Schuster, 2010).

[15] Waterhouse, *Lobbying America* is something of an exception in this regard, in that it does discuss in detail the formation of the Business Roundtable and the restructuring

Despite the apparent empirical rigor of these works, and their general suspicion of sweeping theoretical explanations, the questions they pose (and don't pose), the methods they deploy, and the conclusions they reach are substantially determined by unexamined assumptions. Rather than demonstrating the contingency of business influence on politics, it seems there is an ideological bias to affirm that the political power of business *is in fact contingent*. Ignoring the deeper roots of capitalist class power allows this to be reduced to an effect of business "lobbying." Rather than a structure whose basic function is to reproduce the overall domination of a capitalist class, the state is a (corrupted) pluralist democracy.

It is revealing that none of these accounts make use of the archives of executive branch departments. This is in keeping with the neo-pluralist failure to examine the interaction of particular state agencies and corporate institutions in the formation of business associations. As a result, they have overlooked the ways in which business associations have served as a means to *develop* policy through a cooperative relationship with state officials, and then to build business coalitions in support of such initiatives, rather than for business to simply *impose* a fixed, pre-given ideological agenda. State archives hold a wealth of data and insights on the role of state agencies in the formation of interest groups, and the way state officials and corporate executives have collaborated within such venues to mobilize business. Indeed, these venues have often been important precisely to overcome the deep *reluctance* of business to undertake political projects favored by state officials and corporate allies. Nowhere is this clearer than in the case of "free trade," as we shall see. Similarly, the attack on the New Deal state that emerged over the crisis decade of the 1970s was substantially formulated *within* the state itself. Nor is this function of the state in mobilizing business relegated to periods of crisis. Rather, it is a systematic necessity for the exercise of political authority in the context of relative autonomy. As the state does not manage the economy directly, it

of other business associations from the 1970s through the 1980s. Nevertheless, the basic pluralist assumptions are upheld throughout the work, despite the fact that the evidence Waterhouse himself presents, to say nothing of that which he ignores, tends to contradict these assumptions. For a detailed review of this text, see: Stephen Maher, "The Capitalist State, Corporate Political Mobilization, and the Origins of Neoliberalism," *Critical Sociology*, August 4, 2016.

has to construct mechanisms to integrate corporate power within political processes.

The theory of the integral state posits a far more complex conception of political agency, historical causality, and state power, in which business associations are functionally integrated within wider, evolving institutional relationships. Within this schema, the state bureaucracy is the most active force driving the formulation of policy, and developing institutions for integrating corporate power within the policymaking process and mobilizing business support. Of course, the theory of the integral state *does not* deny the occurrence or impact of corporate lobbying. On the contrary, it seeks to highlight how business associations have functioned as mechanisms through which the state organizes a class-wide consensus around policy. Specific firms and sectors continue to advocate for their own interests—striving to minimize the costs they will face of particular policies or regulations, and to advocate for advantages of all kinds. What is important for understanding the integral state is the way that business associations come to organize and articulate the perspective not of a given firm or sector, but that of *the capitalist class as a whole*. It is these civil society associations that function as part of "the totality of forces organized by the State and by private individuals to safeguard the political and economic domination of the ruling classes."[16]

The theory of the integral state places the phenomenon of "lobbying" within a different theoretical context—specifically, a richer ontology of state and corporate power—which reframes the phenomenon's scope and meaning. In this way, the theory of the integral state does not challenge the significance of corporate lobbying, but offers *a better explanation for it*. Rather than focus on isolated practices of lobbying, this theorization draws attention to the integration of corporate power with the *structure* of the state institutional complex. For example, as we shall see in the case of the Business Roundtable and the President's Export Council, by the 1970s business associations were integral to the specific institutional reproduction of Congress itself. This included greater power over the electoral process with the emergence of the Political Action Committee, and the expansion and superior organization of political advocacy and financial contributions. More significant than determining

[16] Antonio Gramsci, *Selections from the Prison Notebooks of Antonio Gramsci*, ed. Quintin Hoare and Geoffrey Nowell-Smith (New York: International Publishers, 1973), 221.

the outcome of elections, however, was the systematic integration of corporate power with the policymaking and legislative process *between* elections. Business associations served as mechanisms for building and expressing consensus between executive branch agencies, corporate elites, and key Congressional leaders and committees. Furthermore, state and corporate personnel conducted research and analyses, published reports, articulated perspectives, and supplied other inputs that constituted an important foundation for legislation. These activities were in no way exceptional, contingent, or spontaneous, but were integral to the reproduction of the specific, historically existing structure of the legislative process.

Capitalist class hegemony is reproduced through the totality of the state's apparatuses, not only the legislature. These institutions, and the relationships within the state complex, are fluid and evolving. Corporate power and business associations impact upon relations of power within the state administrative apparatus, as well as between the executive branch and Congress. Indeed, the formation of the integral state was intrinsic to the development of the state bureaucracy. As this bureaucracy became more extensive, and corporate capitalism more complex, power was increasingly concentrated in the executive branch. While executive branch agencies are legally prohibited from lobbying Congress, corporations are not. This encouraged state agencies to deepen their integration with corporate institutions in order to coordinate lobbying efforts for their own agendas. Since laws passed by Congress are binding on the executive branch, they serve to shape the structure of power within the bureaucracy. Therefore, the concentration of political authority *within* the bureaucracy, the allocation of power *across* executive branch agencies, and the role of corporations in mediating the relationship between the executive branch and Congress were mutually interdependent institutional dynamics. Positive feedback loops developed as patterns of state and corporate institutional development mutually reinforced one another. By the 1970s, this had facilitated the emergence of a highly autonomous state economic and trade apparatus—which secured the continuation of free trade amidst rising protectionist pressures, alongside an agenda of low taxes, deregulation, and fiscal constraints with the support of a new political consensus between financial and non-financial corporations.

A central aspect of the theoretical approach deployed here is the proposition that *the capitalist state is an active force with its own internal dynamism.* Just as it does not passively respond to interest group or lobbying pressures, neither is the state epiphenomenal of deeper economic laws—though it is fundamentally defined by its embeddedness within the structure of capital accumulation. Nor, for that matter, does the state merely establish the underlying conditions necessary to stabilize accumulation, or simply step in to deal with crises and "market failures." On the contrary, the state is a *systematically creative* agency. The state's active organization of the political hegemony of the capitalist class is not necessary to "correct" an otherwise equilibrated system, but is a creative force that is a basic condition of the social structure.

This conception differs from the "elite pluralist" view, as well as the Marxist conception articulated by Poulantzas whereby the state organizes an "unstable equilibrium of compromise" between the fixed, objective interests of distinct fractions of capital.[17] Though elite pluralism grants that elite interests have a greater impact on state policy than others, it relegates the state to an essentially passive role. Similarly, the Marxist view usually sees the state as merely balancing the fixed interests of external fractions of capital. To be sure, organizing a class consensus involves substantial conflict over policy, and the mediation of different interests. The important point is that integral state venues are not merely spaces where the pre-existing, objective interests of business leaders are *expressed* and *reconciled*, but rather where such people are *educated* and their political interests *formed*. Integral state organizing is a process that creates political interests, and organizes capital in support of them, while negotiating trade-offs and costs among firms and sectors.

The Theory of the Integral State

The concept of the integral state finds its origins in the work of Antonio Gramsci, which he summarized in the formulation "political society + civil society." In western capitalist societies, Gramsci held, the state rules not just through legislation and coercion, but also "complexes of associations in civil society."[18] Gramsci's state theory—contradictory and incomplete though it is—provides important foundations for the study of "civil society" organizations. His approach differs significantly from the concern with outlining the structure and functions of the capitalist state

[17] Poulantzas, *State, Power, Socialism*, 221.

[18] Gramsci, *Selections from the Prison Notebooks*, 243.

that occupied the more complete state theory that emerged during the 1970s, in the pioneering work of Miliband and Poulantzas. Rather than focusing on the specific class linkages and functions of the state apparatus in capital accumulation, Gramsci examined the modalities of state power as it operates through wider networks to construct a hegemonic order. This framework clarifies how institutions that are not necessarily "within" the formal state apparatus, and may even possess considerable autonomy from it, are nevertheless vectors for the operation of state power in securing political order. Such institutions form a "hegemonic apparatus" that supports the legitimacy of the state and that of the broader social system in which it is embedded. This also creates new contradictions, new openings for undermining political authority, and new possibilities for "hegemonic crisis."[19]

Gramsci's distinction between state institutions in the narrow sense and a wider integral state indicates the diffuse quality of state power. The boundary between "civil society" and "state" is thus conceived as blurred and porous: state power extends over, incorporates, and permeates institutions situated within the formally external realm of civil society. Though Gramsci suggests that this wider integral state includes "economic organizations," he does not specifically theorize the relationship between capitalist corporations and either "civil society" or "political society."[20] Nevertheless, it is clear that corporate power, as the primary form of capitalist economic organization, is central to the processes whereby the state organizes class hegemony—and therefore to the integral state. Contact between the formal state complex and civil society takes the form of specific relationships between different firms and business associations and particular state agencies. The place of individual agencies *within* the hierarchy of state apparatuses reflects these "external" linkages with civil society as well as internal state dynamics. It is here that we reach the limits of Gramsci's state theory: he did not devote much attention to the *institutional* ramifications of his notion of the integral state. This includes, notably, the relationship between corporations and state structures, and the specific roles of corporations in the organization and expression of class power.

[19] Gramsci, *Selections from the Prison Notebooks*, 210–76.

[20] Gramsci, *Selections from the Prison Notebooks*, 221.

Subsequent state theorists have not devoted sufficient attention to studying the specific mechanisms whereby states actually organize capitalist class power. This entails substantial conflict, not least as a result of the tension between the economic interests of particular capitalists and the general interest of the capitalist class articulated by the state. Corporations play a uniquely dominant role within civil society, as pluralists themselves would increasingly concede over the 1970s. However, this is not just a consequence of their superior command over resources with which to form civil society organizations. Rather, it is a result of the fact that corporations organize ownership and control of the means of production. It is the institutional structure of the corporation, and not the organizational power of civil society organizations, that is the basis of the social power of the capitalist class. Partly for this reason, as Claus Offe and Helmut Wiesenthal demonstrated in a classic article, it is easier for capitalists to form business associations than for workers to organize trade unions.[21] Offe and Wiesenthal argued that not all "interest groups" are created equal. Rather, there are "two logics of collective action": one that applies to unions, and another to business associations. While unions *form* collective interests as the basis for their power, business associations are organized by their constituents to merely *express* pre-existing, self-evident, measurable economic interests. Business associations are simply aggregations of individual firms pursuing profit maximization—achieving which Offe and Wiesenthal assumed was identical with the systemic interests of capitalism.

Offe and Wiesenthal severely downplay the contradictions involved in politically organizing business. Similarly, the institutional mechanisms through which the state organizes capital are nowhere to be found in their account—nor is the possibility that the state plays an active role in forming business associations even considered. Leo Panitch's analysis of "corporatism," on the other hand, foregrounded the role of the state in organizing tripartite structures consisting of both capital and labor amidst the crisis of the 1970s. Panitch defined this "in terms of an actual linkage between the state and functional interest groups (especially trade unions and business associations) constituted by institutionalized representation in economic policy making," as well as "an element of state

[21] Claus Offe and Helmut Wiesenthal, "Two Logics of Collective Action: Theoretical Notes on Social Class and Organizational Form," *Political Power and Social Theory* 1 (January 1, 1980): 67–115.

control over the groups whereby their autonomy is limited and they are employed as agencies of mobilization or administration of state policy."[22] Clearly, corporatism is a specific historical and institutional phenomenon, and Panitch was primarily concerned with analyzing the impact of these arrangements on trade unions. Nevertheless, aspects of Panitch's theorization—especially the active role of the state in organizing *capital* by establishing linkages with business associations—are relevant for understanding the functioning of the integral state more generally. As the historical evidence presented in this study suggests, though the relationship may not always have been as close or as formal as these corporatist structures, the active organization of business associations, and their integration with state administration, was a continuous characteristic of the American state.

What needs to be explored here is the contested and difficult relationship between class power, the interests of particular capitalists and corporations, and the organizing force of the state. How is corporate *economic* power organized into class *political* hegemony? Answering this question requires not just distinguishing between the organizational logics of business associations and labor unions, but *differentiating among business associations themselves*. While corporations certainly create business associations to advocate for their particular interests, the state also constructs the political hegemony of the capitalist class by forming and mobilizing business associations. These therefore cannot be seen as simply being self-organized by their constituents for the purposes of expressing pre-existing interests. On the contrary, they are embedded within and reproduced through the activity of the state for the purpose of *forming* the class-wide interests of capital, and *mobilizing a constituency that is not already self-mobilizing* around this. The "capitalist class" does not possess political unity or cohesion *as a class* outside of the contradictory state processes through which this is articulated and established. Nor is this simply a matter of "adding up" prior, self-evident economic interests. In fact, the relationship between the competing economic interests of particular firms and the political unity of the capitalist class is a deeply *contradictory* one. This is precisely why the capitalist class cannot rule itself, but requires a relatively autonomous state to organize its hegemony and govern not at the *behest* of capital, but on its *behalf*. To facilitate

[22] Leo Panitch, "Trade Unions and the Capitalist State," *New Left Review* 1, no. 125 (February 1981): 24.

this, the state establishes venues for *educating* capitalists and *creating* a class-wide perspective. Consequently, the political conflicts *within* business associations are often more revealing of the operation of the integral state than those *between* these organizations and the "outside world."

This project contributes to filling these gaps by examining the formation and development of the integral state over the first century of American corporate capitalism. As we shall see, this was not merely a matter of securing abstract "consent" for state rule, but rather constructing specific structures for articulating class power. The emergence of the capitalist corporation, in which the state played a decisive and constant role, also placed extensive new demands on the state. In addition to securing political support from capital, even simply crafting sound policy demanded the formation of apparatuses for organizing corporate power and integrating it within the policymaking process. The state agencies undertaking these functions were nodes within a wider integral state, creating venues for building class consensus and coordinating policy development and implementation. These venues were sometimes "private," as with the national Chamber of Commerce, created in the early twentieth century to support the new Department of Commerce, and sometimes "public," as with the Business Advisory Council set up by Roosevelt to institutionalize corporate support for the New Deal. Over time, corporate institutions developed a range of operations oriented toward reproducing integral state networks—engaging with state officials full-time and participating in "private" yet "political" venues with representatives from other firms. The development of corporate institutions thus created new conditions for the integration of "political society" and "civil society" in relation to the state's task of organizing the capitalist class.

As I define the term, the *integral state* is comprised of the institutional networks and relays that mediate and integrate state and corporate power. This consists of all the mechanisms through which corporate power is organized into class power and articulated to a hegemonic apparatus, including those on the terrain of civil society. These linkages span the coming and going of elected governments, forming durable networks that are deeply rooted in the administrative structure of the state as well as corporate institutions. The specific structure of this matrix at a given point in time constitutes a particular "type" of capitalist hegemony, or "phase" of capitalist development. Forms of hegemony, or phases of capitalist development, are therefore identifiable by reference to particular organizational forms of state and corporate power. The linkages that constitute the integral state permeate and interconnect: (1) the state bureaucracy; (2) the legislature; (3) the industrial policy apparatus; (4) civil society business associations; and (5) corporate governance structures. The historical formation and political functions of business associations must be understood as taking place within this institutional matrix, not as having spontaneously emerged upon the terrain of civil society to exogenously influence a passive state.

The "autonomy" or "independence" of each of these organizational forms can in no way be taken for granted. Similarly, it cannot be assumed that business associations constitute the primary institutional "point of contact" between state and corporation. The political functions of particular firms are the product of specific, path dependent relationships with state agencies. State agencies work with firms to craft policy, build capitalist class consensus, and coordinate the implementation of policy through civil society organizations on the basis of manifold linkages that are logically and historically prior to those constituted through any individual business association. Such integral state forms may be restructured or fall away over time, but the deeper linkages between the state and particular firms that organize and reproduce these venues may persist—and indeed continue to constitute the basis for the formation of new associations. Just as those firms that are the most economically central also possess the greatest capacity for integral state organizing, so too is this centrality reinforced by virtue of these political functions. This active role of the state, and its deep relationships with corporations, is crucial for understanding how specific business associations can come to articulate not merely one sectoral or industry perspective, but rather a class-wide view—as we shall see in the cases of the Business Roundtable, the Committee for Economic Development, the Business Advisory Council, and others.

These linkages between state and corporate power are not merely external to the state, but are integral to the specific reproduction of power within the state institutional complex: they play a role in shaping the *hierarchy of state apparatuses*.[23] This hierarchy establishes what Poulantzas called the "structural selectivity" of the state, which serves to "advance

[23] Poulantzas, *State, Power, Socialism*, 132–34; Clyde W. Barrow, *Critical Theories of the State: Marxist, Neomarxist, Postmarxist* (Madison, WI: University of Wisconsin Press, 1993), 30; Panitch, "The Impoverishment of State Theory."

(or obstruct) particular fractional or class interests."[24] To this one should also add the institutional interests of state agencies themselves. Far from passively channeling external interests, state agencies mobilize power resources, including business, in service of their objectives. The internal unity of the capitalist state is shaped on the basis of integral state linkages whereby corporate power becomes a factor in the *internal world* of the state, both mediating the relationship between apparatuses and constituting a force within distinct apparatuses. The state is thus not a unitary "subject," but a contradictory institutional complex constituted through relationships among its component agencies as well as external linkages to "civil society." Consequently, state policy and structure are the outcome of contested and often conflictual institutional interests, which emerge in relation to the broader dynamics of capital accumulation. While those agencies that are more prominent in the hierarchy of state apparatuses play the largest role in making policy, the complexities of structural selectivity mean that these institutions also operate within a wider field of (integral) state power they do not fully determine.

This points to the fact that the corporation must be conceived not just as an economic institution, but also a political one. This is not the same as seeing corporations as economic institutions that undertake political activity by forming business associations to advocate for their interests on the terrain of civil society. Rather, it points to the fact that through their specific linkages with particular state institutions, corporations come to mediate relations within the state complex itself, while participating in the organization of *class* power. This complicates the concept of relative autonomy, which is predicated on the institutional separation or demarcation of the political and economic "spheres." While preserving the notion of relative autonomy as a necessary institutional expression of the public nature of the state and the private control of capital, the theory of the integral state leads us to consider the complex interpenetration of economic and political forms of power as these are organized within a coherent, if contradictory, hegemonic institutional complex. Nor is the formation of the integral state ontologically or historically "secondary" to the formation of formal state institutions and private corporations themselves. On the contrary, these relays and structures are fundamental to both state and corporate institutions. The emergence of an integral

[24] Bob Jessop, "The Strategic Selectivity of the State: Reflections on a Theme of Poulantzas," *Journal of the Hellenic Diaspora* 25, no. 1–2 (1999): 1–37.

state was an essential factor in the historical development of the state bureaucracy, the reproduction of its internal structure, and its changing relationship with Congress, just as it was foundational to the evolution of corporate organization.

The active state hypothesis is especially important in relation to industrial policy.[25] Indeed, if integral state theory is an attempt to think *beyond* the "military industrial complex," it nevertheless incorporates this dimension of state-corporate integration as well. The theory of the integral state posits that the networks that interpenetrate the firm and bind it to other institutional structures must be seen as integral to its internal reproduction. Similarly, innovation cannot be seen as simply endogenous to a particular firm. Rather, this is the product of a broader institutional structure centered on the state: the *industrial policy system*. The role of industrial policy in the development of the most dynamic companies and sectors has been profound—to the extent that it is impossible to understand the structure, strategy, or market position of these firms in abstraction from this. This system, which took shape during and after World War II, consists of an institutional complex linking state agencies (especially the Department of Defense), National Laboratories, universities, and high-tech engineering-based firms. The result has not been the stifling or overcoming of capitalist competition through the implementation of a "command economy" structure centered on the Pentagon, as some classical theories of the "military-industrial complex" held.[26] On the contrary, the formation and reproduction of this system can only be understood in relation to the competitive dynamics of capitalism. The effect has been the formation of a grouping of nationally based firms centered on the state, among which GE was a key leader for a half-century.

The proposition that the state is a systematically creative force has further implications in relation to industrial policy. That state activity cannot be understood as merely correcting "market failure" means that, in organizing industrial policy, it is supporting activities that are directed

[25] See: Mariana Mazzucato, *The Entrepreneurial State: Debunking Public Vs. Private Sector Myths* (New York: Anthem Press, 2013); Fred L. Block and Matthew R. Keller, *State of Innovation: The U.S. Government's Role in Technology Development* (Oxfordshire, UK: Routledge, 2015).

[26] Seymour Melman, *Pentagon Capitalism: The Political Economy of War* (New York: McGraw-Hill, 1971).

towards ends which business itself did not determine. These practices, and the structures that support them, would not exist without state activity. Industrial policy is not therefore merely a matter of state *subsidization* of existing corporate Research & Development projects and objectives. Rather, the state *directly commissions* R&D projects to fulfill political objectives that are relatively autonomous from competitive market logics. Through these means, the state is a central force in actively determining the nature of the research and investment that corporations embedded within this system undertake. Much of the R&D that generates technologies later commodified by corporations is initially undertaken outside the structure of the firm altogether. Furthermore, to the occasional frustration of corporate executives and state officials, industrial policy in the United States has not been directly aimed at supporting long-term corporate competitiveness, nor helping to improve the bottom lines of particular firms. Rather, the industrial policy system is a means for the state to use the production processes and institutional capacities of corporations to achieve political objectives established within the state complex—especially the development of military technologies. As private corporations are the only entities capable of manufacturing the products and infrastructures necessary to reproduce its global power, the state *depends* upon coordinating with them in this respect.

The complex interconnection of state and corporate power indicated by the concept of the integral state is also crucial for understanding the *internationalization of the state*. Beginning especially in the 1990s, an extensive literature on "globalization" emerged, which is substantially premised on a false dichotomy between the power of multinational corporations and the power of states. According to this view, multinational corporations have usurped the power of states through the development of cross-border "networks" of trade and investment.[27] Similarly, some have suggested that the decline of state power has been accompanied by the emergence of a "transnational capitalist class" (TCC) whose power is articulated through multilateral institutions that exist over and above states,[28] while others take this further to suggest that this amounts to the

[27] Manuel Castells, *The Rise of the Network Society: The Information Age: Economy, Society, and Culture*, Second Edition (Hoboken, NJ: Wiley, 2009); Justin Rosenberg, "Globalization Theory: A Post-Mortem," *International Politics* 42 (2005).

[28] William K. Carroll, *The Making of a Transnational Capitalist Class: Corporate Power in the 21st Century* (London, UK: Zed Books, 2010); William K. Carroll, "Whither

formation of a "transnational state."[29] The TCC is seen as formulating its own general political interests, without state coordination, and then instrumentalizing states to serve its ends. Thus, competitive pressures are apparently giving way to global solidarity and mutual cooperation among this global elite. This is presented as a primary cause of the generalization of neoliberalism across national contexts—in other words, as the result of the *will* of a more or less coherent and organized TCC that acts upon states from without. Nevertheless, some TCC theorists have pointed out that the more concrete the analysis becomes, the more difficult it is to pinpoint the "transnational capitalist class," or to distinguish it from nationally embedded bourgeoisies with international interests.[30]

The concept of the internationalization of the state offers a more substantial basis for understanding processes of global political and economic integration.[31] As Poulantzas argued, this cannot "be reduced to a simple contradiction of a mechanistic kind between the base (internationalization of production) and a superstructural cover (nation state) which no longer corresponds to it." Nor can the state be seen as "a mere tool or instrument of the dominant classes to be manipulated at will, so that every step that capital took towards internationalization would automatically induce a parallel 'supernationalization' of states."[32] This concept was developed further by Robert Cox in his ground-breaking work *Production, Power, and World Order*. Cox's study is distinguished by its attentiveness to "distinctive *forms of state*" and "the characteristics of their historic blocs, i.e., the configuration of social forces upon which state

the Transnational Capitalist Class?," in *Socialist Register 2014: Registering Class*, ed. Leo Panitch, Greg Albo, and Vivek Chibber (London, UK: Merlin Press, 2013); William I. Robinson, *A Theory of Global Capitalism: Production, Class, and State in a Transnational World* (Baltimore: Johns Hopkins University Press, 2004); Leslie Sklair, *Sociology of the Global System* (London: Harvester, 1991); Leslie Sklair, *Capitalism and Development* (London: Routledge, 1994).

[29] Robinson, *A Theory of Global Capitalism*.

[30] Carroll, "Whither the Transnational Capitalist Class?"

[31] Nicos Poulantzas, *Classes in Contemporary Capitalism*; Robert Cox, *Production, Power, and World Order: Social Forces in the Making of History* (New York: Columbia University Press, 1987); Leo Panitch, "Globalisation and the State," in *Socialist Register 1994: Between Globalism and Nationalism*, ed. Ralph Miliband and Leo Panitch (London: Merlin Press, 1993); Leo Panitch and Sam Gindin, *The Making of Global Capitalism: The Political Economy Of American Empire* (London: Verso, 2012).

[32] Poulantzas, *Classes in Contemporary Capitalism*, 78.

power ultimately rests." It is the configuration of these forces, Cox held, that "defines in practice the limits or parameters of state purposes, and the modus operandi of state action."[33] Furthermore, Cox argued that the new international order established after World War II under American leadership entailed restructuring the institutions of nation states themselves. It was this reorganization of states to support and reproduce a new transnational regime that primarily constituted the internationalization of the state.

As Panitch pointed out, there remained an unresolved antinomy in Cox's work. While this theorization, which remains rooted in the materiality of state power and the domestic bloc that supports it, is far more substantial than that of TCC theorists, Cox maintained an "outside-in" conception of the internationalization of the state. According to this view, over time, causality increasingly flowed through the state from consensus reached at international forums to the domestic social formation. Cox even went so far as to depict the state as the "transmission belt" of this international consensus, "adjusting" its internal political relations accordingly.[34] But the mechanisms whereby the state was disciplined to do this remained unclear, shifting "back and forth from social force to ideology to institution to system." Conversely, Panitch emphasized that "the role of each state is still determined by struggles among social forces always located within each social formation."[35] As this book bears out, the internationalization of the state was indeed marked by the empowerment of those apparatuses most involved in reproducing the transnational system, and the restructuring or further marginalization of those agencies which had been oriented toward domestic concerns and constituencies, including labor and smaller nationally-oriented firms. This was achieved by organizing integral state support, especially among the largest and most internationalized corporations whose global networks also served as a crucial material foundation for the informal American empire.

[33] Cox, *Production, Power, and World Order*, 105–6.

[34] Robert Cox, "Global Perestroika," in *Socialist Register 1992: New World Order?*, ed. Ralph Miliband and Leo Panitch (London: Merlin, 1991), 30–31.

[35] Panitch, "Globalisation and the State," 73–74.

However, there was "a more general process at work."[36] As this book shows, state power was restructured not only to meet its growing international responsibilities, but also on the basis of the ability of ascendant apparatuses, especially the Treasury, to mobilize support among business and within the state. Large corporations supported the autonomy of these apparatuses in order to deflect protectionist pressures from small business, but they also backed the emphasis on low taxes and the increased constraints on fiscal policy—especially as the fiscal crisis of the state, and corporate profitability crisis, heated up over the 1970s. The defeat of labor by the 1980s was also a fundamental condition enabling this reorganization of state power. It was through these processes, whereby state power was restructured on the basis of integral state linkages and the dynamics of capital accumulation, that the internationalization of capital and the state took place.

As Panitch and Gindin showed in *The Making of Global Capitalism*, coordinating this process of global integration was the unique imperial responsibility of the American state.[37] Far from existing outside of states, states have been the key authors of globalization—including by participating in multilateral institutions embedded within the American empire. Emphasizing the continuity of the imperial functions of the American state across the phases of global capitalist development, Panitch and Gindin show historically how the postwar Bretton Woods regime (1945–1971), as well as the subsequent neoliberal order which further deepened international integration (1981-today), depended upon the formation of specific state institutional capacities.[38] This "informal empire" promoted global integration based on competitive markets and transnational flows of investment. The present study presents rich empirical evidence to

[36] Panitch, "Globalisation and the State," 72.

[37] Panitch and Gindin, *The Making of Global Capitalism.*

[38] This theorization of imperialism differs from that of the classical Marxists, who held that capitalist firms had a preference for carving out exclusive economic territory for which they seek state protections in the form of tariff walls. This generated inter-imperial rivalry between large national blocs of capital and the states that are predominantly their instrument. While this dynamic to some extent characterized the inter-war period when these accounts were written, as Panitch and Gindin show, contemporary global capitalism has evolved in the contrary direction of free trade, 'national treatment' of foreign capital and economic interpenetration. Thus the United States maintains an 'informal empire.' Nikolai Bukharin, *Imperialism and World Economy*; Vladimir Lenin, "Imperialism: The Highest Stage of Capitalism"; Rudolf Hilferding, *Finance Capital.*

support this theorization of imperialism, and also shows how the global expansion of state power was supported by integral state linkages with corporate power—whose internationalized networks of production and investment constituted a material foundation for the imperial practices undertaken by the American state. Moreover, it illustrates how the global extension of American state power was entwined with the internationalization of the integral state. As I show, state agencies actively worked with US multinational corporations to build support among businesses within other social formations for US hegemony, including through the formation of civil society organizations abroad.

Institutional Marxism

This study is situated within what has become something of a specific tradition within political economy, which takes the notion of "*making*" as the fundamental starting point of historical materialism. The contemporary origin of this lineage lies in the work of the great British historian E. P. Thompson, particularly his classic *The Making of the English Working Class*.[39] A more recent example is Leo Panitch and Sam Gindin's *The Making of Global Capitalism*, the definitive scholarly account of the political economy of the American empire.[40] By beginning from the verb "to make," these works indicate that the foundation of the analysis they contain lies in the concrete unfolding of a specific historical process that is *made*. Seeing history as "being made" implies the presence of specific creative *makers*. This means that history is something that is *created* through the projects and activities of particular people and groups, not the result of the mechanistic unfolding of "laws" or the impersonal and lifeless functioning of static closed systems. And yet, it also emphasizes that these makers themselves must *be made*, since they are integrated within this process of historical eventuation and are therefore also the product of its continuous unfolding. This dialectical interaction between subject and object, as human beings embedded within objective processes simultaneously remain creative agents, captures the essence of what historical materialism is about: the history of the relationship between human

[39] E. P. Thompson, *The Making of the English Working Class* (Penguin UK, 2002).

[40] Panitch and Gindin, *The Making of Global Capitalism*.

beings and matter. To paraphrase Marx, human beings make their own history, but within conditions that are not of their own choosing.[41]

This project may be seen as a contribution to understanding the making of the American ruling class. Just as for the working class, the ruling class is made and re-made through the creative projects undertaken by conscious human beings subject to the systematic pressures of capitalism. To understand the making of the ruling class, one must examine the forms of organized power that sustain its position: primarily, the state and the corporation. Unlike in the case of the working class, the organization of the capitalist class within a coherent, if contradictory, hegemonic structure is a basic task of the capitalist state. While facilitating the organization of large-scale productive property into corporations, the state assembles these competing firms into a power bloc through the formation and reproduction of an integral state.[42] On the other hand, much like in the case of the working class, the political organization of the capitalist class occurs through class struggle. It is within the context of the struggle to discipline the working class, and to maintain the social power and economic stability of capital, that the capitalist class is assembled as a coherent political force through the development of integral state institutions. During crisis points, such as the Great Depression and the decade of "stagflation" across the 1970s, these imperatives motivated the expansion of state capacities to plan and execute the restructuring of class hegemony, and to organize a class consensus around these efforts. Indeed, neither the New Deal nor "neoliberalism" was a coherent body of ideas imported into the state whole cloth. Rather, they took shape as strategic responses in the context of class struggle.

This role of the state in organizing the capitalist class and undertaking policy planning does not only occur during crises. Rather, the creative force of the state is a constant and foundational aspect of the system. State and corporate institutions are made by concrete, living human beings embedded within historical processes shaped profoundly by the pressures of capital accumulation. Neither the industrial policy system, nor class hegemony—nor, for that matter, state and corporate organization themselves—"just occur." Rather, these structures take shape as institutional

[41] Karl Marx, "The Eighteenth Brumaire of Louis Bonaparte," in *The Marx-Engels Reader*, ed. Robert Tucker, Second Edition, 1978, 594–617.

[42] For a detailed theorization of the concept of the "power bloc," see: Nicos Poulantzas, *Political Power and Social Classes* (NLB, 1975); Poulantzas, *State, Power, Socialism*.

forms that must be made and remade through the creative efforts of real human beings as they cope with processes outside of their control and even beyond their understanding. Yet insofar as they are embedded within the overarching structure of capitalist social relations, the formation of these institutional forms is *neither accidental nor inevitable*.[43]

Institutional Marxism (IM) brings together insights from political economy, state theory, and historical institutionalism with the philosophy of critical realism to explain how history evolves through the open-ended operation of distinctly capitalist pressures upon conscious human beings organized into specific institutional formations.[44] If classical Marxist political economy has tended to downplay the causal role of human agency and institutions in the historical development of capitalism, institutionalists have been unable to adequately define capitalism as a historically specific set of social relations with common pressures across different contexts. From this perspective, there is nothing distinctly *capitalist* about the institutional formations they examine.[45] Meanwhile, Marxist state theory has developed an extensive set of tools for grasping the functions of the capitalist state. Yet such analyses have often remained abstract, rather than focusing on the historical processes through which specific states are made and remade, and the institutional mechanisms whereby they organize class power.[46] While Regulation Theory approaches have foregrounded the role of institutions in stabilizing modes of regulation, these are often conceived as static, closed systems. For IM, institutions are not lifeless structures equilibrating static "regimes," but are continually reshaped by human agents, and are a creative and dynamic force within a fluid historical process.[47]

[43] This phrase, which so succinctly summarizes this theoretical orientation, is taken from the very first sentence of Panitch and Gindin, *The Making of Global Capitalism*.

[44] For a full discussion of Institutional Marxism, see: Stephen Maher and Scott M. Aquanno, "Conceptualizing Neoliberalism", *New Political Science* 40, no. 1 (2018): 33–50; Stephen Maher, "Escaping Structuralism's Legacy: The Renewal of Theory and History in Historical Materialism," *Science & Society* 80, no. 3 (June 14, 2016): 291–318.

[45] Hall and Taylor, "Political Science and the Three New Institutionalisms"; Immergut, "The Theoretical Core of the New Institutionalism"; Thelen, "Historical Institutionalism in Comparative Politics."

[46] Bob Jessop, *State Theory: Putting the Capitalist State in Its Place* (University Park, PA: Penn State University Press, 1990); Barrow, *Critical Theories of the State*.

[47] Michel Aglietta, *A Theory of Capitalist Regulation: The US Experience* (New York: Verso, 2000); David Kotz, "Social Structure of Accumulation Theory, Marxist Theory,

The conceptual foundations of IM are Marx's basic model of capitalism, the model of *relative autonomy* from Marxist state theory, and the model of *emergence* derived from the philosophy of Critical Realism. Critical Realism understands empirical phenomena as emerging through the operation of hierarchically ordered generative mechanisms.[48] This model of causation upholds the "directional logic" of more basic mechanisms, while simultaneously preserving the "totally novel" power within each layer. Thus higher order strata are not simply the result of the working out of mechanisms located within lower order strata. Rather, specific casual structures exist "immediately basic" to higher strata.[49] This concept of emergence implies that human societies must be understood as *open systems*. Static, functionalist models cannot explain highly complex open systems, which are characterized by immense variation in the operation of generative mechanisms. The actions of more basic causal mechanisms cannot be expected to have uniform effects, because interactions at higher levels of the causal hierarchy are increasingly contingent and variegated. This means we cannot see capital as a closed *totality* that mechanically unfolds according to a fixed "inner necessity." Instead, IM deploys Marx's understanding of capital as a heuristic for investigating emergent phenomena. It does so by positing a series of generative mechanisms that act upon many-sided, discursively constituted, and institutionally embedded human subjects in the form of experiential pressures. In this view, the historical totality is never complete: it is always in a state of *becoming*, of *being made* by really existing human beings.[50]

and System Transformation," *Review of Radical Political Economics* 49, no. 4 (December 1, 2017): 534–42.

[48] Roy Bhaskar, *A Realist Theory of Science, Second Edition* (Brighton, UK: Harvester Press, 1978); Andrew Sayer, *Realism and Social Science* (London, UK: Sage, 2000); Margaret Archer, *Realist Social Theory: The Morphogenetic Approach* (Cambridge, UK: Cambridge University Press, 1995); Sean Creaven, *Marxism and Realism: A Materialistic Application of Realism in the Social Sciences* (New York: Routledge, 2000); Andrew Collier, *Critical Realism: An Introduction to Roy Bhaskar's Philosophy* (New York: Verso, 1994).

[49] Sean Creaven, *Marxism and Realism*, 32, 41, 59.

[50] E. P. Thompson saw this as a "dialog" between "social being" and "social consciousness," while Jean Paul Sartre similarly asserted that "subjectivity is neither everything nor nothing; it represents a moment in the objective process … and this moment is perpetually eliminated only to be perpetually reborn." E. P. Thompson, *The Poverty of Theory* (New York, NY: Monthly Review Press, 2008 [1978]), 9; Jean-Paul Sartre, *Search for a Method* (New York, NY: Vintage Books, 1968), 33.

This understanding of Marx's model of capital as a heuristic to guide concrete interrogation of emergent phenomena provides the ontological and epistemological foundations for a robust comparative method. Such a method approaches the study of capitalism *in general* through the examination of the *specific* contexts in which it has developed. The objective is to identify the operation of the "transfactual" causal mechanisms (i.e., existing across contexts) that generate such widely varied empirical effects. This heuristic consists of three basic mechanisms: (1) competition; (2) class conflict; and (3) the relatively autonomous state.[51] These pressures are rooted in the basic structure of capitalist social relations: a system of production based upon competitive, profit-based accumulation by individual private producers, and the commodification and exploitation of wage labor.[52] This generates specific forms of struggle between and within classes, and requires the formation of an apparatus (the state) capable of organizing the overall political hegemony of a ruling class internally riven by competitive pressures. Institutions are then developed and reproduced by creative human beings within conditions characterized by a balance of class forces, historically specific competitive dynamics, and in relation to the central role of state power in sustaining or undermining these projects. In this way, IM theorizes emergent phenomena as the historical product of the dialectical relationship between capitalist structural pressures, institutional capacities, and human agency.

[51] These mechanisms, and their role in institutional reproduction, are explicated in: Leo Panitch and Sam Gindin, "Marxist Theory and Strategy: Getting Somewhere Better," *Historical Materialism* 23, no. 2 (2015): 3–22.

[52] This bears some resemblance to the concept of "rules of reproduction" articulated by Robert Brenner, and deployed within the "Political Marxist" tradition by Ellen Meiksins Wood, Charles Post, and Vivek Chibber. Yet while the use of the term varies, as Benno Teschke and Hannes Lacher have pointed out, it has tended towards a 'structuralist' application that is quite at odds with the framework developed here—which emphasizes the heuristic nature of this model of capital, the creative nature of human agency, and the dynamism of institutional reproduction. See: Benno Teschke and Hannes Lacher, "The Changing 'Logics' of Capitalist Competition," *Cambridge Review of International Affairs* 20, no. 4 (2007): 565–80; Robert Brenner, "The Social Bases of Economic Development," in *Analytical Marxism*, ed. John Roemer (Cambridge, UK: Cambridge University Press, 1986); Ellen Meiksins Wood, "Rational Choice Marxism: Is the Game Worth the Candle?," in *Rational Choice Marxism*, ed. Terrell Carver and Paul Thomas (London, UK: Palgrave Macmillan UK, 1995), 79–135; Vivek Chibber, "What Is Living and What Is Dead in the Marxist Theory of History," *Historical Materialism* 19, no. 2 (2011): 60–91.

On this basis, this study makes three kinds of contributions to the way we think about power in contemporary capitalist democracies. First, it illustrates the potential of the Institutional Marxist framework to generate original empirical research, and contributes to building a theory of institutions in capitalist society. Second, it makes contributions to the state theory literature by more clearly theorizing state power, in particular its relation to corporate power and the practices and institutions through which it articulates class power. Finally, in adopting a historicizing approach, the study makes a contribution toward a clearer periodization of capitalist development in the United States. Periods of development can be differentiated by reference to the specific institutional form of capitalist hegemony at a given time. As we shall see through the lens of GE, capitalism in the United States has evolved through four different phases: entrepreneurialism, finance capital, managerialism, and neoliberalism. The state's role in organizing class hegemony is the dominant factor in the transition from one phase to another, reproducing class power on the within particular conditions of competition, class struggle, and institutional development. In this way, this study identifies particular hegemonic regimes not with "policy frameworks" emanating from the consciousness of state planners or imposed by corporate lobbyists, but rather understands these as emerging within the processes of historical contestation that shape the concrete form of organized power.

This demarcation of "phases of capitalist development" characterized by particular "hegemonic regimes" resembles to some extent the Regulation Theory approach. Although this groups together work from a variety of different perspectives, there are important differences between IM and the broad orientation of Regulation Theory. Regulation Theory emerged through a critique of neoclassical economics, and its basis in general equilibrium theory. It sought to illustrate how institutional structures, rather than a self-equilibrated "free market," are necessary to account for the stability of the social order. Regulation theorists therefore largely see institutions as reproducing functionally integrated closed systems, or particular "modes of regulation." These are reproduced in a relatively static fashion, until a breakdown of institutional order forces restructuring during a period of interregnum. Often, the state is understood as a mere background condition that underwrites the reproduction of particular regimes. This stands in marked contrast with the approach developed here, which emphasizes the fluid nature of historical development and the state's creative role in organizing class power across different periods of development.[53]

As the principal institutions organizing and expressing economic power in contemporary capitalism, corporations define and structure class situations, and form the bedrock upon which the state articulates class hegemony. As noted above, the economic power organized by the firm secures the social power of *capitalists*—but not that of a politically unified or coherent *capitalist class*—outside of civil society associations. Clearly, this differs radically from the "theory of the firm" developed in mainstream economics, based in methodological individualism and ahistorical contractualism.[54] Such frameworks see the corporation as a "nexus of contracts" between rational, utility-maximizing individuals created for reasons of efficiency. This deprives the corporation of all historical weight and institutional materiality, collapsing it into a two-dimensional timeless abstraction. Similarly, it obscures all political determinations of corporate strategy and structure, as well as the political power for which corporate institutions constitute a fundamental basis. While there is no doubt that the corporation has facilitated the competitive mobility, allocation, and accumulation of capital, IM sees corporations as specific historical institutions comprised of relations of power.[55] The analysis of the firm must

[53] Aglietta, *A Theory of Capitalist Regulation*; Robert Brenner and Mark Glick, "The Regulation Approach: Theory and History," *New Left Review* I, no. 188 (August 1991): 45–119; Bob Jessop, "Survey Article: The Regulation Approach," *Journal of Political Philosophy* 5 (December 16, 2002): 287–326; Bob Jessop, "Regulation and Politics: The Integral Economy and the Integral State," in *Hegemonie Und Staat*, ed. Alex Demirović, H Krebs, and Thomas Sablowski (Münster: Westfälisches Dampfboot Verlag, 1992); Bob Jessop, "Regulation Theories in Retrospect and Prospect," *Economy and Society* 19, no. 2 (1990): 153–216; Kotz, "Social Structure of Accumulation Theory, Marxist Theory, and System Transformation"; David M. Kotz, *The Rise and Fall of Neoliberal Capitalism* (Cambridge: Harvard University Press, 2015); David Kotz, Terrence McDonough, and Michael Reich, eds., *Social Structures of Accumulation: The Political Economy of Growth and Crisis* (Cambridge, UK: Cambridge University Press, 1994), especially Chapters 1 and 5.

[54] Richard Caves, *Multinational Enterprise and Economic Analysis*, Third Edition (Cambridge, UK: Cambridge University Press, 2007).

[55] Geoffrey Ingham, *Capitalism: With a New Postscript on the Financial Crisis and Its Aftermath* (Hoboken, NJ: Wiley, 2013); Joshua Barkan, *Corporate Sovereignty: Law and Government Under Capitalism* (Minneapolis, MN: University of Minnesota Press, 2013); William G. Roy, *Socializing Capital: The Rise of the Large Industrial Corporation in America* (Princeton, NJ: Princeton University Press, 1999); John Scott, *Corporate Business and Capitalist Classes* (Oxford, UK: Oxford University Press, 1997).

register how networks which systematically interpenetrate and traverse the "formal" corporate body join it with a larger structure of power centered on the state. Indeed, state power shapes, regulates, and underwrites particular forms of corporate governance. Shifts in, and conflicts over, corporate governance are thus inextricably connected to formal state institutions.

Managerialist writers such as Adolph Berle and Gardiner Means, James Burnham, Peter Drucker, and John Kenneth Galbraith saw the "separation of ownership and control" supposedly effected by the corporation as having transcended the class structure and competitive pressures of capitalist political economy.[56] Galbraith argued that the corporate bureaucratization of production had created a vast "technostructure" manned by non-capitalist administrators.[57] More recently, Alfred Chandler Jr. has argued that this "managerial revolution" had replaced the "invisible hand" of the market with the "visible hand" of corporate planning.[58] Pluralists often took up managerialist arguments regarding the "separation of ownership and control" to reinforce their view that ownership of wealth did not result in the monopolization of political power by a unitary elite. Dahl argued that since professional managers, and not owners, controlled corporations, these do not embody private power but are effectively public utilities, as managers were not necessarily motivated by the pursuit of profit. Since ownership confers little power, private control over capital does not challenge pluralist democracy, and the relationship between owners and non-owners does not constitute a primary axis

[56] Adolf A. Berle and Gardiner C. Means, *The Modern Corporation and Private Property,* (New York: Macmillan Co., 1933); Adolf A. Berle, *Power without Property: A New Development in American Political Economy* (Boston: Harcourt, Brace, 1959); Peter Drucker, *Concept of the Corporation* (Oxfordshire, UK: Routledge, 2008); James Burnham, *The Managerial Revolution* (Penguin Books, 1962).

[57] John Kenneth Galbraith, *The New Industrial State* (Princeton, NJ: Princeton University Press, 2015); John Kenneth Galbraith, *The Affluent Society* (Boston: Houghton Mifflin, 1978); John Kenneth Galbraith, *The Galbraith Reader* (London, UK: Palgrave Macmillan, 1977).

[58] Alfred D. Chandler Jr., *The Visible Hand: The Managerial Revolution in American Business* (Cambridge, MA: Belknap Press, 1977); Alfred D. Chandler Jr., *Scale and Scope: The Dynamics of Industrial Capitalism* (Cambridge, MA: Harvard University Press, 1994); Alfred D. Chandler Jr., *Strategy and Structure: Chapters in the History of the American Industrial Enterprise* (Cambridge, MA: MIT Press, 2000); Alfred D. Chandler Jr. and Takashi Hikino, *Big Business and the Wealth of Nations* (Cambridge, UK: Cambridge University Press, 1997).

of social conflict. The corporate form thus underwrites polyarchy, since power is dispersed across manager-controlled organizations as opposed to centralized state control.[59]

On the contrary, the argument presented in the present study follows Maurice Zeitlin and Ralph Miliband in seeing corporations—regardless of the relative power of investors or insider managers at a given point in time—as an institutional foundation of capitalist power.[60] Ownership and control of corporations reside in the same social class, while managerial-controlled firms remain firmly oriented toward profit maximization.[61] Similarly, the larger units of capital constructed through the processes of corporate concentration and centralization, facilitated by the state, brought not the suppression, but the dramatic *intensification* of competitive pressures. Nevertheless, Dahl is correct in noting the somewhat fragmented nature of corporate power—which only becomes *more* pronounced after accounting for the pressures of capitalist competition. Indeed, this is precisely why the capitalist state's function of organizing corporate power into class power is so essential to political order.

Miliband's institutional conception of power led him to situate managers as part of the capitalist class.[62] Poulantzas, on the other hand, argued that Miliband was wrong to consider managers "as one among the distinct economic elites composing the ruling class," which "attributes to them an importance they do not possess." Miliband's insistence against the managerialists that, despite their institutional empowerment within the corporation, managers remained motivated by profit maximization led Poulantzas to accuse him of advancing a "subjective" definition of class, as opposed to one based in the "objective" structure of capitalist

[59] Dahl, *Dilemmas of Pluralist Democracy*; Robert Dahl, *After the Revolution?* (New Haven: Yale University Press, 1970).

[60] Maurice Zeitlin, *The Large Corporation and Contemporary Classes* (New Brunswick, NJ: Rutgers University Press, 1989); Ralph Miliband, *The State in Capitalist Society* (London, UK: Merlin Press, 2009); See also: James O'Connor, *The Corporations and the State* (New York: Harper and Row, 1974).

[61] Edward S. Herman, *Corporate Control, Corporate Power: A Twentieth Century Fund Study* (Cambridge, UK: Cambridge University Press, 1982).

[62] See: Miliband, *The State in Capitalist Society*; Ralph Miliband, *Class Power and State Power* (Verso, 1983); Poulantzas, *Classes in Contemporary Capitalism*.

property relations.[63] Poulantzas claimed Miliband's focus on institutions "prevented him from seeing what is important"—not "differences and relations between economic elites" but rather between "fractions of capital."[64] Yet it is precisely these capitalist institutions that constitute the concrete existence of class domination. Indeed, a major function of the integral state is the crystallization of modalities of ownership and possession of capital through corporate organization. These modalities have taken different forms as capitalism has been restructured across particular phases of development, transforming linkages with the state and redistributing power across the integral state complex.

To understand the relationship between institutional power and capitalist class structure, the Marxist notion of *class position*, defined in terms of objective relations to the means of production, must be supplemented with Max Weber's concept of *class situation*.[65] In this view, social classes are comprised of *types* defined and reproduced by the institutions into which class actors are organized. These formations establish intra-class hierarchies even as they shape the balance of force between classes—securing the dominance of specific strata or groups *within classes* who then exert historical agency as a function of the institutional capacities they command.[66] Those in four distinct, if sometimes overlapping, capitalist *class situations*—managers, finance capitalists, bankers, and entrepreneurs—have possessed different roles and capacities in relation to corporate power over time.[67] Corporate institutions, and the specific

[63] Nicos Poulantzas, *The Poulantzas Reader: Marxism, Law, and the State* (Verso, 2008), 176–78.

[64] Poulantzas, *The Poulantzas Reader*, 177.

[65] Max Weber, *The Theory of Social and Economic Organization*, trans. A. M Henderson and Talcott Parsons (Oxford, UK: Oxford University Press, 1947); Max Weber, *Economy and Society: An Outline of Interpretive Sociology* (Berkeley, CA: University of California Press, 1978).

[66] Offe and Wiesenthal, "Two Logics of Collective Action"; Panitch, "Trade Unions and the Capitalist State."

[67] Scott, *Corporate Business and Capitalist Classes*. The definitions of bankers and managers should be self-evident. "Entrepreneurs" are those who own and directly possess fixed assets. "Finance capitalists" were defined best by Hilferding as those who "sit upon the governing boards of a large number of corporations" and who represent "a kind of personal union, on the one hand, between the different corporations themselves, on the other, between the latter and the banks".

mode of their insertion and combination with other organizations and processes, produce and configure these situations.

What Anwar Shaikh has called "real competition" remains a central disciplinary and regulative force in corporate capitalism, ensuring the central importance of profit maximization regardless of the relative power of particular capitalist class strata within corporate institutions. This competition takes many different forms: over markets, products, technologies, and intellectual property; organizational forms, distribution systems, and labor processes; geographical spaces; investment (i.e., capital markets); and corporate control itself. As Shaikh writes:

> Capital is a particular social form of wealth driven by the profit motive. With this comes a corresponding drive for expansion, for the conversion of capital into more capital, of profit into more profit. Each individual capital operates under this imperative, colliding with others trying to do the same, sometimes succeeding, sometimes just surviving, and sometimes failing altogether. This is *real competition*, antagonistic by nature and turbulent in operation.[68]

Shaikh argues that rather than declining, competition intensifies with corporate size, while generating pressures toward greater internationalization. This also contributes to the increasing complexity of corporate forms, in part through the creation of new products and technologies. However, while helpful in clarifying the pressures of capital accumulation, Shaikh's *Capitalism* contains scant historical analysis, or discussion of any actually existing corporations. IM seeks to identify the effects of these competitive pressures on the *historical* development of concrete institutional forms—which is what makes "real competition" so very *real*.

Understanding the importance of competition for corporate organization involves the recognition that competitive pressures emerge *within* such large corporations, not just *between* them. As Sheikh shows, competition is fundamentally for *profits*, rather than sales or market share. Consequently, competition between capitals primarily takes the form of competition between investment opportunities: low profit rates lead to the withdrawing of investment, while high profits draw increased investment. From this perspective, "the key strategic decision of the capitalist is

[68] Anwar Shaikh, *Capitalism: Competition, Conflict, Crises* (Oxford, UK: Oxford University Press, 2016), 259.

what to invest in and the defining characteristic of capitalist competition is the mobility of investment—mobility over space and between different commercial/financial/industrial activities."[69] As James Clifton argued, these competitive pressures are internalized within large multi-process firms, as corporate planners have to allocate investment across a range of distinct businesses with differential rates of return, capital structures, and long-term growth potential. Within the structure of the multidivisional corporation, these competing investment opportunities are very often organized as particular divisions. Moreover, divisions must also compete for investment against external opportunities for acquisition and expansion. As this indicates, while corporations may in some sense be economic planning systems, they are nevertheless about *planning competitiveness*. Since large firms are the most mobile, with very low internal transaction costs, they have the largest range of investment opportunities—and are therefore *the most* competitive.[70]

On the other hand, corporate structures are inscribed within state power, and there is no guarantee that the most economically efficient organizational modalities will be enacted with the legal and regulatory support of the state—which is ultimately a *political* matter. Environmental and labor regulations, for instance, prohibit corporations from organizing their operations as might be most economically efficient in service of a higher, non-economic notion of the "public good." These regulations are the result of social struggles and exemplify the impact of the relative autonomy of the state on economic organization. Nor is it obviously the case that the current financialized model of corporate governance is inherently more efficient than possible alternatives. To be sure, the dominance of this model today reflects its ability to survive in the context of global competition, but it also reflects a balance of power within the state and capitalist class that is partly the result of distributional processes that are not strictly "rational" from the point of view of the efficiency of capital accumulation. Indeed, many supporters of the capitalist system have argued that this model is *less* efficient than various others they seek to enact. Nevertheless, over time the systematic reproduction

[69] Dick Bryan and Michael Rafferty, *Capitalism With Derivatives: A Political Economy of Financial Derivatives, Capital and Class* (Springer, 2005), 259.

[70] James A. Clifton, "Competition and the Evolution of the Capitalist Mode of Production," *Cambridge Journal of Economics* 1, no. 2 (June 1, 1977): 137–51.

of competitive pressures, and the dynamics of concentration and centralization it encourages, can undermine and eventually overwhelm even the most institutionally powerful actors.

Within this framework, historical "agency" is a function of command over institutional resources whose reproduction is disciplined by the pressures of capitalism. Just as the development of institutional capacities makes it possible for corporations to amass capital on a larger scale, and increases the competitiveness of capital assembled within such institutions by increasing sectoral and spatial mobility, this also expands the agency of those at the top of this power structure to organize and undertake these processes. Though market disciplined, the range of reproduction strategies available to those within the most powerful firms is enlarged by virtue of the institutional capacities they are able to mobilize. Paradoxically, the agency of these actors arises from the same conditions that make these larger units of capital more intensely competitive. While successfully reproducing corporate institutional structures remains dependent on market discipline at many different levels, decisions over *how this is achieved* are concentrated at the top of the institutional pyramid. The greater the institutional resources available to agents situated within these structures, the greater the range of these decisions: in the case of the corporation, what to make and where to make it, how to structure management, strategies for raising finance and allocating capital across internal business operations or technologies, and the like. Thus these actors are thus afforded *agency to compete*. Crucially, the *economic* rationality that underlies hierarchies within the firm also constitutes the basis for *political* power once corporate organization is considered from the point of view of the integral state.

Corporations confer particular power interests on those seeking to preserve or increase the scope of their institutional command. But this does not mean, as this study bears out, that executives have a clear set of "objective interests" they seek to impose on the state. The interests of human subjects within both corporations and the state are formed through institutional processes within highly complex situations characterized by great uncertainty about the effects of different strategies, and partial knowledge about the world. However, executives do have an interest in working with state officials to create a regulatory and policy environment they believe will be conducive to the reproduction of their power, and the "bottom line" of their firm. Those within the relatively autonomous state share these concerns inasmuch as they coincide with the long-term general interest of capital as a whole. This does not extend to supporting the immediate economic interests or even the reproduction of every firm, nor the social power of a particular component of the capitalist class. Nevertheless, in crafting policy, state agencies need to actively cultivate business support for the policies and trade-offs they seek to implement, especially insofar as this entails costs for capital. This is not merely a matter of balancing the objective interests of different components of the capitalist class, but rather *forming* the interests of capitalist elites by integrating them with state policymaking processes and assimilating their individual perspectives within a class-wide view.

Therefore, in organizing class hegemony, the state systematically educates and integrates capitalists within policy processes and state apparatuses that support the power of capital *in general*, while managing the *particular* trade-offs and costs this entails. The flip side of this is that making sound policy also demands that state officials integrate corporate power into the policymaking process. This helps secure "buy-in" for policy initiatives among the most powerful and well-connected, while facilitating the gathering of information about market conditions, the likely effects of any proposed policy changes on the business environment, and a deeper awareness of the existing capacities to carry out a given political agenda. State officials simply lack the expertise, or rather the perspective, necessary to formulate a conception of the general interest of capital without such input. So too is this coordination important for implementing policy—for example, war mobilization or the management of transnational economic governance. Those at the top of these power systems have access to the largest range of information about the problems faced by particular sectors and the likely impact of policy, while also possessing the greatest capacity to influence wider networks. It follows that those occupying such positions command the most important nodes from which to build consensus. The consent of capital for state policy is not an abstract or ephemeral phenomenon; rather, this is organized through the apparatus of the integral state.

The Case of General Electric

The integral state does not form spontaneously, but develops historically through emergent, path-dependent institutional relationships between specific state and corporate institutions. As Marx wrote in the "Critique of the Gotha Program," the notion of the capitalist state *in general* is "a fiction"—there are only concrete *states*, formed through specific historical processes. Nevertheless, Marx wrote, "in spite of their manifold diversity of form," capitalist states have "certain essential features in common" by virtue of their shared basis in capitalist society.[71] This same insight applies to the corporation. While generalizations about "the firm," "capital," "sectors," or "class fractions" can be helpful in hypothesizing the dynamics of capitalism, understanding the structure of class power requires an analysis of the networks, mechanisms, and organs which constitute it. Firms strategically govern economic processes on the basis of a set of historically evolved capacities and relationships, and serve specific functions in the reproduction of state and class power. As such, the story of the institutional evolution of each firm tells us something distinct and novel in that—though all are subject to the same structural pressures that attend ownership of capital—each nonetheless evolves as a unique historical process, in relation to interlocking systems of state, corporate, and class power.

It is certainly true that General Electric represents a single "case," and is just one firm out of many. However, GE's historical role as a cornerstone of the integral state, and therefore its importance for the organization of class power, means that studying it can offer more general insights into the nature of political order in the United States. That not every company has performed the function GE has, including working closely with state officials to form "civil society" organizations to shape and articulate class consensus, makes it exceptionally important for an empirically grounded theory of the integral state. These political functions were rooted in GE's deeper structural integration with state power. This included its embeddedness within the industrial policy system, which contributed to the development of its extensive engineering capacities. This, in turn, compelled GE's administrative decentralization, which was an adaptive response to the diversification that accompanied this technological development. GE's economic centrality was cemented as its range of business operations multiplied, developing links to a wide spectrum of customers, suppliers, and financiers. This allowed GE executives to more closely approximate the perspective of capital "in general," and served to amplify its political significance as those within the state sought to use it as an institutional foundation for organizing capitalist class power.

[71] Karl Marx, "Critique of the Gotha Program," in Robert Tucker, ed., *The Marx-Engels Reader*, Second Edition, 1978 [1875], 537.

GE's function within the integral state initially became especially pronounced as the Roosevelt administration struggled to build support for the New Deal. However, this was the outcome of a historical process reaching back to the joint origins of the modern capitalist state and corporation at the end of the nineteenth century. The institutional development of GE since that time provides a window into the formation of the American integral state, the backbone of class power. By tracing GE's evolution in relation to the formal state apparatus from its formation in the finance capital period (1880–1930), through the managerial period (1930–1979), to the restructuring leading up to the age of neoliberalism (1979–present), the mechanisms and institutions that constitute and systematically reproduce the integral state become clearer. Indeed, the changes and continuities across this historical progression, both in the configuration of state institutions as well as GE's governance structure, illustrate how the anatomy of social power and class rule was established through the organization and integration of state and corporate power. Across these phases, the integral state was established through the interdependent processes of state and corporate formation; it was strengthened through multiple crises; and it was restructured to reflect and support shifting hierarchies within the capitalist class and state organization.

GE's role in the integral state reveals much about the distinctive process of capitalist development in the United States, including the organizational development of the state, financial institutions, and "non-financial" corporations. The modern bureaucratic state and corporation emerged through a series of increasingly large-scale and capital-intensive projects planned and executed by the state. As we shall see in Chapter 2, states initially issued corporate charters allowing for the pooling of capital for the purpose of completing large-scale public projects, particularly infrastructure development. However, after the passage of the New Jersey Corporation Act of 1889 and the Sherman Antitrust Act of 1890, the corporation became a permanent form of *private* power. States would no longer be able to use the ability to revoke charters to control these organizations. Nevertheless, the initial models of private corporate organization were constructed with state support to build and operate the national rail system, which was accompanied by the formation of a national financial system. The railroad companies formed the model for the equally monumental project of electrification, to which GE was central. The technical and administrative capacities that emerged from this formed the basis for the mobilization for World War I, from which emerged a more robust and active state, corporations of increasing size and capacities, and deep-rooted patterns of state-corporate integration.

In this period, capitalist development in the US broadly conformed to the classical model of *finance capital* famously articulated by Rudolf Hilferding in his 1912 book by that title, based on his observations of capitalist development in Germany.[72] While the joint-stock company facilitated the raising of massive amounts of capital, Hilferding argued, in the process industrial capitalists were converted into creditors, or owners of money capital who have no necessary connection with the uses to which their credit is put. Rather than directly owning fixed assets, these industrialists now controlled tradable shares. The banks then acquired critical importance as shareholders, mobilizers of capital, and organizers of cartels. The result was bank control over productive enterprises, secured by placing representatives on the Boards of Directors of corporations they controlled—forming "interlocking directorates." Boards of Directors were in this period the key venues for organizing and expressing corporate control and consolidating inter-corporate networks. In this way, banks commanded their own industrial empires, merging isolated enterprises into firms, and firms into cartels. It was through precisely such a process that GE was formed, as J. P. Morgan wrested control of the company from its founder, Thomas Edison—a conflict that took place over a decade.

Though Hilferding saw this as inevitably leading to the decline of competition, this was hardly the case, as the experience of GE attests. In fact, this period was characterized by fierce competition, especially over organizational forms and intellectual property. It was precisely this that led the state to establish a model of *corporate self-regulation*, whereby a relatively small number of banks and the corporations they controlled organized markets and stabilized prices within broad state-enforced parameters, while still competing intensively for profits through other means. GE and Westinghouse were given substantial control over the Board of Patent Control, a parastate body set up to limit the destructive competition over intellectual property then underway. By this point, some of the distinctive attributes of capitalist development in the US were already apparent. The state's more active role, and the greater decentralization of the financial system than in Hilferding's account led

[72] Hilferding, *Finance Capital.*

to the emergence of managerial corporate structures that were more autonomous from financial power. The administrative, legal, and technical personnel that filled these institutions began to form a stratum of professional managers, who were increasingly linked with state institutions—especially after the establishment of the Department of Commerce in 1903. That integral state organization was essential to the functioning of the new department was indicated by its immediate efforts to form a national Chamber of Commerce to articulate a unified, class-wide perspective among its business constituents.

As surveyed in Chapter 3, the New Deal regulations that followed the 1929 crash marked the end of the finance capital period, formally separating the banks from the governance of industrial corporations. This was accompanied by the restructuring of the integral state around the power of the professional managers, who would maintain their position at the apex of corporate control throughout the ensuing *managerial* era. As bank centrality waned, "non-financial" firms internalized a range of financial functions for which they had previously relied upon their finance capital overlords. That this marked the full emergence of the distinctive American model of corporate organization was registered in Adolf Berle and Gardiner Means' path-breaking study *The Modern Corporation and Private Property* in 1932.[73] They argued that a "managerial revolution" had occurred, whereby a non-owning, salaried managerial class had taken possession of the productive assets of society, rendering the actual owners largely irrelevant to corporate governance. There was more than a grain of truth to this.[74] With the decline of bank power, insiders gradually assumed control of corporations, while also filling expanding state bureaucracies. As shareholdings became fragmented and dispersed, investor pressure on managers was increasingly limited. Corporate insiders now dominated and subordinated Boards of Directors, which had been the key locus of corporate control during the finance capital era.

As the effects of the largest capitalist crisis in history rippled throughout society, and waves of militant class struggle were unleashed, the Roosevelt administration worked with a core group of these ascendant managers to organize a capitalist class consensus around the reforms

[73] Berle and Means, *The Modern Corporation and Private Property*.

[74] See the above discussion of Miliband, *The State in Capitalist Society*; Zeitlin, *The Large Corporation and Contemporary Classes*.

it saw as necessary to save the system. This took place primarily through the formation by executive order of the Business Advisory Council (BAC) within the Department of Commerce in 1933. Gerard Swope of GE emerged as the key representative of the group of so-called corporate liberals who formed the core of this effort, which transitioned directly into, and was tremendously reinforced by, World War II. As discussed in Chapter 4, mobilizing the economy for all-out global war was the largest task the federal government had ever undertaken, and required the development of an industrial policy that went considerably beyond existing state capacities. The extensive coordination with private corporations this required was organized through the formation of the War Production Board, which was headed by GE President Charles Wilson—a position that made him so powerful that he was referred to by the press as the "co-President." State investment poured into manufacturing firms at an unbelievable rate, leading to a doubling of output and the development of historically unprecedented science and research capacities within the new "military industrial complex." GE was at the very center of this powerhouse of technological innovation, spinning off technologies through its different business divisions.

This cemented GE's role as a foundational node of the integral state. While Wilson was head of the "public" WPB, he simultaneously helped form the "private" Committee for Economic Development (CED) alongside GE's Chairman, Phillip Reed, with the support and guidance of the Department of Commerce. The CED sought to mobilize business support for the centralization of industrial policy under the control of the military, as opposed to civilian New Dealers, and for accepting the risks and costs of an unprecedented reduction in tariffs after the war. The integration of business with the new Department of Defense after the war was coordinated by the Office of Defense Mobilization, successor to the WPB but with even greater powers—and again headed by Wilson. Meanwhile, the powerful Atomic Energy Commission (AEC) oversaw the postwar continuation of the Manhattan Project, developing nuclear technologies through a network of National Laboratories, universities, and high-tech manufacturing companies. At the same time, Reed helped organize business support for the postwar international order drawn up in the State Department and the increasingly powerful Treasury Department, covered in Chapter 5. With the success of these efforts, even as American capitalists remained reluctant to invest abroad—and as GE itself absorbed a slew of antitrust suits that dismembered its international cartel system—Reed and the State Department undertook to "internationalize" the integral state. This included expanding the International Chamber of Commerce, headed by Reed, with embassies in different countries coordinating the work of setting up chapters and building support among local capitalists for integration within the American system.

This led to Reed's involvement in organizing business support for the US Information Agency, which spread the idea of American utopia abroad through both "public" and "private" infrastructures and networks. USIA techniques also contributed to GE's large-scale community relations program at home, outlined in Chapter 4. This entailed developing relationships with local media and civil society organizations in towns where the company had plants, as well as issuing its own publications and materials. One aspect of this program was the hiring of Ronald Reagan as the company's spokesman, which included hosting the popular television show *GE Theater* and traveling around the country spreading a "new Right" anti- "Big Government" and "Big Labor" ideology. While GE had been a foremost supporter of the New Deal class compromise with "responsible" trade unions since the 1930s, a major strike in 1947 alarmed management, who came to believe labor had "gone too far." As GE investment moved to the non-union south, supported by a similar shift in state industrial policy, these new "public relations" efforts were focused there. Still, it was the state defense apparatus, on which GE was so dependent, that was most concerned about the fact that the primary union representation for GE workers was the Communist-led United Electrical Workers (UE). Under threat of revoking GE contracts, the AEC urged GE to do more to address what they saw as a serious national security threat, given the sensitive nature of the work GE was contracted to do. However, with the merger of the AFL-CIO in 1955, politically radical trade unionism was effectively domesticated. Unions disciplined labor within the system of managerial hegemony, while securing continually rising living standards in tandem with increases in productivity—and thus without altering the distribution of income.

The managerial hegemony consolidated over the two decades following World War II reflected in certain respects the model Paul Baran and Paul Sweezy developed in their seminal 1966 work *Monopoly Capital*.[75] Baran and Sweezy argued that a self-perpetuating group of

[75] Paul A. Baran and Paul M. Sweezy, *Monopoly Capital: An Essay on the American Economic and Social Order* (New York: Monthly Review Press, 1966).

managers had assumed corporate control, supported by the increasingly massive military industrial complex. Bankers did not dominate industrial enterprises, as in Hilferding's account, and shareholders were mere bystanders. Rather, professional managers administered giant firms characterized by centralized bureaucratic structures. These corporations had achieved financial independence through the internal generation of funds that were at the complete disposal of management, depriving bankers of the privileged position they possessed within the finance capital model. In any case, to Baran and Sweezy, the question of whether shareholders had been subordinated by managerial power was irrelevant, since corporate strategy was bound to adhere not to the preferences of bankers, shareholders, or managers, but the economic laws of "monopoly capital."[76] These ensured not only that manager-controlled firms remained oriented toward profit maximization, but also that the strategies they pursued would be identical with the interests of the largest shareholders, and thus that the two strata formed a "harmonious interest group." Baran and Sweezy believed the working class had been fully disciplined and integrated with this structure. Competition, too, was a thing of the past, while state-corporate economic planning had effectively resolved capitalism's crisis tendencies.

Within just a few years, nearly every aspect of this model would either break down or be revealed as mistaken. In fact, Baran and Sweezy were writing just as global competition was intensifying, and the two-decade-long state-led postwar boom finally running out of steam. The institutional contradictions of the managerial period burst to the fore, as union militancy held wages up despite falling productivity, squeezing profits. Investment fell, leading to economic stagnation. The assimilation of labor to managerial hegemony, it seemed, was not without its contradictions. Nor were relations among these different capitalist class segments so "harmonious" as declining profits led to industrial firms becoming more reliant on external financing, increasing the power of the investors to discipline managers. What James O'Connor in 1973 called "the fiscal crisis of the state," whereby government spending tended to

[76] See also: Miliband, *The State in Capitalist Society*; Zeitlin, *The Large Corporation and Contemporary Classes*.

outstrip GDP growth, intensified.[77] Pressure grew within the state, particularly around the increasingly powerful Treasury Department, for fiscal austerity, tax cuts, and deregulation. As we shall see in Chapter 7, it came to be supported in this by a class coalition that included both the largest industrial corporations as well as the financial sector. In addition to monetary stability, this program aimed to cut corporate costs, improve margins, and restore investment and growth. Far from state spending absorbing a rising surplus, as Baran and Sweezy had believed, the surplus was actually falling (reinforced by rising corporate taxes), and policymakers increasingly saw state spending as further contributing to inflation.

Yet the path to resolve the crisis was far from obvious to either policymakers or business. In fact, "stagflation" dragged on throughout the decade, as state officials struggled to develop a program that could discipline labor, reduce wages, restore profits, and hold together the postwar managerialist model. As had been the case with the transition from finance capital to managerialism over the New Deal and World War II period, the development of the neoliberal program was not a matter of state officials or corporate lobbyists dogmatically imposing a fully worked out ideology. New state capacities were formed to chart a way forward, especially around the Treasury Department, supported by integral state institutions and linkages—most importantly the Business Roundtable (BR). Formed in 1972 by Fred Borch of GE and John Harper of Alcoa at the urging of Treasury Secretary John Connally and Fed Chairman Arthur Burns, the BR consisted of top executives from the most prominent industrial corporations. In many respects the successor to the BAC, the BR explicitly sought to work with state officials to develop, and build a class-wide consensus around, the basic elements of the necessary restructuring. It would remain the most prominent "lobbying" organization throughout the 1970s. But it wasn't until 1979, the last year of the Carter Administration, that the crisis was finally brought to an end with the "Volcker Shock," which provoked a deep recession and broke the back of worker militancy along with inflation.

In supporting the ascent of the Treasury Department, the industrial firms on the BR were joining with the increasingly hegemonic financial sector, with which that agency had long close links. An important part of the material base for this coalition, and GE's role in forming

[77] O'Connor, *The Fiscal Crisis of the State*.

it, was the financialized restructuring of the large industrial corporation, discussed in Chapter 6. Integration with the industrial policy system had led to the *decentralization* of production into semi-autonomous divisions alongside the *centralization* of capital allocation within the firm. Administrative decentralization was an adaptive response to diversification, as the new product lines that resulted from technological innovation were organized into increasingly self-contained business divisions. Top executives became "general" managers, approximating capital *in general*—responsible not for overseeing specific concrete businesses, but rather distributing abstract money-capital across a "portfolio" of business. Operational functions were reserved for lower-level managers, who headed increasingly autonomous and self-contained business units that competed for investment from top planners. External financiers also used their growing power within corporate governance to push forward this restructuring. This was supported within the firm by the corporate financial office, now headed by a powerful Chief Financial Officer closely linked with external investors. So too was rising investor power reflected in the renewed clout of Boards of Directors, and in the inability of the BR to constrain the increasingly assertive SEC regulations and reporting requirements geared toward increasing "transparency" and managerial "accountability" to shareholders.

At the same time, the pressures of corporate internationalization as well as rising competition from Europe contributed to the unravelling of the postwar Bretton Woods system of fixed exchange rates and capital controls. While international economic liberalization and tariff reductions had been a thorny issue among American capitalists since World War II, protectionist pressures had been contained in part by concentrating power within a highly autonomous trade apparatus. GE had been at the vanguard of a group supporting this, as well as successive rounds of tariff reductions. With the onset of crisis, and in the wake of drastic tariff reductions in the early 1960s, the fragile "free trade" consensus was shaken. As discussed in Chapter 8, after the collapse of Bretton Woods in 1971, the Department of Commerce was tasked with constructing an advisory system of unprecedented scope, covering all sections of business right across the American economy, to support the Tokyo Round negotiations that would establish a new global trade regime. GE played an important part in supporting these efforts, which sought both to mobilize business support for the new regime as well as to supply negotiators from the Office of the US Trade Representative with information and technical support. The broad policy framework of liberalization, however, was not itself negotiable. Moreover, "trade" policy would no longer be limited to tariffs; now trade negotiations also focused on "non-tariff barriers." These included areas of policy typically thought to be within the exclusive purview of national governments, including subsidized export credit and national regulatory standards.

International agreements would now constrain states' ability to extend subsidies to particular firms, even as "temporary adjustment assistance." While the American state retained greater autonomy to make exceptions, it also carried a special burden in superintending internationalization. Nevertheless, even in the case of the American state, new disciplines limited non-tariff barriers. This was especially concerning to smaller firms focused on the domestic market, which were hit hard by cheap imports and lacked the ability to compete by restructuring internationally. What was in fact unfolding was a new round of competition over organizational forms to circulate value through globally integrated networks, locating particular stages of production in whatever geographical zones offered the lowest costs. When the Tokyo Round finally concluded in 1979, Carter appointed Reginald Jones, CEO of GE, to head the "President's Export Council," ostensibly the top advisory body on trade. The PEC worked to extend and consolidate the coalition supporting the new agreement and the extensive state restructuring that came with it. The Department of Commerce would now become an enforcement apparatus of the transnational regime—which continued to require extensive collaboration with corporations. In addition to backing this, the PEC appeared to promise smaller firms benefits in the form of increased *exports*, either through state support or by integrating more deeply with the internationalizing networks of the big MNCs as suppliers or contractors.

Though some Commerce officials had hoped the PEC would offer the department the opportunity to reverse its long decline, and take responsibility for coordinating an extensive new export-led industrial policy, this was not to be. Instead, trade policy functions were concentrated within the STR, while Commerce was relegated to overseeing implementation and enforcement. Treasury had become the preeminent state agency, along with its agenda of low taxes, fiscal constraints, and deregulation. A major development of state capacity to organize an expansive new industrial policy was not on the cards. Nor was the Defense Department about to yield control of industrial policy to the Commerce Department. It was a matter, then, of disciplining capital into accepting the new parameters set forth within the multilateral agreements constructed by the STR. Nor did labor have the vision, or the capacity, to counter the international restructuring then unfolding. Along with the Volcker Shock, the new internationalization would help to discipline labor—restoring profits, exiting the crisis, and tilting the balance of class forces decisively toward capital. The *neoliberal* era had begun.

In 1981, the iconic Jack Welch took the helm at GE. Over the Welch years, the company came full circle: from emblem of New Deal managerialism to foremost icon of shareholder value, whereby the primary purpose of corporate strategy was to boost the share price. This reflecting the rising power of investors, and bringing a new discipline to the organization. Thousands of workers would be laid off as management pushed "lean production," while thinning the company's bloated bureaucracy through dramatically advancing the firm's centralization-decentralization. At the same time, Welch dramatically expanded the company's financial unit, renamed GE Capital, which came to make up 40% of the company's profits. While this has been identified with the "hollowing out" of production, there is little intrinsic basis upon which these businesses—which were based partly on the commodification of core capacities of the firm—can be separated from GE's other divisions. Nevertheless, a new range of firms replaced GE at the cutting edge of high-tech production, while GE itself moved further away both from the industrial policy system as well as its longstanding leadership within the integral state—marking a new era in American capitalism.

A Note on Sources

While the data pertaining to General Electric are primarily based on the company's Annual Reports between 1920 and 1980, as supplemented by news reports, biographies of company executives, and other secondary literature on the company, this study draws most extensively on US state archives—indeed several chapters are based almost entirely on these sources. In the summer of 2015, I spent three weeks at the US National Archives in College Park, Maryland, viewing documents for the relevant period for the departments of State, Treasury, Commerce, Energy, War, and Defense, as well as the White House, Office of Management and Budget, Office of the US Trade Representative, War Production Board, Office of Defense Mobilization, and President's Export Council.

This included records for the various business advisory groups embedded within these agencies. Archival records for the Business Advisory Council, including meeting minutes, were included within the Department of Commerce documents until 1961, when that body became "private." I was also able to digitally access documents from the Carter Presidential Library. I received a large quantity of archival records related to the Construction User's Anti-Inflation Roundtable, and its successor, the Business Roundtable, which are not publicly accessible, but which were made available to me by Professor Benjamin Waterhouse of the University of North Carolina Department of History. The conceptual tools for identifying, interpreting, contextualizing, and analyzing the information gleaned from these sources were drawn from the theoretical frameworks addressed in this introductory chapter.

CHAPTER 2

The Making of General Electric in the Era of Finance Capital

This chapter explores the rise of finance capital in the US—characterized by the fusion of finance and industry under the dominance of banks—through the lens of GE's formation and early development. Specifically, it traces the mechanisms through which bank power overtook the early capitalist entrepreneurs, using the decade-long conflict between Thomas Edison and J. P. Morgan as a case study. It shows how the system of finance capital was politically enhanced and legally codified with the enactment of the Sherman Antitrust Act of 1890, and develops a picture of how managerialism emerged from the era of bank control as the loosening of finance capital networks enhanced the power of internal corporate managers. It demonstrates how this evolution was linked with processes of state formation, as an increasingly robust state moved to reduce bank power within corporate governance structures, integrate this strata of managers within policymaking processes, and organize corporate support for the state-building—and empire-building—project. The expansion of the federal bureaucracy was accompanied at each step with the formation of integral state institutions linking state and corporate power, beginning with the efforts of those in the Department of Commerce to form the National Chamber of Commerce in 1912.

© The Author(s), under exclusive license to Springer Nature Switzerland AG 2022

S. Maher, *Corporate Capitalism and the Integral State*, Marx, Engels, and Marxisms,
https://doi.org/10.1007/978-3-030-83772-3_2

Edison, Morgan, and the Creation of GE

The formation of the General Electric Company in 1892 marked the culmination of a long struggle between J. P. Morgan and Thomas Edison. The conflict between the two men is an excellent illustration of the process whereby banks gained control of "key nonfinancial corporations" by the turn of the century.[1] With the rise of bank power from 1879 to 1892, finance capitalist *par excellence* Morgan took control of a series of companies initially owned and operated by inventor-entrepreneur Edison by merging them first with each other, forming the Edison General Electric Company in 1889, and then later with the Thomson-Houston Company to establish the General Electric Company in 1892. Through the creation of GE, Morgan was able to assume control over these assets by reorganizing them into the type of corporate structure that would epitomize what later became known as "finance capital." His ability to achieve this was bolstered by his strong links to capital markets abroad in the City of London, where Morgan operations were very well established.[2]

The "entrepreneurial" age that was eclipsed by the rise of finance capital in no way resembles the supposedly *laissez faire* moment depicted in popular mythology. Prior to the organization of finance capital, the American economy was backward and primitive. As David Harvey notes, the "small-scale of enterprise and fragmentation of economic activity" that characterized this era does not by any means imply "perfect competition." The economy was highly regionalized, and small firms could easily become monopolistic within the economic territories they were able to command as a result of high transport costs and asymmetric, uneven information flows. Capital markets were similarly primitive and localized. The only activities that were large-scale and centralized were government finance and public works, often carried out by early corporations under public charters. Moreover, the unity of ownership and possession characteristic of the "entrepreneurial" model meant that business was hampered by the limited managerial capacities of families or partnerships—a far cry

[1] Miguel Cantillo Simon, "The Rise and Fall of Bank Control in the United States: 1890–1939," *American Economic Review* 88, no. 5 (1998): 1077.

[2] Ron Chernow, *House of Morgan: An American Banking Dynasty and the Rise of Modern Finance* (Boston: Atlantic Press, 1990).

from the extensive professionalized management systems developed by finance capital.[3]

Increasingly in the post-bellum era, direct ownership of fixed assets by individual entrepreneurs was replaced by possession of tradable shares in a corporate organization that controlled such fixed assets. The relationship between owners and assets was increasingly mediated by abstract money capital, as *personal* ownership and control were replaced by *impersonal* ownership. The role of family networks as the basis for mobilizing and allocating capital, and managing assets, was preserved for a time in the form of bank-managed trusts, but the dispersal of these through inheritance and sale soon led economic power to pass to the banks. State-led railway construction laid the initial foundations for national-scale financial infrastructure, as well as the establishment of the corporation as a private entity (as opposed to a quasi-public entity chartered to fulfill a specific purpose for a limited time).[4] The banks that emerged from this process merged enterprises into large national firms, forming overlapping bank-centered corporate webs uniting regional economies into a national market.[5]

The support the state extended the banks during the construction of the railroads was not the exception but the rule, as the development of the financial system took place with the full support of a fragile but expanding state over the late-nineteenth and early-twentieth centuries. Through reorganizations of troubled firms and mergers, bankers were able to secure overall control over corporate structures, exercised through voting trusts and board representation. While the "banks did not exercise control by micro-managing firms," they were nonetheless responsible for "overseeing financial matters (dividends, capital structure, and investment) and appointing top managers" throughout the finance capital period.[6] Over time, however, these networks became looser, broader, and more interdependent. As a result, "non-financial" corporations developed

[3] David Harvey, *The Limits to Capital* (New York: Verso, 2006), 143–4.

[4] William G. Roy, *Socializing Capital: The Rise of the Large Industrial Corporation in America* (Princeton, NJ: Princeton University Press, 1999), 41–77.

[5] John Scott, *Corporate Business and Capitalist Classes* (Oxford, UK: Oxford University Press, 1997); Panitch and Gindin, *The Making of Global Capitalism*, 29–31; Simon, "The Rise and Fall of Bank Control in the United States."

[6] Simon, "The Rise and Fall of Bank Control in the United States," 1091, 1080; This theory of competition is developed in Shaikh, *Capitalism: Competition, Conflict, Crises*.

a greater autonomy from specific banks and became more central in the US than in more bank-centric contexts.[7]

This finance capital period was not characterized by "monopolization" as it is conventionally defined: the squelching of competition by giant trusts and combinations. On the contrary, the organization and integration of a truly national economy through the formation of finance capital enhanced the geographical mobility of capital and generated intense competition, which regulated the reproduction of these institutions. The overlapping bank-centered corporate webs that took shape as banks merged enterprises in which they had a stake linked regional economies into a national market.[8] The case of GE shows how competition intensified as a consequence of corporate institutional development, often taking highly destructive forms (which would only be curtailed with the expansion of the state's capacity to do so). Competition over organizational forms, managerial expertise, intellectual property rights and patents, market share, production techniques, branding, and investment, all reinforced price competition to defend market power.

At the same time, the state possessed only a limited capacity to enforce competitive markets and discipline bank power. Consequently, it encouraged the development of a system of *corporate self-regulation*, through which markets were stabilized through bank-managed trustification, cartelization, and price-fixing. But this did not suppress the competitive dynamics of capitalism, which were the *motivation* for the formation of cartels and trusts in the first place, as capital was amassed on an ever-larger scale. This competition led to crises and contradictions that encouraged the further development of state institutions to oversee and superintend an increasingly complex and large-scale corporate capitalism.

GE offers a compelling window into this finance capital phase of capitalist development in the US. GE was central to the production and "invention" of consumer electrical products through advanced R&D conducted by Edison and his associates, beginning with the light bulb.

[7] Martijn Konings, *The Development of American Finance* (Cambridge, UK: Cambridge University Press, 2011); Charles Post, *The American Road to Capitalism: Studies in Class-Structure, Economic Development and Political Conflict, 1620–1877* (Chicago: Haymarket Books, 2012).

[8] Stephen Skowronek, *Building a New American State: The Expansion of National Administrative Capacities, 1877–1920* (Cambridge, UK: Cambridge University Press, 1982), 121–62.

But it was also at the core of the much larger project of developing, building, and operating new infrastructures and technologies for generating, distributing, and consuming electricity. After the railroad boom, but prior to the construction of a military-industrial complex during World War I (in which GE would also play a major part), electrification formed the crux of state-supported engineering and technology innovation. This was the second major project of the modern capitalist state, which worked to facilitate the involvement of private investors, as it had with the railroads. As we shall see, the formation of GE illustrates clearly how private ownership of public electrical infrastructure served as a foundation for the consolidation of finance capital, as well as for the market power of the industrial corporations that would become increasingly autonomous from the banks as this regime declined.

Edison perfected the incandescent light in 1880. At the time, lighting was overwhelmingly supplied by natural gas. Though electric lighting and power had already found limited applications, such as construction sites and lighthouses in Europe, these used isolated plants that generated only enough power for individual operations. For the light bulb to find a market, an entirely new central-station infrastructure would have to be constructed. While gas utilities provided some precedent, the capital intensity and managerial and engineering expertise necessary to build and operate these new electrical systems went well beyond anything that had come before, with the sole exception of the railroads. What was significant about Edison was not merely that he was the inventor of the electric light, but that he was the inventor of the modern electrical utility.[9] This required not merely technical and engineering work, but also assembling the organizational apparatus necessary to raise investment, and to bring the technologies developed through the R&D this financed to market.

Edison thus became one of "the first American industrialists not intimately connected with the railroads who found it necessary to raise funds on capital markets to build their initial enterprise."[10] The support of financiers allowed him to acquire equity positions in the electrical utilities that would finance the purchase and installation of his electrical

[9] William J. Hausman, Peter Hertner, and Mira Wilkins, *Global Electrification: Multinational Enterprise and International Finance in the History of Light and Power, 1878–2007* (Cambridge, UK: Cambridge University Press, 2008). The account here draws especially on pp. 3–34 of this text.

[10] Hausman, Hertner, and Wilkins, *Global Electrification*, 21–22.

systems. He had no interest in operating the utilities directly, merely in ensuring they would remain loyal customers for electrical equipment and infrastructure owned and designed by his companies and respect his overall interests.[11] In addition to the systems for electrical generation and distribution, Edison also developed products that would use these systems—in turn forcing network providers to build bigger and better electrical systems, provided by Edison, to meet the new demand. The result was the creation of a network incorporating the utilities and Edison's companies that established "both coordination and control across the market."[12] This "benign cycle" would remain a core element of GE's business strategy until World War II.[13]

Within ten years of the perfection of the incandescent light, electric power generation was rapidly being organized on an industrial scale—and being integrated within the finance capital empires of the investment banks. Initially, "this fledgling industry consisted of scores of independent local firms using different technologies and organizational structures, hobbled by local government, dependent on local investors and equipment manufacturers, and engaged in destructive competition." But increasingly through the first decades of the twentieth century, the industry would become "dominated by a few large holding companies using standardized methods of generation and organizational structure, and protected by government agencies."[14] GE's Electric Bond and Share Company would emerge as the most prominent of these holding companies.[15]

[11] William E. Rothschild, *The Secret to GE's Success* (New York: McGraw Hill Professional, 2007), 7–8; Chandler, *The Visible Hand*, 427–28.

[12] Rothschild, *The Secret to GE's Success*, 9–11; Patrick McGuire, Mark Granovetter, and Michael Schwartz, "Thomas Edison and the Social Construction of the Early Electricity Industry in America," in *Explorations in Economic Sociology*, ed. Richard Swedberg (New York: Russell Sage Foundation, 1993), 228.

[13] McGuire, Granovetter, and Schwartz, "Thomas Edison and the Social Construction of the Early Electricity Industry in America," 224–30; Hausman, Hertner, and Wilkins, *Global Electrification*, 52–55; Chandler, *The Visible Hand*, 310.

[14] McGuire, Granovetter, and Schwartz, "Thomas Edison and the Social Construction of the Early Electricity Industry in America," 213.

[15] Norman S. Buchanan, "The Origin and Development of the Public Utility Holding Company," *Journal of Political Economy* 44, no. 1 (1936): 31–53.

Apart from its capital intensity, another distinctive aspect of the electrical industry was its knowledge intensity, making control over intellectual property among the most important keys to sustaining market power. Edison was not simply an individual genius, but was rather the head of a large R&D enterprise that operated out of the legendary laboratories in Menlo Park, and later West Orange, New Jersey.[16] Edison's team raced to acquire a large number of patents in a wide variety of areas (including key components of the telegraph, telephone, and motion-picture projection system) in an attempt to gain control of what he, along with his financial backers, saw as valuable intellectual property. He and his associates established a network of companies to turn these patented technologies into marketable commodities, foremost among them the Edison Lamp Company.[17]

Drexel, Morgan, and Company, along with other investors, including William Vanderbilt, formed the Edison Electric Light Company (EELC) in 1879 to finance these efforts—supporting Edison's experiments at Menlo Park while controlling the resulting patents. It was a paradigmatic example of the emerging separation of legal ownership and possession: Edison controlled the network of operating companies (for now), while Morgan and his allies were the most important financiers. This arrangement afforded Edison "deep pockets," giving him an edge over his competitors and allowing him to further consolidate intellectual property by aggressively litigating patent disputes. He filed for patents even when his claim to an innovation was dubious, gaining and defending control of intellectual property through expensive legal action others could not afford.[18] However, financial problems and delays soon forced Edison to surrender control over EELC to an executive committee controlled by

[16] Hausman, Hertner, and Wilkins, *Global Electrification*, 11; McGuire, Granovetter, and Schwartz, "Thomas Edison and the Social Construction of the Early Electricity Industry in America," 224.

[17] Quoted in: McGuire, Granovetter, and Schwartz, "Thomas Edison and the Social Construction of the Early Electricity Industry in America," 217. According to the Edison papers, the Edison Lamp Company was originally known as the "Edison Lamp Works" when it was formed in 1881. By May of that year, it changed its name to the "Edison Lamp Company." It became a corporation in 1884, before merging with other Edison companies to become the Edison General Electric Company in 1889.

[18] Rothschild, *The Secret to GE's Success*, 5–6.

Morgan associates, and to sell EELC stock, patents, and other assets.[19] While Morgan thereby gained control of the financing arm of the Edison operation, Edison retained power over the Edison Lamp Company, the operating and research business.

The stage was set for the conflict between Edison and Morgan that would subsequently unfold. The struggle for strategic control was marked by the fact that each possessed "differing conceptions of the basic trajectory of the electricity generation business."[20] Edison's fundamental goal through the 1880s was to construct and equip a large-scale, centralized power station: the famous Pearl Street station in New York. This required a long time horizon, major fixed-capital investment, and the construction of networks of supply and demand for an unrealized technology. Conversely, Morgan preferred the more immediate profits to be reaped from smaller scale, isolated power stations servicing individual large electricity consumers (e.g., for industrial purposes). Furthermore, other investors in EELC, including Vanderbilt, had invested millions in fixed capital related to gas utilities, which Edison's central-station plants threatened to render obsolete.[21]

History would prove Edison correct; but it was only his tenacity in maneuvering to exert control over institutional capacities, technologies, and systems of production that afforded him the power to implement his vision. By threatening to resign from the firm—which would mean depriving EELC owners of future patents as well as destroying the value of the current portfolio—Edison was able to strong arm the EELC executive into authorizing $1 million for development of the Pearl Street central-station project. The Edison Illuminating Company of New York (EEIC-NY), forerunner of ConEdison, then obtained a contract for exclusive licensing rights for the entirety of New York City—but only if the new station was completed for less than $250,000 dollars, and if Edison was able to build, equip, and operate four new plants per year after 1881.[22]

[19] McGuire, Granovetter, and Schwartz, "Thomas Edison and the Social Construction of the Early Electricity Industry in America," 218.

[20] McGuire, Granovetter, and Schwartz, "Thomas Edison and the Social Construction of the Early Electricity Industry in America," 218.

[21] McGuire, Granovetter, and Schwartz, "Thomas Edison and the Social Construction of the Early Electricity Industry in America," 218, 222.

[22] McGuire, Granovetter, and Schwartz, "Thomas Edison and the Social Construction of the Early Electricity Industry in America," 222–26; Katherine White, "Preserving the

But the conflict between Morgan and Edison reflected more than just a difference over technology or market strategy. It was symptomatic of deeper, shifting relations of power, as the period of entrepreneurial ownership gave way to the consolidation of bank power. Edison was perennially in conflict with Morgan and the EELC over royalties derived from his patents, and vigorously resisted attempts by the ascendant bankers to merge his operations with the finance capital trusts they controlled.[23] Morgan and the EELC also attempted to eliminate Edison's exclusive production licenses with Edison companies. By striving to sever these exclusive contracts, Morgan was attempting to break the network of organizational linkages that was the foundation of Edison's control of these operations, digesting and remolding them into his finance capital structure.

As repeated sales of securities to raise capital meant Edison and his allies were no longer in control of a majority of EELC stock, Edison's ability to resist Morgan's designs was ultimately rooted in his ability to produce valuable intellectual property, and the recognition of this by a sufficient number of shareholders and directors who initially sided with him against Morgan in confrontations around the EELC board table. In this way, he was able to marshal sufficient support for EELC investments in new central-station projects in Boston and New York City, financed by sales of securities and patents. Morgan increased the pressure on Edison in 1884 by calling in all existing loans to the EELC, and offering new credit only at high rates of interest. Within a few years, Edison's firms were all deep in financial crisis, severely hampering his efforts to extend the network of central-station facilities. By 1886, Edison was forced to sell his remaining shares in EELC to Morgan for "a pittance"—giving Morgan full control of EELC, but not the manufacturing firms.[24] With the help of Henry Villard, a crucial ally of Edison's with longstanding links to German banks, these companies were consolidated into Edison

Patent Process to Incentivize Innovation in the Global Economy," *Journal of Science and Technology Law*, March 18, 2006; Thomas Hughes, *Networks of Power: Electrification in Western Society, 1880–1930* (Baltimore: Johns Hopkins University Press, 1983), 21.

[23] McGuire, Granovetter, and Schwartz, "Thomas Edison and the Social Construction of the Early Electricity Industry in America," 226.

[24] McGuire, Granovetter, and Schwartz, "Thomas Edison and the Social Construction of the Early Electricity Industry in America," 229–30.

General Electric (EGE) in 1889.[25] As the consolidation transferred valuable intellectual property along with Edison's manufacturing operations into the central-station business, Morgan had no choice but to take a minority stake in the larger firm if he wanted to avoid losing all control.[26]

The significant efficiency gains wrought by integrating the manufacturing operations helped put the firm on a sound financial footing, which helped advance Edison's central-station systems—including extending credit to a growing number of local utilities. The competition for effective control of the Edison companies thus had the effect of spurring the tendency toward concentration and centralization of capital, including through the consolidation of operating companies. But it also took the form of competition between such companies, as EGE's strategy of extending credit to utilities was emulated by its two chief competitors, Westinghouse and Thomson-Houston, which began "furiously competing to extend credit and sell equipment to electrical utilities across America."[27]

Crucial to this development of concentrated capitalist competition were transformations in US corporate law by the 1890s. Under the "patchwork system" of general incorporation laws that had emerged from state legislatures by the 1850s, there was little consistency across states apart from the right for investors to act under a common name.[28] This was transformed by New Jersey's Corporation Act of 1889, which allowed businesses incorporated in that state to operate nationally under the extremely liberal provisions of the state law (unleashing immense pressure on other states to follow suit).[29] The effect was the complete "privatization" of the corporation, definitively ending the ability for states to use the old system of corporate charters to control these organizations. Rather than issuing a special grant of incorporation to build

[25] Hausman, Hertner, and Wilkins, *Global Electrification*, 79.

[26] McGuire, Granovetter, and Schwartz, "Thomas Edison and the Social Construction of the Early Electricity Industry in America," 231.

[27] McGuire, Granovetter, and Schwartz, "Thomas Edison and the Social Construction of the Early Electricity Industry in America," 231–32.

[28] Joshua Barkan, *Corporate Sovereignty: Law and Government Under Capitalism* (Minneapolis, MN: University of Minnesota Press, 2013), 56; Martin J. Sklar, *The Corporate Reconstruction of American Capitalism, 1890–1916: The Market, the Law, and Politics* (Cambridge, UK: Cambridge University Press, 1988), 93–105.

[29] Chandler, *The Visible Hand*, 319; Barkan, *Corporate Sovereignty*, 56–57.

bridges, canals, and other public infrastructure, states began to see incorporation as a means to raise revenue through taxes and licensing fees.[30] Whereas previously state legislatures established corporate organization to achieve a specific "social good," the corporation was now an open-ended, state-organized, privately controlled machine for pooling, mobilizing, and investing capital. As states struggled to create the legal framework to define and regulate the structures of finance capital, the corporation emerged as "a legal embodiment of capital separate from the state and stockholders."[31]

Although the US Congress passed the Sherman Antitrust Act the following year in response to popular anger over the cartels and trusts that had come to dominate American industry, when coupled with the generalization of the corporate form via the New Jersey Corporation Act, the result was a major merger wave. Since the Act outlawed cartels and trusts, it encouraged the merger of these into single, large, consolidated enterprises to avoid antitrust prosecution—"the first essential step in the transformation of such federations into modern industrial enterprises by means of administrative consolidation and centralization."[32] Although banks had long been prominent in the organization and governance of corporations, it was only after the Sherman Act served to entrench their position and legally codify the finance capital regime that their power reached its zenith—playing a triple role as investment bankers, commercial lenders, and active institutional investors in the newly consolidated enterprises.[33]

By the end of the 1890s, finance capitalists—from both the industrial and financial side—had formed hundreds of corporations, primarily through mergers. Manufacturers, many of whom (like Edison) had resisted corporatization and attempted to sustain kinship and other personal networks as the basis for organizing production, finally relented and were brought "into the core of the corporate class." J. P. Morgan, on the other hand, "led the financial community into the industrial realm"

[30] Barkan, *Corporate Sovereignty*, 57.

[31] Barkan, *Corporate Sovereignty*, 57.

[32] Chandler, *The Visible Hand*, 320. See also Sklar, *The Corporate Reconstruction of American Capitalism*, 105–45.

[33] Roy, *Socializing Capital*, 197–198.

by "underwriting and controlling" the formation of numerous corporations, including International Harvester, U.S. Steel—and of course, General Electric.[34] Through these linkages, "industrial capital merged with investment capital and sparked the corporate revolution."[35]

The basic organizational infrastructure that would become GE had already been established by the reorganization of Edison's businesses into EGE. Just three years later, in 1891, a move by EGE to take over one of its main competitors, the Thomson-Houston Electrical Company, was transformed by Morgan—who was supposed to finance the merger—into an a opportunity to finally take control of EGE by instigating a reverse takeover of EGE by Thomson-Houston.[36] The new company, over which Morgan had "complete control," was called General Electric.[37] While marginalizing Edison's allies, Morgan supported Thomson-Houston President, Charles Coffin, to be President of the new firm. That the company did not even bear the Edison moniker was a calculated rebuke by Morgan of his rival over the preceding decade.

The merger greatly strengthened the new company's technological and market position. While the "war of the currents" at the end of the nineteenth century culminated in Westinghouse's AC systems winning out over Edison's DC,[38] the fact that Thomson-Houston was a major player in AC allowed the new GE to become the electrical systems and products leader in both markets.[39] GE aggressively pursued and captured the electric lamp market, which was the primary consumer product market prior to the development of electric appliance: GE was able to retain 50% of the American market even after the Edison patents on lamp technology expired in 1894.[40] It was also the leader in the power traction market. Moreover, the company developed efficiencies in manufacturing that lowered its costs substantially. GE soon "dominated the American

[34] Panitch and Gindin, *The Making of Global Capitalism*, 29.

[35] Roy, *Socializing Capital*, 198, 272.

[36] Chandler, *The Visible Hand*, 428.

[37] McGuire, Granovetter, and Schwartz, "Thomas Edison and the Social Construction of the Early Electricity Industry in America," 232.

[38] Rothschild, *The Secret to GE's Success*, 11–18.

[39] Rothschild, *The Secret to GE's Success*, 14–15.

[40] Leonard S. Reich, "Lighting the Path to Profit: GE's Control of the Electric Lamp Industry, 1892–1941," *The Business History Review* 66, no. 2 (1992): 307; Rothschild, *The Secret to GE's Success*, 25.

electrical industry," with more than twice the sales of Westinghouse, its only significant competitor, and soon became known as the "Electric Trust" as a result of what were perceived as anti-competitive practices.[41]

This could not have been achieved without the tremendous advantage afforded by GE's ties to Morgan's banking empire. The expansion of financial markets by the late-19th century allowed corporate entities to issue securities and debt on an ever larger—and indeed highly speculative and unsustainable—scale. This, together with the lack of adequate state regulatory capacity, led to a series of financial crises. The 1893 crisis in particular demonstrated the deep dependency of GE on external investment, and the capacity of Morgan to convert this dependence into power over corporate governance. Nevertheless, Morgan's protection—some would say "bailout"—of the company actually allowed it to emerge from the crisis in an even stronger position.[42]

Though GE had been able to generate a market for its industrial and consumer electrical products by purchasing utility stocks, this strategy was built on credit, and left the company highly leveraged. When the stock market collapsed, the company ran into a cash-flow crisis.[43] A series of bankruptcies rocked central-station utility companies between 1894 and 1896, and few could repay the debts they owed EGE and Thomson-Houston, leaving GE with a vast portfolio of worthless stocks and bonds.[44] GE was asset rich but cash poor, providing an opportunity for the further consolidation of finance capital through acquiring and reorganizing its devalued assets and extending control over the firm. That these assets were the country's core electrical infrastructure—including generation, distribution, consumption, and all the manufacturing activities that sustained these—meant that their value would endure through the crisis, as demand for electricity continued to explode. Indeed, Morgan was able to use the crisis to increase his control over GE while acquiring electrical utilities at fire sale prices—despite the fact that he had once opposed their very construction.

[41] Reich, "Lighting the Path to Profit," 306–7.

[42] Rothschild, *The Secret to GE's Success*, 22.

[43] Rothschild, *The Secret to GE's Success*, 22.

[44] McGuire, Granovetter, and Schwartz, "Thomas Edison and the Social Construction of the Early Electricity Industry in America," 233.

The process whereby Morgan gradually secured control over the Edison operations and reorganized them into GE makes clear the intrinsic and mutually reinforcing link between the state, the development of the financial system, and the formation of corporations. The separation of ownership from control drew firms into financial markets to raise capital, which empowered those amassing and supplying it. This also forced non-financial corporations to develop a set of distinctly financial capacities, thereby themselves taking part in reproducing the financial system in which they were embedded. Given the capital-intensive nature of the project of electrification, as well as the need for a constant stream of investment to support the development or acquisition of new technologies, this sector was particularly close to the finance capital structures then taking shape. GE was a vehicle for establishing private ownership and financialized governance around core electrical infrastructure, which offered a stable revenue stream while allowing the company to leverage these assets to dominate the electrical equipment and manufacturing sector through horizontal and vertical integration.

GE connected finance with the managerial, legal, engineering, and manufacturing capacities necessary to install, operate, and maintain a national electrical infrastructure. At the same time, this allowed it to dominate emerging markets in consumer and industrial electrical products that would utilize these systems. Its development of sophisticated management and administrative capacities within the structure of finance capital in order to execute these functions would eventually put GE at the very forefront of the "managerial revolution" that would emerge with the New Deal. As ascendant finance capitalists organized economic processes on ever-larger scales, they required an expanding layer of professional managers, engineers, scientists, and attorneys. This stratum also supported the great bureaucratic expansion of the American state through the progressive era. The enhancement, within the incubator of finance capital, of state and corporate administrative capacities by this growing layer of professionals established the crucial institutional conditions for the eventual marginalization of bank power.

Managerial Expansion and the Incubator of Finance Capital

The institutional development of corporate capitalism proceeded quickly. The new corporations had to hire and train "whole teams of professional executives" to cope with the vast logistical demands of the "extensive economies of scale and speed" of the operations they oversaw.[45] Banks also increasingly offered management services to firms in which they took an interest.[46] In part, this was necessitated by the particular challenges of organizing and planning Byzantine finance capital networks— which caused repeated crises "because they did not know exactly where, in the midst of their complex organizations, profits were coming from or unnecessary costs being incurred."[47] The failure of the price mechanism to operate efficiently in the context of cartelization meant that bankers had to develop mechanisms for the surveillance of firms they controlled "to evaluate the worth, organization, and prospects of companies."[48]

As GE rose to national dominance in the first decade of the twentieth century, the company instituted the strong, transparent, and highly disciplined financial and managerial systems that became its "hallmark."[49] Serving as GE's first president, Charles Coffin oversaw the formation of a then-unique administrative system in which power was centralized in the hands of top-salaried managers, who oversaw hierarchical, bureaucratic command and control structures; "order was imposed from the top," while top managers themselves "reported to a board of directors dominated by outside financiers."[50]

Boards of Directors were, at the beginning of the twentieth century, the primary forum for the expression of bank power—and the key institutional locus of the fusion of finance and industry that defined finance capital. Yet GE's size and the sophistication of its operations also meant that more than in other firms, the key policymakers "were not the outside directors, not even those who served on the executive committee, but rather its full-time salaried managers, Charles Coffin and his salaried vice presidents." GE's central office "had a larger number of functions than did the staffs on railroads and other industrial enterprises of that day," including large patent and law departments, an early advertising unit

45 Simon, "The Rise and Fall of Bank Control in the United States," 1079.

46 Christopher D. McKenna, "The Origins of Modern Management Consulting," *Business and Economic History* 24, no. 1 (1995): 53.

47 Harvey, *The Limits to Capital*, 149.

48 McKenna, "The Origins of Modern Management Consulting," 53.

49 Rothschild, *The Secret to GE's Success*, 20.

50 Chandler, *The Visible Hand*, 430.

(the "publicity bureau"), and research units.[51] GE pioneered the bureaucratic structures that would later, with broader changes in the American economy, serve as the foundation of managerial capitalism.

Yet, these systems would become generalized only because they proved to be a competitive advantage. GE's robust management and accounting systems boosted its reputation on Wall Street, and it became seen as a "safe haven for investors."[52] While the crisis of 1893 firmly established the crucial "J. P. Morgan connection" with GE, the relative stability this provided, along with its new management practices and the continuing protection of Morgan, led to GE's attracting *many different investors* by selling shares on the stock market.[53] Over the long run, this tended to loosen the company from the rigidities of finance capital, as its own capacities to buy and sell equities and debt on financial markets grew. The increasing complexity of the firm's operations, and the size of its bureaucracy, further empowered internal managers and increased their autonomy from the financier-dominated board.

The sophistication of these administrative practices was evident in, and supported by, the system of corporate self-regulation that developed over the finance capital period. If the Sherman Act illustrated the centrality of the state to shaping the organization of the capitalist economy, it simultaneously revealed how underdeveloped state institutions were at this point. While new state regulatory apparatuses had begun to take shape with the creation of the Interstate Commerce Commission in the 1880s, these "were structured so as to be insulated from democratic pressures, and their range of options was proscribed so as not to generally disturb the structures of power in the regulated industries."[54] Though this regulatory expansion emerged at the urging of the Progressive movement, the main effect of these developments "was to provide state-backed solutions to some of the contradictions of the new patterns of capitalist accumulation," which involved further enhancing the capacities of the capitalist state.[55] Capital would receive the support of the state to regulate itself, organizing markets through bank-dominated networks.

[51] Chandler, *The Visible Hand*, 431–32.

[52] Rothschild, *The Secret to GE's Success*, 23.

[53] Rothschild, *The Secret to GE's Success*, 23.

[54] Panitch and Gindin, *The Making of Global Capitalism*, 35.

[55] Panitch and Gindin, *The Making of Global Capitalism*, 35.

State-sanctioned cartelization allowed GE—in part thanks to its extensive bureaucracy—to control the major markets it had come to dominate. But it was not as if the state simply handed GE control of a large segment of the economy: rather, its market position was the result of the fiercely competitive process described above. This was the basis upon which GE developed "the mechanisms of market control as its most valuable patent rights expired, permitting the company to maintain a high level of profits for half a century."[56] In the absence of a robust and autonomous state regulatory apparatus, the system of corporate self-regulation institutionalized this position—organizing agreements among the biggest firms that reflected and secured the established market power of each in order to limit the most costly and destructive forms of competition.

This is well illustrated by the formation, in 1896, of the Board of Patent Control (BPC). After having bet on an inferior technology in choosing DC over AC, GE's entry into the AC market following the merger of the Edison companies with Thomson-Houston led to an explosion of legal conflicts with both Westinghouse and other patent-holders—costly both for the companies and the court system. Though GE and Westinghouse together controlled over 75% of the American electrical equipment industry, the return of price competition and the surge of patent-infringement suits—the defeat of which were the key to continued market control—led to declining profitability and made it clear that regulatory innovation was necessary to stabilize the market and provide an alternative means to settle such disputes. The federal government encouraged GE and Westinghouse to enter negotiations and come up with a way to resolve the issue. In March 1896, the two competitors reached an agreement to exchange licenses to all patents, except those for electric lighting. GE's dominance over Westinghouse was to be reflected in the form of larger market share.[57]

The BPC institutionalized the pact, which lasted until 1911. The body regulated the electrical industry by giving the GE-Westinghouse accord the status of a parastate agency designed to protect the defined market shares of each firm on the basis of their joint control of intellectual property. All filings for new electrical patents were sent to the BPC to

[56] Reich, "Lighting the Path to Profit," 305–6.

[57] Reich, "Lighting the Path to Profit," 308.

determine if they violated existing patents held by either GE or Westinghouse. In the event of a conflict, the BPC took legal action to stop the new patent from being approved; if the application was not a violation, then either GE or Westinghouse could acquire it. Should the inventor refuse the offer, the BPC would take them to court, which would typically result in the inventor selling the rights at a "nominal price."

GE's control of the electric lamp market was further consolidated the following year, in 1897, with the formation of the Incandescent Lamp Manufacturers Association (ILMA) through an agreement with Westinghouse and 16 smaller companies, altogether making up 95% of sales. The ILMA recognized GE's overwhelming market dominance, now sanctioned by the state. ILMA prices were set based on GE's prices, and GE was allotted 50% of the market to Westinghouse's 12%. The remaining share was divided among other, smaller producers.[58] In 1901, amidst a huge national merger wave, GE moved to take control of the independent producers (which were already deeply dependent on the larger companies) through the formation of the National Electric Lamp Company (NELC).[59] The idea was to avoid prosecution under the Sherman Antitrust Act by buying out most of the independent manufacturers while nonetheless maintaining "the charade that the companies remained independent."[60] With funds surreptitiously supplied by GE, F. S. Terry of the Sunbeam Incandescent Lamp Co. and B. G. Tremaine of the Fostoria Incandescent Lamp Co. quietly acquired most of the other independents, which they consolidated into NELC. By 1911, NELC ran 18 subsidiaries that continued operations under each company's name, coordinated and supported by NELC headquarters in Cleveland. GE acquired 75.2% of NELC stock, with an option to buy the remainder. With NELC's 38% share of the US market complementing GE's 42%, GE was overwhelmingly dominant. Only a few top people at NELC knew about GE's ownership stake—both the public and most employees at NELC believed they were competing with the "electric trust."[61]

58 Reich, "Lighting the Path to Profit," 308.

59 Rothschild, *The Secret to GE's Success*, 27–28.

60 See Rothschild, *The Secret to GE's Success*, 26, and Reich, "Lighting the Path to Profit," 308.

61 Reich, "Lighting the Path to Profit," 309.

GE's control was further extended by various licensing agreements it arranged with Westinghouse and others. This included a series of agreements with equipment producers whereby GE would provide management expertise and patent licenses in exchange for the power to decide which other companies would be permitted to purchase lamp-making products. Additionally, GE contracted with bulb suppliers to purchase most of their output in exchange for a promise to charge smaller producers a higher rate. There was also an international dimension to this cartelization, as GE exchanged patent rights and divided international economic territory with its major competitors, while reserving the massive American market for itself. GE made it clear that it had "no interest in invading foreign lamp markets"—which was in any case unnecessary, since the licensing agreements and equity stakes it had taken in foreign companies ensured it received a steady stream of income from foreign lamp sales anyway.[62]

Though progress at GE's research lab (established in 1900) was uneven, its strategy of buying up patent rights for the inventions of others allowed it to retain its top position. GE acquired patents in the early part of the twentieth century for ductile tungsten-filament and gas-filled lamps, the modern x-ray tube, the process for making silicone, the Calrod heating elements used in electric stoves, and the magnetron tube that would become the basis for the microwave oven. Control over the more efficient tungsten-filament lamp technology allowed GE to compel wholesalers and utilities to accept shipments of the older carbon-filament lamps as a condition for acquiring the newer ones. It also allowed GE to keep the prices of the new lamps high, and forced Westinghouse to take out licenses with GE that continued to limit its market share. After the panic of 1907 forced Westinghouse into bankruptcy and restructuring, it never again posed a serious threat to GE interests.[63]

Meanwhile, GE's growing range of financial functions and capacities was evident in the 1905 formation of the Electric Bond and Share Company (EBASCO). EBASCO was a holding company that controlled electrical utility companies across the United States. It proved to be an exceptionally useful tool for GE to consolidate its market power,

[62] Reich, "Lighting the Path to Profit," 313.

[63] Reich, "Lighting the Path to Profit," 311.

allowing it to reorganize and concentrate the myriad small utility companies and producers under its overall control. EBASCO also enabled GE to geographically spread investment risk, and to develop an efficient and financially strong company in each region through mechanisms of supervision and control established within the holding company. Indeed, through EBASCO, GE was able to provide financial stability to the utilities, expand service provision, and stimulate demand for electrical equipment purchases.[64] GE's position was thus critically supported by its development of management capacities and knowledge systems, which enabled it to provide financial, strategic, and administrative assistance to the utilities.[65] Before long, the power industry was so well organized that any soundly managed operating company had "no difficulty" raising capital—not least due to the proliferation of utility holding companies, EBASCO first and foremost among them.[66]

The electrical utility holding company essentially sought to solve the same problem as Edison's vertical integration strategy had. The challenge, from GE's point of view, was to provide a continuous stream of low-cost capital to the utilities so that "small, isolated, and financially weak" utility companies, which were otherwise unable to amass the capital necessary to purchase, install, and operate the electrical equipment GE manufactured, would be able to do so—and thereby to ensure that there would be markets for consumer electrical products.[67] One way to resolve this dilemma would have been to nationalize the utilities, but GE management remained adamantly opposed to this, fearing the extension of price controls that could limit profits.[68] Instead, through the holding company structure it developed, GE built up electrical utilities by bringing together manufacturing, engineering, and construction operations with investment banks and financial markets, while building *private* institutional capacity and management systems. Yet, the crisis of 1893 had not been forgotten, nor the dangers of over-leveraging by financing

[64] Buchanan, "The Origin and Development of the Public Utility Holding Company," 36–7.

[65] Rothschild, *The Secret to GE's Success*, 29–30.

[66] Buchanan, "The Origin and Development of the Public Utility Holding Company," 37, 50.

[67] Reich, "Lighting the Path to Profit," 43.

[68] Rothschild, *The Secret to GE's Success*, 30.

customers: unlike Edison's strategy, the holding company allowed GE to minimize its own risk and raise additional capital by broadening the investor base.

By virtue of its close relationship with local governments (given that it ran the utilities), EBASCO persuaded regulators to set rates as a percent of investment, which meant that the more the utilities invested in equipment and systems, the more profit they would make. Since GE both owned the utilities and manufactured the electrical systems they purchased and operated, this was a huge boon for the company, ensuring it a stable revenue stream. This made it easier for utilities to attract other investment, especially from small investors, thereby preventing any significant challenge to GE's control.[69] This arrangement effectively maximized the investment available for expanding the electrical infrastructure as rapidly as possible, while maintaining control in private hands. GE poured investment into equipment and systems, coordinating with the utilities through the holding company to plan capacity expansions as the electrical system was swiftly and dramatically scaled up.

All this furthered the development within GE of managerial and financial capacities independent from the banks. In fact, the holding company constituted an ownership structure that was markedly similar to the finance capital networks centered on the big investment banks. Indeed, EBASCO's position as the majority owner of the stocks of operating companies allowed it to "exercise strict control over management policies."[70] As noted above, banks had to develop extensive surveillance, monitoring, and management services functions in order to govern highly complex finance capital systems. That GE placed itself in a similar position vis-à-vis the utility companies indicate the degree to which it was "financialized," not only undertaking industrial production but managing the circulation of investment across discrete business operations. Tellingly, EBASCO was the largest and most important among a large number of public utility holding companies that emerged in this period; but although the others were mostly owned and controlled by banks in the classic

[69] Rothschild, *The Secret to GE's Success*, 29.

[70] Buchanan, "The Origin and Development of the Public Utility Holding Company," 37.

finance capital pattern, EBASCO was the only major case in which a "non-financial" firm took on such a role.[71]

The New American State

The process of constructing a "new American state," which rapidly gained steam at the turn of the century, was closely related to the processes that had led to GE's industrial and financial predominance. Corporate centralization was mirrored in the concentration of power in the executive bureaucracy, which became increasingly autonomous from Congress. The challenges in managing what was already becoming an international capitalist system under the auspices of increasingly large corporations propelled this state-building process, which had "begun in earnest" in the late 1890s.[72] Theodore Roosevelt took an especially strong "interest in building a strong, stable, and professional arm of civil administration under executive control."[73] Indeed, the Progressive era, as Skowronek has noted, was marked by "something of an obsession with the rationalization of governmental forms and procedures." This was expressed in "the construction and control of new administrative systems."[74]

The expansion of the administrative bureaucracy in this period included the establishment of the Department of Commerce, the Bureau of Corporations, the Federal Reserve, the Department of Commerce and Labor, the enlargement of the Treasury Department, and the reorganization of the State Department. Yet, Skowronek's classic account of the process of "building a new American state" pays far too little attention to the fact that this was a decidedly *capitalist* state. If Skorwonek is correct in his assessment that "both the celebratory public interest view and the muckraking private interest view of the early regulatory effort miss the mark," his own view misses the degree to which expanding state institutions emerged to address the needs of a distinctly capitalist society. This meant the state builders had to develop not merely a rational federal

71 Buchanan, "The Origin and Development of the Public Utility Holding Company," 41–42. See Table 1.

72 Richard Hume Werking, "Bureaucrats, Businessmen, and Foreign Trade: The Origins of the United States Chamber of Commerce," *The Business History Review* 52, no. 3 (1978): 328.

73 Skowronek, *Building a New American State*, 183.

74 Skowronek, *Building a New American State*, 177–78.

bureaucracy, but one with the tools to systematically coordinate with and organize corporate power. Building a state, in other words, also meant constructing an *integral state*.

The new Commerce Department was especially concerned with developing mechanisms to systematically coordinate with the new corporate giants. Almost immediately after its formation in 1903, Commerce officials sought to construct an "advisory body" that would integrate corporate power within the state institutions they were constructing. This culminated in the formation of the national Chamber of Commerce in 1912, one year before Commerce and Labor split into separate departments.

Far from being a "civil society" organization spontaneously formed by business leaders to "lobby" the state from without for a corporate agenda formulated autonomously, what in fact was "of paramount importance" in the formation of the national Chamber of Commerce "was the initiative exercised by government bureaucrats."[75] It was Commerce officials, not corporate elites, who took the lead, even overcoming significant *resistance* from corporate executives. Creating a venue for corporate elites to participate in policy development, these officials believed, would ensure "buy in" for the department's political agenda, facilitate the development of effective policy, assist in gathering information, and coordinate advocacy and "lobbying" efforts. Linking major corporate interests with those of the new department could also form a vital base of support in its turf war with the older, more venerable Department of State, while helping it to secure allocations from Congress, thereby supporting its institutional development and ascent within the hierarchy of state apparatuses.[76]

This is not to say that the activities of powerful corporations like GE did not include lobbying Congress on behalf of a legislative agenda—indeed they did. In fact, concerns among Commerce personnel (especially in the Bureau of Manufactures) that such efforts lacked coordination and focus were among of the most important motivations behind their efforts to organize the Chamber of Commerce. The Commerce Department saw its role in establishing the Chamber as creating a venue for a broader and more coherent—class wide—business consensus. And it was a tireless initiative indeed. Only after years of wrangling did Secretary of Commerce

[75] Werking, "Bureaucrats, Businessmen, and Foreign Trade," 322.

[76] Werking, "Bureaucrats, Businessmen, and Foreign Trade," 328.

Oscar Strauss succeed in creating the National Council of Commerce in 1907, comprised of delegates from regional Chambers of Commerce and headquartered in Washington, to facilitate easier contact with Congress and executive branch agencies. Yet even then, capitalists were largely uninterested in active political engagement, apparently convinced "that if they hold their monthly meetings and pass resolutions, the Government should do the balance," as a frustrated Strauss lamented.[77]

Charles Nagel, Strauss' successor at Commerce, believed that the incredible expansion of state institutional capacity then underway would allow him to bring about "a great, correlated, unifying national policy"—while explicitly recognizing that if the state was to regulate business effectively, it needed to create a consultative forum of corporate managers "to guide us right and to show us the possibilities of our own authority."[78] As Nagel put it at a NY State Chamber of Commerce meeting, "the trend is perfectly plain. The story of the departments in Washington alone would tell it... Everywhere we are passing from the passive to the active state. We were mere watchmen; we have become real builders."[79] And in order to do so, he saw that the state needed the support and reinforcement of corporate power: indeed, one of the very things the state "builders" were building were the mechanisms that would coordinate, organize, and politically integrate capital.

The national Chamber of Commerce was finally established in 1912, after President Taft called for a large conference of business leaders in Washington, organized by the Department of Commerce. Power within the new organization lay with an elected 25-person board, and the executive committee it elected. Voting rights were graduated to ensure that bigger organizations had the largest voice. The Secretary of Commerce played the primary role in funneling information from the various conferences and forums of business leaders to the White House, as well as in presenting state agendas to assembled business elites. In this way, the Commerce Department would remain the key institutional node of the integral state until the 1960s, when Treasury and the Federal Reserve would overtake it in some respects—though not its organizational functions in directly convening and liaising with capitalists.

[77] Werking, "Bureaucrats, Businessmen, and Foreign Trade," 330.

[78] Werking, "Bureaucrats, Businessmen, and Foreign Trade," 338.

[79] Werking, "Bureaucrats, Businessmen, and Foreign Trade," 332.

Yet, even as the builders of the new American state sought to organize business and deepen its cooperation with the federal bureaucracy, the expansion of state capacity also enhanced its ability to challenge and reshape structures of economic power. In 1911, state support for the system of corporate self-regulation appeared to shift when a major antitrust investigation dissolved both the BPC and the NELA. Importantly, this did not come as the result of a specific market failure.[80] Rather, in the emerging heyday of politically popular "trust-busting," the Taft administration decided to prosecute GE for its control of the electric lamp market—or at least, to challenge the specific *form* of that control. The state brought a suit against GE and 34 other companies, which was above all related "to GE's relationship with [NELA], which gave the appearance of competition where it did not exist; to price-fixing and market-sharing agreements with Westinghouse, [NELA], and other companies; to the use of process and improvement patents in the suppression of competition; to the preferential agreements with glass bulb and lamp-making machinery manufacturers; and to the distribution system that required wholesalers to accept a variety of lamp types while maintaining prices at levels chosen by GE."[81]

In the end, GE was found to control more than 75% of NELA members.[82] GE management conceded on all points except the company's ability to use patents to establish market power, arguing that patents are inherently monopolistic. The federal judge accepted this argument and arranged a consent decree whereby GE and others were to cease all anti-competitive practices *except* those associated with patent control.[83] GE then requested—and was granted—permission to acquire specific members of the NELA organization and integrate them within GE as subsidiaries. GE also purchased the remainder of NELA stock, and publicly made its ownership known, while terminating the special agreements with Westinghouse and other manufacturers, bulb makers, and machinery suppliers, and agreed to stop setting the prices wholesalers and retailers could charge for GE lamps.[84]

[80] Reich, "Lighting the Path to Profit," 314.

[81] Reich, "Lighting the Path to Profit," 314.

[82] Rothschild, *The Secret to GE's Success*, 28.

[83] Reich, "Lighting the Path to Profit," 315.

[84] Reich, "Lighting the Path to Profit," 315; Rothschild, *The Secret to GE's Success*, 28.

With control of intellectual property firmly established as a legitimate foundation of market power, patent-licensing agreements "now became the vehicle for GE's dominance."[85] Such agreements reached with Westinghouse after the decision specified market share and royalties, and divided up export markets. For its part, Westinghouse offered GE royalty-free licenses and the right to sublicense its patents, agreeing to share technical information while admitting the validity of all GE patents and patent applications. This removed Westinghouse's incentive to conduct Research and Development, and ensured that GE would remain the dominant force in the industry by far.[86]

Thus, while the decision had little effect on GE's domination of the American electric lamp market, it changed the institutional form this domination took, nudging this further in the direction of the modern multidivisional corporation. The lesson was clear: the growing capacity of the state to constitute and regulate competitive markets meant that firms should expect disciplinary action to break up cartel arrangements, even if it would still rely to a large extent on centralized and hierarchical corporate bureaucracies to construct and manage market processes. Rather than networked relations among firms in the form of cartels, economic processes would increasingly need to be reorganized within firms as divisions, while external relations with other firms would be mediated by market mechanisms regulated by the state. It was not "bigness" as such that was the issue, but rather the specific organizational form of economic power that had developed during the finance capital period. It was this organizational form that would be fundamentally challenged, both through conflict and collaboration between state and corporate managers, over the highly turbulent period spanning World War I and World War II.

[85] Reich, "Lighting the Path to Profit," 315.

[86] Reich, "Lighting the Path to Profit," 315.

CHAPTER 3

The Formation of the State-Capital Complex

The managerial corporations that had grown up within the incubator of finance capital increasingly emerged as the dominant force in the American economy, as their capacities dramatically expanded with state support over the World War I years. The final nail in the coffin of finance capital would come through the Great Depression and the New Deal, as the instability of the bank-centric system became clearly apparent—spurring the development of a more robust state that was ever more able to regulate and organize an economy that was not merely national, but increasingly global. The formation of a more muscular—and more autonomous—state would go hand-in-glove with the transition from the finance capital to the managerial era, as it acted to curtail bank power and to restructure the institutional networks that supported it.

Part and parcel of building these new state capacities was constructing integral state mechanisms to support them by integrating the new corporate elite into expanding state institutions. This was particularly critical as policymakers struggled to stabilize an embattled capitalism rocked by unprecedented economic crisis and waves of class struggle from below. Yet organizing capital became more complicated as the increasing autonomy of industrial corporations from bank networks meant that the economy was no longer dominated by a handful of investment bankers, but rather a much broader group of corporate managers. If the New Deal marked the moment when the managerial era came into its own as the successor to

© The Author(s), under exclusive license to Springer Nature Switzerland AG 2022

S. Maher, *Corporate Capitalism and the Integral State*, Marx, Engels, and Marxisms,
https://doi.org/10.1007/978-3-030-83772-3_3

finance capital, this was also accompanied by a new political centrality for GE and its managers—playing a primary role in venues such as Roosevelt's Business Advisory Council (BAC) in organizing class consensus around reforms seen as necessary to save the system. Morgan's boardrooms were no longer sufficient—formal state venues had to be constructed where consensus around policy could be reached among managerial capitalists embedded in large corporate firms from many different sectors.

State managers and corporate executives had little understanding at the beginning of the Great Depression of what it would take to restore accumulation and reduce the unemployment that was at the root of so much of the social unrest in the 1930s. The state's response to the crisis was initially to reinforce the cartels that had constituted the institutional basis of corporate self-regulation—effectively granting them the status of a state apparatus in the form of the National Recovery Administration (NRA), which explicitly aimed to support their ability to set prices. Yet simply keeping prices up was, on its own, hardly sufficient. Nor were the firm-level "welfare" programs that comprised the so-called New Capitalism adequate.

It was only as these efforts failed to address the crisis that the state turned to national welfare programs and fiscal expansion, while working to build support for these measures among the corporate elite. Rather than the rise of a coherent new "Keynesian" doctrine, this shift emerged through a conflictual, and highly uncertain, series of pragmatic responses to an unprecedented crisis. If the BAC was initially created to build support for granting the cartels the imprimatur of state power through the NRA, it ended up serving as a venue for working out the policy program and institutional restructuring that would replace this—giving birth to the managerial regime that would persist until the crisis of the 1970s.

From the Great War to the New Capitalism

By World War I, the growing "trust busting" activism of the state contributed to breaking up the organizational forms that had comprised the structure of finance capital. The increasing confidence of state managers was also reflected in Taft's appointment of Louis Brandeis to the Supreme Court, a major critic of bank power who advocated banning directors from sitting on the boards of competing companies—which would break up the "interlocking directorates" that were so foundational for the organization of finance capital.[1] Moreover, Taft's successor, Woodrow Wilson, "had come to office determined to increase the relative autonomy of the American state from American capital," to which end the state's powers were "considerably enhanced" by the passage of the Income Tax Act, the establishment of the Federal Trade Commission, and the expansion of the departments of State and Commerce.[2]

The Clayton Act that came out of the 1912 Congressional Pujo hearings—the first tentative step toward reducing bank power—did not ban interlocking directorates. Rather, it established a "temporary truce" between bankers and the state that held until the market crash of 1929, after which the state finally intervened to radically reorganize the financial system and bring an end to the finance capital system. In part, this new activism was a reflection of the expanding capacities of state institutions; it was also a response to the repeated crises that had so blatantly pointed out the inadequacy of finance capital to provide enduring economic stability. The fear these trends aroused among finance capitalists was reflected in Morgan's sudden withdrawal from the Boards of Directors of 30 companies in 1914, including that of Westinghouse (while remaining on the board of GE). Though the move was intended to placate the Wilson Administration, almost immediately "Congress began to work on legislation that would eliminate bank control."[3]

Much like the way the Sherman Antitrust Act marked the end of the entrepreneurial era, the dissolution of finance capital was hardly automatic: state power played a decisive role in these economic reorganizations, even though in both cases the decline of the earlier regime was already noticeable, and crucial institutional conditions for its successor were already in place. Just as bank-centered finance capital networks had already loosened considerably by the 1930s, so had increasingly well-developed state and corporate bureaucracies supported the formation of a more decentralized financial system. Yet it was direct state intervention after the 1929 crisis that formally broke up the finance capital networks of bank power and codified the autonomy of the industrial corporations.

[1] Simon, "The Rise and Fall of Bank Control in the United States," 1082.

[2] Panitch and Gindin, *The Making of Global Capitalism*, 45–46.

[3] Simon, "The Rise and Fall of Bank Control in the United States," 1083.

The establishment of the Federal Reserve System in 1912 facilitated the expansion and decentralization of financial markets, while ensuring that the state would no longer have to rely on Morgan, as it had in the 1907 financial crisis, to act as its conduit in fire-fighting financial conflagrations. The growing role of the state in constructing and reproducing financial markets further facilitated the development of GE's institutional capacities to pool capital from many different investors, which had already reduced the firm's reliance on Morgan. The development of state power thereby increased the extent of *impersonal* ownership of the corporation, freeing control of economic assets from particularistic finance capital networks and subjecting the firm to greater market discipline and control—and further entrenching the power of professional managers. As it took on the coordinating and regulatory functions of the banks, the state's institutional capacities likewise expanded, further cementing the "fusion of government and financial power."[4]

While the growth of state capacities and the development of the financial system enhanced the autonomy of industrial corporations from the banks, the linkages between these corporations and the state continued to grow, along with the size and complexity of industrial firms. This process was radically accelerated with the entry of the United States into the Great War. Securing the production of war materiel required an unprecedented degree of economic planning, and therefore demanded extensive coordination between corporate managers and state bureaucrats. While profit-driven corporate managers would directly oversee production, it was geopolitically oriented state personnel in rapidly growing bureaucracies who took the lead in the overall planning of industrial mobilization.

The War Industries Board (WIB), the War Labor Board (WLB), and the War Finance Corporation (WFC)—all created under the Departmental Reorganization Act—constituted the major mechanisms for wartime state-corporate economic coordination. The WIB—which was gradually given "more and more authority over the entire economy"[5]—had broad authority to secure a steady supply of war materiel, as well as to support non-war industries to ensure these were not excessively affected

[4] Panitch and Gindin, *The Making of Global Capitalism*, 43–44.

[5] David Loth, *Swope of G. E.: The Story of Gerard Swope and General Electric in American Business* (New York: Simon and Schuster, 1958), 85.

by the war. Its powers included establishing price controls, standardizing products, and developing and implementing new mass production techniques while rapidly up-scaling American industrial production. By the end of the war, "the government operation was of such a magnitude that it compared to even the largest industrial corporation as that corporation compared to a village garage."[6]

This effort relied upon the participation of the growing stratum of professional managers from private industry to serve in the bureaucracy, where they helped to formulate and implement war production plans. One such man was the future president of GE, Gerard Swope, who resigned from his position at the company (while continuing to receive his salary) to serve as a "dollar-a-year" man with the WIB Purchase, Storage, and Traffic Division. In this capacity, Swope oversaw and coordinated, alongside General Hugh Johnson, a vast logistical supply operation, bringing the managerial expertise he had acquired at GE. Though the planning apparatus was always intended to be temporary, the links between corporate managers and state personnel formed during the war served as the basis for stable and enduring networks that would be sustained long after it was over, as we shall see.

With massive government borrowing to pay for the war making it difficult for private corporations to attract capital, the government set up the WFC, headed by Wall Street banker Eugene Meyer Jr., to extend credit to war industries, mostly by giving loans to private banks that provided financing to these firms.[7] The WFC also provided loans to the European Allies, which funded "massive imports of US munitions, food, raw materials, and manufactured goods during the war," leading to a doubling of US exports.[8] After the armistice, as the wartime boom lapsed into postwar recession, its activities were greatly expanded "to assist in the transition to peacetime conditions."[9] This included extending $41 million in loans to electrical utilities, which indirectly helped finance

[6] Loth, *Swope of G.E.*, 86.

[7] Committee on the History of the Federal Reserve System, "War Finance Corporation (1918–1939)" (Federal Reserve Bank of St. Louis, January 11, 1956), National Archives College Park, MD.

[8] Panitch and Gindin, *The Making of Global Capitalism*, 45.

[9] Committee on the History of the Federal Reserve System, "War Finance Corporation (1918–1939)."

purchases of GE-manufactured equipment.[10] It also extended financing to GE directly, by way of Swope negotiating an $11,000,000 loan on easy terms with the new Reconstruction Finance Corporation.[11] The International General Electric Company loaned WFC funds to "responsible foreign corporations" to finance purchases of GE products.[12]

During the war, the federal government also embarked upon an unprecedented effort to arbitrate industrial relations. The WLB pressured "strategic employers," including GE, to institute collective bargaining in the form of firm-specific "works councils" to diffuse worker grievances.[13] As war broke out in Europe, the Electrical Industry Trades Alliance (EITA) had sought to organize skilled workers in Schenectady, NY, the heart of GE's manufacturing operation.[14] In this context of developing industrial conflict, the WIB worked, along with the WLB, to ensure labor discipline both with the carrot, by ensuring a supply of consumer products, and with the stick, by banning strikes and freezing wages. The WLB even implemented a "work or fight" rule in 1918, which threatened unemployed men with immediately being drafted.[15]

Although the armistice brought an end to these agencies' involvement in mediating industrial relations, it did not resolve the underlying class conflict that had required this management in the first place. This was hammered home as labor unrest erupted at GE facilities, part of a national wave of strikes aiming to preserve wartime wage gains and force union recognition.[16] The retreat of the state from mediating labor-capital relations threw responsibility for disciplining labor back on to corporate managers, who proved in many cases not to be particularly broad-minded

[10] Hausman, Hertner, and Wilkins, *Global Electrification*, 129.

[11] Loth, *Swope of G. E.*, 102.

[12] General Electric Company, "Twenty-Ninth Annual Report," Annual Report, 1920, 8.

[13] Kim McQuaid, "Young, Swope and General Electric's 'New Capitalism': A Study in Corporate Liberalism, 1920–1933," *The American Journal of Economics and Sociology* 36, no. 3 (1977): 324.

[14] McQuaid, "Young, Swope and Genereal Electric's 'New Capitalism,'" 324.

[15] Gerald Shenk, *"Work or Fight!": Race, Gender, and the Draft in World War One* (London, UK: Palgrave Macmillan, 2005).

[16] McQuaid, "Young, Swope and General Electric's 'New Capitalism,'" 324–25.

in their approach.[17] Nevertheless, it became clear that business would have to do something to address the rising tide of labor mobilization after the war.

Based on his performance at Wilson's "National Industrial Conferences" of 1919–1920, where he had issued a strong call for labor conciliation, Owen D. Young—appointed Chairman of GE in 1922—was well on his way to becoming the leading spokesman for the so-called New Capitalism. Proponents claimed this would ameliorate labor problems through the opportunities that would be unleashed by "mass production, invention, and industrial 'self-regulation' under governmental auspices"—all of which would sustain new firm-level measures to pacify labor.[18] Since the WLB had enshrined labor's right to collective representation, the first step seemed to be for employers to soften their opposition to collective bargaining and set up "company unions" they could control. With the eruption of the postwar strike wave, these views moved into the mainstream of the discussion among the management of the largest firms and state officials.[19]

When Young replaced the 80-year-old Coffin as GE Chairman in 1922, he appointed Swope as the company's president. Swope and Young put the New Capitalism into practice at GE, building on "works councils" (in which management worked with worker representatives to formulate work rules and other matters), adding life insurance, loan, and pension programs (with GE managing the Pension Trust itself), promoting worker stock ownership, and offering company-guaranteed mortgages to higher-ranking personnel.[20] These programs had the additional effect of enhancing the power of internal managers, which was supported by the increasing fragmentation of equity holdings among a steadily growing number of stockholders—nearly 50% of which, company reports proudly noted, were women.[21]

[17] Richard W. Gable, "Birth of an Employers' Association," *Business History Review* 33 (January 1, 1959): 535–545.

[18] Josephine Young Case and Everett Needham Case, *Owen D. Young and American Enterprise: A Biography* (Boston: David R. Godine, 1982), 195.

[19] Case and Case, *Owen D. Young and American Enterprise*, 192–208.

[20] McQuaid, "Young, Swope and General Electric's 'New Capitalism,'" 326; Rothschild, *The Secret to GE's Success*, 39–54.

[21] General Electric Company, "Twenty-Ninth Annual Report," 10.

By 1917, firms like GE "were becoming managerial" in that "career managers who were beginning to make decisions at the top as well as middle and lower levels were beginning to look on themselves as professionals."[22] While in the finance capital era, the Board of Directors was the key locus of corporate rule—as the institutional link between industry and finance—with the decline of bank control by World War I boards increasingly became the backwaters they would remain until the 1990s. Though major investors still made up the majority of board members, by the start of the war Coffin, "the veteran professional manager," had become the board's Chairman. And after the war, "the number of insiders on General Electric's board grew larger and the number of financiers declined." Moreover, over time "senior managers of other large industrial enterprises" gradually replaced the remaining financiers.[23]

GE's centrality as an institutional foundation of the integral state was closely related to these developments inside the corporation. It was the president, Swope, who was responsible for all policy and strategy decisions in GE. Though he "consulted" Young, the latter "never became involved in directly running the company."[24] However, the chairman hardly sat idle. Well-connected politically and widely respected, Young maintained relationships with the most important industrialists, financiers, and politicians. Although he was a Democrat, he often worked closely with Republicans and was especially close with Herbert Hoover, who was Commerce secretary through the 1920s. As the central axis of the integral state, the Commerce department played the leading role in "reconciling the vast complex of business interests through a multitude of public–private conferences, inquiries, and committees operating in accordance with Secretary Hoover's corporatist notion of an associative state."[25]

Young's articulation of the "new capitalism" contained a similarly discernable statist emphasis. As he put it in a famous speech at Harvard University in 1927, the rise to prominence of a "new management" that was "free of buccaneering proclivities" would facilitate, with the support of a "Government of Business," a "voluntaristic network of trade associations," leading to an era of opportunity and economic stability with

[22] Chandler, *The Visible Hand*, 453.

[23] Chandler, *The Visible Hand*, 451–52.

[24] Reich, "Lighting the Path to Profit," 320.

[25] Panitch and Gindin, *The Making of Global Capitalism*, 51.

an increasingly equitable distribution of income through employee stock ownership programs like GE's.[26] Young's extensive involvement in the integral state included serving as a top advisor to Calvin Coolidge on international banking issues, and he was instrumental in the development of both the Dawes and Young Plans for German reparations through the 1920s. He also sustained close contacts with Franklin Roosevelt, who even tried to get Young to run for the Senate. In 1929, Young was named *Time* magazine "Man of the Year" and was repeatedly suggested as a presidential candidate in the press.

Meanwhile, except for a dip during the recession of 1922, GE's plants, labor productivity, assets, and profits all grew rapidly, while it managed to nimbly sidestep occasional antitrust actions throughout the decade. The core of GE's business remained electric lamps, an industry it controlled with relative ease as falling costs transformed the incandescent lamp into a mass-market product over the 1920s. Given the company's overwhelming dominance, investors were increasingly hesitant to provide capital for lamp producers not incorporated within the GE umbrella. At the same time, improvements in lamp efficiency, reduced prices, and falling energy costs aided the company's efforts to shed its image as the "Electric Trust."[27]

The massive investment it received during and after the war years drew large numbers of scientists to staff GE's Research Lab.[28] GE's integration into the military-industrial complex supported the expansion of its engineering and advanced R&D capacities, generating technologies which it "spun off" as marketable commodities through its divisional structure. GE was therefore a vehicle through which state defense spending was channeled into the development of new product lines, and ensuring that advanced technologies remained in the hands of US firms. Along with strategic acquisitions, such R&D allowed GE to provide an "expanding array of new electrically powered products, devices, and systems." This in turn provoked a "need for more electricity to be generated, transmitted, and distributed by the electric utilities," which would then "have to purchase bigger and improved systems to expand their networks."[29]

[26] McQuaid, "Young, Swope and General Electric's 'New Capitalism,'" 329.

[27] Reich, "Lighting the Path to Profit," 317–18.

[28] Rothschild, *The Secret to GE's Success*, 24.

[29] Rothschild, *The Secret to GE's Success*, 58–59.

GE, it seemed, would continue to grow in proportion with the skyrocketing consumption of electric power, controlling as it did essentially every aspect of the production, distribution, and consumption of electrical equipment and products.

Key to this enhanced "benign cycle" was an innovative credit-based retail strategy, and a huge intensification of the firm's marketing efforts. Both Swope and Young were convinced that the "sales effort" was just as essential to profits as product development and production.[30] By extolling the virtues of electric living, GE sought to create greater demand for electrical products, virtually all of which it manufactured. Electricity could now be used for cooking, refrigeration, washing and drying clothes, air conditioning, and much more. The electric stove-maker Hotpoint, as well as the Hurley Manufacturing Company, which produced electric washers and driers, were taken over by GE and integrated within its expanding home appliance business. In 1927, the "Monitor Top" refrigerator was added to its product lines, along with electric fans and vacuum cleaners. The advertising effort to associate GE with "Progress" in the public mind—a new strategy in American capitalism—was clearly a success by the 1930s, by which time GE's brand was as omnipresent in American homes as the American flag.

The retail system Swope devised relied heavily on the company's sophisticated financial and management functions, and allowed GE to control distribution of its products without directly owning retail or wholesale outlets. This was supported by the establishment of the GE Credit Company (GECC) in 1932 to provide financing to franchised dealers.[31] GECC leased products to licensed retailers nationwide, with each granted exclusive territory. That the dealers and distributors who physically sold the products never actually owned them allowed GE to set prices at the retail and wholesale level. Moreover, in addition to being supported by a national advertising program, merchants were supplied with business, accounting, and sales training, as well as training in repair and maintenance services. Since authorized retailers were the sole providers of GE factory-authorized parts, the margins for parts and service business remained high, making the system highly lucrative for retailers.

[30] Reich, "Lighting the Path to Profit," 320.

[31] Rothschild, *The Secret to GE's Success*, 61.

An antitrust suit against GE in 1924, focusing both on its patent-licensing agreement with Westinghouse, which institutionalized GE's market dominance and inhibited price competition between the two firms, as well as Swope's agency distribution system (which was claimed to be an evasion of the 1911 consent decree on price fixing), was dismissed by a Federal District Court. Although the government appealed to the Supreme Court, the result was the same: GE's control of intellectual property was held to be a legal foundation for protecting its market dominance through such practices.[32]

The antitrust suit itself revealed significant differences among state apparatuses, depending on their specific functions, in relation to the central place of a powerful corporation like GE within the integral state. Nonetheless, this did not hinder the integral state's development, with GE as a central player. This was especially seen in the growth of the trade promotion capacities of the departments of State and Commerce through the 1920s. As the head of Commerce's Division of Regional Information understood it, this was designed to support the "aggressive expansion policy" of American corporations.[33] Though EBASCO had some pre-World War I foreign investments, these had been "very limited."[34] In 1917, encouraged by the State Department, EBASCO undertook its first major foreign investments in utilities abroad, developing electrical infrastructure in US-allied Latin American states. These large public works projects closely resembled what would later be called "international development" programs, and were closely coordinated with the state.

It was during the allegedly "isolationist" 1920s that GE really globalized, becoming one of the first examples of what we would today think of as a multinational corporation. In addition to extending loans through the WFC for GE electrical equipment and products, the state directly encouraged GE to implement the holding company model it had pioneered in the US with EBASCO elsewhere around the world. In 1923, EBASCO organized the American & Foreign Power Co. to handle most of its foreign business. By the close of the 1920s, it had become "the largest multinational enterprise in public utilities" with 47,000 employees,

[32] Reich, "Lighting the Path to Profit," 321.

[33] Panitch and Gindin, *The Making of Global Capitalism*, 51.

[34] Hausman, Hertner, and Wilkins, *Global Electrification*, 144–45.

virtually all of whom were stationed abroad.[35] This foreign investment came with the practices, standards, and institutional forms developed by EBASCO in the US, as well as the incorporation of new territories into American-dominated financial and political systems.

GE's administrative systems and practices thus became central to the expansion of a nascent American empire. The global expansion of American capitalism brought with it the imposition of American institutional forms, standards, and practices were upon new local contexts. As the American & Foreign Power Company explained its procedures, it sought:

> (1) To investigate and to acquire properties; (2) To rearrange the contractual relations with the governing authorities so as to open the way to development; (3) To reorganize the financial structures of the operating companies to permit improvements and plant additions at the lowest practicable cost; (4) To prepare plans for development and construction of new power plant capacity and modern transmission and distribution systems [typically supplied by GE]; (5) To apply the latest, most modern commercial development to the property, in the process selling new electrical merchandise in well-lighted, attractive stores; (6) To introduce new operating and accounting methods, so as to improve efficiency while upgrading service and lowering operating costs.[36]

Although GE distributed its interest in EBASCO to its shareholders in 1925, it maintained a "network" relationship with both that company and American & Foreign Power, with Young sitting on its board long after the spin-off. Among other things, this meant that "typically the utilities managed by American & Foreign Power purchased GE equipment" on an ongoing basis.[37]

GE's financial operations and capacities were essential to organizing and regulating international markets in the face of the relative institutional weakness of the American state. Although the state supported the extension of American power abroad by encouraging corporations to internationalize, its ability to effectively establish and police global capitalist markets in the interwar period was limited. This was apparent in the operations of the International General Electric Company (IGE),

[35] Hausman, Hertner, and Wilkins, *Global Electrification*, 182–87.

[36] Hausman, Hertner, and Wilkins, *Global Electrification*, 185.

[37] Hausman, Hertner, and Wilkins, *Global Electrification*, 171, 182.

established by Swope as a wholly owned subsidiary of GE responsible for exports and foreign licenses. True to the classic pattern, over the 1920s the firm organized cartel agreements, underpinned by foreign direct investment. This allowed GE to control the actions of competing firms, and in effect to set prices.[38]

At the end of 1924, the Convention for the Development and Progress of the International Incandescent Lamp industry was signed, under the guidance and stewardship of IGE's European representative J.M. Woodward. IGE's leadership role in organizing these arrangements indicated the sophisticated nature of GE's management and administration compared with other major firms, as well as its global reach. As Woodward reported at the close of the negotiations, "I must say without being misunderstood that the European parties are entirely amateurish, for reasons which arise from their historic division of interest. They realize this, and that realization coupled with their still active mistrust of each other has caused them to accept our leadership and to invite its continuance."[39] As GE took large equity stakes in the major electrical equipment manufacturing companies in England, France, and Germany and kept minority interests in European public utilities, Siemen's head of finance, Max Heller, complained in a note to Young in November 1929 that "the whole world belongs to the Americans."[40] Given this, it is easy to see how state managers would depend upon the perspectives and input of corporate executives when making policy or conducting diplomacy; no doubt this is part of the reason they were urged to globalize in the first place.

The Phoebus Agreement initiated in 1925 was perhaps the most administratively sophisticated component of the vast international electrical cartel. Established under the rubric of the Swiss Corporation Phoebus SA, and incorporating 90–95% of the industry, the agreement controlled factories and retailers, fixed prices, and regulated output. This required constructing the institutional infrastructure to administer production quotas among the participants, and to manage the exchange of technical information and sharing of patent rights.[41] The organization consisted of a General Assembly that set policy, an Administrative

[38] Rothschild, *The Secret to GE's Success*, 67.

[39] Reich, "Lighting the Path to Profit," 324.

[40] Hausman, Hertner, and Wilkins, *Global Electrification*, 171.

[41] Reich, "Lighting the Path to Profit," 325; Rothschild, *The Secret to GE's Success*, 68.

Board that issued the rules to carry out the policy, and a Board of Arbitration that adjudicated disputes. It also developed a testing lab, which was necessary to assure consistent quality among the members' products (i.e., to ensure firms were not "cheating" by selling cheaper, sub-standard products), and a marketing division that promoted the use of electric lighting.

Although GE did not join Phoebus, the lack of an international trade and investment framework meant that it was up to the largest and most powerful firm—deeply connected to the American state—to oversee international regulation of the industry. GE's involvement was absolutely essential to the functioning of the cartel—including the direct involvement of IGE in negotiating and administering the arrangements. In fact, GE's international dominance, including cartel agreements with major European producers, made joining the arrangement unnecessary. This was especially the case in view of its substantial equity stake in the principal cartel members: GE was generally "the largest single shareholder by far" in these firms, which gave it "a very strong voice in company policies."[42] Dividend payments from these holdings also supplemented the financial gains GE wrought from lamp sales via licensing fees—even where other cartel arrangements prevented GE from exporting lamps themselves. Meanwhile, GE's decision not to formally join Phoebus helped it to avoid a worrying FTC investigation initiated by the Senate into GE's role in the electrical industry, which threatened to break up the company.

By the 1930s, amidst the Great Depression, the expiration of patents, and the international tensions leading up to World War II, the Phoebus agreement was rendered a dead letter. Unlicensed producers were now free to use relatively up-to-date lamp technology without regard for licensing agreements, forcing GE to shift its strategy to acquiring new patents on improvements, allowing it to maintain a competitive edge. This prevented GE's competitors from producing state-of-the-art lamps and implementing the most efficient production methods through the rest of the decade. Japanese producers did attempt to break into the American market, supported by extremely low-wage labor and a devalued yen. But GE's market position and comfortable margins enabled it to rebuff the invasion by introducing an "economy" lamp (called "Type-D"), which, although priced the same as the Japanese product, was of much higher

[42] Reich, "Lighting the Path to Profit," 326.

quality. GE was also able to get the courts to exclude some Japanese lamps on the grounds that they had some similar markings to those produced by GE, infringing on the company's copyrights.

The breakdown of international order, rooted in domestic and international contradictions that states could not resolve, contributed to the generalized crumbling of the "new capitalism" edifice. But this had been underway almost since the moment it was announced in the early 1920s. These cracks were rooted in the contradictions and limits of corporate self-regulation, which began to show signs of weakness as "dominant enterprises in oligopolistic or capital-intensive industries proved unable to transcend industry or firm-specific matrices."[43] The international cartel agreements that held the system together at the global level were highly unstable, straining under competitive contradictions and capitalism's crisis tendencies. Domestic "human engineering" programs were also faltering, as attempts to integrate workers within corporate structures through equity ownership and pension programs failed and labor organization spread.

GE's management wasn't merely shirking responsibility for capitalism's social ills when it wrote in its 1927 Annual Report that, despite the rhetoric espoused by Swope and Young, "it is difficult for any one company… to do anything comprehensive in eliminating, or, indeed, even affecting to any great extent" the problem of unemployment.[44] But if, as the report concluded, "neither one company nor one industry can solve it," this begged the question which most capitalists and indeed state actors were not yet ready to answer conclusively: what force but the state could do so?[45] Despite Swope and Young's best efforts, the faltering of firm-level measures signaled the need to formulate a national welfare model, organized and implemented by the state. However, even as they came to lead the corporate elite in recognizing the need for an increased role for the state in coordinating the economy, they remained committed to corporate self-regulation throughout the decade, jealously defending managerial power against state encroachment.

[43] McQuaid, "Young, Swope and General Electric's 'New Capitalism,'" 330.

[44] General Electric Company, "Thirty-Sixth Annual Report," Annual Report, 1927, 16.

[45] General Electric Company, "Thirty-Sixth Annual Report," 16.

Capitalist Crisis, State Formation, and the "Planning Impulse"

The stock market crash of 1929, and the ensuing Great Depression, put the final nails into the coffin of the "New Capitalism." Nevertheless, GE's ownership of core aspects of the electrical infrastructure allowed it to weather the storm. Electric lighting was no longer a luxury, but a necessity. This afforded GE great stability even in the worst of times. Electrical utilities, among GE's most important customers, would remain sound investments and continue to add capacity. Similarly, amidst the collapse of appliance and heavy equipment sales (as the crisis struck the Insull utilities empire), which forced the company to lay off 50% of the workforce, GE could still count on strong lamp sales as an "extremely important" source of profit. GE was also able to prevent prices falling, both through Swope's retail system and through the strength of industrial cartels. State support for these cartels was longstanding, as we have seen, and had become more significant in the electrical equipment sector over the 1920s. The National Recovery Act of 1934 would further extend overt state support for industrial self-regulation and price fixing, which played a major role in these firms' ability to survive the crisis years.

This stability allowed GE to serve as an important basis for coordinating early efforts at crisis management. Beginning soon after the Depression hit, Swope and Young relied upon means that J.P. Morgan would have found familiar and arranged "numerous covert salvage operations of bankrupt financial institutions." Young played an especially key role in mediating negotiations between investment bankers and the Insull utilities empire, which was by then in full collapse. Young also helped organize "committees on industrial cooperation" made up of executives from major corporations, like Walter C. Teagle of Standard Oil New Jersey and Alfred P. Sloan of General Motors, as well as leaders of the major representatives of business unionism, William Green and Matthew Woll of the AFL. In these forums, Young argued for generalized reductions in tariffs to both bankers and politicians, to relieve the agricultural depression and prevent what he saw as a tendency toward isolationism. As he put it, tariffs meant that the US would "retain the surpluses that we might otherwise market to the world and which, so long as they stay with us, destroy our own prosperity."[46] This too was a sign of the

[46] McQuaid, "Young, Swope and General Electric's 'New Capitalism,'" 331.

weakness of the American state, whose role in "superintending" global capitalism would, in the future, be essential for preventing such retreats to protectionism during crises.[47]

By 1932, it was clear to Young that business could not, on its own, resolve the crisis. In an influential address at Notre Dame University that year, Young called for state action to stabilize the banking system, restore agricultural buying power, and ameliorate growing class conflict through enhanced social security measures.[48] Soon after, Young became one of a small group of business advisors for FDR's presidential campaign who aimed to resolve the crisis through an expanded system of state-corporate coordination. Yet unlike many in the new administration, who would strive to establish a more active public planning apparatus, Young believed state power should be extended to support the existing system of corporate self-regulation and private cartelization.

As it became apparent that at least some of the reformers wished to go further than this, Young began to retreat from the call for "planning" altogether. This had some very personal causes, as a 1933 Senate investigation had associated Young with a banking scandal linked to J.P. Morgan. Within a month, Young was warning of the dangers New Deal "collectivism" posed to individual freedoms. This antagonism was not helped by the fact that the holding company structures set up to finance electrical utilities came under particular regulatory scrutiny, which would eventually result in the Public Utilities Holding Company Act of 1935 that gave the new SEC (established the year before) "primary jurisdiction over utility holding company finances and operations."[49] The establishment of the Tennessee Valley Authority, alongside the overall growth of state-owned utilities, also engendered worries within GE of full electrical utility nationalization.[50]

As Young's outright rejection of the New Deal led him to fade away from those who sought to support and influence the reforms, Swope emerged as among the most prominent figures within the integral state. Though he is often credited as a key architect of New Deal programs,[51]

[47] Panitch and Gindin, *The Making of Global Capitalism*.

[48] McQuaid, "Young, Swope and General Electric's 'New Capitalism,'" 331–32.

[49] Hausman, Hertner, and Wilkins, *Global Electrification*, 201.

[50] Rothschild, *The Secret to GE's Success*, 122.

[51] Rothschild, *The Secret to GE's Success*, 39–56.

it was in fact Swope's efforts to mobilize the capitalist class behind the Roosevelt administration's agenda that were most significant. The true significance of the famous "Swope Plan," on which many believe the New Deal was based, derives not from the genius of the man for whom it is named, but rather from his location within integral state networks binding together state and corporate power—and especially his critical role in reproducing these networks through the Depression era. As Swope himself insisted when he first articulated the plan, "there is nothing new or original in what I am proposing."[52] Like those of "other late Hooverian and early Rooseveltian economic advisors," Swope's ideas were basically modeled on Wilson's War Industries Board.[53]

It was, in short, not the novelty of the ideas, but the structure of power and the circumstance of crisis that explains their resurfacing and association with Swope. In the face of unprecedented crisis and class upheaval, the state sought to organize and integrate the managerial elite within its policy networks, circling the wagons to restore social stability and protect class power. In such circumstances, long-held notions within the Department of Commerce of an "associative state" to actively coordinate the economy were revived, most prominently by Secretary of Commerce Daniel Roper. Indeed, Roper had been involved in Wilson's massive expansion of the federal bureaucracy, and likely saw Swope's plan as a sign of movement by a vanguard group of capitalist managers toward the more active state Commerce had favored for years.

The Swope Plan was first articulated in early 1931 at a meeting of the National Electrical Manufacturers Association (NEMA), in a speech entitled "The Stabilization of Industry."[54] Dominated by GE and Westinghouse interests, NEMA had since the 1920s organized the cartelization of the industry, with the partial support of the Department of Commerce, through a series of formal and informal agreements and understandings.[55] As it turned out, this was a perfect venue for unveiling the Swope Plan, which called for the repeal or radical revision of antitrust legislation to

[52] Loth, *Swope of G. E.*, 203.

[53] Kim McQuaid, "Competition, Cartellization and the Corporate Ethic: General Electric's Leadership During the New Deal Era, 1933–1940," *The American Journal of Economics and Sociology* 36, no. 4 (1977): 418.

[54] Loth, *Swope of G. E.*, 201–2.

[55] Ralph G. M. Sultan, *Pricing in the Electrical Oligopoly* (Boston: Harvard University Press, 1974).

form a legal NEMA-like cartel in every industry, authorized to come to binding agreements on prices and output "under loose governmental supervision" by a new Federal Trade Commission.[56] Perhaps unsurprisingly, when his speech ended, "he was greeted not only with applause but with very strong indications that his own association would put the plan into operation as a test without waiting for further action elsewhere."[57]

Yet the Swope Plan's "vague guarantees of protection against unemployment, disability, death, and retirement," with no provisions for employee representation in trade association decision-making, was not nearly enough to quell class upheaval. After "several months of ill-organized wrangling,"[58] the Roosevelt administration finally produced its restructuring plan in the form of the National Industrial Recovery Act (NIRA), which created the National Recovery Administration (NRA).

Though both were rooted in the experience of the WIB, Swope's vision differed from that eventually put forward by the administration, hewing more to the model of corporate self-regulation. As Sklar notes, there were essentially two kinds of regulation considered within the range of "effective political opinion" since the Wilson administration: "statist," which amounted to "government direction of the market with corporations treated as public utilities and agents of public policy," and "nonstatist," which meant "indirect government regulation of a corporate-administered market."[59] Whereas the Swope Plan was definitively in the "nonstatist" camp, the NIRA was more statist. The NIRA afforded the state greater enforcement powers than the Swope Plan, and allowed workers to collectively bargain under leadership of their own choosing. After all, "what distinguished the new Democratic administration from its Republican predecessors was above all the sense that the American capitalist system could not be restored by trying to reconstruct it with capitalists themselves acting as the main agents of the state." For the reformers, the Depression made it crystal clear that this had "obscured problems which were rooted in the very industrial, financial,

[56] Loth, *Swope of G. E.*, 203.

[57] Loth, *Swope of G.E.*, 205–6.

[58] McQuaid, "Competition, Cartelization and Corporate Ethic," 418.

[59] Sklar, *The Corporate Reconstruction of American Capitalism, 1890–1916*, 324.

and class structures of modern capitalism, and left the American state with insufficient relative autonomy or capacity to attend to them."[60]

In practice, however, the NRA plan did not differ substantially from the Swope Plan. The limits of state capacity meant that the program ultimately "reverted to the corporatist model introduced in World War I."[61] As one administration official put it, the NRA was "merely the trust sugar-coated," having merely "pinned a policeman's badge" on sectoral trade associations to regulate themselves.[62] Government supervision was merely "cursory," while labor and consumer interests failed to acquire a substantial say.[63] Based on NEMA inputs, the NRA established codes of "fair competition," including price levels, enforced by the new Federal Trade Commission. Selling below the listed price was declared an illegal "unfair trade practice." NEMA then "took up the task of NRA code enforcement with gusto"; indeed, the body even prepared a letter to the NRA in 1935 outlining the many "unfair trade practices" the enforcement powers of the NRA should be extended to combat.

It is easy to see why managers at GE and other big firms would support such a program, which helped manufacturers maintain relatively high prices "during the unprecedented collapse of electrical equipment orders during the 1930s."[64] Nevertheless, dominated and torn asunder by competing capitalist interests, the NRA "system of state-sanctioned industrial self-regulation" was crumbling after just its first year.[65] Aimed solely at supporting the cartels in preventing deflation by keeping prices up amidst collapsing sales, and not accompanied by fiscal expansion or increases to wages that could boost effective demand, restore profits, and resolve the crisis, the failure of the NRA was all but predetermined.

At the same time, the stock market crash brought an end to the "temporary truce" between the banks and the state established in the 1920s, with another round of Congressional investigations challenging

[60] Panitch and Gindin, *The Making of Global Capitalism*, 55.

[61] McQuaid, "Competition, Cartellization and the Corporate Ethic," 418; Panitch and Gindin, *The Making of Global Capitalism*, 58.

[62] Alan Brinkley, *The End Of Reform: New DealLiberalism in Recession and War* (New York: Knopf Doubleday Publishing Group, 2011), 46.

[63] McQuaid, "Competition, Cartellization and the Corporate Ethic," 418.

[64] Sultan, *Pricing in the Electrical Oligopoly*, 28–31.

[65] Panitch and Gindin, *The Making of Global Capitalism*, 58–59.

finance capital in 1932–1934. Apart from focusing public attention on the "corruption" of the finance capitalists—especially conflicts of interest facing banker-directors, and the fate of small shareholders beholden to their decisions—a series of major reforms was passed "that would further reduce the power of bankers."[66] These included the Securities Act and the Glass-Steagall Act, both passed in 1933, as well as the Securities Exchange Act (establishing the SEC) the following year. While the effects of the Securities Act on finance capital were minimal, the Glass-Steagall Act was more substantial. The Act forced banks to decide whether they wanted to be commercial or investment banks. Practically, choosing the "commercial" option meant restricting equity holdings and limiting seats on the boards of industrial corporations, while selecting "investment" meant reduced leverage since the bank would no longer be able to accept consumer deposits.

The act thus effectively separated financial institutions from corporate boards, formally bringing the finance capital regime to an end and reversing the fusion of banking and industrial capital. However, while reducing the power of the *banks*, the state simultaneously protected and broadened the *financial system*. The possibility for such an intervention was not only the consequence of the expansion of state capacities, nor can it be explained solely in terms of the exceptional circumstances presented by the crisis. Rather, as we have seen, the deeper economic bases of bank dominance had undergone a longer-term erosion. Just as the development of state capacities facilitated the decentralization of the financial system, so too had the growth of corporate bureaucracies and the fragmentation of shareholdings—to say nothing of state industrial policy—empowered internal managers vis-à-vis bankers. The growing capacities and autonomy of the state, the development of the financial system, and the supremacy of industrial firm managers were deeply conjoined historical processes.

The demise of finance capital also meant that the coordinating function of the bankers, especially critical in times of crisis, was now left entirely to the state. Even if it had wanted to, Treasury could no longer simply call J.P. Morgan and wire him a blank check to resolve a crisis, as it had in 1907. Capitalism was now much bigger and the capitalist class much broader. State managers had to wrangle a much wider group of capitalists and navigate far more diverse interests. As Brinkley wrote:

[66] Simon, "The Rise and Fall of Bank Control in the United States," 1090.

> Roosevelt himself seemed to believe that the "business world" was a single coherent entity capable of reaching a collective decision on its relationship to government... There may have been a time when such assumptions had at least some validity – when J.P. Morgan, John D. Rockefeller, and a few others could make an "arrangement" with government and ensure the compliance of most of their colleagues in finance and industry – but if so, that time had long since passed. The corporate world had great centers of power, to be sure, and there were reasons for political leaders to try to placate them, as they often did. But there was no central leadership of that world and, indeed, no real community of interests that any central leadership could represent.[67]

The failure of Swope and Young's secretive efforts over 1929–1933 clearly indicated that the state would need to take the lead in organizing such a "community of interests" among competing capitalist firms. This required developing new capacities to play a deeper and more profound role in coordinating fractious corporate interests—and made capitalists like Swope and Young, who sat atop one of the "great centers of power" in the new managerial elite, even more important. This was reflected in FDR's establishment of the Business Advisory Council (BAC) within the Department of Commerce by executive order in June 1933—just nine days after the passage of Glass-Steagall. Headed by Swope, it was made up of the "more far-sighted businessmen with a broad public conception of the obligations of business," by in large the same managerial vanguard that had emerged out of World War I.[68] As Secretary of Commerce Roper put it, "no other group or affiliation of business men... has had the composite experience of working with the Federal Government."[69]

Funded entirely by corporate donations, the BAC was "*in* the government – but not *of* it."[70] It was, rather, a central organ of the integral state, traversing and linking state and corporate power. Commerce officials were not required to attend meetings, and members could choose their own successors. The BAC established committees to discuss New

[67] Brinkley, *The End Of Reform*, 90–91.

[68] Brinkley, *The End Of Reform*, 41; Robert M. Collins, "Positive Business Responses to the New Deal: The Roots of the Committee for Economic Development, 1933–1942," *The Business History Review* 52, no. 3 (1978): 371.

[69] Collins, "Positive Business Responses to the New Deal," 376.

[70] McQuaid, "Competition, Cartellization and the Corporate Ethic," 419.

Deal programs and offer feedback to the administration. It became a "locus for the planning impulse among America's businessmen," and "a bastion of those who dreamed of a business commonwealth – a system involving national planning and regulation of industry, with government cooperation but without government control."[71] Like his predecessors at Commerce, Roper held expansive visions of an "associative state," and hoped that the integral state linkages then being formalized within the BAC would be but the first steps in the formation of a "National Advisory Council to include in its membership representatives of all groups in the economic and social structure of the country."[72]

Swope had also moved toward increasingly corporatist ideas, now arguing that the NRA needed to be replaced by a "National Chamber of Commerce and Industry" with greater capacity to enforce business codes.[73] This more active state involvement was depicted as part of the "scientific evolution of capitalism," whereby the chaos of competitive markets would be replaced by private economic planning structures overseen by specially trained managers, with the support and coordination of the state. Yet these ideas were highly unpopular among business leaders, who worried about the costs, and feared that the expansion of such a public power could eventually challenge their own—especially under conditions of intense class upheaval. Liberal New Dealers were similarly skeptical, fearful of creating another platform for business to criticize the administration.[74] It was conservatives like Roper who were the warmest supporters of such a vision.

The designation of the BAC as an "advisory" body tends to obscure its true nature and create the impression that corporations had "captured" the state. The reality is closer to the inverse: the BAC represented a key mechanism whereby *the state* organized *capital*. The BAC provided a platform for those segments of the capitalist class most favorable to the administration's agenda to advocate and organize under the supervision and guidance of state managers, while flattering these capitalists that they were "advisors." Though Roper served as a conduit between the BAC and the administration, providing information on the political

[71] Collins, "Positive Business Responses to the New Deal," 375.

[72] Collins, "Positive Business Responses to the New Deal," 375.

[73] McQuaid, "Competition, Cartellization and the Corporate Ethic," 418–19.

[74] McQuaid, "Competition, Cartelization and the Corporate Ethic," 419.

dynamics among leading segments of the capitalist class, as FDR himself put it the BAC, was "useless from the point of view of facts and policies and... only good for the dissemination of morale and a few ethical fundamentals."[75] This became especially clear in March 1935, after BAC's entreaties to Roosevelt that the NRA be renewed were unsuccessful—with the Supreme Court declaring it unconstitutional amidst sharp criticism from progressives and small business.[76]

As the administration stumbled toward what has become known as the "Second New Deal" beginning in 1935,[77] there was even less support among capitalists for this round of reforms than there had been for the "first" New Deal. This was especially the case for the provisions extending labor rights, like the Wagner Act, which "legalized unionization campaigns, collective bargaining and the right to strike, and established quasi-juridical procedures for securing recognition and settling disputes." Such measures were imposed upon capital by an increasingly robust state, which was forced to make concessions to labor in the face of waves of class struggle from below. Even though the Wagner Act contained strict limits on the right to strike, and the limited benefits of the Social Security Act passed the same year would serve to reinforce labor market discipline, business opposition to these measures was vocal and widespread. Under these conditions, maintaining close relations with business (even those segments in the BAC that were most favorable to the administration's agenda) was difficult for the administration—despite the fact that FDR himself "offered virtually no support to the Wagner Bill."[78]

Although there was hardly enough of a support base among the capitalist class to enact such policies unless the state was compelled to do so by labor struggles, Swope's efforts to win over business in forums like the BAC did not end, despite being temporarily pressured to recede into the background during the most contentious years. The BAC remained the primary mechanism whereby the administration coordinated with, and attempted to maintain, a base of support among the capitalist class for its agenda, however small that base may have been at times. Swope also remained personally close with Roosevelt throughout

[75] Collins, "Positive Business Responses to the New Deal," 374.

[76] Brinkley, *The End Of Reform*, 88–89.

[77] Panitch and Gindin, *The Making of Global Capitalism*, 59.

[78] Panitch and Gindin, *The Making of Global Capitalism*, 60.

the New Deal period, and continued to be a major supporter of the Social Security system, which remained controversial even among the relatively supportive BAC. He even privately supported the Tennessee Valley Authority, which had earned the concentrated ire of most of his managerial peers—including those at GE.[79]

Swope and Young, along with a minority of other corporate leaders, had realized the inadequacies of firm-level measures to deal with the crisis. In the face of rising unemployment, which undermined the wage gains, profit-sharing arrangements, and works council plan they had advanced under the banner of the "New Capitalism," Swope and Young had even been open to allowing GE plants to be peacefully organized by "respectable" unions. Similarly, from his position on the NRA's Industrial Advisory Board, Swope developed a "majority rule" provision in labor-representation elections that he believed would help AFL and CIO organizing efforts—at the expense of more radical socialist unions—and advocated for union representation on company boards.

Nevertheless, the enactment of the Second New Deal led BAC members to doubt their influence on policy, increasingly believing that Roosevelt simply ignored the council unless it proved politically useful.[80] Roper himself resigned in advance of the 1936 election. Although dreams that it would become a national coordinating body for an extensive economic planning regime were dashed, disappointing those (like Roper) with more far-reaching goals, the council was nevertheless reconstituted. There was simply no other way for the state to perform its function of organizing the capitalist class amidst an ongoing crisis but to systematically consult business and integrate its perspectives into the policymaking process. This was true for both technical and political reasons: to ensure there was sufficient buy-in for policies among the most important and well-connected members of the capitalist class, as well as to acquire the necessary information to craft sound policy. Moreover, despite the rancor on the BAC, the difference between members and non-members was pronounced: whereas the latter more or less hysterically rejected the New Deal out of hand, members tended to accept the Roosevelt policy framework and engaged in bargaining over the particulars.

[79] Collins, "Positive Business Responses to the New Deal," 374; McQuaid, "Competition, Cartellization and the Corporate Ethic," 420; Rothschild, *The Secret to GE's Success*, 30.

[80] Collins, "Positive Business Responses to the New Deal," 373.

As economic conditions improved over 1936 and 1937, the mood among business shifted. The BAC began advocating a balanced budget as an essential priority, despite Roper's efforts at "lobbying" the BAC that continued deficit spending was essential to the recovery. When Roosevelt announced a return to massive deficit spending in April 1938, Swope and Young used their "highly publicized" advisory roles to call on Roosevelt to implement the measures necessary to end the recession and restore "business confidence."[81] Yet this was pushing on an open door: in the context of Swope's activities on the BAC, the real target of this appears to have been other capitalists; and indeed, Swope and other pro-New Deal businessmen stepped up their efforts to bring others around. Since "converting administration liberals was like bringing coals to Newcastle," as BAC member Ralph Flanders put it, "the real need, deeply felt, was to convince their fellow businessmen of the efficacy of a wisely administered fiscal policy. But the work of conversion was difficult."[82] This effort was supported by economists like John Kenneth Galbraith, who was the ghostwriter of a BAC plan entitled *Toward Full Employment*—and whose ideas of a managerial technocracy bore more than a little of the imprint of this era.

If the 1933 Glass-Steagall Act had brought a formal end to bank control, the Chandler Act of 1938 further drove a stake into the heart of the old system of finance capital. The act barred investment banks from reorganizing publicly traded corporations, which was thenceforth to be undertaken by trustees. This prevented investment banks from taking control of firms through restructuring, which had been common.[83] The state's reduction of the power of the House of Morgan pleased others on Wall Street, who sought to limit the ability of the Morgan to use the New York Fed to achieve their *particular* interests.[84] Thus, the increased relative autonomy from the dominant centers of financial power the state achieved through its institutional expansion, coupled with the broadening of shareholdings and the emerging power of non-financial managers, allowed it to discipline the concentrated power of private banks

[81] McQuaid, "Competition, Cartellization and the Corporate Ethic," 421.

[82] Collins, "Positive Business Responses to the New Deal," 379.

[83] Simon, "The Rise and Fall of Bank Control in the United States," 1091.

[84] Panitch and Gindin, *The Making of Global Capitalism*, 57.

and construct market mechanisms that were more adequate to a broader base of capitalist interests.

By 1939, Swope and his allies on the BAC began to find that "a majority of businessmen had made their peace with the New Deal," as many former opponents began to see the merit in the Social Security Act, reducing their pension benefits by the exact proportion the program paid out. Swope's efforts received more than a little help from the recession and the lack of alternative proposals from conservative corporate leaders, to say nothing of the decline of the social movements that had been so threatening in the mid-1930s. With the return of labor peace, the White House organized, with the help of Swope, "what it called a 'grand truce' with capital during the first months of 1938."[85] Young also began to advocate for the creation of a National Chamber of Commerce and Industry, which Swope had presented five years earlier, perhaps hoping to preserve the electrical cartel despite the invalidation of the NRA. But Swope and Young would wait in vain for the administration to enact a more robust mechanism for state-corporate economic planning, as "Rooseveltian rhetoric was not followed by legislation which would have forced increasingly refractory businessmen into compliance."[86]

The defeat in Congress, with the support of the Chamber of Commerce, of Roosevelt's 1938 Executive Reorganization Bill, which was "designed to enhance the planning and coordination capacities of the executive branch," marked the definitive end of these ideas. The competitive dynamics of capitalism ensured that although calls for economic coordination were ubiquitous among the reformers, "the dream of economic harmony was by the late 1930s little more than a hazy vision, quickly and decisively repudiated whenever it threatened to take concrete form."[87] With the failure to realize a system that would "combine the public control and planning with the advantages of private ownership," to say nothing of the subsiding of the crisis, Young once again stopped supporting Democratic candidates, while Swope's visits to the White

[85] Sklar, *The Corporate Reconstruction of American Capitalism, 1890–1916*, 431–41; Mizruchi, *The Fracturing of the American Corporate Elite*, 34–36; McQuaid, "Competition, Cartellization and the Corporate Ethic," 421; Panitch and Gindin, *The Making of Global Capitalism*, 61–62.

[86] McQuaid, "Competition, Cartellization and the Corporate Ethic," 421.

[87] Brinkley, *The End Of Reform*, 46.

House became ever less frequent.[88] Although this "halted the momentum" of the New Deal, the dramatic expansion of the American state's institutional capacities would not be simply rolled back: "federal civilian employment almost doubled; and the seventeen new administrative agencies... were as many as had been set up in the previous three decades." Yet these new capacities in no way indicated "a dichotomy of purpose and function between state and capitalist actors, since they were mainly oriented to working with regulated industries to stabilize or rejuvenate private markets and stimulating private capital accumulation."[89]

Part and parcel of the largest peacetime expansion of the state in its history was the continued development of a state-capital complex, whereby the concentration and centralization of capital in the hands of large corporations—now dominated by internal managers—was reflected in the concentration of political power in an executive branch with which they were closely integrated. Those in the state sought to enhance its ability to organize corporate power into *class* power, though the process whereby it did so was messy and uneven, and fraught with conflict from corporate capitalists who were unhappy with the costs this entailed—especially as class struggle from below forced the state to make compromises with an unruly working class, which it then imposed on individual firms.

Though the state-capital complex would continue to expand, this would not take the form that Roper, Swope, and now Young hoped for. Neither private cartelization overseen by a passive state, nor a more active planning apparatus would take root. Rather, by the end of World War II, a state-organized innovation system comprising key state agencies, the universities, an extensive network of national laboratories, and major industrial corporations would constitute the pivotal nexus of technological development, while markets increasingly mediated relations between, and even within, firms. The central role of the state in technological innovation, together with its role in regulating output via demand management, constituted the economic planning regime Galbraith would call the "Industrial System"[90]—one in which, however, market mechanisms would still play a major role.

[88] Sklar, *The Corporate Reconstruction of American Capitalism, 1890–1916*, 324; McQuaid, "Competition, Cartellization and the Corporate Ethic," 421.

[89] Panitch and Gindin, *The Making of Global Capitalism*, 62.

[90] John Kenneth Galbraith, *The New Industrial State* (Princeton, NJ: Princeton University Press, 2015).

This was registered within GE, as senior managers began to urge their subordinates to refrain from taking part in NEMA meetings where price fixing and other cartel arrangements were discussed.[91] As its capacities increased, the state no longer needed to lean on such institutions. The rise of the state, it seemed, would not merely deal the deathblow to the bank power that was the beating heart of the system of finance capital, but would also discipline industrial managers and impose competitive market structures. The extension of market mechanisms was therefore not the result of the retreat of state power, as *laissez faire* ideology would have it. Quite the opposite: it was the product of the *growth* of state administration. Similarly, as we shall see, the internationalization of American capital was intrinsically linked to the internationalization of the American state.

[91] Sultan, *Pricing in the Electrical Oligopoly*, 33–34.

CHAPTER 4

The Golden Age of Managerialism and the State Industrial Policy System

During the finance capital era, financiers merged isolated entrepreneurial firms into large corporations, and then organized these into horizontally networked cartels and trusts centered on investment banks. As we saw, with the decline of the investment banks, the development of state capacities, and shifts in state regulation, these networks were restructured into autonomous, centralized corporations governed by professional managers. The two decades after World War II saw the maturation and consolidation of this structure of managerial hegemony. The key foundations for this were the state industrial policy system that emerged from the war to play a profound role in the development of the managerial corporation, the postwar economic boom, and the consolidation of so-called "business unionism."

As a result of its integration with the system of interlocking state-corporate investment that developed from wartime planning, GE's engineering, manufacturing, and administrative capacities underwent tremendous expansion. Whereas other firms divested from wartime operations with the cessation of hostilities, GE burrowed even more deeply into the industrial policy system, spinning off military technologies into consumer and industrial product lines that formed the basis for a range of operating divisions. The administrative decentralization GE implemented through an unprecedented postwar reorganization was an adaptive response to the resulting diversification, and therefore reflected the company's integration

© The Author(s), under exclusive license to Springer Nature Switzerland AG 2022

S. Maher, *Corporate Capitalism and the Integral State*, Marx, Engels, and Marxisms,
https://doi.org/10.1007/978-3-030-83772-3_4

with this industrial policy system. This model internalized competitive pressures within the firm, enhancing discipline, increasing efficiency, and squeezing more value out of operating divisions.

To be sure, the support of the state industrial policy system reinforced the market dominance of large high-tech manufacturing firms like GE—not just subsidizing existing research and development, but focusing investment on the kinds of early-stage research for which there was little market incentive. However, as this suggests, the development of the industrial policy system was not simply the result of corporate lobbying. Rather, it was the state that took the lead in constructing the systems of investment, research, and production necessary to support its new informal empire. Nor did the state act as a singular monolith: in addition to managing military production and R&D, the industrial policy apparatus crystallized a balance between competing nodes within the state which sought to politically mobilize business around distinct interests and agendas.

Through such means, the integration of corporate power helped stabilize the hierarchy of state apparatuses, atop which initially sat the State Department and the new Department of Defense. As head of the War Production Board (WPB), and later the Office of Defense Mobilization (ODM), GE President Charles Wilson worked to institutionalize a consensus among business around what was in effect a compromise between the military and New Dealers in the administration. In what has often been misleadingly called "military Keynesianism," the state maintained full employment and macroeconomic stability not through an extensive welfare state, but military spending, which also supported a group of engineering-based firms like GE.[1] This helped prevent a postwar recession. Later, as the Treasury Department took on a more important role, the Committee for Economic Development (CED), in many ways descended from the WPB, built a corporate consensus around its ascent, even as it came to rival the State Department.

Meanwhile, business unions increasingly absorbed within the state labor-relations apparatus helped to preserve the existing distribution of

[1] This is not to say that the goal of military policy was to smooth out the domestic business cycle: the primary goal of military industrial policy was to produce the material foundations for US geopolitical dominance. The priority at the Fed was not full employment, but inflation by the early 1950s. Nevertheless, the expansion of military spending helped secure the technological and market dominance of US firms.

income by tying wage gains to productivity increases. These unions limited their horizons to wage and benefit increases, neither challenging managerial control over investment and the labor process, nor advancing a political vision beyond corporate capitalism. Despite the emergence of "pattern bargaining" in some sectors, industrial conflict remained largely fragmented at the firm level and took the form of bureaucratic procedures negotiated by state, union, and corporate experts. This served to regularize industrial conflict and discipline workers, as the willingness and capacity of unions to educate, engage, and mobilize their members faded away.

With the active support of the state, GE and a group of "moderate" firms formed alliances with "responsible" business unions, which helped crush radical alternatives, like the Communist-led United Electrical Workers (UE). However, it was the state that pushed GE to aggressively confront UE, concerned about the sensitive nature of GE's military-related research and production, while the company dragged its heels. When GE did challenge UE, it did so partly through its cutting-edge "community relations" program, which drew on methods pioneered within the US Information Agency—in which GE President Philip Reed was a leading participant, as we shall see in the next chapter. USIA and GE propaganda programs drew on the latest psychological theories, and new techniques for polling and surveying workers and communities, to develop a "new right" political discourse. Moreover, they sought to find ways to utilize mass communications systems and technologies to disseminate these messages. GE spokesman Ronald Reagan became a leading figure in this effort, spreading the word both in person and through his role in hosting the popular television show *GE Theater* as the ground-breaking potentials of that medium were only just becoming apparent.

At the same time, the company increasingly shifted investment and production from the traditional northern industrial heartland to the union-free, "open shop" south, supported by similar regional shifts in the industrial policy system. Local "boosters" in the so-called "Sun Belt" states competed to establish a favorable "business climate," including building universities and other infrastructure. GE's position at the center of the WPB and ODM led it to play a central role in sustaining integral state networks nationwide, linking nationally organized corporate power to local business associations as state investment poured into the region through the industrial policy system. By the 1970s, these networks formed an important foundation for the Business Roundtable, as the state sought to deal with was by then clearly a crisis of managerial capitalism.

Managing War Production

If World War I had initiated the development of an institutional complex linking the state with manufacturing corporations to organize war production, World War II brought this to an entirely new level.[2] As during World War I, GE was at the center of this state-corporate planning structure. This began with the passage of the Lend-Lease Act in 1940, which extended credit to the UK for the purchase of American-manufactured armaments. The result was a massive stimulus to US companies, which converted their production capacities from consumer, commercial, and industrial applications to manufacturing military hardware. Yet this "involved not only the unprecedented production of ships, planes, tanks, guns, and ammunition; it required sweeping transformations in the entire economic structure and fundamental changes in the Government itself."[3] In addition to the tremendous growth and empowerment of the military establishment, American production doubled during the war years, and technological development surged with exploding state investment in advanced R&D.[4]

Contracts were awarded to corporations based not on competitive bids, but rather on a "cost-plus" model, whereby the government would pay up front for whatever it needed, covering the initial investment and paying for all output before anything was even produced. In this way, large engineering-based firms were effectively incorporated within a state system of investment and economic planning centered on the military, which also included public universities and a national network of government-funded laboratories. Naturally, this contributed tremendously to the growth of the engineering capacities of the firms integrated within the system, in addition to generating a tremendous surge in technological innovation.

[2] Brian Waddell, *Toward the National Security State: Civil-Military Relations During World War II* (Westport, CT: Praeger Security International, 2008), 153.

[3] United States Civilian Production Administration, *Industrial Mobilization for War*, (Washington, D.C.: Government Printing Office, 1947), xiii.

[4] Arthur Herman, *Freedom's Forge: How Business Produced Victory in World War II*, (New York: Random House, 2012), 337.

In the first year of the war, GE invested $78 million expanding its facilities—while the state contributed $120 million.[5] Like other companies, during the war GE "simply took direction from the military, and it used its considerable talents to design and manufacture an astounding array of weapons and systems."[6] GE made propulsion plants for warships, turbo-superchargers for airplanes, searchlights and military radios, radar sets and naval gun directors, turbines for naval ships, torpedoes, and electric lighting. It also developed propulsion systems for the Navy, as well as the first radar system, and advanced radio communications equipment. It produced some of the first American-made jet engines, and contributed to making the atomic bomb as well as the first nuclear submarines.[7]

The industrial mobilization effort was coordinated with executives from major corporations, who served as "dollar-a-year men" or Without Compensation (WOC) employees within the ad hoc planning bureaucracy. Largely drawn from the same group of "corporate liberals" who had supported the New Deal over the 1930s, these executives were paid one dollar per year to participate in wartime industrial planning—though they retained their corporate salaries. This "helped strengthen the bond" between this corporate bloc and the New Dealers, while broadening corporate buy-in for the mobilization effort and leading liberals in the administration to soften their criticisms of big business. The shifting focus of state capacities, away from "overt regulation" and toward macroeconomic stabilization and targeted industrial policy, further reinforced synergies between the state and large corporations.[8]

Since the state is not a singular entity, but a contradictory institutional assemblage, the war planning apparatus also served as a framework for competing state nodes to mobilize corporate power on behalf of their particular agendas. New Dealers in the administration "distrusted military planning" as well as "the corporations and businessmen upon whom the military relied so heavily." Additionally, such figures "assumed that the tools of governance developed for handling the continuing depression could be easily shifted to organizing the economy for war."[9] They

[5] Herman, *Freedom's Forge*, 248.

[6] Rothschild, *The Secret to GE's Success*, 74–76.

[7] Herman, *Freedom's Forge*, 248.

[8] Brinkley, *The End Of Reform*, 173.

[9] Waddell, *Toward the National Security State*, 26.

saw the integration of "corporate liberals" within the war mobilization apparatus as a way to counterbalance the power of the military and generate momentum toward a postwar corporatist economic planning system, whereby fiscal policy would be used to maximize output and employment. Liberals accordingly wanted the state to aggressively expand production—both to prosecute the war and to ensure full employment after the war—and blamed delays on corruption and abuse within the WOC system.[10]

The military, for its part, simply lacked the institutional capacity to coordinate with corporations in the ways necessary to implement a viable industrial policy, and strove to limit the civilian economic planning apparatus to carrying out this subordinate function. It initially sought to mobilize support from capitalists—especially small business and financiers—who held the "essentially conservative belief that war production must be promoted carefully, to avoid disrupting the fragile equilibrium of American industry" which could lead "to the same problems of overproduction" they believed had caused the Great Depression.[11] The integration of corporate power within the war planning system institutionalized an accommodation between these two, whereby the state would undertake massive investment, but this would remain under military control: what would later be referred to as "military Keynesianism." Over time, the vociferousness of New Dealers' anti-corporate criticism receded even as overall military control of industrial policy was protected.[12]

The industrial planning apparatus initially took the form of the National Defense Advisory Commission (NDAC) left over from World War I. In January 1941, Roosevelt concluded that "advice and encouragement"—the extent of the NDAC's power—"would no longer do the job," and thus that "a new body was needed that could make decisions and issue directives, with a single head in charge of mobilizing American industry for the war effort."[13] This took the form of the Office of Production Management (OPM), headed by former General Motors President William Knudsen and dominated by corporate dollar-a-year men. Among these was GE's Philip Reed—a "dollar-a-year man par excellence" who

[10] Brinkley, *The End Of Reform*, 191, 196.

[11] Brinkley, *The End of Reform*, 191, 196.

[12] Waddell, *Toward the National Security State*, 26.

[13] Herman, *Freedom's Forge*, 127.

served in a wide range of positions and capacities, including in the UK Lend-Lease Office.

The OPM worked in conjunction with an array of corporate advisory committees, which provided policy input, organized consensus among business, and supported the administrative capacities of the emerging industrial policy system. Information supplied by these committees allowed the OPM "to decide upon and implement policies affecting industry," as they "offered readily available expertise, and a business-friendly source of policies with which firms would be that much more likely to comply."[14] However, as Waddell shows, although the OPM had broad responsibilities on paper, it was unable to effectively make and implement decisions, nor adequately coordinate among its constituencies. Moreover, extensive linkages between manufacturing corporations and the military establishment, which extended back to World War I, led to criticism from liberals that the OPM was "virtually the civilian auxiliary of the War and Navy Departments."

Nevertheless, the efforts of the OPM laid the basis for its replacement by a more authoritative body, the War Production Board (WPB), created by Roosevelt in 1942 and headed by Sears Roebuck Vice President Donald Nelson. Reed served as Deputy Director of the Materials Division. "As I understood my job," Nelson wrote, "it wasn't up to me to *tell* industry how to do its job; it was our function to *show* industry what had to be done and then to do everything in our power to enable industry to do it." To accomplish this, Nelson continued to expand the WOC system, while Roosevelt issued an executive order suspending antitrust prosecutions against companies deemed essential to the war effort. By 1942, "over ten thousand business executives… had moved into offices, cubicles, and even converted bathrooms in the hopelessly overcrowded headquarters of the war agencies."[15]

Liberals vociferously criticized what they perceived to be corrupt relationships, as "dollar-a-year" men directed contracts toward firms at which they were employed. The primary source of such pushback was Senator Harry Truman's Special Committee to Investigate the National Defense Program, which issued a report "mildly critical of the dollar-a-year men generally and of [Phillip] Reed in particular." The Truman Committee

[14] Waddell, *Toward the National Security State*, 33, 38.

[15] Brinkley, *The End of Reform*, 190–91.

sought "to abolish [WOCs], or at least enforce a rule that 'no person shall be employed in any position in which he will make decisions directly affecting the affairs of his own company.'" This would have defeated the entire purpose of the WOC system, which was intended to draw on the expertise and political connections of corporate managers—*especially* in order to facilitate coordination with their own firms and sectors. And, as Secretary of War Henry L. Stimson wrote in his diary, "You have got to let business make money out of the process, or business won't work."[16]

Despite these criticisms, administration liberals came to see the WPB as a mechanism for exerting greater civilian control over wartime industrial policy, while the military resisted any attempts to expand the WPB's power. As liberals pointed out, carefully restraining the ramping up of war production was also a convenient "vehicle for maintaining the Old Wall Street-Army combination."[17] In an attempt to end the "feud" between the WPB and the military, Nelson appointed investment banker Ferdinand Eberstadt, seen as a close ally of the military, to the agency. Eberstadt created the "Controlled Materials Plan" (CMP), which tightly circumscribed the authority of the WPB over purchasing.[18] Nevertheless, the CMP was "the most ambitious attempt ever mounted in the United States to allocate, coordinate, and monitor the flow of scarce materials for the entire industrial economy."[19]

Under the CMP, the WPB delegated a fixed quantity of controlled materials to the military, which divided it among its prime contractors, who would in turn divide the materials among their subcontractors. The CMP was therefore a top-down distribution model that relied on centralized coordination within the WPB between the military and the largest firms. Thus in carving this institutional space away from the military, the CMP actually boosted the power of the WPB. Partly because of the lack of resistance from the military, the CMP "quickly established itself as the most efficient and successful of the WPB's many undertakings,"

[16] Quoted in Herman, *Freedom's Forge*, 84.

[17] Brinkley, *The End of Reform*, 196.

[18] Brinkley, *The End Of Reform*, 195.

[19] Robert Cuff, "From the Controlled Materials Plan to the Defense Materials System, 1942–1953," *Military Affairs* 51, no. 1 (January 1987): 1.

which only further increased the desire within the military to restrict its authority—"an inclination actively cultivated by Eberstadt himself."[20]

Nelson, on the other hand, sided with administration liberals in seeking to expand the WPB's power and persuaded Roosevelt to appoint Charles Wilson (president of GE) as head of its Production Executive Committee in September 1942. "Although no liberal himself," Wilson "had the support of many New Dealers because he believed above all in expanded production," while Eberstadt and the military continued to cling to the view that industrial stability required more cautiously scaling up wartime production.[21] The conflict that ensued between Wilson and Eberstadt dominated the WPB through the end of 1942 and early 1943. While the military establishment feared greater civilian authority, New Dealers believed that Wilson—perhaps uniquely—had the clout to restrain the growing power of the military. As New Deal liberal Mordecai Ezekiel wrote Vice President Henry Wallace in 1942, "if we let [Wilson] go down, there will be nothing left to stop the Army-Eberstadt-Baruch clique from obtaining complete power and control over the organization of industry for the war, and probably for the peace as well."[22]

What Ezekiel did not see was that the "Old Wall Street-Army combination" was being replaced by a new, much more extensive set of linkages between the military and the industrial corporations that had become the center of economic power in the United States. When Wilson was subsequently appointed Executive Vice President, he "assumed effective operating control of the WPB," which "increasingly spoke with one voice."[23] Although Wilson supported boosting state investment for war production, as the New Dealers had hoped, he nonetheless "soon proved almost as unwilling as Eberstadt had been to challenge the military's control of purchasing or its opposition to reconversion."[24] Wilson's rise within the WPB entrenched a nexus of power binding the military and a core group of large corporations around a robust military-controlled industrial policy, with which New Dealers would have to come to an accommodation.

[20] Brinkley, *The End of Reform*, 195.

[21] Brinkley, *The End of Reform*, 196.

[22] Quoted in: Brinkley, *The End of Reform*, 196.

[23] Waddell, *Toward the National Security State*, 53.

[24] Brinkley, *The End Of Reform*, 198.

Coinciding with Wilson's appointment was the formation of the Committee for Economic Development (CED) within the BAC, nurtured especially by Secretary of Commerce Jesse Jones. The CED was comprised of many of the same corporate managers who dominated the industrial planning apparatus, including Wilson. The CED's "basic philosophy... was a version of business liberalism not much different from that held by its forerunners of the 1930s."[25] Like these predecessors, it sought to organize a *class wide* perspective: it was "committed to the idea that the health of the postwar American (and world) economy as a whole was of more importance than the immediate market environments of particular sectors."[26]

The CED's integral state role was also signaled by its orientation toward the state, which, like the BAC before it, distinguished it from other business associations. As Undersecretary of Commerce Edward Noble put it at a BAC dinner, insofar as the notoriously conservative and staunchly anti-New Deal National Association of Manufacturers (NAM) and the Chamber of Commerce persisted in their "rejectionist stance," they "fell into disrepute, not only with the Executive Branch of Government but also with Congress and the people as a whole."[27] On the other hand, the "discreet symbiosis" the CED pursued with the state "paid dividends." Unlike the rejectionists, the CED sought to "create an agenda and organize a 'positive business program' for postwar industrial development, economic growth, and social stability... in cooperation with federal officials and, simultaneously, with the NAM, the USCC, and other capitalist organizations."[28]

The CED supported the WPB by organizing a corporate consensus around the "new liberalism," and coordinating the consolidation and entrenchment of the wartime economic planning apparatus under military control after the war. This meant joining the military in opposing any moves toward postwar demobilization that would dismantle the industrial planning apparatus, thereby also supporting liberal calls for increased state

[25] Collins, "Positive Business Responses to the New Deal," 389.

[26] Brinkley, *The End Of Reform*, 173.

[27] Edward Noble, "Speech by Undersecretary of Commerce Edward Noble at BAC Dinner," April 14, 1940, Record Group 40, Entry UD 11, Box #3, National Archives College Park, MD.

[28] Kim McQuaid, *Uneasy Partners: Big Business in American Politics 1945–1990*, (Baltimore: Johns Hopkins University Press, 1994), 20.

investment to expand production. While the CED "Field Development Division was to encourage and monitor plant-by-plant business planning through the establishment of a network of regional and local committees; the Research Division was to 'bring to light information...to aid in bringing into being an economic climate more favourable to continued high employment."[29] All this laid the groundwork for the state-corporate consensus around the postwar "military Keynesian" interventionist state.

The Industrial Policy System and Corporate Decentralization

Though for liberals the WPB experience served ideologically not as a model, but a warning of the state's inability to effectively coordinate production, it nevertheless laid the foundations of "a vast, cartelistic partnership between the armed forces and private industry, largely invulnerable to political attacks; a national security state, which forged intimate partnerships with the corporate world, constantly blurring the distinctions between the public and private."[30] The so-called "New GE" that emerged from the war was a creature of this wartime production apparatus, which had transformed it from a company focused on developing and installing the technologies, systems, and infrastructures for electrical generation, distribution, and lighting into a high-tech, diversified conglomerate. Whereas in the prewar years the company produced products and services in just three industries, by the end of the war this number had reached twenty-one.[31]

Nevertheless, after the war business remained broadly skeptical of the costs that sustaining a "military-industrial complex" would entail. Many executives called for tax reductions.[32] Neither were corporations automatically behind eliminating the tariffs that had protected American industry since the nineteenth century—a core part of the "free trade" order envisioned by the ascendant State Department. GE executives, however, continued to play prominent roles in building support

[29] Collins, "Positive Business Responses to the New Deal," 388.

[30] Brinkley, *The End of Reform*, 199.

[31] Rothschild, *The Secret to GE's Success*, 77.

[32] Clarence Y.H. Lo, "Theories of the State and Business Opposition to Increased Military Spending," *Social Problems* 29, no. 4 (April 1982): 427.

among capital for these policies and programs through integral state organizations like the CED, the BAC, and the International Chamber of Commerce (ICC). Reed's cooperation with the State Department in advocating for "free trade" was particularly noteworthy, given that this entailed the state dismantling the empire of cartels and trusts GE had built over a half-century that had allowed it to dominate global markets.

While Ford and General Motors also took part in wartime production, and had diversified accordingly, with the end of hostilities these firms divested from these operations. GE, on the other hand, effectively became a machine for "spinning off" technologies generated within this state innovation system into marketable commodities. Though GE extolled the fact that the firm "grows from within," nurturing its own new businesses rather than expanding through mergers and acquisitions,[33] this in fact reflected the institutional structure of the state industrial policy system. At the core of the new GE were its state-supported engineering operations, which spawned various consumer and industrial businesses as top management invested in developing and marketing technologies they believed had promising non-military applications. To be sure, the technological sophistication of the electrical infrastructure, equipment, and lighting industry had required GE to develop extensive research capacities from the start—the first in American industry to do so. But it was GE's structural integration with the state industrial policy complex that led to the development of the company's engineering operation into the force it became.

The propulsion systems GE developed with government support and patented formed the basis for core postwar businesses powering ships, aircraft, and locomotives. These technologies, which continued to be purchased by the Air Force and Navy, led to the creation of GE's jet engine business, still one of its most important operations. The company also developed a military electronics operation, which served as the basis for postwar expansion into a number of industrial markets—including industrial controls, industrial computers, and telecommunications businesses. It thus played a leading role in boosting productivity across US manufacturing through automating plants and new applications of electronics and early computer technology. State support was likewise crucial to GE engineers' improving silicones and producing a range

[33] Ralph J. Cordiner, *New Frontiers for Professional Managers* (New York: McGraw-Hill, 1956), 29–31.

of new materials for military and industrial applications, including "the core competencies that led to GE's innovations in plastics and artificial diamonds."

Yet although GE depended on the state for its competitive edge and the development of high-tech products, its place within the industrial policy system was primarily the result of political needs determined within the state. Whether battleship drive systems, sophisticated radar technologies, or nuclear weapons, it was GE's capacity to physically build and manage the products, technologies, and systems necessary for the material reproduction of empire—not its "capture" of the state in search of subsidies—that accounted for its position within the industrial policy apparatus.[34]

As no consumer products were manufactured during the war, these businesses received a major boost from the pent-up demand after it ended. Growing middle class purchasing power and suburbanization unleashed huge possibilities for profitmaking, as the country was literally transformed. "Middle class" consumption was underpinned not least by the contributions of GE industrial technologies to boosting productivity, which supported both the expansion of the managerial stratum and rising wages for unionized workers. This was reinforced by accompanying cultural shifts as consumerism became normalized—and GE products became the very symbol of a new, post-political American "modernity":

> Entire cities were created, and massive highway and telecommunications networks were built. In short, the issue was not *what* to build but *how* to build it and get it to market as quickly as possible. This caused a huge surge in the construction of manufacturing and commercial buildings, providing GE with major growth opportunities for its industrial and commercial businesses and creating a need for new electrical systems. Nuclear and

[34] Lee Clarke, "The Origins of Nuclear Power: A Case of Institutional Conflict," *Social Problems* 32, no. 5 (June 1985): 482–86. For a strong articulation of the "capture" thesis, arguing that the AEC was "completely subservient" to corporations, see: James Allen, *Atomic Imperialism* (New York: International Publishers, 1952). Others, like Useem, saw a pre-existing "consensus" among private corporations and the state, thus erasing the processes of institutional contestation whereby the state organized capital behind its geopolitical strategy. See: Michael Useem, "Corporations and the Corporate Elite," *Annual Review of Sociology* 6 (1980): 41–77.

> gas turbines were added to the GE mix, and these businesses also grew dramatically.[35]

While the company's major contractor segment benefitted directly from the housing boom, GE engineers transformed state-funded wartime electronics and telecommunications breakthroughs into a huge new range of consumer products, including radios, televisions, and microwave ovens. Moreover, all this continued to reinforce GE's "Benign Cycle" by increasing demand for the infrastructures necessary for electricity production and distribution, still among GE's core businesses—now including state-supported nuclear power as well.[36] State support for the firm's engineering and research functions had the effect of "creating new skills and facilities, particularly in the electronics field, …doubling the number of its plants, and …tripling the number of employees" over the war years. The firm again doubled in size over the 1950s, from $2.2 billion to $4.4 billion.[37]

By the late 1950s, the state was still GE's largest customer, accounting for over 20% of corporate sales, and the firm had become the second-largest provider of military hardware.[38] More important than the *level of state consumption*, however, was the *form of state investment*, which targeted advanced R&D the firm would not have undertaken based on market incentives alone. As former GE executive William Rothschild observed:

> Although government business had a low return on sales, it had very positive cash flows, and it required little in terms of investment dollars because

[35] Rothschild, *The Secret to GE's Success*, 79.

[36] Ralph J. Cordiner, *New Frontiers for Professional Managers*, (New York: McGraw Hill, 1956), 10–11; Rothschild, *The Secret to GE's Success*, 90–91.

[37] In fact, this realization came late at GE relative to some other major firms, which had begun to decentralize as early as the 1920s. Unlike Westinghouse, GE's ability to weather the Depression made it somewhat impervious to pressures for restructuring during the crisis years. Chandler Jr., *Strategy and Structure*, 300, 365, 368; Ronald G. Greenwood, *Managerial Decentralization: A Study of the General Electric Philosophy*, (Hive Publishing Company, 1982), 26.

[38] Cordiner, *New Frontiers for Professional Managers*, 20–21; Rothschild, *The Secret to GE's Success*, 88; Thomas F. O'Boyle, *At Any Cost: Jack Welch, General Electric, and the Pursuit of Profit* (New York: Knopf Doubleday Publishing Group, 1999), 57, 152.

> the government often owned the facilities and made all the investments. This gave U.S. companies such as GE a major competitive advantage.[39]

State contracts stipulated specific research and engineering activities to be undertaken by the firm, and state personnel closely monitored and oversaw work in progress. GE's cutting-edge engineering operations were so interpenetrated with the state innovation system that it could be hard to tell where one ended and the other began. Though GE engineers received their paychecks from GE, and the technologies they developed could become the intellectual property of the company, their positions were financed through state investment; they worked in facilities owned by the government, on projects closely overseen by state personnel, and in collaboration with scientists and engineers from universities, government labs, and the state.

The Atomic Energy Commission (AEC), created in 1946, played a substantial role in this institutional nexus. The Commission, an "unusually powerful regulatory agency," oversaw the reorganization of the Manhattan Project after the war into a permanent state-corporate science apparatus, the "backbone" of which was the National Laboratories system funded by the state and operated by a combination of universities, corporate contractors, and the state itself.[40] As the authors of the Atomic Energy Act—which created both the AEC and the Congressional Joint Committee on Atomic Energy [JCAE]—observed:

> never before in the peacetime history of the United States has Congress established an administrative agency vested with such sweeping authority and entrusted with such portentous responsibilities… The Act creates a government monopoly of the sources of atomic energy and buttresses this position with a variety of broad governmental powers and prohibitions on private activity. The field of atomic energy is made an island of socialism in the midst of a free enterprise economy.[41]

[39] Rothschild, *The Secret to GE's Success*, 80.

[40] Richard G. Hewlett and Francis Duncan, *A History of the United States Atomic Energy Commission, Volume II: Atomic Shield (1947–1952)*, (University Park, PA: Pennsylvania State University Press, 1972), 76, 223–26; Clarke, "The Origins of Nuclear Power," 483.

[41] Richard Hewlett and Oscar Anderson, *A History of the United States Atomic Energy Commission, Volume I: The New World (1939–1946)*, (University Park, PA: Penn State University Press, 1962), 4–5.

It may not have been "socialist," but the AEC was responsible for planning state investment in advanced R&D broadly related to nuclear energy and weapons projects, and coordinating the oversight of state-corporate research activities by the military and other state officials.

This was supported by the JCAE, "the most powerful congressional committee in the history of the nation," which served as "almost a unicameral legislature within the bicameral Congress."[42] Congress gave the panel exclusive jurisdiction over "all bills, resolutions, and other matters" related to civilian and military nuclear power, and made it the only committee in modern times to have legislative authority.[43] Though ostensibly created for "oversight" of the AEC, in fact "the rationale for establishing the joint panel," articulated by Senator Brien McMahon, was "to assist the [AEC] with new laws when new laws are required, to assess its operations and alter its powers and structure when necessary, to be ready to adapt it to continuously changing circumstances."[44] This "had the effect of blurring the line between the JCAE and the executive agency it was tasked with overseeing, making the panel, in essence, a 'legislative-administrative hybrid'."[45] The JCAE was therefore more accurately seen as a legislative *support* for the AEC. The AEC, an executive branch agency, was thus given unprecedented direct legislative power. A relatively small community of administrators, legislators, and scientists with privileged access to classified information came to exert nearly unlimited power over the development of nuclear technology.

In addition to supplying much of the investment to develop civilian nuclear technology, the government owned the fissionable material used in commercial and military reactors. This meant that GE and Westinghouse incurred essentially no cost to develop the nuclear energy

[42] Christopher Davis, "9/11 Commission Recommendations: Joint Committee on Atomic Energy—A Model for Congressional Oversight?," CRS Report for Congress, (Congressional Research Service, August 20, 2004), 2; Harold Green and Allen Rosenthal, *The Joint Committee on Atomic Energy: A Study in the Fusion of Government Power*, (Washington, D.C.: The National Law Center, George Washington University, 1961), 288; Herbert Jasper, "The Oversight Role of the Joint Committee on Atomic Energy," CRS Memorandum, (Congressional Research Service, 1975), 5.

[43] Davis, "9/11 Commission Recommendations," 14.

[44] Davis, "9/11 Commission Recommendations," 7–8.

[45] Davis, "9/11 Commission Recommendations," 15–16., quoting Green and Rosenthal, *The Joint Committee on Atomic Energy: A Study in the Fusion of Government Power*, 259.

infrastructure and to monopolize that industry.[46] Yet the AEC-JCAE was hardly the passive plaything of corporations seeking economic gain. On the contrary, the AEC-JCAE "*actively* pursued nuclear development with the aim of creating a strong military, buttressed by a civilian nuclear program."[47] Commission planners saw the civilian nuclear program as a means to carry out military R&D, legitimating these activities while defraying certain costs onto non-military state agencies and private capital. In other words, it facilitated the "development of military technologies without sending the bill to the military."[48] As the official history of the Commission concluded, a key dilemma it faced was "how to give first priority to weapons and production and still strike a proper balance in research and development."[49]

In the absence of state leadership, there was little reason for private capitalists to invest in developing a civilian nuclear infrastructure. Indeed, "if left to market forces, there would have been no demand for nuclear-generated electricity, and the United States would probably not have a civilian nuclear industry."[50] This conclusion is borne out by the fact that GE and other producers continued to lose money on nuclear plants until the 1970s, when new orders ground to a halt.[51] That nuclear power "offered little economic advantage" even meant that state officials had to overcome the utilities' "persistent nuclear aversion."[52] If the "operative goal" of the AEC-JCAE "was not the production of energy," the utilities "seemed to have been turned into a tool of the state," even though the state "could not directly control the utilities."

The Office of Defense Mobilization (ODM), created in 1950, played an even more important role in consolidating the structure of power emerging around state industrial policy, picking up where the WPB left off. After his responsibilities on the WPB came to an end in 1945, Wilson

[46] Richard Hewlett and Jack Holl, Atoms for Peace and War: Eisenhower and the Atomic Energy Commission 1953–1961, (Berkeley, CA: University of California Press, 1989), 494.

[47] Clarke, "The Origins of Nuclear Power," 483.

[48] Clarke, "The Origins of Nuclear Power," 485.

[49] Hewlett and Duncan, *A History of the United States Atomic Energy Commission, Volume II*, 66.

[50] Clarke, "The Origins of Nuclear Power," 483.

[51] Rothschild, *The Secret to GE's Success*, 94.

[52] Clarke, "The Origins of Nuclear Power," 483.

briefly returned as GE's President. Just two years later, he was appointed by Truman to serve as head of the ODM, which was described by *Business Week* as a "super mobilization agency."[53] The extensive powers he assumed led others in the press to refer to Wilson as the "co-president."[54] As laid out in a Department of Defense document, the ODM "directs, controls, and coordinates all mobilization activities of the Executive Branch of government, including but not limited to production, procurement, manpower, stabilization, and transport activities."[55]

Though explicitly set up to meet the military needs of the Korean War, the ODM participated in the much broader task of "constructing a permanent national security state and defense economy, if not an incipient 'garrison state.'"[56] At the core of this was the close institutional relationship between the leading engineering-based corporations, universities, and the military. As during World War II, a core principle of the ODM was that, "to the maximum extent possible, private enterprise shall be relied upon to take the steps necessary to meet the requirements of the mobilization base, with Government aid when appropriate."[57] Personnel for the various WOC positions within the ODM were often drawn from within the BAC, with which the agency developed a close "advisory" relationship.[58]

[53] Quoted in: Paul G. Pierpaoli, "Truman's Other War: The Battle for the American Homefront, 1950–1953," *Organization of American Historians Magazine of History*, Spring 2000, 17; Alfred L. Scanlan, "The Defense Production Act of 1950," *Rutgers Law Review* 5, no. 8 (1951): 518–29.

[54] Pierpaoli, "Truman's Other War," 17.

[55] Vincent Rock, "Statement of Agency Responsibilities and Programs Concerning the Mobilization Base," September 4, 1952, Record Group 469, Entry UD 643A, Box #4, National Archives College Park, MD.

[56] Pierpaoli, "Truman's Other War," 16.

[57] Office of Defense Mobilization, "Providing and Maintaining the Mobilization Base," September 19, 1952, Record Group 469, Entry UD 643A, Box #4, National Archives College Park, MD.

[58] "Minutes of General Council Meeting of the Business Advisory Council for the Department of Commerce," October 22, 1954, Record Group 56, Entry 198, Box #106, National Archives College Park, MD; "Minutes of General Council Meeting of the Business Advisory Council for the Department of Commerce," December 8, 1954, Record Group 56, Entry 198, Box #106, National Archives College Park, MD.

The creation of the ODM "did not stem from the state implementing business' plans."[59] Rather than the corporate "capture" of the state, the ODM pointed to the state's ongoing reliance on these firms, GE perhaps first and foremost, for organizing and implementing a class consensus.[60] The ODM was formed as the Truman administration stumbled through what conservatives believed was the onset of the postwar recession they had long feared. As deficits and inflation mounted, Truman fumbled with an ineffective mix of wage and price controls and tax increases, before sharply increasing military spending. In addition to coordinating state investment with military planners, the ODM would allow economic controls, should they still be necessary, to be negotiated and implemented by Wilson.

However, it was geopolitical concerns, and especially the need to construct an extensive new imperial state, that primarily motivated the ODM's creation. In fact, "plans for higher military spending originated with Dean Acheson, Paul Nitze, and other top officials in the Department of State."[61] The ODM was a means for Truman "to mobilize the nation, including big business, into supporting the administration's extensive military buildup."[62] The CED, which included many of the same corporations, worked to build business support for the ODM. Indeed, the BAC only reluctantly accepted that "the assumption of new government functions in recent years, and the need for large defense outlays… will require tax burdens at heights which are unprecedented except in brief periods of all out war"—continuing to insist that this "may restrict or distort the nation's economic progress."[63]

Despite its growing prominence, the State Department did not challenge military control over industrial policy, but rather carried out functions that the military had neither the capacity nor the desire to fulfill. The emergence of a more militaristic generation of leaders within the

[59] Lo, "Theories of the State and Business Opposition to Increased Military Spending," 433.

[60] Business Advisory Council, "Draft of Tax Policy Statement," November 1952, Record Group 56, Entry 198, Box #106, National Archives College Park, MD.

[61] Lo, "Theories of the State and Business Opposition to Increased Military Spending," 433.

[62] Lo, "Theories of the State and Business Opposition to Increased Military Spending," 433.

[63] Business Advisory Council, "Draft of Tax Policy Statement."

department reflected and complemented the rapid growth and centralization of military administration in the new Department of Defense. The scale of the reorganization of state military and intelligence systems was indicated by the passage National Security Act of 1947, which merged the Departments of War and the Navy under the control of the Secretary of Defense, along with the new Department of the Air Force, and created the CIA, NSC, and Joint Chiefs of Staff.[64] Corporations opposing this as a result of "perceptions of the costs of the rearmament program" sought to "strengthen like minded officials within government in their bureaucratic battles with other officials." But these groups "influenced only a limited set of national security decision makers."[65]

The Golden Age of Capitalism and "The New GE"

The development of the industrial policy system exerted mounting pressures on GE's rigid, hierarchical, and centralized bureaucratic structure. Before the war even ended, Ralph Cordiner, former President of Schick Razor who had worked with Wilson on the WPB, was appointed Special Assistant to GE's President. In this capacity, his "major assignment was to develop a plan for overhauling the management and organization structure of the corporation," a project undertaken within the company's powerful Advisory and Operations Committees. After three years of study, he "called for a complete reorganization."[66] When he took over as president, he oversaw the "great restructuring of 1951," which reshaped GE from a centralized and functionally departmentalized structure built around a single business (i.e., divided into functional units which handled sales, legal, engineering, finance, production, etc.) into a decentralized, multidivisional conglomerate.[67]

[64] Stephen A. Cambone, *A New Structure for National Security Policy Planning* (Washington, DC: Center for Strategic and International Studies, 1998), 228–32.

[65] Lo, "Theories of the State and Business Opposition to Increased Military Spending," 433–34.

[66] Greenwood, *Managerial Decentralization*, 16; Thomas W. Evans, *The Education of Ronald Reagan: The General Electric Years and the Untold Story of His Conversion to Conservatism* (New York: Columbia University Press, 2007), 26; Cordiner, *New Frontiers for Professional Managers*, 45.

[67] Westinghouse had decentralized over the 1930s, not least as a result of the fact it had experienced the pinch of the Great Depression much more intensely than GE

The new multidivisional structure was characterized by a hierarchical division between *investment* and *operational* functions. The firm would now be comprised of "a general office whose executives would concentrate on entrepreneurial activities," and "autonomous, fairly self-contained operating divisions whose managers would handle operational ones."[68] Each division would oversee specific product lines, including developing and maintaining their own suppliers, customers, and strategic plans, while meeting the overall financial objectives of the company.[69] Divisions were then subdivided into an even larger number of product departments. Top executives were now known as "general managers," supposedly capable of directing *any* particular business, who allocated capital among divisions on the basis of abstract "objective" quantitative measures—primarily profit, growth, and return on investment.[70]

Decentralization was an "adaptive response" to the administrative challenges of diversification, as top executives had neither the time nor the industry-specific knowledge to be directly involved in the operations of each business.[71] The challenge involved in managing a multiplying range of heterogenous businesses was exponentially greater than growing around a single industry: while "expansion in a single line of business only increased the scale and scope of existing routine and procedures... diversification into new lines of products with new markets and sources of supplies brought a whole new range of tactical and strategic decisions." Top executives therefore required "a way of evaluating performance in some hundred different businesses without becoming involved in the operational details of each of them."[72] These equivalencies were increasingly seen in terms of quantitative exchange-value determinations: what

had. Greenwood, *Managerial Decentralization*, 18; See: Chandler, *Strategy and Structure*, 368–69.

[68] Chandler, *Strategy and Structure*, 299; Greenwood, *Managerial Decentralization*, 22.

[69] Rothschild, *The Secret to GE's Success*, 88; Chandler, *Strategy and Structure*, 311.

[70] Even though GE's decentralization went further, and happened later, than other companies he surveys, Chandler notes that this process of top management coming exclusively to handle entrepreneurial activities did not go as far at GE as it did elsewhere. This would increasingly shift over the 1970s. (See Chandler, *Strategy and Structure*, 368.).

[71] Chandler, *Strategy and Structure*, 299–314; Greenwood, *Managerial Decentralization*; Cordiner, *New Frontiers for Professional Managers*, 44–45.

[72] Cordiner, *New Frontiers for Professional Managers*, 98.

made qualitatively distinct production processes *comparable* was their money-value as determined by rates of return.

One can identify in this the roots of the *financialization* of the industrial corporation, as it was restructured from a *system of production* to a *system of investment*.[73] This had three dimensions: (1) conversion of top corporate planners into 'investors,' or bearers of abstract money-capital; (2) gradual reorganization of corporate governance as an internal capital market; and (3) empowerment of financial operations over the rest of the organization. The process whereby "the top team was now less the captive of its operating organizations" also required "the financial offices [to] provide more and better data," which led to the rapid growth and increasing power of these financial units.[74] The quantitative metrics they provided constituted *general criteria* on the basis of which *general managers* could evaluate internal and external operations alike: both assessing the past and present performance of internal operating units and evaluating "new areas for development or expansion in which operating unit executives would have comparatively little interest or knowledge."[75]

Diversification and decentralization therefore brought the gradual displacement of Weberian bureaucratic structures by financial controls and the internalization within the firm of competitive market discipline. It also resulted in the deepening penetration of the money-form within the firm, as it came to more substantially mediate relations between top executives and operating managers. This, in turn, further enhanced the dominance of the abstract over the concrete. Thus, "'measure' meant that the correct response to the question, 'What is it we make in Louisville' eventually wasn't 'refrigerators'; it was 'money.'"[76] As one semi-official account of the reorganization put it, Cordiner's "theory of decentralization was based on a concept somewhat akin to the theory of atomistic competition. That is, each self-sufficient activity of the corporation would operate

[73] Greta R. Krippner, *Capitalizing on Crisis* (Boston, MA: Harvard University Press, 2011); Neil Fligstein, *The Transformation of Corporate Control*, (Boston, MA: Harvard University Press, 1993).

[74] Chandler, *Strategy and Structure*, 310; O'Boyle, *At Any Cost*, 52.

[75] Chandler, *Strategy and Structure*, 310.

[76] O'Boyle, *At Any Cost*, 52.

on its own within the overall framework of the rules of a free-enterprise system."[77]

The byzantine, rule-bound nature of Cordiner's decentralization makes it clear that even as GE lurched toward the formation of an internal market, the organization was still strongly characterized by the rigid, centralized, bureaucratic structure of the managerial firm. This became painfully obvious as the "mind-boggling complexity" of Cordiner's model "spawned gridlock of truly monumental proportions." Eventually, the "assumption that a manager could manage anything was proven wrong," as it had meant that hordes of new managers "were placed in situations without the proper experience and understanding of the business and they relied heavily on ungrounded measurements."[78] This led some to speculate that Cordiner had merely "embraced the concept of 'professional managers' as a rationale for moving his loyalists into jobs they were unfamiliar with."[79] Though it was true that internal discipline was a part of Cordiner's strategy—including breaking the power of lower-level managers he referred to as "warlords"—the company's rapid growth also meant that it had a real need to produce large numbers of highly trained administrators.

As such, Cordiner's Chief of Staff, Harold Smiddy, worked with academics and management consultants to develop the first company-operated management institute in Crotonville, New York.[80] This was "a very intensive, continuous 13-week program," with a curriculum that represented the most sophisticated elaboration of "managerial science."[81] In 1956, the facility trained 4,000 people.[82] By 1959, *Time* reported that 32,000 students were attending GE "company schools," a number greater than "most U.S. universities" and fully 11% of the workforce.[83] Crotonville inculcated graduates not merely with the supposed ability to manage "scientifically," but also with a particular sense of loyalty to

[77] Greenwood, *Managerial Decentralization*, ix.; Cordiner, *New Frontiers for Professional Managers*, 59.

[78] Rothschild, *The Secret to GE's Success*, 107.

[79] O'Boyle, *At Any Cost*, 51–52.

[80] Rothschild, *The Secret to GE's Success*, 98, 103, 108.

[81] Evans, *The Education of Ronald Reagan*, 70.

[82] Cordiner, *New Frontiers for Professional Managers*, 73–74.

[83] "Atomic Energy: The Powerhouse," *Time Magazine*, 12 January 1959.

"the GE way"—striving to cultivate a willingness among graduates to "dedicate their lives to the company."[84] The reputation of GE's management training programs also meant that graduates were in high demand elsewhere, increasing GE's centrality to inter-corporate networks. This allowed the company to market these programs through its Management Consulting Services, armed with materials produced for Crotonville—including Cordiner's book *New Frontiers For Professional Managers*, which became one of the sacred texts of managerialism.

The emergence of the new "managerial science" reflected the power of internal managers within corporate governance, the defining feature of the managerial period. The fragmentation of stock holdings, once concentrated in investment banks during the finance capital era, across a large number of small shareholders left external investors unable to mount a coherent challenge to internal managers. Cordiner even pursued a conscious strategy of maintaining a large number of small shareholders "so that GE could not be controlled by any one individual or investment group."[85] This meant splitting the stock whenever the price surpassed $100 per share, ensuring small investors would be able to purchase stocks while deterring those seeking to speculate on asset values. Encouraging employee stock ownership was another way Cordiner stove to prevent the concentration of shareholder power, implementing a program whereby the company threw in 50 cents for every dollar invested by an employee. In addition to preventing the development of an oppositional bloc of shareholders, as employees typically support management in conflicts with outsiders, this also increased employee discipline, leading workers to identify more closely with the firm's financial success.[86]

The shift in power from financiers to internal managers was reflected in the decline of Boards of Directors, which became "as much captives

[84] Rothschild, *The Secret to GE's Success*, 113. As a former top GE executive who participated in the Crotonville program put it: "While serving in the U.S. Army, I studied the art and science of brainwashing, and I even wound up giving lectures on the topic. When I returned to GE, I concluded that the Crotonville approach bordered on brainwashing. The combination of the intensity, isolation, and indoctrination of the GE perspective was very similar to the approach used by the Chinese and Viet Cong in brainwashing U.S. prisoners" (Rothschild, 105).

[85] Rothschild, *The Secret to GE's Success*, 89.

[86] Michael Useem, *Investor Capitalism: How Money Managers Are Changing the Face of Corporate America* (New York: Basic Books, 1999).

of the professional entrepreneurs as were the stockholders."[87] In addition to the fragmentation of shareholdings, this was underpinned by the ability for managers to rely on retained earnings to finance investment, as well as the role of state investment in supporting GE's core engineering operations.[88] Similarly, the growing internal complexity of firms placed a premium on insider knowledge. GE came to view the Chairman of the Board as merely "represent[ing] the President in such areas as financial affairs, public and governmental liaison, and international matters," much in the same way that "Executive Vice Presidents represent the President in relationships with a specific group of Operating Divisions."[89]

Nevertheless, GE's centrality within the capitalist class was reinforced by establishing a Board composed almost entirely of outside directors—only two of the nineteen men on the board, GE's President and Chairman, were company executives. As Cordiner put it, board members were "national, and come from a wide variety of businesses and industries, including education, food, agriculture, mining, manufacturing, marketing, banking, and transportation."[90] The wide cross section of networks and contacts that converged on the GE Board—reflecting in part the diversity of its operations, and the customer and supplier networks that came with them—was an important institutional foundation of its capacity to organize a capitalist class *political* consensus, and thus its prominence within the integral state.

The growth of this managerial layer within state and corporate bureaucracies underpinned a distinct "middle class" ethos. Thanks to state economic intervention, and the scientific governance of corporations by professional managers, economic crisis, class conflict, and even material scarcity were, according to managerial ideology, things of the past. As Cordiner put it, any "wasteful frictions" between workers and capitalists, as well as between corporations and other institutions, resulted merely from the "national obsession" with "concepts of old world capitalism and

[87] Chandler, *Strategy and Structure*, 313; Greenwood, *Managerial Decentralization*, 24.

[88] Doug Henwood, *Wall Street: How It Works and for Whom* (New York: Verso, 1998).

[89] Cordiner, *New Frontiers for Professional Managers*, 67–68.

[90] Cordiner, *New Frontiers for Professional Managers,* 15.

old world socialism" and their "obsolete assumptions as to the nature of economic life in the United States today."[91]

The US had "evolved a wholly new form of capitalism"—"people's capitalism"—and had become "the first nation in the world to break through the ancient barriers of scarcity into an economy of abundance."[92] Scientific managers had no particular side in any conflict over power or resources, and were thus uniquely capable of objectivity: they were merely "employees hired by the share owners through their elected directors to manage their business in the balanced best interest of all concerned."[93] In fact, the state also had a hand in the development of this ideology: as we shall see in the next chapter, the notion of "people's capitalism" was a product of the US Information Agency, with which Reed was closely affiliated. The USIA would take up Cordiner's call "to communicate to the rest of the world" the "unique experience" of post-historical American reality.[94]

The State, Managerial Hegemony, and the New Company Unionism

Despite the projections of managerialist ideology, capitalism had hardly rid itself of its contradictions—least of all class. Underpinning the social stability and rising standards of living for the "middle class" were relatively high rates of unionization. The consolidation of managerialism over the 1950s rested upon an alliance between a group of corporations connected to the state industrial policy system, and "business unions" embedded within these firms as well as the state labor-relations apparatus. This corporatist arrangement routinized and stabilized industrial conflict through top-down mechanisms that secured labor discipline within the structure of managerial hegemony. Though the American Federation of Labor (AFL) embraced the business unionism model, the Congress of Industrial Organizations (CIO) initially sought to challenge it. One of the unions at the forefront of this was the Communist-led United Electrical Workers (UE), the third largest and most radical of the CIO unions.

[91] Cordiner, *New Frontiers for Professional Managers*, 2.

[92] Cordiner, *New Frontiers for Professional Managers*, 1.

[93] Cordiner, *New Frontiers for Professional Managers*, 17.

[94] Cordiner, *New Frontiers for Professional Managers*, 1.

In the wake of the CIO-led postwar strike wave, in which UE played no small part, GE was at the center of an effort to develop class-wide strategies for resurrecting New Deal corporatism through an alliance with "responsible" unions. When Wilson tapped Cordiner in 1941 to plan GE's reorganization, Cordiner was simultaneously appointed to work on a BAC "Technical Subcommittee composed of industrial relations experts who are on the firing line in daily contact with employer-employee relationship problems," in order to develop "the fundamental principles which should govern a sound industrial relations policy for the nation."[95] Joining Cordiner in these tasks at GE was labor-relations Vice President Lemuel Boulware. Despite widespread support for the UE strike, no workers in plants Boulware supervised had participated—leading to his promotion by Wilson, who tasked him with investigating the company's failure to contain the labor action. The post-mortem outlined with horror that while workers "appeared vigorously to support the union's demands," so too did "community leaders, politicians, and merchants in areas where GE had plants."[96] Even state and local governments seemed dangerously out of control. The problem, in other words, was larger than simply one of collective bargaining at GE plants. From the company's point of view, that workers and community members were "likely to learn about events affecting their wages and working conditions only through union communications" was indicative of the GE's "failure to communicate."[97]

Yet GE was reluctant to combat even radical trade unionism in its own plants. It was the AEC that insisted repeatedly over 1948 that GE be more aggressive in attacking the UE if it expected to continue receiving state investment for developing sensitive nuclear technologies. The AEC explained in no uncertain terms that it "could not tolerate a situation in which union officials of suspected loyalty could exercise discipline over members working in atomic energy." Therefore, "as the Commission saw it, General Electric as contractor had the responsibility for correcting the situation" by revoking recognition of UE. While the company promised

[95] Walter White, "Confidential Memorandum to Mr. W. L. Batt from Walter White," October 10, 1940, Record Group 40, Entry UD 12, Box #2, National Archives College Park, MD.

[96] Herbert Roof Northrup, *Boulwarism: The Labor Relations Policies of the General Electric Company*, (Ann Arbor, MI: University of Michigan, 1964), 21.

[97] Northrup, *Boulwarism*, 31.

to do so—at least "providing the Commission gave its full cooperation and support"—it reversed course just a few months later, insisting that "the Commission would have to take the initiative in withdrawing recognition of the UE." When the AEC subsequently decided to open atomic energy facilities to unionization, it simultaneously "agreed that General Electric should be directed to withdraw recognition" from UE. Though the UE filed a suit against GE and the AEC for breach of contract, the case was dismissed on April 25, 1949, "with the finding that the Commission had exercised its authority according to the Atomic Energy Act."[98]

Meanwhile, United Auto Workers (UAW) raids on UE locals began shortly after UAW President Walter Reuther reversed his earlier pledge and signed a non-Communist affidavit in 1947. Under the Taft-Hartley Act, passed just weeks previously over Truman's veto, signing such an affidavit was necessary to appear on the ballot in elections overseen by the National Labor Relations Board (NLRB). Unions that refused to comply, such as UE, were left isolated and vulnerable, as compliant unions could organize NLRB elections in which the dissenters were not eligible to participate. Aggressive raiding left UE leaders with little choice but to sign anti-Communist affidavits, the very last CIO union to do so. When CIO President Philip Murray still refused to publicly oppose raids on UE-organized shops, UE dissociated itself from the CIO—leading Murray, Reuther, and others to declare the UE "expelled" from the organization. Simultaneously, the CIO established a new union, with no locals and no members, to replace UE: the International Union of Electrical, Radio and Machine Workers (IUE).

The CIO then sent a telegram to every company with which UE had a contract, supporting the withdrawal of all recognition for the dissident union. GE led the way in doing so; others followed suit. As UE entered dire financial straits, the United Steel Workers and UAW "poured thousands upon thousands of dollars into the war on the UE," backed by financial contributions from the CIO. GE and Westinghouse also invoked the "employers' rights" enshrined in Taft-Hartley to petition for NLRB elections, and gave CIO organizers "free run of the

[98] Hewlett and Duncan, *A History of the United States Atomic Energy Commission*, 343–47, 460–65.

plant to carry on a campaign on the inside."[99] The House Un-American Activities Committee and House Committee on Education and Labor intensified the climate of intimidation by conducting hearings at which union members, shop stewards, officers, and staff representatives would be called to appear.[100] According to a GE policy issued in 1953, justified under powers claimed under the Atomic Energy Act, any worker who pled the Fifth Amendment in such hearings would be fired.[101]

Over the 1950s, what would become known as "Boulwarism" came into its own. Based on a detailed assessment of workers' attitudes and union strategies, as well as broad collaboration with state officials, behavioral psychologists, and corporate executives organized through the US Information Agency, BAC, and other venues, Boulware devised an "Employee and Community Relations Program." It was premised on the understanding "that it was not enough to win over company employees on narrow labor issues"; rather, workers should "pass on GE's essentially conservative message to others."[102] In Boulware's words, GE's employees should become "mass communicators." Crotonville now incorporated "numerous" sessions on economics and politics to reinforce the Boulwarism agenda.[103] The fundamental objective was to counteract "union communications" according to which "restrictions on managerial freedom to manage, to innovate, or to effectuate necessary change can be made to seem reasonable, fair, and constructive of employee interests." Such ideas were described as "the facts of economic and competitive needs and the unvarnished truth."[104]

The resources and organizational capacities GE was able to bring to bear in promoting its "unvarnished truth" far surpassed those of UE. The company's program—which "involved use of all the resources available, aimed at all the audiences involved"—was coordinated by three thousand "employee relations managers" who reported directly to Boulware,

[99] James J. Matles and James Higgins, *Them and Us: Struggles of a Rank-and-File Union*, (Englewood Cliffs, NJ: Prentice Hall, 1974), 199–201; Northrup, *Boulwarism*, 46.

[100] Northrup, *Boulwarism*, 44.

[101] Matles and Higgins, *Them and Us*, 217–19.

[102] Evans, *The Education of Ronald Reagan*, 4.

[103] Rothschild, *The Secret to GE's Success*, 104.

[104] Northrup, *Boulwarism*, 32.

and whose "loyalty and enthusiasm for their leader knew no bounds."[105] The ideological apparatus these managers oversaw operated on a vast scale, as the company "developed a managed-news program that was the envy of corporate America." Newspapers in towns or cities where GE plants were located published positive articles about the company, which was often among their largest advertisers and the city's largest employer. However, the "most impressive publications" were the four produced by the company itself, each of which had nationwide distribution. GE also held "book clubs," either "at the plants or in nearby homes of employees." After all, spouses "often influenced the employees to accept GE's positions."[106]

As a collective bargaining strategy, the basic approach of Boulwarism was simply not to bargain. Management would issue an offer, which was considered final, unlike what Boulware called the "trick offers" companies often *referred to* as final before undertaking a bargaining process that gave unions the opportunity to gain concessions. Moreover, the same offer would be made to unionized and non-unionized employees, a strategy calculated to demonstrate that collective bargaining was a futile endeavor: quality employment packages were not "concessions" to be wrung from a reluctant and greedy corporation, but rather issued "voluntarily" by paternalistic managers. Offers were not the result of struggle, but rather the outcome of "scientific" assessment of "objective facts" by specialized managers.[107] This was held to be different from the bad old capitalism, ruled by selfish financiers, as well as labor unions, which were prone to acting "unscientifically" in seeking to maximize benefits to their members.[108]

After making an offer, the company then set about the task of "Job Marketing," or using the techniques of modern advertising, advanced psychological theories, and propaganda methods refined within the national security state to sell the contract directly to workers. This was intended to minimize the mediation of unions, and employed "virtually all media, from television and radio, to newspaper, plant publications

[105] Northrup, *Boulwarism*, 33; Evans, *The Education of Ronald Reagan*, 12.

[106] Evans, *The Education of Ronald Reagan*, 50, 54, 73.

[107] Cordiner, *New Frontiers for Professional Managers*, 1–39; Northrup, *Boulwarism*, 31–32.

[108] Lemuel R. Boulware, *The Truth About Boulwarism: Trying to Do Right Voluntarily* (Bureau of National Affairs, 1969), 87.

and personal contact," as Judge Irving Kaufman put it in a landmark decision finding Boulwarism to be in violation of labor standards.[109] Extensive surveys and focus groups allowed company messages to be carefully tailored for specific audiences in undertaking the "regrettable and distasteful but vitally necessary task… to correct any unwarranted confidence in any unsound proposals by union officials."[110] If the "economic facts" of a profit-based, competitive system of production were taken as given, GE managers had a major advantage in the argument.

General Electric, the National Security State, and the New Right

The integration of the major labor organizations within managerial hegemony was consummated with the merger of the AFL and CIO in 1955, though by this time "few substantial differences remained between the two federations."[111] As first AFL-CIO President George Meany put it, "we do not seek to recast American society in any particular doctrinaire or ideological image. We seek an ever rising standard of living."[112] It was perhaps fitting that the AFL-CIO was born precisely as state repression peaked with the passage of the Brownell-Butler Communist Control Act, which established a "Subversive Activities Control Board" that could strip unions determined to uphold a "Communist line" of bargaining rights. For its part, the IUE evolved into "a hopeless mess of dishonesties, confusion, and ineffectiveness in which all semblance of democracy and the principles on which it was founded have disappeared," as founding Secretary-Treasurer James Click would later put it.[113]

[109] Cited in: Evans, *The Education of Ronald Reagan*, 46.

[110] General Electric Company, "Year-End Review: Where We Were, Where We Are, Where We Are Trying to Go in Employee Plant Community and Union Relations," General Electric Company Employee Relations News Letter, December 31, 1954, pg. 3–4. Cited in: Northrup, *Boulwarism*, 27; see also 31–35.

[111] Nelson Lichtenstein, *State of the Union: A Century of American Labor*, Revised and Expanded Edition, (Princeton, NJ: Princeton University Press, 2002), 147.

[112] Lichtenstein, *State of the Union*, 147.

[113] Northrup, *Boulwarism*, 47.

That workers were split between UE and IUE "permitted Boulware and his successors to divide and conquer."[114] In fact, the consolidation of business unionism coincided with the start of a broader phase of GE's community relations program. If the most hysterical and vicious McCarthyism was by then in decline, it was replaced by a more genteel and popular successor in the form of GE spokesman Ronald Reagan. Especially significant was *General Electric Theater*, a television show hosted by Reagan created in 1953. Fully sponsored by GE, the show ran for ten seasons, becoming the country's top-rated Sunday prime-time program. Having served as the President of the Screen Actor's Guild, Reagan could draw on a veritable fount of ideological power to support the show: Hollywood celebrities.[115]

While the regular appearance of movie stars on the show boosted the popularity of *GE Theater*, Reagan's regular public association with such personalities solidified his own celebrity status, making him an even more valuable commodity for GE. While GE sponsored the programming that brought Hollywood royalty right into one's living room, so too had it created the very technologies that made such modern miracles possible. "In engineering, in research, in manufacturing skill, in the values that bring a better, more satisfying life," each segment began, "at General Electric, progress is our most important product."[116] GE became synonymous with "progress," and even American national virtue itself, enhancing the value of its "brand" while supporting the conservative political messages Reagan delivered.

Reagan also spent considerable time on the road, touring each of GE's 130 plants across 43 states to speak to captive audiences on the shop floor, while reaching their neighbors and families through community groups such as Rotary Clubs and Moose Lodges. The connections GE built through Boulware's Community Relations program ensured these events were prominently covered as major events in local media. GE ads regularly featured the "all-electric home" the company had supplied the Reagans with, which featured all the latest "gadgets."[117] Over time, the line between advertising and political propaganda was increasingly blurred,

[114] Rothschild, *The Secret to GE's Success*, 120.

[115] Evans, *The Education of Ronald Reagan*, 58.

[116] Quoted in: O'Boyle, *At Any Cost*, 26.

[117] O'Boyle, *At Any Cost*, 26.

as Reagan became (in the words of one GE executive) "a missionary to spread the word of the threat of organized labor and big government and to stress the merits of free enterprise."[118]

That Reagan spent a large amount of time in the south was explained by GE's expanding investments there. Smaller southern capitalists, especially represented by NAM, the Chamber, and the southern Democratic Party, had held back the New Deal tide at the Mason-Dixon line. By the 1950s, this was ironically encouraging the integration of the region with the national economy, as the low-wage and union-free zone began to attract investment from northern-based corporations.[119] Southern and southwestern states offered business a range of subsidies, as well as more favorable ground for NLRB contests and contract negotiations. GE was among the first to begin relocating production there—an explicit part of Boulware's labor-relations program.

While GE plants in the traditional industrial heartland were increasingly threatened with closure, the company made new investments in Alabama, Arkansas, Georgia, Kentucky, Maryland, North Carolina, Texas, and Virginia. Municipalities and states across the "Sun Belt" began to compete for state and corporate investment, striving to create a favorable "business climate" by cutting taxes, reducing regulations, and passing anti-union "right to work" laws, while building the educational and other infrastructure that would attract military contracts.[120] Given that "there were many U.S. cities that were non-union and wanted the new jobs, especially GE jobs," the company gained significant leverage when its "leaders showed that they were willing to move plants."[121]

State investment through the industrial policy system played a pivotal role in this restructuring. As we saw, GE's adoption of the conglomerate form, where the auto companies did not, reflected its particular embeddedness within the industrial policy system. The same was true for GE's early relocation to the south, a move the auto companies would not

[118] Rothschild, *The Secret to GE's Success*, 116.

[119] Tami Friedman, "Exploiting the North–South Differential: Corporate Power, Southern Politics, and the Decline of Organized Labor after World War II," *Journal of American History* 95, no. 2 (September 2008): 323–48.

[120] Elizabeth Tandy Shermer, *Sunbelt Capitalism: Phoenix and the Transformation of American Politics*, (Philadelphia, PA: University of Pennsylvania Press, 2013).

[121] Rothschild, *The Secret to GE's Success*, 120.

follow for decades.[122] Beginning in the late 1940s, the federal government "channelled a vast share of national resources" toward improving the public services and infrastructure in the south.Between World War II and 1952, military expenditures "were concentrated in the Great Lakes states, in the Northeast, and in the emerging centers of West Coast military production, California and Washington." After 1952, the relative share of military contracts going to these areas declined, while that of the south and southwest grew.[123]

As a result, wholly "new areas of industrialization sprang up… dominated by defense-related firms," especially those on the ODM and CED.[124] Although this generated rapid economic growth in the southern states, it "simultaneously eroded the traditional bases of political and social leadership" in the region—and therefore fomented social conflict.[125] Regional small capitalists, and the Democratic politicians they supported, welcomed federal money, but insisted on retaining local control. Meanwhile, the CED "systematically" established "deep connections with small business associations and municipal governments nationwide and focused on directing the power of both, overlapping, groups of residents to campaign for industry."[126]

Local CED networks mobilized and "overhauled" moribund local business associations, especially Chambers of Commerce, to resurrect atrophied—in some cases practically non-existent—Republican political apparatuses. New linkages between national business associations and local "boosters" developed the capacity of municipal associations and governments to compete for investment. Once elected, corporate-backed "boosters" restructured state governments, subverting troublesome legislatures by developing more robust and autonomous state bureaucracies. They also set up "advisory groups" to connect with and reinforce

[122] Kim Phillips-Fein, "'If Business and the Country Will Be Run Right:' The Business Challenge to the Liberal Consensus, 1945–1964," *International Labor and Working-Class History* 72 (Fall 2007): 202.

[123] Jeffrey Crump, "The Spatial Distribution of Military Spending in the United States 1941–1985," *Growth and Change*, Summer 1989, 52–53, 57.

[124] Pierpaoli, "Truman's Other War," 19.

[125] Bruce J. Schulman, *From Cotton Belt to Sunbelt: Federal Policy, Economic Development, and the Transformation of the South, 1938–1980*, (New York: Oxford University Press, 1991), 112.

[126] Shermer, *Sunbelt Capitalism*, 85–86.

national and local integral state networks, and to mobilize local Chambers and other business associations. The result was that "boosters and outside executives largely dictated the terms for new or continued investment."[127]

That most CED members were Republicans already indicated the extent to which the "corporate liberalism" label never quite fit this group.[128] As early as 1952, Reed joined a small group of fourteen businessmen urging General Eisenhower to run on the Republican ticket in hopes of reinvigorating that party.[129] He would remain a key advisor throughout Eisenhower's presidency. At the same time, the BAC's Labor Policy Committee, headed by Cordiner, issued a confidential report to Secretary of Commerce Weeks concluding that Taft-Hartley "has been partial to unions and has failed to carry out the intent of Congress." The report advocated expanding state powers to enforce injunctions against strikes, protecting "employers' freedom of speech" and the "right to lock out" workers, defending "open shop" laws, escalating anti-Communist attacks, and increasing the use of damage suits against unions.[130] Cordiner also urged others to adopt GE-style community relations programs, exhorting "industry to work through its own employees and in its plant communities in a campaign of education."[131] Meanwhile, the BAC Committee on Taxation worked with the Treasury Department to flesh out its basic low tax, low spending, and low deficit orientation.

[127] Shermer, *Sunbelt Capitalism*, 85–86.

[128] Mizruchi, *The Fracturing of the American Corporate Elite*, 42.

[129] Business Advisory Council for the Department of Commerce, "Chairman's Report for 1953," January 29, 1954, Record Group 56, Entry 198, Box #106, National Archives College Park, MD; "Minutes of General Council Meeting of the Business Advisory Council for the Department of Commerce," January 14, 1953, Record Group 56, Entry 198, Box #106, National Archives College Park, MD; Walter White, "Memorandum to Council Members," November 12, 1953, Record Group 56, Entry 198, Box #106, National Archives College Park, MD.

[130] "Confidential Report of the Labor Policy Committee of the Business Advisory Council to Secretary Weeks," May 9, 1953, Record Group 56, Entry 198, Box #106, National Archives College Park, MD.

[131] "Minutes of General Council Meeting of the Business Advisory Council for the Department of Commerce," October 22, 1953, Record Group 56, Entry 198, Box #106, National Archives College Park, MD.

This meant rolling back the welfare state where possible and keeping military spending to a "responsible" minimum.[132]

As this suggests, Commerce continued to play an important role in facilitating capitalist political activism and in building class-wide consensus. It also acted as a critical intermediary between corporations and the broader state complex, the "point of contact" between state and corporate power *in general*. A primary task of the department was systematically organizing the relationship between the state and business, including regularly convening capitalists through the BAC. In the words of its Executive Committee, the BAC "played a dual role, one to give advice to Secretary Weeks and the other equally important, to carry back to scattered communities an understanding of problems faced by the Administration and to be ambassadors of good will for the federal officials with whom they came in contact."[133] All the major political initiatives over the 1940s and 1950s were launched out of the BAC, from Cordiner's labor strategy groups to the CED.

Nevertheless, Commerce was relegated to an ancillary role in relation to the consolidation of the power of the new national security state over industrial policy. It had played little role in the ODM and was marginal to the more important linkages that had now emerged between the CED, the State Department, and the Department of Defense. While the BAC had been central to organizing capitalist support for the New Deal, it was the CED that played the major role in building consensus around "free trade" and "military Keynesianism," supported by the ascendant Defense and State departments.[134] The main torchbearers of the corporatist "planning impulse" were now on the CED.[135] While Commerce officials had

[132] See for instance: "Minutes of General Council Meeting of the Business Advisory Council for the Department of Commerce," May 7–8, 1954, Record Group 56, Entry 198, Box #106, National Archives College Park, MD; Business Advisory Council, "Draft of Tax Policy Statement," November 1952, Record Group 56, Entry 198, Box #106, National Archives College Park, MD. "Minutes of General Council Meeting of the Business Advisory Council for the Department of Commerce, Hot Springs, Virginia, May 8 & 9 1953," May 20, 1953, Record Group 56, Entry 198A, Box #17, National Archives College Park, MD.

[133] "Minutes of General Council Meeting of the Business Advisory Council for the Department of Commerce," March, 19, 1953, Record Group 56, Entry 198, Box #106, National Archives College Park, MD.

[134] Mizruchi, *The Fracturing of the American Corporate Elite*, 37.

[135] Shermer, *Sunbelt Capitalism*, 85–86.

once dreamed of leading an "associative state," it was the Department of Defense and Department of State which had become the most prominent hubs of state-corporate integration.

In addition to providing economic and technical input, GE also worked *politically* to organize consensus around the policy frameworks that emanated from the state agencies to which it was so closely connected. These relationships were increasingly supported by the CED, whose top-down structure was specifically geared toward organizing business around the formation of a new imperial state at home and abroad. As we shall see in the next chapter, policy devised by its powerful Research & Policy committee, which was embedded within the most prominent state apparatuses, established the basis for a consensus built across the organization. Apart from its prestige within the state, that the CED was a highly exclusive forum, containing only a limited number of increasingly powerful "multinational" corporations, also made it a more adequate space for developing a consensus among these firms, which could then be extended "downward" through the BAC and other forums.

This was also true of Cordiner's "Links Group," formed out of the committees on labor relations he had led within the BAC. Made up of fellow CEOs who faced CIO unions, the Links Group strategized around a narrower set of political interests than what would have been possible within the BAC. Boulware, too, assembled "public affairs" or "government relations" executives—by then a common post within major corporations—into an informal group he called the "Wise Men." His secretary privately kept a membership list of 20–30 such executives, who met monthly at the University Club in New York. Though Boulware "set the agenda and often attended personally," Virgil Day, Boulware's protégé and one of the most politically connected GE executive s, was the regular attendee for GE.[136] Just as Cordiner and Reed had played pivotal roles on the BAC and CED, in meetings of the Wise Men "it was clear that the lead company was General Electric."[137]

Boulware's "Wise Men" were effectively corporate political officers whose full-time job was to participate in the integral state. It was, in a sense, a fully privatized and routinized form of the WOC system: a broader set of state-integrative functions were assimilated as permanent

[136] Evans, *The Education of Ronald Reagan*, 98.

[137] Evans, *The Education of Ronald Reagan*, 99, 103.

features of corporate bureaucratic structures, rather than being fulfilled in an ad hoc fashion. The proliferation of such positions points to the entrenchment of a vast integral state structure, as well as the increasing complexity of managing state-corporate relations. Indeed, "all of the men [present in meetings of the "Wise Men" were familiar with the corridors of power in Washington, D.C., and in the state capitals throughout the nation." Each was embedded in the layers of "lawyers and lobbyists" that constituted the integral state from the local to the national level, and which formed important institutional foundations for the political parties.

To be sure, Cordiner's and Boulware's efforts remained definitively non-partisan. However, enmeshed within these networks was an emerging group of conservative political consultants, some of whom would go on to play key roles in the Goldwater campaign and the subsequent "conservative revolution." Their connections to the national integral state brought these individuals "sustaining incomes between campaigns," aiding them in constructing the new Republican Party political apparatus. Moreover, the Wise Men group worked to mobilize business on behalf of a distinctly conservative agenda. This was apparent from its founding of the National Investor Relations Institute, which—"following the GE model"—encouraged companies to lobby Congress and "to use their shareholder mailing lists to promote important corporate issues such as tax and regulatory reform."[138]

Efforts to rebuild the Republican Party were spurred on by the "slaughter" suffered by the GOP in the 1958 mid-term elections—"the worst defeat ever for a party occupying the White House." That year, as Cordiner became chair of the BAC, GE initiated what was effectively Reagan's first national campaign, based on "a plan hatched by Ralph Cordiner and Lemuel Boulware" at a strategy meeting "held on a small island off Florida."[139] Reagan would be taken out of GE plants "almost entirely," and would instead focus nearly exclusively on "community engagement." After the meeting, Boulware wrote a seven-page memo to Jack S. Parker, who would take over for Boulware after he retired from GE.[140] The "plans for succession and political engagement" outlined in

[138] Evans, *The Education of Ronald Reagan*, 99, 103; Alexander Laskin, "Investor Relations as a Public Relations Function: A State of the Profession in the United States," *Journal of Public Relations Research* 26 (2014): 200–214.

[139] Evans, *The Education of Ronald Reagan*, 83, 84.

[140] Northrup, *Boulwarism*, 66.

the document were "unique in American corporate history," in that "it would do nothing less than convert the company into a giant political force" that would outlast Boulware's departure.

Boulware continued speaking regularly at integral state venues, like the NAM and local Chambers, within which smaller, regional capitalists were organized, in order "to urge corporate executives to disseminate his message."[141] J.J. Wuerthner, manager for public affairs at GE's "Electronics Park" in Syracuse, played an important role in coordinating these efforts. As chair of the Government Affairs Committee of the Manufacturers Association of Syracuse, he headed a "seminal task force" of corporate managers on political organizing. His 1959 book *The Businessman's Guide to Practical Politics* became an ideological centerpiece of this mobilization, serving as a key part of the "eleven-week courses in practical politics" Wuerthner designed.

By the end of the decade, Boulware's weekly *Employee Relations News Letter*, initially mailed to the company's 15,000 supervisors and managers, had been requested by "several times" that number, including "columnists, teachers, clergymen, politicians, and other businessmen." Though this number had declined by the time of Boulware's retirement in 1961, by then another intellectual lodestone for the new right had emerged in the form William F. Buckley's *National Review*. Buckley himself had long been a reader of Boulware's newsletter, and wrote to Boulware that he had been "one of the people most responsible" for the founding of the *National Review* and the progress the new conservatives were then making.[142]

The patterns of state-corporate integration formed through the World War II mobilization and planning effort thus proved durable indeed over the decades that followed. During the 1950s, the military consolidated its power over the state industrial policy system, as well as its linkages to a core group of cutting-edge corporations. In these years, such high-tech manufacturing firms began to redirect investment toward the non-union, low-wage south. The competitive dynamic this set off was favorable to business and the military alike, as states competed to create a "favorable business climate" and support the construction of the infrastructure for advanced R&D. This integration of the south with

[141] Boulware, *The Truth About Boulwarism*, 103.

[142] Evans, *The Education of Ronald Reagan*, 105.

the corporate-dominated national economy was supported by the efforts of erstwhile "corporate liberals" to build closer connections with state governments and local business associations, forming the basis for a resurgent Republican Party.

This was fundamentally built upon the organizational infrastructure initially developed by the WPB for war mobilization, and later carried forward by the ODM with the support of the CED. The corporations that spearheaded this process of economic integration were themselves largely creatures of the state industrial policy system. The shift in investment by these firms, including GE, toward the south and southwest was likewise inseparable from the similar redirection of state investment within the industrial policy system. So too was it bound up with and enabled by institutional restructuring and capacity building at the state level. Even "new right" ideology itself, and the techniques whereby it was formulated and disseminated, were developed within integral state venues, in particular the USIA, as we will see in the next chapter. It was the national integral state, constructed by an active state, that made possible the coordination of a nationwide business strategy for reconstructing American political and economic federalism.

CHAPTER 5

From Class Interest to National Interest: General Electric and the Making of an Informal Empire

The process whereby the state organizes the capitalist class is highly contradictory and contested. It is not managed by a single central authority, but rather takes the form of divergent and even conflictual institutional practices often only loosely articulated to each other. During the war years and after, an industrial policy system took shape that formed a key foundation of the state-corporate power structure. This formed the basis for a "military Keynesian" compromise between New Dealers and the military, which secured Defense Department hegemony over an industrial policy system integrating large, international, technology-focused corporations with state power. This chapter examines the internationalizing dimensions of this power structure: the institutional mechanisms through which the state organized a domestic class consensus around, and on that basis constructed, a global "informal empire."

Just as integral state organs had promoted industrial mobilization for war and the subsequent consolidation of the industrial policy system, so too were they essential to organizing corporate support for plans formulated within the State and Treasury departments for postwar international order. State managers worked actively to build a corporate consensus around aid for European reconstruction, reductions in US tariffs, increased autonomy in negotiating trade agreements and carrying out anti-inflation macroeconomic stabilization, and for establishing and

© The Author(s), under exclusive license to Springer Nature Switzerland AG 2022

S. Maher, *Corporate Capitalism and the Integral State*, Marx, Engels, and Marxisms,
https://doi.org/10.1007/978-3-030-83772-3_5

managing a new transnational economic governance regime. The significance of these efforts is highlighted by the considerable risks this restructuring entailed for many capitalists in the form of increased competitive pressures, higher taxes, and the breakup of international cartels. The centrality of GE to this effort was particularly striking given that the company was then absorbing a litany of devastating Department of Justice antitrust suits, which completely broke down the cartels that enabled it to dominate global markets over the previous half-century.

Building a new imperial state required developing an enlarged conception of the "national interest" that incorporated a responsibility for overseeing the international system. The capitalist class consensus around this was articulated through a range of state practices that operated at a considerable remove from the immediate economic interests of particular capitalists. Far from the state serving as the instrument of a dominant bloc of corporations, what was most noteworthy about this process was the significant state *autonomy* it exhibited. Yet if the project of constructing a new global order relied upon the unique planning capacities of state institutions, the latter nevertheless had to solicit information and cooperation from corporations. While the State Department developed and mobilized support for the Marshall Plan, the Treasury led similar efforts in relation to the Bretton Woods economic regime.

Despite the rise and fall of a series of integral state organizations, a cluster of specific firms remained at the center of these efforts, GE perhaps most of all. Even those organizations most amenable to the state's imperial agenda, such as the CED, remained conflicted. Firms with close links to the state were key to making the case for global empire within these integral state venues. Just as it had been crucial to institutionalizing the "military Keynesian" compromise, the CED had to bridge the contradictions between supporting the rise of the monetary apparatus, with its anti-inflation orientation, and simultaneously sustaining high levels of military spending to fuel the industrial policy system and support US global power. Organizing support for the new imperial state also extended to increasing the autonomy of the trade policy apparatus, which helped deflect challenges from protectionist forces among business and in Congress.

Nevertheless, individual capitalists were able to secure short-term "special case" exemptions from tariff cuts. Although this unevenness might make it seem as if:

> the American state made compromises that undermined the liberal objectives it had set for itself… this would be to take too idealized a view of the American imperial project. 'Liberalization' was a process; pragmatic compromises were part of making progress within the overall project. Moreover, this was not just a matter of 'two steps forward, one step back'. Interventionist domestic policies and regional trade protection from US exports were not contrary but essential to the imperial project's long-term success.[1]

The Bretton Woods era was not so much characterized by a global system that had attained an internal equilibrium, only later to be overturned by a new (neoliberal) political paradigm. Rather, it was a moment in the broader, long-term *process* of "making global capitalism," whereby the global economy was gradually integrated—forming markets, building states, and liberalizing cross-border flows of capital, as capital penetrated every region of the world.

Relative Autonomy, the Integral State, and the National Interest

Postwar planning within the American state began even before the US entered the war. At that time, neither state officials nor corporate executives had anything like a clear conception of the "informal empire" that would eventually emerge from the ashes of the conflict. What was clear, however, was that the US would be the most powerful country in the world, and would have a substantial say in how the international system would be reconstructed. To meet this challenge, the state mobilized vast institutional resources to study possible options for forging a more stable postwar capitalist world order under American hegemony.[2] This would replace the old system of inter-imperial rivalry, wherein the internationalizing tendencies of capital were contained within exclusive economic territories dominated by individual imperial powers, with an economically and politically integrated capitalist "Grand Area" overseen by the United

[1] Panitch and Gindin, *The Making of Global Capitalism*, 98.

[2] Panitch and Gindin, 68–69; Harry Magdoff, *The Age of Imperialism: The Economics of US Foreign Policy* (New York: Monthly Review Press, 1969); Giovanni Arrighi, *The Long Twentieth Century: Money, Power, and the Origins of Our Times* (New York: Verso, 1994).

States. This was to include Europe, the British Empire, and as much of Asia as possible. State planners sought to identify "the basic needs of such a system" which "any discussion of the national interest necessarily had to address."[3] Planning was concerned with the operations of individual firms only insofar as these were relevant to developing an overall picture of this geo-economic structure. The fundamental logic of the American "national interest" would henceforth incorporate the need to stabilize a dynamic, globalizing capitalism, even if disagreement remained possible over the *means* through which to do so.

Postwar planners came to realize that if the new world were to be more stable than the prewar one had been, the ad hoc agreements among lawyers, corporations, and states bridging across divergent national legal and regulatory structures that had held together the world system would have to be replaced. So too did constructing a new American "informal empire" mean going well beyond simply insisting on an "Open Door" for US investment into colonial spaces managed by other powers, as had been US policy prior to the war. What was needed was a vast and largely unprecedented multilateral institutional architecture to enforce "a general system of rules for mediating the international and national economic responsibilities of all states"—in short, "a new rule of law in the international economy."[4] Rather than states jockeying to protect the domination of economic spaces by their own national capitalist classes, political order would be established through a system of transnational governance administered by a *condominium of states*.

This vision of world order was shaped by the activism of key nodes within the American state which devised, won support for, and then implemented the drastic political and economic restructuring it entailed. To be sure, the tremendous expansion of the American state over the New Deal and especially World War II constituted an important foundation for this project. However, in order to *articulate* a new vision for world order, *organize* a consensus among capitalists for this unprecedented project, and then *superintend* this world order, entirely new—and

[3] Laurence H. Shoup and William Minter, *Imperial Brain Trust: The Council on Foreign Relations and United States Foreign Policy* (New York: Authors Choice Press, 2004), 173.

[4] Panitch and Gindin, *The Making of Global Capitalism*, 74; Robert Cox, *Production, Power, and World Order: Social Forces in the Making of History* (New York: Columbia University Press, 1987); John Gerard Ruggie, *Winning the Peace: America and World Order in the New Era* (New York: Columbia University Press, 1996).

unique—state capacities would be required. This would prove difficult. Indeed, the long-term and system-wide perspective necessary to construct a new global imperial order placed even many of the relatively far-sighted and broad-minded "corporate liberals" on the CED at odds with moving beyond the "Open Door" policy. In this struggle, GE's corporate leadership would play a central role in organizing a class consensus around the hegemonic designs drawn up by planners in the State and Treasury departments.

This was facilitated by the changing role of GE's Chairman of the Board of Directors, which, as Cordiner himself described it, increasingly became that of representing GE "in such areas as financial affairs, public and governmental liaison, and international matters."[5] Throughout his time at GE, Reed was embedded within the State Department and was a major proponent of trade liberalization—especially in relation to Great Britain, which planners saw as "vital" to promoting a similar model of "free trade" with the rest of Europe and beyond. During the war, Reed served under Ambassador Averill Harriman in the Lend-Lease Mission to the United Kingdom; when this morphed into the Mission for Economic Affairs, Reed was appointed as its "Minister." In this capacity, he worked with "administration multilateralists" to secure "obligations on Britain to eliminate trade barriers along with the USA after the war."[6] After the war, Reed supported efforts to generalize this orientation to other countries, including as economic consultant for the US delegation to the San Francisco Diplomatic Conference for founding the United Nations. The following year, he simultaneously gained a seat on the Council on Foreign Relations (CFR) Board of Directors and was made Chair of *both* the CED's powerful Research and Policy Committee (R&P) *and* the US Associates of the International Chamber of Commerce (ICC).

This signified not the "capture" of the state by private power, but rather Reed's centrality in generating support for state policy.[7] The scale of the research and other intellectual labor required to understand, not to

[5] Cordiner, *New Frontiers for Professional Managers*, 67–68.

[6] Charlie Whitham, "The Committee for Economic Development, Foreign Trade and the Rise of American Corporate Liberalism, 1942–8," *Journal of Contemporary History* 48, no. 4 (October 2013): 853–54.

[7] The classic study of the CFR, which includes an extensive review of the documentary record, is Shoup and Minter, *Imperial Brain Trust*. While I draw on their study, Shoup and Minter's conclusions differ sharply from my own. They essentially take the classi

mention reshape, the world system was unprecedented and extended well beyond the administrative purview or coordinating capacities of private corporations. Whole academic departments were formed to meet the massive demand for regional and global knowledge. These were often networked with the state through Council on Foreign Relations (CFR) research groups, which, in the words of its own later annual reports, served "as training ground for members called upon to serve the government in important positions."[8] The CFR also initiated its massive "War & Peace Studies" project to support State Department planning, while the creation of that department's "Advisory Committee on Postwar Foreign Policy" in December 1941 brought CFR researchers directly into the state. Notably, little direct input was solicited from corporate executives. Of the fourteen people appointed to the Advisory Committee—half of whom were government officials, and half private citizens—none were active managers of any corporation, very much unlike the "dollar-a-year man" system at work elsewhere in the state.

The CFR hardly functioned as an instrument through which a politically coherent capitalist class imposed its pre-formed interests on the state, as Shoup and Minter suggested in their classic study. The truth was closer to the opposite: what made CFR study and discussion groups "unique and extremely important" was that they were able "to provide a forum" for academics, state officials, and businessmen to "meet and reach a consensus."[9] The CFR provided a "network of contacts linking together all those involved in the making of foreign policy, in or out of government" and also facilitated "contacts and the integration among foreign policy leaders."[10] Yet it was state apparatuses that defined problems and established broad agendas and priorities for research and discussion within the CFR. By holding conferences and meetings, producing publications, and other such activities, the CFR created space for discussion and consensus formation among policy "experts" and corporate executives largely concerned with other matters. In this way, it served

"instrumentalist" view: that the CFR was a means for capitalists to impose their will upon the state and control policy. As we shall see, this was far from the case.

[8] Council on Foreign Relations, "1950 Annual Report", New York, cited in: Shoup and Minter, *Imperial Brain Trust*, 35.

[9] Shoup and Minter, *Imperial Brain Trust*, 21.

[10] Shoup and Minter, *Imperial Brain Trust*, 57–58.

to educate businessmen about global political and economic realities, thereby contributing to the very *formation* of their interests.

The CED constituted the primary link between business and the CFR, which had only "minimal" links to the NAM and the Chamber of Commerce).[11] Consequently, inputs from business would reflect something closer to a viable general consensus, mediated by "representative" executives and framed by large firms embedded within the industrial policy system, rather than parochial advocacy by individual companies. At the same time, the state, assisted by the CFR, played a significant role in shaping the CED's positions, working to organize big capital behind the policies devised by leading state agencies. This took place primarily through the CED's powerful Research & Policy Committee (R&P), which was effectively the CED "Central Committee."

Despite the CED's formal "independence" from the state (in contrast to the BAC), "it was decision-makers of the government that drove and ultimately determined policy initiatives" in often quite gruelling R&P meetings of academics, corporate executives, and state officials.[12] That the CED looked "to scientific 'objectivity' and not political ideology to foster methods of cooperation between state and business" is revealing in this regard. The organization presented its "basic objective" not as advocating for particular interests, but rather as being "to *develop*, through objective research and discussion, findings and recommendations *for business and public policy* which will contribute to the preservation and strengthening of our free society."[13] Its appeal to the capitalist's own expertise was that in "recognizing that a civilized world cannot be had for the wanting, but has its price, we have sought, as businessmen should, policies to get it at no more cost than necessary."

On this basis, the CED emerged as the most important mechanism for building consensus among business for European reconstruction through the Marshall Plan, and the "Bretton Woods" multilateral trade and investment regime, developed by the State and Treasury departments. But the process whereby it did so was marked by tensions between these agencies,

[11] Shoup and Minter, *Imperial Brain Trust*, 109–10.

[12] Whitham, "The Committee for Economic Development," 870.

[13] Emphasis added. Marion Folsom, "The Economic Situation in Western Europe" (Committee for Economic Development, November 1952), Record Group 469, Entry UD 643A, Box #2, National Archives College Park, MD.

as the work of the Treasury in designing an international financial architecture over the 1940s led it to increasingly rival the State Department's role in postwar planning. Unsurprisingly, the de facto "sharing" of policy planning between the two agencies "was dogged by miscommunication and conflict."[14] Just as the State Department had done through the CFR, Treasury brought "some of the country's brightest young economists on board" who produced "an alternative international economic policy to the State Department's."

As Secretary of State Dean Acheson put it, State's "moralistic, pacifist, and laissez-faire" orientation resulted from the fact that it "had no ideas, plans, or methods for collecting the information or dealing with the problems" with which Treasury was concerned. While State continued to cling to the old "Open Door" policy, insisting simply on "free trade," Treasury saw that "trade could only be liberalized on the basis of an international monetary arrangement that would also allow for economic growth and domestic accumulation in other countries."[15] Nevertheless, the distance between the Treasury and State should not be overstated. The Treasury strongly supported liberalizing trade, even if it also recognized that full employment and economic growth "would depend more on accumulation at home than exports abroad."[16] Indeed, the "free-trade" agenda espoused by Secretary of State Cordell Hull had "remained government orthodoxy throughout the war and imbued all foreign policy discussions and diplomacy, especially with Britain, a vital agent in achieving postwar economic liberalization."[17]

As mentioned above, GE's Reed was pivotal to the trans-Atlantic US-UK alliance, and given his close connection to the State Department, it should not be surprising that he strongly articulated a "free trade" position. As he saw it, although "there is a penalty, at least initially" to promoting free trade and reducing tariff barriers, "to take the initiative in such a move should be the main response of the US."[18] The priority given by the State Department and Reed to removing tariff barriers is

[14] Whitham, "The Committee for Economic Development," 849.

[15] Panitch and Gindin, *The Making of Global Capitalism*, 71.

[16] Panitch and Gindin, *The Making of Global Capitalism*, 72.

[17] Whitham, "The Committee for Economic Development," 849.

[18] Phillip Reed, "Taxes and Trade: 20 Years of CED Policy," May 9, 1963, Record Group 56, Entry 198, Box #2F, National Archives College Park, MD, 47.

perhaps best understood as being aimed at "winning Congressional and business support… and preventing isolationist opinion from looking too closely into what would be entailed in the vaguely defined 'new international responsibilities' the American state was embracing for the postwar world."[19]

Just getting business to subscribe to the broad logic of liberalization proved extremely difficult, even among the relatively homogenous "corporate liberals" on the CED. As Reed reported later:

> the record of one of the earliest meetings of CED trustees preserves a warning that trade policy might be a rocky road. One trustee noted that 'violent emotions' tend to be stirred up by what he described as 'free trade and protective tariff questions… He wanted to know if the other trustees thought it possible that CED could work in this field and maintain its objectivity.[20]

Fortunately from Reed's perspective, "it could and did, although the forecast that some rather insistent feelings might show themselves was entirely correct."[21] As Reed said, this meant "we can speak as businessmen without speaking for business – we can speak for the general interest, but still speak as businessmen."[22]

In the end, the CED articulated a consensus that coupled a central and explicit commitment to the radical tariff reductions pushed by Reed and the State Department with support for the new global financial architecture developed by the Treasury Department. State personnel were actively engaged in shaping this consensus. Top Treasury planner Harry Dexter White, in particular, was "a key figure in shaping CED minds on financial policy."[23] While free traders were "forced to accept a level of short-term protectionism and tariffs to nurture the fragile economies of Europe," "the Keynesians and protectionists in business and Congress were forced to concede a greater level of US intervention in leading the world economy."[24] This was initially articulated in the first R&P trade

[19] Panitch and Gindin, *The Making of Global Capitalism*, 70–72.

[20] Reed, "Taxes and Trade: 20 Years of CED Policy," 43–44.

[21] Reed, "Taxes and Trade: 20 Years of CED Policy," 44.

[22] Reed, "Taxes and Trade: 20 Years of CED Policy," 41.

[23] Whitham, "The Committee for Economic Development," 851.

[24] Whitham, "The Committee for Economic Development," 866.

policy statement, issued in 1945 under the leadership of its first Chairman, Ralph Flanders.

This statement found its origins in April 1943, when the State Department's Will Clayton, an ardent free trader who "personified the business-government symbiosis," urged the CED to adopt a position on international trade. Shortly thereafter, the R&P commissioned a confidential report on "International Trade and Domestic Employment" from Calvin Hoover, a prominent New Dealer, Keynesian, and Dean of Duke University's Graduate School of Arts and Sciences.[25] In preparing the report, Hoover solicited input "from a group of leading lights," including academics and former state officials, most of whom were affiliated with the CFR (as was R&P Chairman Flanders).

Hoover presented the first draft to the R&P at a meeting in January 1944, and was subsequently cross-examined for six hours.[26] The central conclusions of his draft borrowed from the Commerce Department's 1943 publication *The United States in the World Economy*, arguing that "stable domestic employment was a *precondition* of advancement towards liberalized world trade" and that "in the current world to propose that we simply embrace free trade was senseless." By the time the second draft was considered ten months later, the Bretton Woods conference had already concluded. As the only major study of these CED meeting minutes observed, Hoover continued to resist pressures, including from Clayton, to see trade as the key to resolving issues of domestic employment, asserting that "if international trade is considered as a panacea, it will fail."[27]

White attended the next meeting weeks later to reinforce this position, and "specifically to tackle the CED over the Bretton Woods proposals and gain their support in the business community," a task at which he proved "especially persuasive."[28] White supported R&P Chairman Flanders in challenging the notion of "the CED acting as a champion of the worldwide liberalization of trade."[29] That there was no dissent from

[25] Whitham, "The Committee for Economic Development," 851.

[26] Karl Schriftgiesser, *Business Comes of Age* (Harper & Brothers, 1960), 119, cited in: Whitham, 853.

[27] Whitham, "The Committee for Economic Development," 855–858.

[28] Whitham, "The Committee for Economic Development," 860–61.

[29] Whitham, "The Committee for Economic Development," 860.

the "substantial government presence," including "a heavyweight contingent of government economists with multilateralist credentials" and top officials that "devised policy options for the State Department regarding postwar problems," indicated the contours of the consensus that was then emerging.[30]

In a letter to Hoover in late January, White proclaimed the latest draft report "an exceptionally good piece of work" which "should prove very useful in securing public support for an enlightened international economic policy."[31] The report concluded that "a simple policy of unilateral lowering of conventional trade barriers by all countries would not, of itself, be adequate and permanently effective in expanding world trade." Instead, it called for the creation of "new types of international institutions" that would "set up working rules which would limit the field of operations of national controls and prescribe the types of action permissible for such controls."[32] The primary objective of such rules and protections—"in part facilitated by the new types of international economic institutions, and in part carried out by the governments themselves"—was "freeing nations from having to choose between domestic full employment and unregulated foreign trade."[33]

The final draft of the policy statement was put before the R&P in January 1945, finally approved at the February meeting, and issued in March. Its three central recommendations mirrored the Treasury Department's "White Plan" almost exactly, except that they left aside the question of European reconstruction and made more explicit the focus on reducing tariff barriers. As the statement read, the CED sought a policy that would support "the maintenance of dependable currencies and dependable relationships among currencies," "a substantial reduction in the restraints upon world trade, including the reduction of both tariff

[30] Whitham, "The Committee for Economic Development," 858, 860.

[31] Harry Dexter White, "Harry Dexter White to Dean Calvin B. Hoover," January 29, 1945, Record Group 56, Entry A1 360-O, Box #15, National Archives College Park, MD.

[32] Calvin Hoover, "International Trade and Domestic Employment," November 1, 1944, Record Group 56, Entry A1 360-O, Box #15, National Archives College Park, MD, 25.

[33] Hoover, "International Trade and Domestic Employment," 25.

and non-tariff barriers," and finally "development of rules of conduct for world trade."[34]

The approval of this position was perfectly synchronized with the administration's efforts to shepherd Bretton Woods through Congress, which Roosevelt had asked to ratify the proposals in February. The administration "faced bitter opposition from American bankers and conservatives," but "just as the proposals looked set for defeat on Capitol Hill, the CED was invited to intervene in the debate on behalf of the administration." The publication of the policy statement—the result of a year and a half of intensive consensus-building efforts by state actors—thus dramatically revealed that "the administration now had its business champions for the Bretton Woods proposals."[35]

The CED statement declared it to be a basic matter of *principle* that "a restrictive course by America toward foreign trade is contrary to American interest" as "it will be followed by restrictions abroad." The policy statement therefore "recommended":

> that the United States, in the long-range interests of its citizens and those of other nations, take leadership in an international program for the extension of world trade on a basis which will improve world levels of living through an increased exchange of goods and services among nations and increase world productivity through the wide dissemination of improved techniques of production.[36]

The key step to achieving this was for the US to take "the lead in a program to bring about a great reduction in the artificial barriers to trade between nations whether they take the form of tariffs, direct governmental controls over trade subsidies, or restrictive business agreements." Thus "the protective tariff of the United States should be lowered... by the continuation of negotiations under the Reciprocal Trade Agreements Act." More radical was the call for "a major horizontal cut in all

[34] "Trade Policy: A Key to Free World Economic Strength," by Philip D. Reed, in Reed, "Taxes and Trade: 20 Years of CED Policy," 43.

[35] Whitham, "The Committee for Economic Development," 862.

[36] Committee for Economic Development, "Revised Draft Policy Statement: International Trade, Foreign Investment and Domestic Employment," February–March 1945, Record Group 56, Entry A1 360-O, Box #15, National Archives College Park, MD.

duties to be adopted by the United States *regardless of whether other countries follow suit or not*." Such a drastic, across-the-board, unilateral cut was necessary to prevent individual US capitalists from undermining the general interest: "An attempt to revise this tariff downward item by item would almost certainly lead to logrolling by special interests against the national interest and result in only minor reductions." Therefore, "only the bold action of a large flat reduction seems likely to succeed."[37] Nevertheless, it was acknowledged that "a major horizontal cut in tariffs might cause hardship in special cases and necessitate some provision… to ameliorate the effects in cases of extreme hardship, perhaps through temporary subsidies to ease the adjustment to the new conditions."[38]

As this makes clear, "if there was ever a case where the advantages of relative autonomy were manifest, allowing a capitalist state to act on behalf of capital but not at its behest, it was in the extensive public campaign the US Treasury undertook to get the Bretton Woods agreement endorsed by Congress over the bankers' opposition."[39] However, what is also significant is the degree to which, paradoxically, this autonomy was itself a function of the capacity for state agencies to mobilize dominant blocs of corporate power in support of it. While it may be the case that passage by Congress of the Bretton Woods proposals "was not assured until the Treasury struck a last-minute agreement with the representatives of the American Bankers Association and leading Wall Street banks,"[40] this was itself no doubt facilitated by the support mobilized via the CED. President Harry Truman himself later hailed the intervention by the CED as "unequivocally… determinative in passing the Bretton Woods Bill."[41]

That the R&P statement specifically mentioned the Reciprocal Trade Act is significant. Initially passed in 1934, the Act delegated Congress' constitutional authority over tariffs to the president, thereby "institutionalizing in trade policy the executive's greater relative autonomy from particular capitalist interests, with the effect of insulating the state 'from

[37] Emphasis added. Committee for Economic Development, "Revised Draft Policy Statement".

[38] Committee for Economic Development, "Revised Draft Policy Statement".

[39] Panitch and Gindin, *The Making of Global Capitalism*, 79.

[40] Panitch and Gindin, *The Making of Global Capitalism*, 79.

[41] Whitham, "The Committee for Economic Development," 861–62.

unwanted protectionist pressures'."[42] This helped block efforts by protectionists in Congress, as well as on the BAC and other integral state venues, to restrain the liberalizing thrust of US trade policy. However, for that very reason it also remained deeply controversial among business. Sustaining this configuration of state power, and the policy framework it secured, depended upon the capacity of the state to mobilize business in defense of it. The autonomy of the state trade policy apparatus may have been substantial, but it was nevertheless relative.

The CED approved publication of Hoover's report pending one last round of discussion in April 1945. Though described in its introduction as "a synthesis of the present opposing views about the Bretton Woods proposals," the report reaffirmed that the R&P accepted these arrangements and sought merely to work out the details. The main complaint expressed in the document was that the IMF not be used as an open-ended source of long-term financing, as this would likely damage its role in stabilizing the international economy. But the report did not reject postwar aid for reconstruction. Rather, it suggested that this function be clearly relegated to the International Bank for Reconstruction and Development, in the interests of the stability and political viability of the international economic institutions that were to facilitate global integration. Moreover, the report expressed a need for *temporary* currency and exchange controls "as a condition of orderly currency relationships within the framework of long-term self-interest of ourselves and others," even though controls would "alter what otherwise would have been the free flow of trade and investment."[43]

With Bretton Woods passed, the CED then became "chief business advocate of the Marshall Plan."[44] Though the question of aid to Europe, "one of the most important focuses" of State Department-CFR planning, had been left aside so as not to jeopardize passage of Bretton Woods, it was now safe to take this up.[45] Such an extensive aid program was hotly contested among corporate executives already nervous about continued

[42] Panitch and Gindin, *The Making of Global Capitalism*, 70.

[43] Ralph Flanders, "The Bretton Woods Proposals: A Statement on National Policy By the Research Committee of the Committee for Economic Development," March 1945, Record Group 56, Entry A1 360-O Box #15, National Archives College Park, MD.

[44] Whitham, "The Committee for Economic Development," 867.

[45] Shoup and Minter, *Imperial Brain Trust*, 35.

high levels of defense spending and the state's dramatically enlarged international responsibilities. As a result, in 1947 the State Department formed the Committee for the Marshall Plan to Aid European Recovery (CMP) as part of an "all-out public relations blitz" to sell the reconstruction plan. The CMP was an "ad hoc committee comprised [of] a coalition of corporate and labor interests and a liberal elite closely linked to the internationalist 'foreign policy establishment'," stitched together by the State Department and CFR. Put bluntly, it was "a propaganda operation, seemingly independent of, but responsive to, State Department suggestions and advice" that would undertake Congressional lobbying and public advocacy.[46]

This began by assembling an all-star cast of former state officials, including former Secretary of War and Secretary of State Henry Stimson, and former Secretary of War Robert P. Patterson, who became Chairman of the Executive Committee. Averell Harriman, then-Secretary of Commerce, led this effort, bringing a number of "prominent people"—including his old colleague, GE's Reed—onto the Executive Committee. Reed and Harriman also formed the "public education committee," which advertised in newspapers, wrote articles, set up a radio program, and organized CMP chapters across the east coast. No doubt GE's extensive community relations programs contributed to this effort. As Representative Charles A. Plumley of Vermont put it, "there was never such propaganda in the whole history of the nation as there has been for the Marshall Plan."[47]

The corporate executives represented on the body were selected primarily from the CED, comprising eight of the nineteen total CMP members. This overlap, and the role of the CED in organizing business support for the State Department's and CMP's objectives, was evident from a policy statement the R&P issued in February 1948. Entitled "An American Program of European Economic Cooperation," the statement "strove to arouse business and Congressional support for the Marshall Plan" by insisting that "the benefits to us would be enormous in expanded trade, increased security, and, above all, greater protection to our free

[46] Michael Wala, "Selling the Marshall Plan at Home: The Committee for the Marshall Plan to Aid European Recovery," *Diplomatic History* 10, no. 3 (July 1986): 247–49.

[47] Wala, "Selling the Marshall Plan at Home," 252, 264.

society." "Today," the statement insisted, "national policy must concern itself with external affairs to an extent never before experienced."[48]

This ability to mobilize such an important bloc of corporate power also reinforced the State Department's growing prominence and lent substantial political clout to its agenda: "The sheer eminence of its members, with their frequent contact with Congressmen and Senators, and the perpetual public appearances of its most prominent supporters allowed the CMP to succeed in convincing Congress that the foreign policy establishment backed the Department of State and its plans for the [Marshall Plan]."[49] According to a *Fortune* magazine poll, the Marshall Plan passed in 1948 with the support of 95% of business, even as it found support among only 45% of the public at large.

The State Department and the Ideological State Apparatus

The consensus reached within the CED marked the effective end of the State Department's five-decade-long commitment to the Open Door policy. While its stature had grown in the process of envisioning and constructing a postwar world order, as it did it was also transformed—by processes of institutional learning, by the shifting international context it confronted, and by the evolution of the organization of state power. The Treasury and the Federal Reserve increasingly took the lead in forming economic policy, particularly after the "independence" of the Fed was institutionalized with the 1951 Treasury-Fed Accord—which created "a free market in government securities" and thus ended the Treasury's power to determine bond prices by fiat. As this pivotal reorganization of state power would institutionalize constraints on elected officials' ability to engage in deficit spending, the CED followed the Treasury Department in supporting it.[50] Meanwhile, military planning capacities continued to expand, including through the establishment of the RAND

[48] "An American Program of European Economic Cooperation: A Statement on National Policy by CED" (Washington, DC: CED, February 1948), 9–11 and 28–29, quoted in: Whitham, "The Committee for Economic Development," 867.

[49] Wala, "Selling the Marshall Plan at Home," 248.

[50] Panitch and Gindin, *The Making of Global Capitalism*, 86–87.

Corporation in 1948. These planning functions were increasingly coordinated between State and the new Defense Department, which, along with the CIA and NSC, had been established by the National Security Act of 1947.

The growth of the military bureaucracy and the rise of the state monetary apparatus as the key node promoting economic internationalization contributed to a reorientation of the State Department's role and function, which:

> ...now shifted towards securing adequate natural resources to sustain domestic accumulation, and creating conditions abroad that would attract US foreign direct investment and ensure its security. And yet more important was the broader role it would now play in taking responsibility for the reconstruction of the other core capitalist states, promoting the decolonization of their former empires, and trying to ensure that both of these historic developments occurred in a manner consistent with their integration into global capitalism.[51]

This shift was complemented by the emergence of a more hawkish generation of leaders within the department, including Secretary Dean Acheson and Director of Policy Planning Paul Nitze. The new orientation was articulated most clearly in NSC-68, a joint effort with the Department of Defense as well as the National Security Council that became "the seminal blueprint for waging the Cold War."[52] The document "advocated the direct militarization of American foreign policy, a tripling of military spending, and increased intervention into areas in the global periphery (Africa, Asia, Latin America) being vacated by European powers to preclude Soviet adventurism." This was necessary as "the United States was now involved in a total war, a permanent struggle that erased the old distinction between war and peace."[53]

Broad scepticism among capitalists about the costs of empire continued, as concerns of return to postwar recession were stoked by inflation, ballooning deficits, and Truman's ineffective wage and price controls. Considerable tensions and disagreement persisted within dominant business associations, and even the CED issued a public statement

51 Panitch and Gindin, *The Making of Global Capitalism*, 87.

52 Pierpaoli, "Truman's Other War," 16.

53 Waddell, *Toward the National Security State*, 149.

calling for tax reductions. This was reflected in Truman's own initial ambivalence. Although he would undertake a massive increase in defense spending with the creation of the ODM the following year, in his 1949 inaugural address he promised to balance the budget, decrease the national debt, and combat inflation while peddling a decidedly scaled-back version of the New Deal he termed the "Fair Deal." It was the Korean War and Truman's adoption of the policy of Cold War as articulated within NSC-68, that afforded "a central motive force for the new national security state." Just a few months after the inauguration, Truman publicly declared a "Cold War" in a blistering, "crusading" speech that was part of "a full-scale, all-out public relations blitz of the nation's key opinion makers."[54]

This "blitz" had both national and international dimensions. By the late 1940s, confronting the considerable popularity of the radical left in Europe, including Communist Parties, and winning the support of political and economic elites for the American empire had become central concerns of the State Department. This was not so much about undermining the power of labor as it was about promoting an American-style "New Deal" corporatist state abroad—just as the CED had been doing at home. With the support of the state, GE promoted the "Anglo-American Productivity Council," chaired by Reed, which organized visits by trade unionists and business managers to GE factories to observe "modern" labor relations at work. So too was it important to confront the appeal of radical politics, and the alternative path to modernity the Soviet Union appeared to offer, in the global periphery. The "economic development" of these societies should follow a capitalist path, fuelled by the private investment of American capitalists.

Although the CMP was dissolved with the passage of the Marshall Plan in 1948, core functions were reorganized and extended through the US Information Agency (USIA) Advisory Commission on Information (ACI). The Commission's objective was "to formulate and recommend to the Secretary of State policies and programs for the carrying out of the informational aspects" of US foreign policy; "to report to the Secretary of State quarterly on all informational programs and activities carried on under the authority of the United States Information and Educational Exchange Act of 1948"; and "to report to the Congress semi-annually

[54] Waddell, *Toward the National Security State*, 137.

on all information programs."[55] Like the "Advisory Committee on Postwar Foreign Policy," the ACI brought together academic psychologists, corporate managers, marketing executives, and state officials to develop an ideological consensus along with the infrastructures and networks to promote it far and wide.

Through the ACI, the State Department crafted messaging, and worked with local capitalist classes and political elites to create the legal, administrative, and ideological conditions to support US hegemony. As Secretary of State Webb put it at one meeting:

> We will be going through quite a critical period, I think, in utilizing all the ingenuity of the American business community and the Governmental agencies concerned with the economic and the restoration of what some of us refer to as the international legal framework for commerce and trade that has been pretty well destroyed by the events of the last 10 years or so. All of that has to take place if we are going to accomplish the two main objectives of our foreign policy, the first of which is to erect a military shield against aggression which we and our friends are going to accomplish at a very great expenditure... The second thing is to organize the free world community behind that shield, which means, of course, economic, social, political, military organization.[56]

A review of ACI minutes reveals that a range of State Department personnel attended nearly every meeting, from high-level political appointees and strategists to lower-level bureaucrats. Once again, GE's Reed was the primary business representative. The first meeting, which took place in 1948, addressed issues related to the reorganization of the State Department then underway—a topic which turned out to be a major focus of the group's discussions. This was in part because the government was then preparing the Hoover Report (different from the CED report), an extensive plan for rationalizing the byzantine executive branch bureaucracy. Bringing capitalists into this process, both to lend their organizational expertise and to build their personal identification

[55] Edward W. Barrett, "Memorandum for Matthew J. Connelly," August 29, 1950, Record Group 306, Entry P212, Box #3, National Archives College Park, MD.

[56] "Minutes of the Joint Meeting of the U.S. Advisory Commission on Information and Its Advisory Committees (General Business, Radio, Press & Publications, Film)," November 30, 1951, Record Group 306, Entry P212, Box #4, National Archives College Park, MD, 3–4.

with State Department objectives and interests was thus important. In many cases, these resembled sales meetings, in which strategies for selling State Department policies were devised.

As President Truman himself had put it in calling for a global "Campaign of Truth" in 1950, the US "must use every means at our command, private as well as governmental, to get the truth to other peoples" to win "the minds of men."[57] Indeed, the Educational Exchange Act of 1948 specifically stated that the USIA must utilize, to the maximum extent, "the services and facilities of private agencies, including existing American press, publishing, radio, motion picture, and other agencies through contractual arrangements or otherwise."[58] In keeping with this logic, the State Department would extend aid to American corporations in developing and gaining control of the means of mass communication internationally.

But these programs were hardly about simply giving handouts to US media corporations. On the contrary, this reflected the State Department's geostrategic concern "to assure the predominance of American business in the communication field."[59] A condition for the State Department to mobilize private communications infrastructures was that these be under the control of American corporations. The program therefore amounted to recognition of the geopolitical significance of control over increasingly global means of mass communication. If these were to be in private hands, fulfilling State Department objectives in this area required systematic cooperation between the state and private corporate owners.[60]

As the State Department noted, since "the problems connected with setting up a committee consisting of representatives of private enterprise as a whole were too complex" the department would establish a General Business Advisory Committee (GBC) within the USIA, made

[57] Quoted in Tanner Mirrlees, *Hearts and Mines: The US Empire's Culture Industry* (Toronto: UBC Press, 2016), 80.

[58] Mirrlees, *Hearts and Mines*, 79–80.

[59] Mira Wilkins, *The Maturing of Multinational Enterprise* (Cambridge, MA: Harvard University Press, 1975), 256–57.

[60] Philip Reed, Letter, May 7, 1946, Record Group 306, Entry P212, Box #2, National Archives College Park, MD. Philip Reed, "Selling Ideas in a Troubled World," Speech Delivered at Harvard Business School Association, Boston, Massachusetts, June 7, 1952, Record Group 306, Entry P211, Box #5, National Archives College Park, MD.

up of a group of executives who could coordinate with other capitalists on the department's behalf.[61] Reed, the GBC Chairman, framed the committee's role as being to "consider ways and means whereby American private business, as distinguished from government, can complement and augment the government's program in this great and vital undertaking."[62] This included using business to "appraise the kind of message that we put into the apparatus, what we are saying to the world, who says it and the task of getting the right people to say it."[63] Such well-connected firms could also work through "business groups who have representatives abroad" in order to ensure "the right people say it."[64]

At its earliest meetings, the GBC explicitly considered the limits of how far this could—and should—go. In his introduction of the program at its first meeting, Reed sketched out what he saw as some of the critical questions the assembled businessmen should take on:

> Is it appropriate to suggest to business, in one segment or another of it, that a particular program be implemented by them? And if so, what is the best way of getting at it? How should the State Department approach it? Or should it be approached at all by the State Department? Or should it be launched by some trade association group or some business group outside of the government? That is the program.[65]

In hindsight, the concerns motivating the "Campaign of Truth" probably exaggerated the fragility of the American "informal empire" that was then taking shape. Deep institutional linkages and material interests, to say nothing of military power, ultimately upheld both American hegemony and the capitalist processes of production and investment that it regulated and stabilized. However, just as FDR had seen the BAC as "useless

[61] Frank Oram, "Advisory Committee Progress Report," January 7, 1952, Record Group 306, Entry P218, Box #11, National Archives College Park, MD; U.S. Department of State, "Press Release," March 7, 1951, Record Group 306, Entry P218, Box #11, National Archives College Park, MD.

[62] U.S. Department of State, "Press Release," March 7, 1951.

[63] United States Advisory Commission on Information, "Stenographic Transcript," August 29, 1956, Record Group 306, Entry P212, Box #8, National Archives College Park, MD, 70.

[64] United States Advisory Commission on Information, "Stenographic Transcript," August 29, 1956, 94–95.

[65] Frank Oram, "Advisory Committee Progress Report," 1.

from the point of view of facts and policies" but had still found it "good for the dissemination of morale," so was a similar logic at work in the case of the ACI. As Reed put it:

> not less than 50% of the value that was hoped to be derived from the organization of these panels was... this briefing of important influential people from a good many different fields in the philosophy and in the planning and the execution of this information program... If somehow knowledge of the work of the information organization could be more widely disseminated, particularly to people who are opinion leaders who are influential, than that in and of itself might do a considerable amount of good in generating a better understanding of the activity and support for it in this country.[66]

Aside from general support, it was unclear how business could contribute significantly to developing the program. As Reed wrote, "the enthusiasm of the men who comprise the various panels cannot be maintained unless a way is found to permit all of them to make worthwhile contributions."[67] Corporate managers certainly wanted to express opinions and receive information about international politics and the state's global political objectives, but Reed had a difficult time convincing the committee "to interest itself in its prime assignment." If State wanted participation from business, Reed said, "you have to sell them first."[68]

The State Department, for its part, also found the GBC useless for providing concrete policy inputs. State Department personnel were far better informed about international relations and geopolitics than corporate executives; asking the latter for technical input in crafting a specific program—as opposed to organizing capital around a broad agenda or new policy paradigm—was largely a futile exercise. As an internal debrief put it, "From the standpoint of [the State Department], what benefit did we get from this meeting, except for some good public relations and

[66] Department of State, "Transcript of Proceedings: U.S. Advisory Commission on Information," April 9, 1952, Record Group 306, Entry P212, Box #4, National Archives College Park, MD, C14.

[67] Sigurd Larmon, "Sigurd Larmon to Philip Reed," December 31, 1951, Record Group 306, Entry P211, Box #5, National Archives College Park, MD.

[68] Philip Reed, "Philip Reed to Erwin Canham," October 9, 1951, Record Group 306, Entry P211, Box #5, National Archives College Park, MD.

understanding of our program? Frankly, as for suggestions, guidance, and advice, the answer is: None."[69]

When the GBC suggested that the NAM should be approached to participate, it was made testily clear that this was not only something the department normally did as "basic to our operations," but was in any case not of much help:

> we had already approached the NAM on two occasions with no success so far. We are still trying, but find that, so far, the most effective way is to work through individual companies. The second suggestion, that by telling companies we need their cooperation we would find that they would come up with their own ideas, has proven to be, unfortunately, unrealistic. Prior to and subsequent to the Advisory Committee meeting, we had met with representatives of industry, had asked for their cooperation and ideas, and had even made a few suggestions. No original ideas resulted. A few of the companies cooperated, but only after we had kept going after them on an individual basis.[70]

The Department's conclusion that working through individual companies, like GE, was more effective than going directly to the business associations like the NAM was significant. As we have seen, even the business associations that were most inclined toward cooperation with the state, and were thus the most prominent, were riven with tensions over the expansion of the American state's imperial responsibilities and administrative systems. This is important for understanding why, even as "business associations" and "advisory groups" came and went, a core group of firms—GE perhaps most prominently of all—had been at the center of the institutional networks integrating state and corporate power since at least the 1930s.

Just a few months after the initial meetings of the GBC, Reed concluded in a letter sent to all Committee members that it had largely failed, and henceforth "should regard ourselves as a panel of consultants to the State Department and to the Commission on Information," to be

[69] Frank Oram, "Advisory Committee Progress Report," 2.

[70] Frank Oram, "Advisory Committee Progress Report," 2–3.

called upon on an ad hoc basis.[71] Every member of the GBC replied with agreement.[72] Yet as Reed reported to his handlers at the State Department, "I think I can discontinue the formal existence of the Committee without leaving any irritation," since "my relations with these individuals are preserved to the extent there are individuals in that group whom I can look to and call in from time to time to help out."[73] Even if the GBC went dormant, the broader ACI continued to function with Reed's very active participation, and to serve as a link to business. This also helped to maintain Reed's connections to the central foreign policy apparatuses, as well as his (and GE's) status within the capitalist class. ACI meetings even took place in GE's Connecticut boardroom and Reed's suite at the Sheraton-East Hotel in New York City.[74]

These programs were far from being entirely ineffective. State support for American media companies, to say nothing of the manufacturers of the physical infrastructures of mass communication, surely had an effect on their global predominance. So too were these networks and techniques useful to GE for its domestic "community relations" programs. For the rest of the decade, the ACI continued to develop the messaging that would sell American capitalism abroad, which it dubbed "People's Capitalism." As Reed explained:

> this is an attempt and an opportunity to recapture and to put new values and new understanding on the term 'capitalism.' That is what we are; we have been ducking it, and it has a very unhappy connotation and by associating people, the word 'people' with 'capitalism'... my reaction to it

[71] Philip Reed, "Letter From Philip D. Reed to Members of the General Business Committee," May 23, 1952, Record Group 306, Entry P218, Box #11, National Archives College Park, MD.

[72] "Digest of Comments Received in Reply to Letter of May 23 to Members of the General Business Committee, U.S. Advisory Commission on Information," June 25, 1952, Record Group 306, Entry P218, Box #11, National Archives College Park, MD.

[73] Department of State, "Transcript of Proceedings: U.S. Advisory Commission on Information," April 9, 1952, C22.

[74] See, for example: United States Advisory Commission on Information, "Meeting Agenda," November 13, 1956, Record Group 306, Entry P212, Box #8, National Archives College Park, MD; and: United States Advisory Commission on Information, "Agenda and Participants," May 26, 1958.

> has been exceedingly favourable everywhere I have gone or used it or seen it.[75]

This recalls Cordiner's use of the ideology of "People's Capitalism," including in his canonical text *New Frontiers for Professional Managers*. As much as the ACI may have contributed to the development of GE's "community relations" program in the US, it also sought to globalize that model across Europe, Asia, Latin America, and the Middle East, while tailoring it to the specific cultural and ideological conditions in each context.

American Hegemony, Class Power, and the Internationalization of the Integral State

The State Department was also concerned with advancing the deeper material foundations of the US empire. Amidst the retreat of American capital from European investment after the postwar wave of antitrust suits, the State Department persisted in striving to build capitalists' global networks and to organize capitalist classes abroad into business associations embedded within and supportive of American hegemony. That GE had long been among the most internationalized firms meant that Reed would be especially useful in these efforts. Business associations such as the ICC, of which Reed became Chairman in 1949, and the Business Council for International Understanding (BCIU), of which he was also a prominent member, were important mechanisms for organizing this international "civil society."

However, the rootedness of capitalist classes within particular states ensured that this would be full of contradictions, especially given that the "constellation of class and ideological forces in Europe was so different from that in the US."[76] Establishing an informal empire whereby the American state would articulate the general interest of *global* capital required accommodating the interests and strategies of capitalists and political elites elsewhere, insofar as these states "could not and did not become replicas or branches of the American state." This tension was

[75] United States Advisory Commission on Information, "Stenographic Transcript," November 7, 1957, 21, Record Group 306, Entry P212, Box #8, National Archives College Park, MD.

[76] Panitch and Gindin, *The Making of Global Capitalism*, 90.

reflected in the strength of industrial and financial capital in the US, on the one hand, and the initial radicalism of European working classes, on the other—"the crucial matrix that determined European capitalist classes' accommodation to the new imperial relationship."

The social democratic compromises in Europe that emerged from this matrix were primarily a result of the balance of forces within each social formation. Yet they also reflected the force of the American state in the reconstitution of European states. American capitalists found the social democratic compromises that accompanied the US-promoted internationalization of the New Deal costly, as they felt they were footing the bill for European largesse in the form of reconstruction aid. States receiving Marshall Plan aid would be allowed to remain "committed to the mixed economy," but the US would insist that "market forces be represented more liberally in the mix" as W.F. Duisenberg, the first head of the European Central Bank, put it.[77] Meanwhile, Reed argued to American capitalists that continued aid, and toleration of even "irresponsible" policies, were necessary to combat the rise of the radical left and smooth the integration of Europe within the new American empire.

In 1949, Deputy Assistant Secretary for Public Affairs Howland Sargeant wrote to Reed asking him to identify the causes of, and more importantly to help overcome, opposition among US capitalists to aid for the UK under the postwar majority Labour government, which they instinctively saw as unfriendly to capitalist interests. Since such dissent among American business encouraged Labour's domestic opponents in the UK, who were demanding a more laissez-faire economic policy, it also aroused fears within the State Department that such an outspoken sentiment would undermine Labour's active role in supporting the UK's (and its colonies') integration into the US informal empire. Remarking on the apparently rising dissatisfaction with the British government among the US business elite and in the corporate press, Sargeant asked for Reed's help in building support for the trans-Atlantic alliance:

> What are the causes of the dissatisfaction? Certainly included is the belief that after a series of comparatively expensive programs of aid from the United States the British economic position is still regarded as 'desperate', [and] a wide-spread belief that Britain has pursued unwise policies

[77] Quoted in: Panitch and Gindin, *The Making of Global Capitalism*, 96.

> which has led her to sacrifice possible economies in production and distribution in order to obtain what are described as 'socialistic reforms.' ... I do not need to elaborate to you the kind of use that is being and will be made of such attitudes and resulting public criticisms by those who wish to encourage a belief that a split in the Western groups of democratic nations is inevitable.[78]

In his reply to Sargeant, Reed explained that many in the corporate elite believed that "American aid has saved the Labour government from collapse," and that "further aid would simply postpone the day of reckoning." He then laid out the nature of the accommodation with European social democracy he believed necessary:

> While it is dead clear that we must not be placed in the position of seeming to force the Labour Government to abandon its socialistic convictions, any further economic assistance to Britain (stock piling, increased ECA allowances, etc.) would in my judgement be acceptable to the American people only if coupled with a voluntary declaration by the British Government of its intention to take steps which are in line with American views as to what is necessary.[79]

Reed squarely disagreed with Sargeant that criticism of the economic model advanced within the UK was undesirable. He perceived in the UK Labour Party's social democratic program a threat to the basic structure of private ownership, competitive markets, and the profit motive. Therefore, for reasons of principle as well as pragmatism, American policymakers and businessmen should proclaim loud-and-clear that such a system was destined to be economically damaging. That "capitalism" as Reed defined it was the only possible road to economic stabilization was a reality that should be reinforced by American policy.[80]

[78] Quotes from: Howland Sargeant, "Howland Sargeant to Philip Reed," September 27, 1949, Record Group 306, Entry P211, Box #5, National Archives College Park, MD. For more context regarding the nature and evolution of Reed's relationship with Sargeant, and his successor Edward Barrett, see: Edward W. Barrett, "Edward W. Barrett to Philip Reed," September 14, 1951, Record Group 306, Entry P211, Box #5, National Archives College Park, MD; Edward W. Barrett, "Edward W. Barrett to Philip Reed," April 30, 1951, Record Group 306, Entry P211, Box #5, National Archives College Park, MD.

[79] Philip Reed, "Phillip Reed to Howland Sargeant," August 31, 1949, Record Group 306, Entry P211, Box #5, National Archives College Park, MD.

[80] Philip Reed, "Phillip Reed to Howland Sargeant."

Just as the internationalization of the American state provoked new internal contradictions within the American capitalist class, so did it bolster the capacity for fractions of the European elite "to install policies that would have been impossible to pursue on the basis of the domestic alignment of forces."[81] If this meant bolstering the position of more conservative forces within these societies over time, officials within State wanted a temporary postwar peace with social democracy—premised, of course, not upon socialism, but rather private ownership and management of industrial and financial corporations—seeing this as an important condition for the integration of these societies within the American empire. Whatever compromises needed to be made in the short run in the post war era, this was the strategy the American state should be "developing over a fairly long period of time."[82]

The State Department organized several around-the-world trips for Reed in the early 1950s, in which he worked to assure European capitalists that the American state and capitalist class were ready and able to take responsibility for rebuilding the core capitalist economies and integrating these within a world system it would manage and defend. Reed's role as informal ambassador was supported by embassies in each country, which arranged meetings between Reed and important financial, industrial, and political elites. The agenda for these international trips was determined by State Department and embassy staff, and had little to do with the particular interests of GE. With all the political work Reed was expected to do, he jokingly requested that he also be permitted "to spend some amount of time in each place talking with the representatives of the International General Electric or our agents through whom we conduct our business."[83]

A key objective of these trips abroad was to support the development of the ICC. Generally, the State Department would coordinate meetings for

[81] Panitch and Gindin, *The Making of Global Capitalism*, 90.

[82] Howland Sargeant, "Howland Sargeant to Philip Reed," September 27, 1949, Record Group 306, Entry P211, Box #5, National Archives College Park, MD.

[83] Philip Reed, "Philip Reed to James E. Webb," December 6, 1950, Record Group 306, Entry P211, Box #5, National Archives College Park, MD; Philip Reed. Harold B. Minor, "Harold B. Minor to Washington, Visit to Athens of Philip D. Reed, Chairman of the Board of General Electric, Member of the U.S. Advisory Commission on Information and President of the International Chamber of Commerce," Telegram, October 20, 1949, Record Group 306, Entry P211, Box #5, National Archives College Park, MD.

Reed with elites in each country through the ICC branch. In places where there was no such branch, Reed's meetings were arranged by "groups which have agreed to act as the organizing body for purposes of the visit," who presumably could be recruited into the task of forming such a branch. Finally, where even these groups did not exist, "the majority of the planning to be done will be in the hands of the representatives of the International General Electric Company or their agents."[84] Thus, although the international connections GE had established were an important foundation for these state-led efforts to deepen international "civil society" integration, ideally there would be other organizations reflecting a broader elite consensus within particular local contexts to work with. The *ongoing work* of ICC branches was developing and maintaining relationships with the broadest possible base of capitalists who supported the organization's objectives—above all, free trade within the American imperial system.[85]

Upon returning from his 1950 trip, Reed forcefully articulated the strong need for American global leadership in making global capitalism at the ICC "Midwest Power Conference" entitled "The Role of the Modern Businessman." While stressing that "no one is more deeply convinced than I of the necessity of reducing over-all government expenditures," Reed insisted that "the effect of cutting ourselves loose from these overseas expenditures would be so shattering to the morale and economic state of the world"—which would not only be to the benefit of "Russia and her evil objectives," but would also require the United States to "enlarge and accelerate at once our military defense program in all its phases." This outcome, Reed declared, "would be worse than profitless. It would be downright tragic from every standpoint."[86]

Reed also made clear that GE had a direct interest in the expansion of global capitalism: "whether we are considering the European Recovery Program, or the so-called Point Four Program or Economic aid to Asiatic countries, or for that matter the future wellbeing of our own country, electric energy is always a foundation stone and not infrequently the key stone of the structure." Foreign Direct Investment to

[84] Philip Reed, "Philip Reed to James E. Webb," December 6, 1950.

[85] John Begg, "John Begg to O.C. Anderson," Memo, September 12, 1951, Record Group 306, Entry P211, Box #5, National Archives College Park, MD.

[86] Philip Reed, "The Role of the Modern Businessman," Speech to the All Engineers Dinner, Midwest Power Conference, Chicago, Ill, April 5, 1950, 3.

Europe and the periphery surely would continue to flow to the electrical sector—assuming, of course, that the capitalist states of Europe currently expanding social democratic programs continued to allow public utilities, such as electricity, to be privately owned and operated. It was also for this reason that Reed saw the urgency in a program "for explaining simply, clearly, objectively, the reasons why our system of private enterprise is just as right for the utilities of a country as it is for the steel, or automobile or clothing industries." This was, of course, part of the mission of the USIA, which Reed had played such a large role in supporting.

Reed was happy to report that he received "a very definite impression that the trend today is away from government ownership or control of industry and in the direction of encouraging private enterprise." He intimated that "this was stated to me flatly by high officials in several governments and broadly inferred by others"—though he explicitly excluded the UK from this trend, "where the Labour Government was too firmly committed to change."[87] He highlighted the cases of Australia and New Zealand, which he believed suggested the balance of political forces were shifting toward capital, given that in each case "a socialistically inclined Labour government was turned out by a party which promised less taxes, less government spending and more encouragement of private enterprise." Reed built up to a powerful counterrevolutionary rallying cry:

> I suggest to you, gentlemen, that these events present to businessmen of all countries an opportunity and responsibility unparalleled in our lifetime. I believe the crucial moment has arrived – airmen call it the point of no return – when the system of competitive enterprise based on individual initiative can be saved for the benefit of the world's people or lost for a very long while, perhaps forever.[88]

In order to heed the call of history at this pivotal moment, Reed called on businessmen everywhere to "assist their governments in working out programs for the elimination of unsound controls and the creation of a climate favourable to expanding investments, jobs, and output." Achieving this agenda, in other words, did not require capitalists to work *against* states. Indeed, the State Department and other key agencies had been working to create a world order based on precisely these ideals since

[87] Philip Reed, "The Role of the Modern Businessman," 5–6.

[88] Philip Reed, "The Role of the Modern Businessman," 7.

the end of the war, supported by mechanisms for garnering the necessary cooperation and political organization of capital. Through such organizations as the ICC, Reed argued, the American state and allied corporate elites could create an international civil society that would form the basis for the American state to articulate a global capitalist consensus—albeit one that reflected global political and economic hierarchies—which would ensure an era of collective peace and prosperity without precedent in human history.[89]

Extolling the significance of the American defense effort for building a trans-Atlantic class basis for US empire was part and parcel of all this, as was seen in Reed's comments at a luncheon of the elite American Club of Paris in 1951. Despite rumblings of dissent in the US about defense expenditures amidst a flagging economy, he insisted the tide was shifting: "Today it is a different story," Reed said, "public opinion is strongly back of all-out defense mobilization." With former GE President Charles Wilson in place at the head of the new ODM—a position that bestowed upon him "unprecedented power"—Reed told his audience that this would ensure that "the next twelve months will see unparalleled progress both in production and military training for all services."[90]

At the same time, Reed urged European states and capitalist classes to take their share of responsibilities. What was required was "the assumption by each party of its rightful share of the burdens involved":

> There seems to be in some quarters over here a conviction that the United States is a country of endless resources and can be looked to indefinitely for whatever economic assistance is needed. Nothing of course could be further from the fact… I very much doubt that the free world can build, in time, a military force of such strength as effectively to deter Russian aggression without some sacrifice of standards of living in every country. Certainly our standard of living in the United States will suffer. Already our taxes are at or above the level of World War II, and they will be still higher before the year is out… My point is that all belts must come in to an unpleasant degree.[91]

[89] Philip Reed, "The Role of the Modern Businessman," 8.

[90] Philip Reed, "What Are We Waiting For?," Speech for the American Club of Paris, January 11, 1951, Record Group 306, Entry P211, Box #5, National Archives College Park, MD, 4.

[91] Philip Reed, "What Are We Waiting For?", 6.

Reed's 1951 Paris speech painted the long-term goal in messianic global terms: "someday, God willing, we shall see much more clearly that the compartmentalization of free and friendly people into small and frequently uneconomic political units, is standing directly athwart the material, cultural, and spiritual development of mankind."[92] Flowery language aside, the internationalization of the integral state indeed meant that the "national interest" articulated by the American state would need to register the specific interests of other nation states and their capitalist classes—even as it exerted its own force within these social formations.

Capitalist Dissent at Home to the New Imperial State

Despite Reed's best efforts, considerable unease persisted among significant sections of capital over liberalization and the formation of an imperial state. To complement the World Bank and IMF, Will Clayton—the State Department's most ardent "free trader"—had negotiated an "International Trade Organization" at the first postwar multilateral trade negotiations in Geneva. Yet in 1948, Truman decided not to ask Congress to endorse the proposal. In addition to persistent opposition from protectionist forces on the BAC and in Congress, the ITO Charter failed to find support from "even the most internationally oriented US capitalists." Even the ICC, consistently the strongest supporter of free trade multilateralism, saw the ITO Charter as a "dangerous document" as it "appeared to institutionalize permanently" provisions for full employment and economic development.

More significant, however, was the "marked lack of enthusiasm in the administration, and especially the State Department." This ambivalence was rooted in the Charter's "failure to provide sufficient openings and protection for US foreign investment"—which would "become a central element in the multitude of bilateral trade treaties signed by the US government in the 1950s." Clayton himself "was quite content to go no further than the commercial chapter of the ITO," known as the General Agreement on Tariffs and Trade (GATT). The GATT was in itself quite radical: in addition to sweeping tariff cuts, it "set out long-term liberalizing goals, and set ground rules for non-discriminatory treatment of

[92] Philip Reed, "What Are We Waiting For?", 8.

national and international investors," while also leaving plenty of room for temporary trade restrictions. Although short-term protections could be negotiated to handle "special cases," the overall thrust was toward greater liberalization.[93]

Even with the ITO a dead letter, opposition to liberalization continued to register strongly on the broader BAC, as well as in Congress, through the 1950s. Consequently, "corporate liberals" supported the concentration of power in the trade and economic apparatuses, which were insulated from Congress and individual capitalists seeking to avoid the costs of restructuring. This helped ensure that oppositional forces remained unable to "deflect the American state's strategic orientation towards trade policy."[94] Meanwhile, corporate liberals strove to broaden the consensus around such policies, including on the BAC. Short-term protections were held out to incentivize broader buy-in for liberalization. If business wanted the opportunity to appeal for limited protections, it needed a seat at the table; but earning such a seat meant accepting the basic liberalization framework.

Until the late 1950s, when Reed and other liberal internationalists came to dominate the BAC Committee on Foreign Economic Policy, it constituted the primary base of opposition to tariff reduction advanced by the CED group. The Committee on Foreign Trade, meanwhile, expressed scepticism toward the emergence of an extensive trade policy apparatus under the control of the President, which appeared excessively autonomous from the immediate concerns of business. This was evident in the committee's pushback against Eisenhower's "Randall Commission," which sought to rationalize, centralize, and further empower this apparatus, granting the executive wider latitude in negotiating and implementing trade agreements. State solicitation of corporate input in trade policy would of course continue, but the ability for business to meaningfully oppose liberalization would be further constrained. This centralization, backed by the CED, gave the state additional room to continue restructuring the international trade regime, including drastic reductions in tariff protections for US business.

Meanwhile, the BAC's 1952 Tax Policy Statement reflected the basic framing that would dominate its discussions on the issue throughout the

[93] Panitch and Gindin, *The Making of Global Capitalism*, 93–94.

[94] Panitch and Gindin, *The Making of Global Capitalism*, 94.

rest of the decade, largely the remit of its Committee on Taxation. It accepted that it was neither possible nor desirable to reverse the expansion of state power that had occurred over the New Deal and World War II, and accepted the need for the US to take responsibility for managing a world system that was already deeply interdependent. It was simply impossible, either geopolitically or economically, for the United States to maintain some kind of autarkic self-sufficiency. Accepting this reality also meant that a tax system well beyond what had existed previously in peacetime was a permanent, or at least indefinite, necessity.

The question became how to minimize its burdens on business, which most BAC members agreed were excessive, while negotiating trade-offs among firms and sectors. As the document stated:

> It is now apparent that, even after desirable reductions in military and civilian expenditures, the country is faced with a need for long-continued taxation at levels which may restrict or distort the nation's economic progress. The assumption of new government functions in recent years, and the need for large defense outlays to counter the threat of further communist aggression, will require tax burdens at heights which are unprecedented except in brief periods of all-out war. The destructive effects of such taxation can be kept in bounds only under a system of taxation specifically designed with that objective in mind.[95]

This set the BAC definitively to the right of the CED—but despite these differences, it remained within the basic policy framework established by the state. These were the parameters of the hegemonic consensus.

Since 1934, the expansion of presidential power to negotiate and implement trade agreements had taken place under the Reciprocal Trade Agreements Act, which had to be periodically renewed and extended by Congress. Eisenhower sought a more permanent resolution, which would establish even wider presidential authority on firmer footing. Asking Congress to extend the Act yet again, the president also called for a commission to study US foreign economic policy more broadly. As a result, the extension Congress granted in 1953 also provided for the creation of a bipartisan Commission on Foreign Economic Policy. Eisenhower appointed Clarence Rendall of the Inland Steel Company to chair

[95] Business Advisory Council, "Draft of Tax Policy Statement," November 1952, Record Group 56, Entry 198, Box #106, 1.

the Commission, along with six top executives from finance and industry, five Senators, and five Representatives.

Eisenhower's instructions to the Commission were clear: "to find acceptable ways and means of widening and deepening the channels of economic intercourse between ourselves and our partners of the free world."[96] Over October and November, the Rendall Commission carried out a series of closed hearings with industry, labor, and academic experts, as well as soliciting policy guidance from the State Department and other agencies, before finally producing an 800-page report in February 1954. This naturally provoked a vigorous debate on trade policy and the imperial state among business leaders. Although Rendall, through Commerce Secretary Weeks and Treasury Secretary Humphrey, asked the BAC to appoint a representative to appear before the commission, "after considerable discussion" the council opted to decline. Instead, it appointed its own Special Committee "on tariff aspects of foreign economic policy" to report at a special meeting where a private discussion would be held on the subject.[97]

The confidential BAC report was presented at a special meeting at the Department of Commerce.[98] It was essentially a protectionist document, which expressed deep concern about tariff reductions.[99] Acknowledging "great progress has been made toward economic recovery by most nations of the world," the report emphasized that "the continued soundness of our domestic economy is essential to further progress"—which meant that the health of the *American* economy "must be our prime consideration." The report left little ambiguity as to how this should be interpreted,

[96] Walter White, "Memorandum to Council Members," November 2, 1953, Record Group 56, Entry 198, Box #106, National Archives College Park, MD.

[97] The outcome of these deliberations would then, along with the approved version of the committee's report, be passed on to Secretary Weeks "for such use as he might wish to make of them with Mr. Rendall and other interested officials." Accordingly, "Secretary Weeks was asked to communicate with Mr. Rendall and ask him to withdraw the invitation and give it no publicity." "Minutes of General Council Meeting of the Business Advisory Council for the Department of Commerce," October 22–24, 1953, Record Group 56, Entry 198, Box #106, National Archives College Park, MD, 8–9.

[98] Walter White, "Memorandum to Council Members," November 2, 1953.

[99] Reed took part on the special committee, which met over October and November. Though it is hard to know from the documentary record what positions Reed took in these discussions, the overall thrust of the report is clearly at odds with positions Reed expressed both publicly and in more intimate settings, including on the CED.

calling for "the reasonable and legitimate protection of our domestic economy." It also explicitly rejected unilateral tariff reductions of the sort supported by the CED, insisting that "to jeopardize our economic strength for the sake of setting an example could be disastrous, not only to us, but to those whom the action was intended to aid." Though supporting the extension of the Reciprocal Trade Agreements Act for a limited two-year period, the report insisted that trade agreements reached during this limited period "should be reciprocal and not of the sort in which the United States gives much and gets little or nothing in return."[100]

If the Special Committee resisted tariff reductions, the Committee on Taxation joined the Department of Treasury in advocating for a policy that would leverage American foreign investment to intensify competitive pressures on states to reduce taxes and trade barriers. In response to a request by Undersecretary of Commerce Marion Folsom at the annual BAC retreat in Pebble Beach, the Committee on Taxation issued a report on foreign investment and the tax structure. The report called for more incentives for foreign investment, including the elimination of US taxes on income already taxed by foreign governments. The existing structure allowed corporations to receive a tax credit to offset income taxes paid abroad, thereby ensuring a fixed tax rate on all foreign investment (so long as the US tax rate was higher than that paid to foreign governments). Eliminating this, and asserting the principle that all income should be taxed only in the country where it is earned, was expected to have the effect of setting off competition among states for investment by reducing taxes, and "thus provide a real incentive for the international flow of capital."[101]

The contrast with the CED—both procedurally and in policy terms—is striking. Just weeks after the formation of the BAC Special Committee to address the Rendall Commission, Howard Peterson, Chairman of the Fidelity Bank of Philadelphia, placed before the CED R&P, of which he was Chair, the second draft of a proposed statement on "United States

[100] "Minutes of Special Council Meeting of the Business Advisory Council for the Department of Commerce," November 12, 1953, Record Group 56, Entry 198, Box #106, National Archives College Park, MD.

[101] Business Advisory Council for the Department of Commerce, "Report of Committee on Taxation," December 15, 1953, Record Group 56, Entry 198, Box #106, National Archives College Park, MD, 4.

Tariff Policy." That the R&P had turned down the first draft pointed to the significance of the scepticism among business, even the "corporate liberals" on the CED, toward the restructuring the administration was pushing forward.

After the failure of the first draft, Peterson personally went to each of the proposal's opponents and attempted to persuade them to sign on—expressing a willingness to make small changes to the draft, "but not in principle." Peterson's comments upon submitting the second draft to the R&P are revealing:

> Gentlemen, if you approve the draft statement before you it will probably cost CED the resignation of several of its most respected trustees, and about a quarter of a million dollars in corporate contributions. But we believe these recommendations are in the national interest and that you should adopt them.[102]

Clearly, this suggests not an organization striving to pressure the state to implement an agenda developed autonomously, nor to "capture" state power to serve particularistic interests. Rather, it reveals the extent to which the CED was a mechanism for organizing the "general interest" of capital, despite the opposition of individual firms. The CED was about *building* consensus, not *expressing* the pre-existing political views of capitalists.

Peterson's efforts were a success, as the R&P adopted the second draft in January 1954. In sharp contrast to the BAC position, the statement recommended "continued liberalization of United States trade policy on the basis of the following declarations: (1) of principle, (2) of common sense in the application of principle, (3) of national interest, and (4) of free world interest." This framing explicitly addressed the need to balance the "national interest" with "free world interest." Whereas the BAC had so strongly asserted that domestic economic needs be put first, the CED continued to emphasize that the national interest had to be seen as including taking responsibility for the world system as a whole.

Moreover, the statement asserted first and foremost a defense of liberalization *in principle*—though accepting that the application of this principle would have to account for trade-offs and temporary protections dictated by "common sense." While acknowledging "that policy should

[102] Reed, "Taxes and Trade: 20 Years of CED Policy," 44.

be fair to those who may be affected adversely by tariff reduction," the statement stressed that the painful aspects of international integration could not simply be avoided indefinitely. The essential point was crystal clear: "As the strongest economic power the United States has a special responsibility for liberalizing trade. The direction our tariff policy takes will help determine whether the free world moves ahead to widening markets and expanding production, or whether it moves in the opposite direction."[103]

The pressure from Peterson to pass the statement did result in "losses, and some reduction of dollar support, but not as much as had been anticipated"; indeed, "nearly all strayed people and lost money came back."[104] That those who left ended up returning further points to the way the CED functioned as an integral state mechanism, *articulating* and *shaping* the interests of capital, rather than merely *reconciling* or *expressing* the pre-existing "objective interests" of given firms or class fractions. Individual capitalists' political interests, and levels of knowledge, were fluid and developing. The state's leadership in devising and implementing policy pertained just as much to the education of capitalist managers about their own class interests through forums like the CED as negotiating trade-offs among different firms.

As Reed himself summarized what he took to be the key lesson of the episode:

> We learned at least as much about CED as we did about trade policy. The lesson seems to have been that we will come to narrow places in this and in other policy roads that all of us can not (sic) get through in the same way at the same speed… but that – and this is the main thing – even though some pretty stringent disagreement persists in a policy area, the very great majority of us are nevertheless united in our basic view of the civilized society and world that we are after, and that we should continue to work together on policies to get it at not too high a price.[105]

Over time, the BAC did largely come around to this view, even if it remained much more divided than the CED. By March 1954, ongoing and intense disagreement over the Rendall Commission report released

[103] Reed, "Taxes and Trade: 20 Years of CED Policy," 45.

[104] Reed, "Taxes and Trade: 20 Years of CED Policy," 44.

[105] Reed, "Taxes and Trade: 20 Years of CED Policy," 45.

the previous month, and the apparent failure of the Special Committee to exert much influence over its contents, led the BAC to form a new Committee on Foreign Economic Policy. Reed was nominated to participate on the Committee, which was chaired by the powerful and well-connected retired General Lucius D. Clay. Like Reed, Clay was close to Eisenhower, and had been among the group that had urged him to run in 1952. This signaled a shift in the political balance in the organization toward a consensus view that was more accommodating toward the administration's position on trade.

The new committee first considered a proposal for "the termination of economic aid" to Europe, agreeing with the Randall Commission that this was not a good idea. It also "agreed with the Commission's recommendation against cartels and international agreements," even as the onslaught of antitrust suits brought against GE and other firms was intensifying. Tariff reductions remained a thornier issue, the debate over which extended beyond the allotted time and had to be cut off.[106] The confidential report the Committee issued that October bore the traces of what seems to have been a tortured process of compromise and negotiation. "We must recognize that the business community has direct and varied, even conflicting, interests in the foreign economic policy of our country," the report began, "Management naturally desires to approach the problem from the long range national interest, but there are differing convictions as to where national interest lies."[107]

The fact was, "historically, a large segment of American industry, involving heavy investments of capital, first grew and prospered under a protective tariff," making such protections hard to part with. This was particularly the case since, "assisted by aid from this country, Europe has rebuilt extensively since the end of World War II, and as a result much of its machinery, equipment, and production techniques now compare favourably with our own."[108] Given the strength of these protectionist

[106] "Minutes of General Council Meeting of the Business Advisory Council for the Department of Commerce," March 17, 1954, Record Group 56, Entry 198, Box #106, National Archives College Park, MD, 2.

[107] Business Advisory Council for the Department of Commerce, "Report of Committee on Foreign Economic Policy," October 22, 1954, Record Group 56, Entry 198, Box #106, National Archives College Park, MD, 1.

[108] Business Advisory Council for the Department of Commerce, "Report of Committee on Foreign Economic Policy," 1.

impulses, it is perhaps not surprising that the committee did not go all the way to the CED position, articulated in the 1953 R&P statement, in support of taking the lead in pursuing drastic, and even unilateral, tariff reductions. As stated in the BAC committee's report,

> A unilateral lowering of tariffs will contribute only in small part to the freeing of trade, until a more generally favourable climate can develop throughout the free world, and therefore any tariff reductions made by the United States, resulting in increased imports, should be truly reciprocal in character…

The Committee nevertheless recognized that "our position of world leadership carries with it definite obligations" and therefore "we must continue to seek a way to bring the free countries even more closely together, and to improve the economic conditions which prevail in this free world." Although this meant that "it is in our interest to increase our efforts to develop a greater freedom of exchange of goods and services between countries of the free world," the Committee balanced this with an insistence that "the most vital contribution the United States can make to the well-being of the free world and the promotion of its trade is the maintenance of a healthy and productive American economy."

As the economies of Europe and Japan recovered, relatively cheap labor meant relatively cheap imports, which intensified competitive pressures on American producers with unionized workforces. In the case of GE, the labor costs of its own unionized workers had of course not been a problem during the war, given that it was operating under cost-plus contracts from the state. The continued expansion of the industrial policy system after the war likewise cushioned profits and ensured large subsidies for R&D. Once these technologies were spun off as consumer products, however, costs became an increasingly significant factor. As we saw, this contributed to GE's move to relocate production to non-union southern states. This strategy would ultimately be internationalized, as the integration of global finance under American hegemony reduced the costs of moving investment globally.

The overriding strategy within the state was to create unstoppable inertia behind trade barrier reductions and to subvert the ability for individual capitalists to undermine this agenda. This did not go unnoticed in the BAC committee's report, which complained that "neither the [Randall] Commission's report nor the President's message [to Congress calling for a restructuring of the trade policy apparatus] provides any mechanism… whereby an industry which is suffering from or threatened with serious injury may apply for a suitable increase in the tariff."[109] Not only had the state jeopardized US business interests by pursuing liberalization without applying sufficient pressure on other states to follow suit, now the administration wanted to further limit the ability for affected capitalists to challenge additional reductions to trade barriers. Despite these concerns, the committee in the end *supported* the Randall Commission's recommendations, provided that "no further tariff reductions are made without the producers affected thereby being given full opportunity to be heard." As the report noted grimly, "past practice has not uniformly accorded such an opportunity."[110]

Yet if—as the report itself acknowledged—these complaints had hardly found a receptive audience in the past, further increasing the autonomy of the key agencies responsible for trade policy would hardly seem like an effective way to remedy this. Similar concerns about growing state autonomy were expressed in relation to the GATT, which came before Congress the following year. As expressed at a March 1955 BAC meeting featuring a presentation on GATT by Deputy Assistant Secretary of Commerce for International Affairs Marshall Smith, "upon the approval by Congress of the GATT organization plan, the President is then authorized to sign regulations without Congressional consultation made within the limits of the organization plan." Moreover, that "this is on the basis of an international agreement, not a treaty" meant that the Senate's power to "advise and consent" would also be neutralized.[111] Concerns about this assertion of expansive state autonomy were outlined in a report to Secretary Weeks prepared by the Committee on Foreign Economic

[109] Business Advisory Council for the Department of Commerce, "Report of Committee on Foreign Economic Policy," 8.

[110] Business Advisory Council for the Department of Commerce, "Report of Committee on Foreign Economic Policy," 8.

[111] Business Advisory Council for the Department of Commerce, "Minutes of General Council Meeting, March 17, 1955," March 24, 1955, Record Group 56, Entry 198, Box #106, National Archives College Park, MD.

Policy.[112] Ultimately, this dissent would prove unable to halt economic liberalization or the growing autonomy of the trade policy apparatus.

The acrimony on the BAC points to the heightening tensions between it and the state that would lead the Council to formally split from the state and become "independent" just a few years later, in 1961, shortly after Kennedy assumed the Presidency. Nevertheless, both before and after the divorce, the same messy consensus persisted around free trade that had reigned since the definitive end of the "Open Door" policy. Disagreements were centered around state institutions, which bore sovereign responsibility for making and implementing policy. Doing so in a viable way depended on soliciting input from, as well as organizing a consensus among, corporations. This inevitably resulted in "common sense" compromises around "the implementation of principle," in the words of the CED. The broad thrust of the policy was toward liberalization, yet this was to be implemented in a way that ensured political stability and recognized the necessary unevenness it would entail. What was *not* up for discussion was the *direction of change*.

Antitrust, MNCs, and the Contradictions of "Free Trade"

As we saw, GE in the first half of the twentieth century built an global cartel network based on international agreements, interlocking directorates, and foreign investments. Not only did its participation in cartels "not curb General Electric's expansion abroad," but they were "designed to stabilize the world's lamp business," from which GE benefitted, as "the industry's gain was the company's: through IGEC's investments, its royalties, and its service charges, GE shared in the success of the foreign lamp makers."[113] However, in the decade after the war, the international operations of American corporations "underwent penetrating scrutiny" from the Department of Justice, the Federal Trade Commission (FTC), and Congressional hearings. The cartels that had stabilized the world market for a half-century were now "seen as violations of the Sherman Anti-Trust

[112] Business Advisory Council, Committee on Foreign Economic Policy, "Business Advisory Council Report on H.R. 1," March 17, 1955, Record Group 56, Entry 198, Box #106, National Archives College Park, MD.

[113] Wilkins, *The Maturing of Multinational Enterprise*, 66.

Act" and were broken up by an increasingly powerful, confident, and autonomous state.

The DOJ argued "that international arrangements made by corporations restrained free competition, restricted exports and imports, divided world markets, curtailed world production, and deprived American independents of the benefits that would otherwise flow from free vigorous competition."[114] GE was perhaps the single biggest target of these antitrust actions: "the cases against General Electric spanned a dozen years and wrecked havoc with that enterprise's international business," as both it and IGE "were found guilty of participating in cartels in lamps and electrical equipment."[115] By the time the DOJ's antitrust actions subsided as the 1950s drew to a close, the "international business empire that had been developed since the 1880s and that Gerard Swope and Owen Young had so carefully constructed during the 1920s had been torn asunder," and was "left in shambles."[116]

GE largely retreated from international investment until the early 1960s, when it had to start "almost from scratch."[117] GE was hardly alone in this hesitation, as "US banks and corporations" in general "were not much inclined to invest in Western European countries" in the decade after the war.[118] That GE's withdrawal lasted nearly a decade longer indicates the special significance for that company of ending the cartel system. Yet the objective of the DOJ's antitrust actions was not to prevent American firms from investing abroad, but rather to eliminate restrictive agreements that aimed to control prices. The growth of state capacities, and its ability to construct and regulate competitive markets, had now allowed for the internationalization of the Sherman Act which had such a substantial impact on the formation of the modern corporation domestically. The consequences were to encourage the reorganization of horizontal cartel networks into vertically integrated, managerial-dominated, "multinational" firms, whose involvement in any one sector—but not overall size—would be constrained by law.[119]

[114] Wilkins, *The Maturing of Multinational Enterprise*, 263–64.

[115] Wilkins, *The Maturing of Multinational Enterprise*, 294.

[116] Wilkins, *The Maturing of Multinational Enterprise*, 295.

[117] Wilkins, *The Maturing of Multinational Enterprise*, 295.

[118] Panitch and Gindin, *The Making of Global Capitalism*, 90.

[119] Wilkins, *The Maturing of Multinational Enterprise*, 264.

It may appear paradoxical in this context that Reed was at the center of the State Department's simultaneous efforts to internationalize the integral state. Of course, GE and other firms targeted by these prosecutions hardly welcomed the costs they would entail. Yet these prosecutions were not part of a coordinated strategy launched by the State Department or the Treasury. Just as there were tensions between Treasury and State, the activities of the juridical apparatus were only loosely connected to these agencies.[120] Indeed, neither the departments of State and Treasury, nor Commerce, played a substantial part in formulating antitrust policy. In fact, in launching a "rash of antitrust cases" the DOJ in many respects "acted at variance with U.S. policies seeking to prompt foreign investment."[121]

What little coordination did exist between the DOJ and other state agencies was merely "haphazard" and "informal."[122] This mostly took the form of the State Department, along with the military and intelligence apparatus, securing immunities for specific firms based on national security imperatives, particularly control over oil resources, in the context of a "vigorous antitrust policy" "advocated and enforced" by the Truman and Eisenhower administrations.[123] While the DOJ did maintain linkages with integral state bodies, especially the BAC, this was mostly about disseminating information about antitrust law and juridical philosophy rather than forging a collaborative partnership. The result of this uncoordinated process was that massive multinational corporations would dominate the global economy, while *price* competition in each specific *product market* in which these giant firms were involved would be protected. This helped ensure competitive pressures would operate between individual firms as well as *within* them, since the distribution of investment resources across particular businesses by internal managers across divisions would remain responsive to price signals, and therefore profit levels, that emerged from market competition regulated by state power.

[120] Richard B. Bilder, "The Office of the Legal Adviser: The State Department Lawyer and Foreign Affairs," *American Journal of International Law* 56 (1962): 633–84.

[121] Wilkins, *The Maturing of Multinational Enterprise*, 292.

[122] Sol Linowitz, "Antitrust Laws: A Damper on American Foreign Trade," *American Bar Association Journal* 44, no. 9 (September 1958): 856.

[123] Burton Kaufman, "Mideast Multinational Oil, U.S. Foreign Policy, and Antitrust: The 1950s," *The Journal of American History* 63, no. 4 (March 1977): 937–59.

In fact, far from working to interpret antitrust statutes to break up big companies, the DOJ was more concerned with devising arguments to justify their continued power over the global economy in the context of intensified price competition. Though antitrust law limited the share of a single market or sector a given firm could possess, so long as corporations diversified, and prices in each market were thus established competitively, the DOJ argued that there was no antitrust violation. To pass a law that would impose a maximum size on firms as such, the DOJ reasoned, would seem to mean limiting economic growth itself.[124] This pattern of antitrust enforcement reinforced the development of the conglomerate form and corporate decentralization, as large firms pursued growth through acquisitions across unrelated sectors.[125]

In May 1955, Attorney General Herbert Brownell attended a BAC meeting to discuss the "Attorney General's National Antitrust Committee Report." The goal of the commission had been "to crystallize and bring together into a consistent whole the guideposts of a sound antitrust policy," particularly as regarded its applicability to the emergence of the new "multinational corporation."[126] Purporting to offer "a substantial clarification of national anti-trust policy," the opening line of the report said it all: "What benefits should the business community expect from the Report of the Attorney General's National Antitrust Committee?".

In contrast to the charges coming from Congress, the report emphasized that the DOJ "adopts the reasoning of the Supreme Court decisions which distinguish mere size or bigness from monopoly power and monopoly power from monopolization."[127] The report continued:

[124] See, for instance: S. Chesterfield Oppenheim, "The Attorney General's National Antitrust Committee Report," May 7, 1955, Record Group 56, Entry 198, Box #106, National Archives College Park, MD; "Minutes of General Council Meeting of the Business Advisory Council for the Department of Commerce, May 6–7, 1955," May 19, 1955, Record Group 56, Entry 198, Box #106, National Archives College Park, MD; George Wyeth, Jr., "Business Advisory Council for the Department of Commerce, Memorandum for All Council Members," October 30, 1958, Record Group 56, Entry 198A, Box #17, National Archives College Park, MD.

[125] Louis Hyman, "Rethinking the Postwar Corporation," in Kim Phillips-Fein and Julian E. Zelizer, *What's Good for Business: Business and American Politics Since World War II* (Oxford, UK: Oxford University Press, 2012).

[126] Oppenheim, "The Attorney General's National Antitrust Committee Report," 15.

[127] Oppenheim, "The Attorney General's National Antitrust Committee Report," 7.

> The driving force behind American competitive enterprise has been the rivalry of firms aimed at maintaining or improving their position in the market. Market pressures and competitive behaviour feed this drive. It seems to me that there is no way of limiting size by placing an arbitrary ceiling on it without limiting growth. … Successful competition by normal growth or lawful business practices should not be penalized.[128]

The DOJ left little doubt that it understood that "any attempt to brand fewness of sellers as illegal per se would be the precursor of a reorganization of important sectors of our industrial order," and thus completely unrealistic.[129] The DOJ's objective, then, should be to protect functioning competitive markets embedded within an institutional matrix of interlocking state and corporate power, in which a relatively small number of large firms could competitively sell goods and allocate capital. The contradictions of this were brought out by the fact that alongside the reassurances for large firms, the report also indicated that the "Fair Trade" laws that had protected GE's retail business were also on the chopping block. While granting that "Fair Trade laws reflect some legitimate aims in protecting substantial investments," the report nonetheless stated flatly that the "Committee's belief that resale price fixing is at odds with the most elementary principles of a competitive enterprise system," the integrity of which required "preserving price competition at the dealer levels."[130] Within a few years, "Fair Trade" laws would be eliminated, forcing the restructuring of GE's domestic retail operations and increasing pressure from cheap foreign exports.

Despite the overall pro-business tone of the report, the DOJ was aware that business was likely to be made uncomfortable by discussion of antitrust. Business fears, it turned out, were well-founded: in 1959, Senator Kefauver announced hearings that would ultimately uncover collusion between GE and Westinghouse to fix prices for TVA contracts in a scheme that would become notorious as the "Great Electrical Conspiracy." Last-ditch efforts by GE to avoid a conviction—including hiring Eisenhower's recently retired Attorney General—failed. Nine companies and fourteen corporate officers pled guilty to criminal

[128] Oppenheim, "The Attorney General's National Antitrust Committee Report," 7.

[129] Oppenheim, "The Attorney General's National Antitrust Committee Report," 8.

[130] Oppenheim, "The Attorney General's National Antitrust Committee Report," 13–14.

antitrust charges, the first time such charges had held in US history.[131] The beginning of the end of the managerial era was at hand.

But it is important to recognize that, like the abolishment of the Fair Trade laws, this was not an exception, but precisely in line with the logic of the DOJ's antitrust stance. The crimes for which GE was prosecuted—and managers convicted—resembled the practices that had been commonplace throughout the earlier finance capital era, when the state relied on private firms to implement corporate self-regulation. What this illustrated more than anything was, first, the increasing capacity of the state to enforce regulations on even the most powerful private firms; and second, that the state was *not* simply the instrument of dominant firms, but rather had gained significant autonomy from them. Moreover, in line with the DOJ report, the prosecution and its outcome revealed the compatibility of doctrines of market competitiveness with the overall dominance of the economy by a small number of conglomerated firms.

That GE eliminated its international division in the restructuring that followed the wave of antitrust actions signified the extent to which the international economy had become integrated within American hegemony by that time: the ability of the American state to enforce a global "rule of law" meant that the firm no longer needed to distinguish between "international" and "domestic" operations. As the cartels and trusts into which the company's international operations had been organized were broken down, its international business could be governed by the same administrative logics as its domestic business. Processes of production and investment spanning vast geographical distances were now integrated corporate functions, reorganized within sector-based operating divisions with no explicit geographical component.

Along with the shift toward conglomerate organization, the formation of a highly autonomous imperial state—which both *supported* and was *supported by* a group of the largest MNCs—helped ensure that this corporate bloc would join the financial sector in seeking to promote capital mobility, rather than preserving protections for domestic manufacturing. Investment, and not exports, became the crux of trade policy. As the relationship between "general managers" and corporate business operations was increasingly mediated by finance, the former focused ever more exclusively on investment functions. Over the next decade, the evolution of

[131] McQuaid, *Uneasy Partners*, 109.

industrial managers into financiers would take great steps forward, and the institutional infrastructure of global finance would constitute an even more fundamental basis for the internal organizational coherence of the firm—helping to solidify a broader alliance between industry and finance.

CHAPTER 6

The Financialization and Internationalization of General Electric

Over the 1960s, the Golden Age of capitalism finally began to run out of steam, and would subsequently crash in the decade of crisis that unfolded across the 1970s. Though Kennedy and Johnson juiced the economy through military spending, cutting taxes, and Great Society programs, there was no avoiding the conclusion as the decade reached a close that the New Deal state, and postwar managerial regime, were facing deep contradictions. With productivity growth slowing, profits were squeezed as capital was caught between union wage militancy and intensifying foreign competition. The result within the firm was the acceleration of existing tendencies toward internationalization, financialization, and decentralization. Centralized corporate planning hierarchies were replaced with flexible financial controls and market discipline on increasingly autonomous business divisions. This internal corporate restructuring was connected with, and reinforced by, a new wave of concentration and centralization of equity in the hands of big "institutional investors," which increasingly emerged as a counter-balance to the power of internal managers.

Even before the eruption of full-scale economic crisis, the growing capacities of the state made possible greater conflict with even the most powerful firms, while also allowing for the intensification of market mediation and discipline. If this had been apparent in the deluge of antitrust

© The Author(s), under exclusive license to Springer Nature Switzerland AG 2022

S. Maher, *Corporate Capitalism and the Integral State*, Marx, Engels, and Marxisms,
https://doi.org/10.1007/978-3-030-83772-3_6

cases after the war, the Great Electrical Conspiracy marked the high-water mark, as top executives were for the first time sent to prison for antitrust violations. This foretold a political crisis in the relationship between business and the state, which would be intensified by cutbacks in state investment amidst a looming "fiscal crisis of the state."[1] While state budgets had long tended to grow faster than GDP, the two-decade-long boom had allowed confronting this problem to be put off indefinitely. As growth slowed, pressures for restructuring intensified. Far from countenancing tax increases to support continued spending, state officials and their corporate allies insisted that cuts were necessary to control inflation and ensure sufficient levels of investment. In the context of a mounting profitability crisis, taxation and regulatory costs appeared ever more onerous.

Nevertheless, GE's embeddedness within the state industrial policy system remained essential to its organizational structure and market dominance. Hi-tech production continued to be the foundation of GE's internationalization, as its foreign subsidiaries undertook massive infrastructure projects all over the world, often funded by US aid dollars under the rubric of "international development." GE was in *the business of empire*: it was a global, state-supported, and profitable infrastructure production machine. Like other "multinational corporations," it also constructed the cross-border flows of investment and networks of production that were the crucial institutional foundations of global economic integration. However, amidst the intensifying fiscal crisis of the state, military spending began a precipitous decline as a percent of GDP in the wake of the Vietnam War. At the same time, the firm faced new pressures to grow faster than the economy as a whole. In this context, the firm used the extensive financial capacities it had developed to manage its global operations as a basis for marketing financial services—which was a relatively fast-growing sector.

[1] James O'Connor, *The Fiscal Crisis of the State* (New York: St. Martin's Press, 1973).

The Great Electrical Conspiracy and the Crisis of the State-Capital Relationship

In 1890, Friedrich Engels lucidly described the contradictions that could emerge with the development of the modern legal profession and state juridical apparatus:

> As soon as the new division of labor which creates professional lawyers becomes necessary, another new and independent sphere is opened up which, for all its general dependence on production and trade, still has also a special capacity for reacting upon these spheres. In a modern state, law must not only correspond to the general economic condition and be its expression, but must also be an *internally coherent* expression which does not, owing to inner contradictions, reduce itself to nought. … All the more so the more rarely it happens that a code of law is the blunt, unmitigated, unadulterated expression of the domination of a class – this in itself would offend the 'conception of right.' … Thus to a great extent the course of the 'development of right' only consists, first, in the attempt to do away with the contradictions arising from the direct translation of economic relations into legal principles, and to establish a harmonious system of law, and then in the repeated breaches made in this system by the influence and pressure of further economic development, which involves it in further contradictions.[2]

In the early 1960s, these contradictions contributed to a *political* crisis of the state-capital relationship, which would only be resolved with the formation of new integral state institutions in the 1970s to coordinate the management of the *economic* crisis that had by then emerged. Over two world wars, the New Deal, and the postwar construction of a new informal empire, the institutional capacities of the American state grew to make it by far the most powerful capitalist state in world history. This enabled it to act more autonomously from the input of particular capitalists—and for certain apparatuses to pursue a relatively hermetic institutional logic, with minimal regard for other interests expressed and organized within the integral state complex. As the onslaught of antitrust cases after the war that broke up the international cartels attested, this was nowhere truer than for the juridical apparatus, which included not

[2] Friedrich Engels, "Letter to Joseph Bloch, September 21–22, 1890," in *The Marx-Engels Reader*, ed. Robert Tucker, Second Edition, 1978, 762–63.

only the courts, but also the executive branch enforcement apparatus, including the Department of Justice, the Federal Trade Commission, the Securities and Exchange Commission, and others.

If the postwar antitrust onslaught was about internationalizing the Sherman Antitrust Act—and thus the juridical apparatus itself—the prosecution of the "Great Electrical Conspiracy" was the consequence of the growing institutional power, rationalization, and confidence of that apparatus, wherein conceptions of "right" were developed within the courts and the legal profession at a considerable distance from the immediate economic interests of particular firms, and even without directly considering the general interests of the capitalist system. The growth in the capacities and resources of the juridical apparatus created space for this institutional rationality to develop more autonomously from particularistic interests, and made it possible for the resulting "conception of right" to be more actively and systematically enforced.

However, these apparatuses and practices were not fully autonomous from the structures and logic of the capitalist society in which they remained very much embedded. The contradictions between the working out of abstract principles of right and the material foundations of corporate power and class rule reverberated through the state and the legal profession. This was particularly the case given the close ties between specific agents within the juridical apparatus and the centers of corporate power. Although the health of specific firms—particularly those found to have violated the law—may not have been of immediate concern to state officials, the antitrust prosecutions occurred in response to pressures, questions, and challenges thrown up by the pressures of a globalizing capitalism, including the emergence of multinational corporations. The restructuring this juridical apparatus imposed would, over the long run, intensify and deepen market competition, and in fact be functional to the stability and vitality of the overall capitalist order.

Yet from the point of the juridical apparatus—and much to the chagrin of those working in other state agencies—this was hardly the result of a "grand plan" for global capitalist restructuring. Rather, it was the product of the gradual and uneven working out of hegemonic legal doctrines in relation to novel situations. The legal problems that developed around these giant new economic structures, and the integration of the world market into a singular global capitalism under US hegemony, confronted the juridical apparatus with the need to develop new "conceptions of right" in competition, to redefine the geographical, political, and economic scope of its powers, and the like—questions which were thus by no means fully abstract, nor divorced from the *real* means of enforcement this apparatus possessed.

In 1971, Lewis Engman, Assistant Director of President Nixon's "Domestic Council," penned a memo to Domestic Affairs Advisor John Ehrlichman summarizing the "extensive amount of material" compiled by the Domestic Council Committee on Antitrust Policy "on existing antitrust law and enforcement policy... based upon comments from interested agencies and departments." As Engman's memo observed:

> Although Federal Government antitrust policy has a continuing effect upon the day-to-day operations and development planning of countless American business firms, this policy has never been a coordinated part of overall economic planning of the Federal government. The Antitrust Division of the Justice Department has operated as the litigation-oriented defender of competition without the need or the desire to concern itself with the far-ranging implications of its enforcement program.[3]

Thus, Engman stated, "antitrust enforcement by the government is litigation-oriented and is not carried out as a part of an overall economic policy, since the FTC is an independent regulatory agency and the Antitrust Division views itself as an independent prosecutor."[4]

A decade earlier, in September 1959, the Senate began hearings to investigate allegations that General Electric, Westinghouse, Allis Chalmers, Federal Pacific Electric, and numerous smaller companies had conspired to fix prices in bids for government contracts for turbines, switchgear, and other heavy equipment. Though this had gone on for many years, the investigation was only initiated when the Tennessee Valley Authority (TVA) noticed that it had received identical bids from 47 different manufacturers three years in a row. The TVA was a state agency established during the New Deal for planning, financing, and operating large-scale public works projects, which at the time had the largest electrical generating capacity in the United States. Moreover, "other government agencies – at the state, local, federal levels – had the

[3] Lewis A. Engman, "Lewis Engman to John Ehrlichman," Memo, September 1, 1971, Record Group 56, Entry A1 718, Box #9, National Archives College Park, MD.

[4] "Lewis Engman to John Ehrlichman."

same experience," though they had not brought this to the attention of regulatory authorities.

At that time, GE controlled 40–45% of the electrical equipment market, and Westinghouse about 30–35%. Allis Chalmers and Federal Pacific each had 10%. Thus, GE and Westinghouse—but especially GE—played the central roles in organizing the scheme. Executives would meet in secret at public locations to determine the amount of the winning bid, as well as a mid-range bid, which most firms would offer, and a low bid for each government solicitation. To avoid detection, the winning firm would rotate according to a fixed schedule tied to the changes in the phases of the moon. The system was calculated so that over time, each company would maintain its existing market share. Regulatory authorities estimated the cost to taxpayers at $175 million each year.[5] Once the Senate hearings revealed the illegality, the juridical apparatus had both the institutional responsibility, and the capacity, to vigorously enforce the antitrust doctrines it had developed since the war: "Ike's Justice Department wanted blood."[6]

GE hired Eisenhower's recently retired Attorney General, Herbert Brownell, to "talk turkey" with the Justice Department, going beyond the "pious statements" Cordiner and other executives delivered to the Senate. But this had no effect. The Justice Department "hammered offending corporations in ways almost never seen since the 1930s." Federal indictments were handed down in June 1960. A mere week before the 1960 election, nine companies and more than 50 executives pled guilty or no contest to criminal antitrust violations. For the first time in US history, 70 years after the enactment of the Sherman Antitrust Act, antitrust enforcement went beyond civil complaints and penalties to levying *criminal* charges—and delivering guilty verdicts. Executives would actually go to prison for antitrust violations, which thereby "ceased being a gentlemen's misdemeanour."

In addition to the dozen second-tier executives who went to jail, 300 more got suspended sentences. Seven vice presidents and divisional managers at GE, Westinghouse, and two other firms served 60-day sentences. Millions were paid in fines—perhaps not enough to seriously

[5] John Barnhill, "Great Electrical Equipment Conspiracy," in *Encyclopedia of White-Collar & Corporate Crime*, ed. Lawrence Salinger, vol. 1, 2 vols. (Thousand Oaks, CA: Sage, 2005), 377–78.

[6] McQuaid, *Uneasy Partners*, 109.

damage these companies' bottom-lines, but massive by historical standards. Utilities and state governments subsequently filed 2,000 civil suits against the conspirators, tying GE up in litigation for much of the rest of the decade.[7] GE had from its origins developed the capacities to govern capitalist markets—which, as we saw, the state had relied upon and even promoted. Now, an increasingly muscular state was tearing apart and reforming these structures and practices at home and abroad, aggressively expanding the operation of the coercive force of price competition.

"It was the darkest period in General Electric's history, a time when the Justice Department pondered breaking up the company, so manifold and wanton were the transgressions."[8] *All* of GE's top management was fired. Cordiner resigned as President in 1961 and stepped down as Chairman two years later. GE's close relationship with the utilities was also "shattered." In place of the old clientelist networks GE had worked to maintain with the utilities, partly through linkages with state governments, utilities were now "required to seek bids from foreign companies, such as Siemens, Hitachi, and Toshiba."[9] This further intensified competitive pressure, including from Japanese firms supported closely by that state—support that, as we shall see, would become an increasing focus in trade talks over the 1960s and 1970s.

It was just over a year into Kennedy's presidency when the convictions were delivered. During final sentencing in February 1961, a judge accused top GE executive Ralph Cordiner of being "an unindicted co-conspirator against the free-enterprise system." Cordiner was not just *any* capitalist: he was the very personification of the entire managerial order. Cordiner occupied not only the top of GE's managerial structure, but also the summit of capitalist class prestige. As was customary for top GE executives, Cordiner was an eminent *political* figure, and was at the time serving as chair of the BAC. Indeed, the managerial period had seemed to reach its apotheosis when Cordiner was proclaimed GE's first "Chief Executive Officer" in 1958, combining for the first time in the company's history the offices of president and chairman of the board, between which power had been shared since 1913. Nothing could have more

[7] McQuaid, *Uneasy Partners*, 109; O'Boyle, *At Any Cost*, 53–54.

[8] O'Boyle, *At Any Cost*, 53–54.

[9] Rothschild, *The Secret to GE's Success*, 124.

clearly signified the unchallenged dominance of "insiders" over external financiers—the defining attribute of managerial capitalism.

Although the prosecution had been brought under Eisenhower, tensions between the state and business did not recede with the new Democratic administration—quite the contrary. Kennedy's quick embrace of raising the minimum wage and expanding the number of workers it covered only further raised corporate suspicions. However, he eagerly displayed his "seriousness" to business by appointing "business-friendly conservatives to important cabinet positions," while "marginaliz[ing] liberal firebrands like Arthur Schlesinger Jr. and John Kenneth Galbraith when it came to economic policy."[10] Simmering as well were the contradictions generated by the ascent of "multinational" corporations in the context of the federal nature of the American state. The giant corporations, primarily located in the northern states, dominated the national economy and were the primary constituents of the integral state coalitions around free trade and industrial policy. But it was smaller capitalists, without international operations, who most felt the pinch of increased competition that resulted from liberalization.

In the wake of the Great Electrical Conspiracy, these contradictions exploded into a full-blown political crisis. Since its earliest days, Commerce had been associated with protectionist policies, and was anchored in the most nationally oriented elements of the capitalist class. It continued to actively build this constituency, which over time increasingly came to consist of smaller businesses. Kennedy's Commerce secretary, Luther Hodges, was himself a small southern capitalist, having owned a textile mill in North Carolina before becoming governor of that state. These "regional and class alliances" led Hodges to "distrust large corporations," "especially northern industrialists." After the antitrust verdicts, Hodges assumed Cordiner would either step down or be fired by GE's Board. When neither occurred, Hodges forced him to resign as BAC chair, and replaced him with Roger Blough of US Steel.

Though many executives on the BAC were furious, the Republican Party lined up behind Blough.[11] Hodges also insisted on his right to approve members of the BAC, as well as on the appointment of twenty smaller capitalists to the body. Additionally, he demanded control over

[10] Waterhouse, *Lobbying America*, 22; McQuaid, *Uneasy Partners*, 102.

[11] McQuaid, *Uneasy Partners*, 22.

BAC meeting agendas and mandated that government officials address each one, which were also to be opened to the press. As it was, top government officials nearly always attended meetings—indeed, one of the primary functions of the body had been bringing state officials to inform and seek advice from members, while the ability to interact with such leaders was among the key "perks" of BAC membership. Moreover, the Commerce secretary was already (formally, at least) tasked with nominating and approving BAC members, as well as setting meeting agendas. Hodges' move seemed to be another alarming example of the growing assertiveness of the state vis-à-vis capital.

When BAC members complained, Hodges threatened to release all the confidential BAC minutes to the Justice Department to investigate possible antitrust implications of association meetings. Given the scale of the recent antitrust prosecution, this threat was not taken lightly. Clearly, the BAC could not continue under such circumstances even if it had wanted to. Since 1933, it had been a venue for candid discussion among corporate managers and state officials. That this very openness was now threatening the core interests of members was a violation of the trust that was a condition for the organization's basic functioning. Council leaders, led by Blough, informed Kennedy in July 1961 that the BAC was permanently "disaffiliating" from the Commerce Department, and would instead operate as a "purely private" body. Though one of Hodges' assistants present at the meeting declared, "Gentlemen… you have just murdered yourselves," the truth was closer to the opposite: in fact, it was Hodges who had dramatically overstepped and Commerce that would pay the price. Kennedy fired Hodges shortly thereafter.

The BAC severed its formal existence within the Department of Commerce in July 1961, becoming simply the Business Council (BC). Although it was formally "independent," the BC "remained as quasi-public as ever," continuing to function as "a recruitment center for corporate expertise" and a mechanism for building consensus; its meetings were still addressed by high-level administration officials out of the view of the press. Indeed, the "BC simply left its Commerce Department offices and moved to new accommodations down the street," as "new economic liaison committees were created to replace the old ones." Less than two weeks after the split with Commerce, Harold Boeschenstein (owner of the Owens-Corning Fiberglass Company) called Secretary of the Treasury C. Douglas Dillon to propose a meeting "to find out if

[the] Secretary had anything on his mind they could help out with."[12] It is surely not much of an exaggeration to suggest that Kennedy himself "worked feverishly to mend fences with the individual CEOs at the Business Council."[13]

After Boeschenstein's call, Dillon spoke with President Kennedy to determine if he had any objection to Treasury establishing a new relationship with the BC in light of the conflict with Commerce. Edward Gudeman, who had worked under Hodges and was now Acting Secretary of Commerce, was perhaps unsurprisingly "opposed to [Treasury] having contacts with the BAC." Kennedy, however, "didn't wish to make the disagreements between the Department of Commerce and the Council into an overall disagreement with industry." Thus, Kennedy "felt [Treasury] should go ahead with Boeschenstein and his friends and then particularly should try to find something substantive they could get their teeth in and that would be helpful to the Administration."[14] Far from approaching Treasury with policies for which it sought to "lobby," the BC left it to state officials to drive the agenda and devise areas of work to be undertaken. It sought an open-ended affiliation with Treasury, whereby its members could be integrated with policymaking processes in one of the leading state agencies.

The move by the new BC, mere weeks after the divorce with Commerce, to deepen its relationship with the Treasury Department reflected the hierarchy of state apparatuses, and was part and parcel of the expanding institutional ecosystem around Treasury that supported its growing policy scope. With the split from Commerce, the BC moved into what would thenceforth remain the default integral state modality: both *private* and *political*. This denoted the precise contact point between the public and political power of the state, on the one hand, and the private and economic power of the corporation, on the other. As such, it reflected the structure of relative autonomy, as the state organized the political power of the capitalist class "at a distance" from the immediate

[12] "Notes of Telephone Conversation, Harold Boeschenstein to Secretary Dillon," August 1, 1961, Record Group 56, Entry 198, Box #1C-F, National Archives College Park, MD.

[13] Waterhouse, *Lobbying America*, 23.

[14] Douglas Dillon, "Memorandum for Mr. Fowler," August 2, 1961, Record Group 56, Entry 198, Box #1C-F, National Archives College Park, MD.

economic interests of individual firms. It also permitted the BC more flexibility in its linkages with the state, doing away with the requirement that Commerce mediate and organize its relationship with the overall state complex. Developing this integral state relationship with Treasury despite the BC's formal separation from the state required a new juridical rationalization. Secretary Dillon advised the BC that "it would be treated as… 'a government-formed advisory committee'" even though this was "not technically" the case.[15]

The primary preoccupation of the new Kennedy Administration was the large, and growing, balance-of-payments deficit, which was putting pressure on the international role of the dollar. US corporate investment abroad had by that time fully taken off after its postwar pause, as the US-led reconstruction of Europe had succeeded in creating the conditions for investment and growth. The establishment of full currency convertibility meant that US corporate investment could now jump the tariff barrier established by the European Economic Community, and thereby access the whole European market while easily repatriating profits. However, in order to establish subsidiaries abroad to leap over tariff protections, US corporations borrowed funds on well-developed US capital markets, which exacerbated the balance-of-payments deficit—a problem Kennedy found "too great to ignore" even though he sought to further reduce tariffs and boost export competitiveness.[16]

Treasury took the lead in working on this problem, for which it drew upon the integral state mechanisms it was forming with the BC. To restrict the capital outflows that were at the heart of the imbalance, it proposed an end to the deferral of tax on the foreign profits of American MNCs—which was "universally opposed by business."[17] Accordingly, this was at the top of the agenda Treasury set for the new BC. The initial strategy was to attempt to *restrain* what was then seen as "excessive" foreign investment *without* jeopardizing the international economic integration that had been the overriding objective of the postwar project of "making global capitalism."

[15] Henry Fowler, "Lee White from Under Secretary of the Treasury Fowler," June 18, 1962, Record Group 56, Entry 198, Box #1C-F, National Archives College Park, MD.

[16] Panitch and Gindin, *The Making of Global Capitalism*, 113.

[17] Panitch and Gindin, *The Making of Global Capitalism*, 125.

At a two-day meeting in May 1962, the Special Committee on the Balance of Payments was established between Treasury and the BC. Announcing its formation at a special meeting of the BC, Blough described it as "the most important assignment ever undertaken by a committee of the Council."[18] The committee was to "act as a continuing advisory and consultative body as long as it is useful rather than one designed to develop a particular report on a given situation at the time and, then, retire from the field." Following Blough's announcement, Fowler outlined the new depreciation tax credit that had been worked out by the BC and Treasury in what Secretary of the Army Elvis Stahr called a "sexy speech,"[19] while Blough "pointed repeatedly during the press conference to the establishment of the committee and the announcement of the new depreciation guidelines as elements of an improved government-business climate."[20]

Through the mechanism of the new Committee, business—both "bankers and manufacturers"—would be encouraged to take "voluntary actions" to "limit capital outflows from the United States." Treasury officials would also use it to work with corporate managers and encourage them to raise capital abroad, with the further hope that this would lead to the greater development of European capital markets. Treasury believed that this would not only help to "build up more efficient capital market facilities in Europe" but would also assist with "the concomitant need to persuade European nations to relax exchange controls." Furthermore, such internationalization might contribute to easing balance-of-payments pressures by "encouraging and developing increased investment in the United States capital securities markets by European institutions and individual investors, including the listing on foreign stock exchanges, particularly in Europe and Japan, of the shares of major American corporations."[21]

[18] Henry Fowler, "Memorandum for the President: 'Business Council Meeting,'" May 15, 1962, Record Group 56, Entry 198, Box #1C-F, National Archives College Park, MD.

[19] Elvis Stahr, "Elvis Stahr to Henry Fowler," May 11, 1962, Record Group 56, Entry 198, Box #1C-F, National Archives College Park, MD.

[20] Fowler, "Memorandum for the President: 'Business Council Meeting.'".

[21] Henry Fowler, "Memorandum for the Secretary," August 30, 1962, Record Group 56, Entry 198, Box #1C-F, National Archives College Park, MD.

Treasury's efforts to address the balance-of-payments issue were not rooted in the narrow interest of particular US capitalists, firms, or sectors. In many respects, Treasury's efforts to obtain cooperation with voluntary limits on capital outflows *contradicted* the profit-maximization strategies of certain firms. The scale of the challenge Treasury faced in getting corporations to comply was indicated by the report of the BC Special Committee on the Kennedy "Trade Expansion Bill," issued at the same two-day meeting. It included a strong statement on the Treasury Department's efforts up to that point to promote voluntary restraint on capital outflows:

> Since the end of World War I the United States has inherited the mantle of world leadership. Now, the United States dollar is the international currency. Now, the United States is the world's banker. Now, American military strength preserves the peace and provides security for all. The United States can maintain this status only by achieving a balance of payments position which is invulnerable to temporary declines in our export surplus or temporary movements of foreign funds out of the United States. This can be accomplished only by a continuing expansion in foreign investment by United States private enterprise. This is why the United States, ever since World War I, has consistently followed the policy of encouraging such foreign investment, which has not yet even approached the magnitude required for America's future greatness and security. ... American tax policy should not ask American business to operate abroad under conditions less favourable than those of its competitors, nor with penalties on expansion of operating and export businesses through retained earnings. ...Each proposed provision of the Tax Bill should be rejected if it would tend to curtail expansion of legitimate operations abroad.[22]

Treasury was certainly not attempting to stop US MNCs from expanding abroad. Rather, it wanted to shift the locus for financing this expansion to European capital markets, which it saw as "the most necessary next step in the making of global capitalism."[23] Fowler believed that accomplishing this depended on both "persuading a sufficient number of American corporations of the long-run advantages of them floating new issues in European markets" and "securing the cooperation of the Wall

[22] "Business Council, Report of Special Committee on the Trade Expansion Bill," May 7, 962, Record Group 56, Entry 198, Box #1C-F, National Archives College Park, MD.

[23] Panitch and Gindin, *The Making of Global Capitalism*, 126.

Street underwriting bosses, who, quite naturally, have resisted the idea on the ground that it will result in a loss of business for them." Accordingly, Treasury "invited the Foreign Investment Committee of the Investment Bankers Association to meet with us to make a start toward securing Wall Street support." And naturally, "all of these ideas, suggestions, and examples of current practices are fruitful sources of subject matter to explore in depth with the Business Council Balance of Payments Committee," Fowler concluded.[24]

For the remainder of the decade, the state continued to stumble through the balance-of-payments crisis in the face of an increasingly internationalized capitalism that it could not simply control. Attempts to secure voluntary restrictions on capital flows were reinforced with the threat of mandatory controls, including the 1963 Interest Equalization Tax designed to tax capital outflows. But the degree to which financial markets were already integrated meant that this was bound to generate contradictions. While it deterred Europeans from borrowing in the US, it also encouraged US banks to enter the unregulated Eurodollar market. Although this improved the balance of payments, it undermined domestic interest rate ceilings that were central to the New Deal financial regulatory framework, and thus "made the management of monetary policy at home much more difficult." Moreover, as controls failed to recognize that the US balance of trade was not so much a problem in itself as a reflection of the structure of US hegemony, they actually "aggravated speculation against the dollar" by reinforcing "the prevailing assumption… that only the achievement of US trade surpluses could make the dollar secure."

The persistence of inflationary pressures and balance-of-payments deficits eventually led the Johnson administration in 1968 to impose mandatory controls on the outflow of capital. Yet maintaining fixed exchange rates proved difficult, "as speculation built up around possible adjustments… to cope with the emergence of simultaneous recessionary and inflationary pressures." As "coordinated central bank interventions" among core capitalist states to protect interest rates became "more and more onerous," the basis was laid for the abandonment of Bretton Woods altogether in 1971. Yet this reflected not the decline, but the reassertion of the central role of the US in superintending global capitalism. Indeed,

[24] Fowler, "Memorandum for the Secretary," August 30, 1962; Henry Fowler, "Draft Letter to Roger Blough from Under Secretary Fowler," November 21, 1962, Record Group 56, Entry 198, Box #1C-F, National Archives College Park, MD.

"just as the US Treasury had been central to the establishment of new forums and mechanisms for the international management of the 'dollar crisis' within the Bretton Woods framework, so was it now central to that framework's dismantling."[25]

For its part, GE cooperated closely with the Treasury Department in addressing the balance-of-payments crisis. For one thing, that state investment through the industrial policy system was so important to GE ensured that it was particularly inclined to comply with "voluntary" government directives right through the crisis years of the 1970s, and that it would remain helpful in organizing capitalist support for these measures. Additionally, the company's massive exports of large-scale infrastructure and capital goods, subsidized by export credits extended by the Export–Import Bank, also ensured that its US operations contributed positively to the balance of payments.

In 1965, the company reported with pride that its "U.S. operations increased their favourable contribution to the payments balance and took new steps toward further improvement."[26] In addition to direct exports, GE's multinational operations included subsidiaries it managed or in which it had a controlling stake. To finance these subsidiaries, the company set up the General Electric Overseas Capital Corporation "in cooperation with the voluntary program of the U.S. government to improve the nation's payments balance." This entailed borrowing $50 million abroad to finance a portion of the company's international operations, further ensuring GE would make a net positive contribution to the balance of payments.[27] So too did this increasingly multinational scope solidify the company's support for liberalization. The company worked to promote the exports of other, smaller companies "by providing General Electric overseas know-how, manpower and distribution facilities for U.S. companies wanting this aid in developing export business."[28] GE's efforts to organize smaller capitalists around export goals, and to integrate these firms within the global value chains controlled by big MNCS, would remain a major aspect of its efforts to extend the consensus around liberalization to smaller firms.

[25] Panitch and Gindin, *The Making of Global Capitalism*, 125–30.

[26] General Electric, "1965 Annual Report," 1.

[27] General Electric, "1965 Annual Report," 3.

[28] General Electric, "1965 Annual Report," 3.

In July 1965, coordination between the BC and the Treasury Department was expanded through the creation of the BC Treasury Liaison Committee, chaired by Boeschenstein (who, we recall, had reached out to the Treasury Department immediately after the BC's 1961 split from Commerce). Committee meetings were held at the Treasury Department in Washington DC, with the Secretary and other top Treasury officials in attendance. As was the case with the Balance of Payments Committee, Treasury established areas of work and developed meeting agendas, covering policies on taxation, regulation, trade, monetary policy, and more.

The increasing closeness of the Treasury to the trade policy apparatus was apparent from the regular presence at these meetings of officials from the Office of the Special Representative for Trade Negotiations (STR). Multilateral trade negotiations were a significant focus of these meetings, as the radical tariff reductions of the Kennedy Round raised anxieties among capital that the state would act without sufficiently accounting for the concerns of—and costs to—particular firms. Meetings began with a Treasury or USTR presentation, followed by a discussion with the assembled businessmen in which the perspectives of specific industries and firms were assimilated to a broader systemic framework. This was referred to as the "general economic outlook," developing which was a key objective of each meeting.

The integral state function of the new committee included sustaining policy consensus among capitalists, and within the state, across presidential administrations. Thus, the September 20, 1968, meeting "opened with some discussion of the desirability of assuring a smooth transition and continuity of policy during an election year – regardless of the outcome of the November elections."[29] The meeting the following May, after Nixon's crushing defeat of Humphrey, made clear what the basic elements of this desired continuity were, as well as the mechanism whereby the program was derived. Attended by Paul Volcker—then serving as a Vice President of Chase Manhattan Bank—and Treasury Secretary David Kennedy, the meeting featured a lengthy discussion of the Treasury's tax proposal. It covered technical aspects of the policy, as well as a strategic discussion of the "Congressional outlook" for the

[29] Treasury Department, "Summary of Meeting of the Treasury Consultative Committee of the Business Council," September 20, 1968, Record Group 56, Entry A1 736, Box #5, National Archives College Park, MD.

bill. The final portion of the meeting consisted of a "response by the Business Council group," which was divided into three parts: the "business community's response to the tax program"; "probable effects of the program, with special reference to business profits and plant and equipment spending"; and finally, "methods of rallying support for the program."[30]

The Treasury Department, in other words, laid out its tax proposal as well as the strategy to secure its passage through Congress and build support among business. The first step was gaining the support of the BC. Building on the work Treasury had done with the BAC, the Liaison Committee was thus a mechanism for maintaining consensus between business and the state, even across administrations, toward reducing spending and deficits, cutting taxes, and pursuing trade liberalization. As postwar managerial capitalism fell into crisis, such committees, insulated from public scrutiny and the flux of electoral outcomes, would become increasingly important in developing policy and organizing a consensus among the capitalist class.

GE and the Crisis of Managerialism

Despite GE's cooperation with the voluntary Treasury program, it may be surprising, given its historical importance to such integral state networks and efforts, that it participated neither on the BC's Balance of Payments Committee nor the Treasury Liaison Committee. In fact, it seemed almost entirely absent from the public-facing leadership of the new BC altogether. Partly, this was the result of the significance of the disgrace to the company that came with the Great Electrical Conspiracy—indeed, nothing on that order of corporate criminality had been prosecuted previously, and it had come as a shock to the public.

Nevertheless, GE remained a constant feature of the integral state, and Cordiner continued to attend meetings and functions of the BC and other business associations, along with other current and former GE executives. The prosecution of the conspiracy had done nothing to disrupt the structural centrality to the capitalist class that came with GE's diversification, which required systematically interacting with a range of suppliers and

[30] Treasury Department, "Agenda for the Meeting of The Department of the Treasury Liaison Committee of the Business Council with Secretary Kennedy," May 28, 1969, Record Group 56, Entry A1 736, Box #5, National Archives College Park, MD.

customers across many different sectors, possessing knowledge of a wide array of different businesses and markets, and maintaining a diverse Board of Directors. GE's prominence also remained anchored in the firm's embeddedness within the industrial policy system, as well as its extensive internationalization. Together, these factors practically ensured that over the long run, the company's political leadership would return—and it did, as we shall see.

GE was already deeply concerned in 1961 about "constant pressure exerted on price levels by foreign producers with substantially lower wage and salary costs, as well as significant tax and depreciation advantages." To cope with this, management initiated a "vigorous Company-wide cost-control program."[31] When Fred Borch ascended to the top position two years later, worries were clearly growing about how "the rise of international competition has made it imperative that U.S. producers learn to compete not only against domestic competitors but also against foreign producers enjoying advantages in wage, tax and other differentials." However, Borch assured:

> General Electric people are meeting this challenge. Costs are being scaled down aggressively. New steps are being taken toward increased automation. A stronger linkage is being established between research and development and the wants and needs of customers. And individual employees recognize that they must compete successfully in their work with employees of other manufacturers all over the world.[32]

State-supported R&D remained key to GE's competitiveness, but this would have to be more effectively linked to innovative product lines and labor-saving technologies. This was merely the first hint of the emphasis on cost cutting in the face of economic stagnation and rising labor costs that would intensify over the following decade. On the heels of Russia's Sputnik space program, the optimism of the postwar moment was gradually being replaced by the feeling that American industry was facing daunting challenges. These could only be met through an increased effort on the part of individuals and companies alike to outcompete rivals, along with restructuring political and economic institutions to adjust to the new

[31] General Electric, "1961 Annual Report," 1.

[32] General Electric, "1963 Annual Report," 1.

reality. The complacency that had characterized the managerial era would have to be discarded in favor of a renewed striving for national success.

Borch had started out with GE as a financial auditor, before spending most of his career in sales and marketing—a background that highlighted how much the company was changing, even as so much stayed the same. While top managers were increasingly concerned with investment, operational tasks were devolved to divisional and sub-divisional managers. Over his years at the helm, Borch doubled down on the financialized restructuring of the firm from a system of production to a system of investment, while expanding into financial services markets, even as the company remained fundamentally oriented toward selling high-tech equipment and consumer products generated within the industrial policy system.

In his first years, Borch established the "Growth Council," effectively an internal think tank "consisting of some of the best minds inside and outside the company." The Council's objective was to "identify market opportunities that were growing faster than the GNP and in which GE had unique abilities and might gain a competitive advantage."[33] While the conglomerate form allowed GE to weather the boom-and-bust cycles of individual businesses by balancing investments and earnings across different sectors, this also meant that it was difficult for the company to grow more quickly than GDP as a whole. The Growth Council was tasked with devising a strategy whereby it could do so: locating growth sectors and linking these with existing capacities GE had developed which could serve as foundations for expansion into new markets.

Already in 1961, GE observed a growing "tendency of consumers to spend a lower percentage of their disposable personal income on consumer durables and more in the broad area of 'services'." As such, it had begun to expand its offerings of product-related services, as well as "projects for increasing its contributions for transportation, banking and other service industries."[34] Building on this, Borch requested that the Growth Council examine service as well as industrial opportunities. The overall strategy the Council produced was based on leveraging GE's easy access to credit and financialized management systems to enter new markets, including developing a range of financial service products.

[33] Rothschild, *The Secret to GE's Success*, 127–28; O'Boyle, *At Any Cost*, 225; General Electric, "1964 Annual Report," 1; General Electric, "1968 Annual Report," 1.

[34] General Electric, "1961 Annual Report."

In addition to substantially expanding the company's internationalization, it proposed nine areas for investment, four of which were "product areas" and five "service areas." The product areas included nuclear energy, business computers, commercial jet engines, and polymer chemicals; the service areas were entertainment, community development and housing, medicine and medical technology, education, and personal and financial services.[35]

During the mid-1960s, the initial phase of the Growth Council strategy was rolled out in the areas of nuclear power, computers, and internationalization.[36] The latter was of particular concern, as the company pursued a "highly diversified approach to world markets," which included power systems, railroad infrastructure, locomotives, steam turbines, steel mill systems, information technologies, military hardware and electronics, industrial processes and components, and consumer goods.[37] To manage this, Borch organized four "Area Divisions" to coordinate corporate regional strategy across the product divisions: Latin America, Europe, the Mediterranean, and the Far East. Each of these was "assigned a Division-level Manager who guides the development of the best ways to serve the Area's customers – whether by overseas affiliates, U.S. product departments serving directly, or through the IGE Export Division."[38]

GE was by then moving full speed ahead with rebuilding its international operations after the setback of the postwar antitrust onslaught. Between 1952 and 1962, exports grew threefold, and they increased another 24% in 1962.[39] The attraction of investment abroad was amplified by the "continuing squeeze between depressed prices and increasing costs" that came with slowing growth at home, the earliest signs of the full-blown profit squeeze crisis this would later generate.[40] If GE had initially emerged through the project of electrifying the United States,

[35] Rothschild, *The Secret to GE's Success*, 127–46; General Electric, "1968 Annual Report," 1.

[36] General Electric, "1964 Annual Report"; General Electric, "1965 Annual Report."

[37] General Electric, "1964 Annual Report," 14.

[38] General Electric, "1964 Annual Report," 20.

[39] General Electric, "1964 Annual Report," 1, 20.

[40] General Electric, "1964 Annual Report," 1.

a century later electrification remained at the core of its highly diversified global operations. GE installed, operated, and maintained atomic and non-atomic power generation, transmission, and distribution equipment in more than 100 different countries.[41] In 1965, the company even won a contract from the AEC "to develop and build the first nuclear power system for operation on the moon."[42]

This tremendous increase in GE exports "resulted primarily from the Company's leadership in advanced technologies,"[43] which were a product of GE's continued integration with the state-organized industrial policy system. A 1960 Senate Judiciary Committee report found that more than 50% of GE's R&D from 1950 to 1959 was financed by the state ($1.5 billion out of $2.87 billion). GE's 1961 Annual Report boasted that "more than 50 major laboratories nation wide," many subsidized by the state or in partnership with public universities, "serve[d] the research and development needs of specific operating components" of the company. Its R&D expenditure in this period "exceed[ed] that for any other company," constituting the "most extensive research and development activities of any company in the United States and, presumably, the world."[44]

While this was all very profitable, the ends which state investment served were determined not by "markets," but political interests articulated by the state. GE products and technologies played a central role in the violent pacification of the global periphery, including the "bitter warfare in Vietnam" for which it stepped up production of "jet engines, flight controls, armament systems, and other vital equipment."[45] GE also produced crucial infrastructure for "international development," supported by aid and loans from the American state. Indeed, export sales "benefit[ed] in part from U.S. foreign-aid programs which require that dollar credits be used in this country."[46] If the Third World was in some sense "dependent" on the core capitalist countries, one concrete form this

[41] General Electric, "1963 Annual Report," 16.

[42] General Electric, "1965 Annual Report," 11.

[43] General Electric, "1962 Annual Report," 20; General Electric, "1964 Annual Report," 14; General Electric, "1965 Annual Report," 16.

[44] General Electric, "1961 Annual Report," 1961, 20.

[45] General Electric, "1965 Annual Report," 1.

[46] General Electric, "1963 Annual Report," 16.

took was reliance on GE capital, technical expertise, and technologies. But for both core and periphery, locomotives, turbines, power systems, and industrial materials and components—to say nothing of jet engines, bombs, targeting systems, and other military technologies—were essential to the reproduction of an integrated global capitalism. This made GE essential.

GE also played "a major supporting role" in the Apollo program to put a man on the moon by 1970, providing "supplies and services to assist NASA"—an agency that, from the very start, depended on extensive support from high-tech manufacturing firms.[47] To accommodate its expanding work in this area, GE formed the "Missile and Space" division, which covered production related to spacecraft, satellites, and re-entry vehicles. This was in addition to a new "Command Systems" division, which incorporated projects related to the Apollo program, information and control systems, and military communications systems. The company also established the "Defense Programs Operation," which coordinated all of its increasingly sprawling military and space-related operations, "serving the government's aerospace and defense needs on a unified basis."[48] Given that these activities were now spread across multiple large divisions, this would facilitate the servicing of government contracts from one centralized administrative node.

R&D remained the beating heart at the center of the firm's businesses, as GE engineers continued to find ways to commodify and "spin off" state-supported technological development into other consumer and industrial product lines. GE's jet engine business grew over the 1960s, partly as a consequence of continued orders for military airplanes. Military and space program contracts also facilitated the company's move into electronics, which would find applications well beyond the initial purposes of missile guidance, firing, and tracking systems; military computers; undersea technologies including sonar, mine-detection, and communications; and a range of nuclear weapons-related technologies.[49] These included medical electronics, broilers, lamps, circuits, materials, as well as business computers and much more.[50] Particularly noteworthy was the

[47] General Electric, "1962 Annual Report," 4.

[48] General Electric, "1962 Annual Report," 4.

[49] General Electric, "1961 Annual Report," 4.

[50] General Electric, "1962 Annual Report"; General Electric, "1963 Annual Report."

progress in television technology, eventually leading to the development of color TV, radio remote control, and later advanced infrared remote control technology.[51]

A perennial problem for GE was ensuring that the fruits of such state-supported R&D were spun off into consumer and industrial products as efficiently as possible. GE continued to work at "finding new ways to speed the transition between laboratory and market," including by establishing the Research and Development Center in 1965 for this "express purpose." This center contained three units: a Corporate Planning Operation, which connected the company's overall strategic planning with the R&D center; a New Businesses Development Operation, which assessed opportunities to develop R&D work into new businesses; and the TEMPO organization, which integrated corporate and military planning. TEMPO provided state planners with GE's perspective on industrial policy, while also facilitating the flow of information from state industrial policy planners to corporate executives to support longer-term corporate planning and capacity development.[52]

GE's financial capacities and operations were central to the overall Growth Council strategy. During the Borch years, the organization of the GE Credit Company (GECC) was rationalized, such that it became central to the firm's core structure, consolidating GE's financial operations within its divisional organization. The Growth Council sought to find ways to commodify GE's extensive financial capacities as "services" to be sold on the market, as well as to leverage them in competition with other industrial firms in non-financial sectors. This further challenged the "watertight" separation between financial and non-financial firms that was the basis for the New Deal regulatory architecture. As a former executive put it:

> The council's vision was to build on GE's internal capabilities and create a fully integrated, consumer-focused financial package. ... The concept was to use the insurance, pension, investment, and lending skills of the company and create a package to be offered by [GECC]. This included offering credit, health and life insurance, mutual funds, and investment advice based on GE's internal skills and systems.[53]

[51] General Electric, "1963 Annual Report," 2.

[52] General Electric, "1965 Annual Report," 18.

[53] Rothschild, *The Secret to GE's Success*, 139.

Financial services were thus not "added on" to GE's industrial operations, but were at the core of the company's existing operations. In fact, New Deal regulations actually created competitive advantages that *encouraged* industrial firms to enter financial markets. The Glass-Steagall Act's separation between consumer and investment banking barred consumer banks from offering insurance and investment products, while prohibiting investment banks from taking deposits or offering banking services. Financial firms were therefore unable to offer "one-stop" integrated financial services packages such as those marketed by GE in the US (although they were doing so in the relatively unregulated Eurodollar market). Similarly, "Regulation Q" ceilings on bank deposit interest rates contributed to the growth of a market for privately issued corporate debt, as large depositors sought to secure higher returns.[54]

GE's ability to cheaply raise capital as a result of its AAA bond rating thus made independently raising capital easy, and factored centrally into Growth Council strategy. In addition to financing new acquisitions and investment, GECC also facilitated GE's transformation of corporate debt into consumer debt on a large scale, effectively leveraging its industrial assets to extend credit that would finance consumption of the output of those very industrial assets. Nor was GE the only firm that followed such a path: when business responded to slower growth by increasing investment and undertaking a wave of mergers, this was financed not by bank loans or retained earnings, but through these private bonds. Financialization was thus a powerful lever for industrial concentration and centralization. As of the early 1970s, the three largest banks issued less consumer credit than either the three largest manufacturing firms or the three largest retailers.[55] By that time, GECC was diversified to the extent that financing GE-manufactured products was a *minority* of its operations.

Beginning in the mid-1960s, the company began to roll out some of the Growth Council's more ambitious schemes.[56] Especially successful were the company's medical technologies. Crucially, these businesses "benefit[ted] from increased health programs spurred by Medicare,"

[54] Panitch and Gindin, *The Making of Global Capitalism*, 139.

[55] Panitch and Gindin, *The Making of Global Capitalism*, 121.

[56] General Electric, "1965 Annual Report"; General Electric, "1966 Annual Report"; General Electric, "1967 Annual Report."

created in 1965 as part of Lyndon Johnson's "Great Society." By 1968, GE became "the nation's largest producer of professional medical apparatus," developing and producing X-ray technology, pacemakers, and other medical electronics.[57] In keeping with its focus on expanding into the service sector and finance, GE also successfully marketed a range of financial and management services to hospitals.

Another fruitful Growth Council venture, which also relied heavily on the firm's financial capacities and functions, was commercial jet engines. Though GE had long been a major producer of military jet engines, Pratt & Whitney dominated the civilian market. Since the airlines and airplane manufacturers had an incentive to rely on a single engine supplier, as this minimized service costs, there were significant barriers to entry. However, GE's financial capacities allowed it to offer the airlines "a deal they couldn't refuse": if the airlines insisted that GE engines be installed on any aircraft they operated, GE would purchase the aircraft and lease them to the airlines. GE would thus take on all the investment in core air travel infrastructure, which it would thereby own, and charge the airlines rent to operate. Through this strategy, GE captured 75% of the commercial jet engine market.[58] This illustrates the synergies between the company's industrial and financial operations: not only did the latter create demand by extending consumer credit, but these capacities also gave GE an edge in competition with other firms.

Conversely, a plan to employ a similar leasing strategy to compete with IBM in personal and business computer markets became a colossal, and notorious, failure. IBM had set up a leasing business, similar to GE's commercial jet engine strategy, such that companies did not need to invest their own capital to use computers. The company also offered extensive service and software support. At the time, GE was IBM's largest private customer and was also emerging as a major supplier of computerized controls to the military as well as a leader in automating its own manufacturing operations.[59] This seemed to put the company in a position to challenge IBM. Yet GE underestimated the costs of switching from IBM's systems, which was not simply a matter of installing new hardware, but

[57] General Electric, "1968 Annual Report," 12.

[58] Rothschild, *The Secret to GE's Success*, 134.

[59] Rothschild, *The Secret to GE's Success*, 129.

also retraining personnel, writing new software, and dealing with compatibility issues. As a result, neither other companies nor the state were eager to make the move to new systems. To make matters worse, Borch insisted on replacing GE's own IBM systems with the GE ones. As a result, not only did the venture end in a humiliating failure, but the setbacks to GE's other operations meant that it served as a model for why others chose not to switch from IBM. The company was unable to extricate itself from this quagmire until 1970, when it successfully sold the business to Honeywell.[60]

It was becoming clear by the late 1960s that some of the new ventures represented significant overreach for GE. While the company reported "unprecedented growth" in sales over the first half of the decade, this was "profitless growth."[61] Various reasons were given for this: start-up costs, overcapacity, and, not least of all, "labor-related factors"—including a lengthy strike in Schenectady, N.Y., and "numerous shorter strikes that not only reduced sales at some plants but also caused component shortages and thus delayed shipments at other plants."[62] Export growth, too, slowed temporarily as the midpoint of the decade passed. A particularly thorny issue was the "turnkey pricing" strategy GE had utilized for nuclear power plant construction. According to this model, the company quoted utilities a single price "to design, build, and install nuclear systems."[63] While this increased demand for nuclear power systems, since it assumed all risk from the utilities, the strategy backfired massively.

With a large backlog in orders, as inflationary pressures mounted by the late 1960s—and with construction wages rising especially rapidly—the prices GE had contracted to build the plants proved far too low to be profitable, resulting in huge losses.[64] This was no doubt one reason why GE played a leading role in forming the "Construction Users' Anti-Inflation Round Table," a primary antecedent of the Business Roundtable, which sought to better organize highly fragmented and

[60] General Electric, "1970 Annual Report," 4.

[61] General Electric, "1966 Annual Report," 1; Rothschild, *The Secret to GE's Success*, xiii, 151.

[62] General Electric, "1966 Annual Report," 1.

[63] Rothschild, *The Secret to GE's Success*, 93.

[64] General Electric, "1967 Annual Report," 5; General Electric, "1968 Annual Report"; General Electric, "1969 Annual Report,"; General Electric, "1970 Annual Report."

structurally weak construction contractors to resist the wage demands of construction unions. The problems were made even worse as victories won by the growing environmental movement resulted in increasing regulatory costs. Though GE stopped accepting turnkey orders in 1967, the backlog extended well into the next decade.[65] Ironically, it was only in the 1970s, once no new reactors were being built, that the industry became profitable. Since each reactor was unique, only the original manufacturer could provide service and maintenance for existing reactors, effectively granting them monopoly power.[66]

Like many other corporations as the postwar boom began to cool over the later 1960s, GE's initial response to its falling earnings ratio was to increase investment—which was ratcheted up to $1 billion over 1966–1967, approximately equal to the combined total for the preceding five years.[67] This was cushioned by state contracts at home and abroad. Municipal projects in the US and other core capitalist countries complemented GE's "international development" projects across the periphery. This included "major orders for rapid transit equipment and large municipal lighting installations around the world."[68] GE's military and space orders peaked in the late 1960s, after which space and military spending was reduced both as a percent of GDP and in absolute terms. This was initially due, in large part, to the rhythms of the war in Indochina. The company assured its shareholders that "by far the largest portion of this business remains based in long-term defense and aerospace programs which would not be affected by a cease-fire." However, even as sales of military electronics equipment and jet engines were still growing, "space systems and services" fell, "reflecting the diversion of government dollars to more immediate military programs."[69]

The depth of GE's integration with the industrial policy system was by no means reducible to winning or losing a particular contract, or the duration of a military conflict or space program initiative, and would no doubt endure any periodic fluctuations in funding. With its engineering

[65] General Electric, "1967 Annual Report," 5; General Electric, "1970 Annual Report," 13.

[66] Rothschild, *The Secret to GE's Success*, 94.

[67] General Electric, "1967 Annual Report," 1.

[68] General Electric, "1967 Annual Report," 13–14.

[69] General Electric, "1968 Annual Report," 5.

and high-tech manufacturing capacities, to say nothing of its portfolio of intellectual property, GE was as integral to the network of national laboratories, universities, and military planning that constituted the industrial policy system, as that system was to the organizational structure and market power of GE.[70] Even a "stable business" in state contracts would support the reproduction of critical engineering and research capacities—and would continue to create "new opportunities" through "spin-off activities applying space technologies to civilian problems."[71]

Yet it became ever harder to square the push to grow faster than GDP with the reduction in military spending that would persist until the late 1970s. Throughout the 1960s, GE maintained a rough balance among its four key product areas: consumer products, defense and aerospace, industrial components and materials, and heavy capital goods. Though at the beginning of the 1960s, each of these areas accounted for roughly 25% of sales, defense and aerospace sales steadily declined as a percent of the total. While consumer products and heavy capital goods each continued to account for around a quarter of sales throughout the decade, industrial components and materials expanded to nearly a third by the late 1960s, while defense and aerospace shrank to under 20%—and to half that by the end of the 1970s.[72] GE management would become increasingly concerned about these trends over time, particularly as the slowdown of the late 1960s turned to crisis in the 1970s.

Nevertheless, in the 1960s GE filed an average of more than three patents *per day*. By 1968, the company had 170 operating departments focusing on separate aspects of world markets, including 3,000 categories of products and 200,000 different models and sizes. These were produced in 280 manufacturing plants in 33 US states, Puerto Rico, 5 Canadian provinces, and 22 other countries.[73] This created further impetus toward replacing the firm's highly complex Weberian administrative systems with flexible financial discipline and competitive markets.

[70] Mariana Mazzucato, *The Entrepreneurial State: Debunking Public vs. Private Sector Myths* (New York: Anthem Press, 2013); Fred Block, "Innovation and the Invisible Hand of Government," in *State of Innovation: The U.S. Government's Role in Technology Development*, ed. Fred Block and Matthew Keller (Routledge, 2015); Seymour Melman, *Pentagon Capitalism: The Political Economy of War* (New York: McGraw-Hill, 1970).

[71] General Electric, "1968 Annual Report," 5.

[72] The figures here are derived from GE's Annual Reports, 1960–1980.

[73] General Electric, "1968 Annual Report," 5.

At the same time, Cordiner's decentralization had caused the corporate finance function to grow "tremendously in stature and influence," since "decentralization required more financial controls to keep tabs on the separate departments."[74] Decentralization had thus generated new demands for *enlarged* administrative capacities, albeit located in the increasingly powerful corporate financial apparatus.

The push for decentralization became more forceful as the extent of the company's overreach became obvious at the end of the 1960s, having failed to generate greater profits despite increasing revenue by over $3 billion in three years. Not only were many of the ventures outright failures; even those that succeeded took much longer to do so than planners had anticipated. This, in turn, negatively impacted the company's credibility on Wall Street. To appease financiers and resolve funding problems as the company's cash position suffered, Borch appointed Reginald Jones as the firm's first Chief Financial Officer (CFO) in 1968. This signaled a dramatic consolidation of power within the firm's financial unit. Whereas "corporate finance had been a back-office function performed by treasurers or controllers, whose duties were confined to tasks like bookkeeping and preparing tax statements," the CFO was now the company's second-in-command, controlling vast institutional resources.[75]

Borch and Jones worked to systematically implement a formal model of "portfolio management," which signaled a critical shift in the "conception of control" within the company toward financialized management: the firm had evolved from a "system of production" to a "system of investment."[76] Furthermore, Borch and Jones' portfolio management model entailed not just *acquisition*, but also *divestment*. The sale of the failed computer business to Honeywell was in this respect "the first step toward the adoption of the company's strategic portfolio management systems." From that moment on, "GE's many divisions would be viewed as a portfolio of companies – analogous to an individual's stock portfolio – which

[74] O'Boyle, *At Any Cost*, 52.

[75] Dirk Zorn, "Here a Chief, There a Chief: The Rise of the CFO in the American Firm," *American Sociological Review* 69, no. 3 (June 1, 2004): 346; C. Fritz Foley and Michael Lemm, "The Role of the Chief Financial Officer," Harvard Business School Technical Note, June 2016.

[76] Neil Fligstein, *The Transformation of Corporate Control* (Cambridge, MA: Harvard University Press, 1993).

would be reviewed periodically for their strategic fit."[77] These businesses were not permanent components of a giant organization destined to become only larger, but rather flexible investments that could be freely restructured or sold off.

One way Borch sought to accomplish this was by marketizing the financial and management services provided by the functionally divided centralized corporate structure to the decentralized operating divisions. With the "Great Reorganization," Cordiner had "created a very large staff organization to provide consulting services to the decentralized units." This was necessary to build the capacities of the divisions as they became more autonomous, but it was also a means for continued centralized discipline and surveillance. Though "consulting services were free," operational managers often "resented being forced to use the staff organizations," as "these same individuals conducted the management and functional audits." This led to "many confrontations between corporate staff and the operating management."[78]

Borch resolved this by deepening market discipline. He divided the central corporate staff into two groups. The Executive Staff consisted of essential centralized functions for the firm as a whole: accounting, finance, legal, investor relations, executive manpower, and employee relations. The other was Corporate Consulting Services (CCS), which became an autonomous business unit that engaged in market exchanges with other such units within the firm. Individual operating units were expected to develop the services offered by CCS within their own functional divisions—including engineering, manufacturing, executive education, marketing, advertising and sales promotion, and strategic planning functions. To the extent that they continued to need centralized support to fill gaps in these capacities, business units could purchase such services from CCS. These services were also marketed externally to GE's customers and suppliers, as well as to non-profit organizations—further deepening the commodification of the company's financial capacities.

Cleaving CCS off as an autonomous business unit meant that it would have to cover its own costs and would thus face greater market discipline. Similarly, making business unit managers pay for CCS services, rather than granting these "for free" from central management, would force them to

[77] Rothschild, *The Secret to GE's Success*, 153.

[78] Rothschild, *The Secret to GE's Success*, 143.

be judicious in using such services. The expectation was, "if CCS had to sell its services and charge competitive prices, the size of its staff would be reduced, and only those who had unique skills and abilities would survive."[79]

Ironically, however, not only was CCS able to cover its expenses, it actually generated enough income to *grow* its operations. Nor was this just a matter of market "efficiency." For one thing, business unit managers opted for CCS services, even if its prices were not necessarily the lowest, partly as a result of their existing relationships with CCS personnel. These path-dependencies thus tended to resist market restructuring, despite pressure from the top. Nevertheless, by the end of the 1960s, "Borch's decentralization, as well as his endorsement of fee-based corporate services, contributed to making GE more like a confederation of independent, often competing businesses than like a single, coherent company."[80]

With the appointment of Jones as CFO, Borch created another task force and commissioned McKinsey & Company to develop a strategy to trim and rationalize the bureaucracy.[81] The task force sketched out a plan for further decentralization that aimed to overcome the limits of the Cordiner model. Cordiner had implemented a rule that product departments automatically had to be split into smaller units once their annual revenue exceeded $50 million. The task force found that this had generated not market efficiency, but administrative fragmentation. As a result, "many departments were internal suppliers and not 'businesses' at all," as they had no clear competitors or customers outside of the internal circuits in which they were embedded. The group suggested that the company's 125 product departments be reorganized into 43 "strategic business units," which must "serve real external markets" with "clearly identifiable customers and competitors."[82] Crucially, they should "be able to control their own destinies and initiate actions without having to rely on other GE organizations."

[79] Rothschild, *The Secret to GE's Success*, 144–45.

[80] Rothschild, *The Secret to GE's Success*, 146.

[81] O'Boyle, *At Any Cost*, 53.

[82] Rothschild, *The Secret to GE's Success*, 154.

According to the new model, top planners and external experts would present the "Big Picture," which would consist of overall corporate financial goals and objectives, to the SBUs at an annual conference. On this basis, SBU managers would then develop business plans autonomously and present them to top managers. In doing so, they were encouraged to "imagine that they were making a presentation to an investment banker to get funds for their business."[83] Business units were then given feedback on their strategies, which were reviewed by the CFO to make sure they "would help the company meet its investor and shareholder expectations."[84] Accomplishing this required further developing the planning capacities of the SBUs, which was accomplished by hiring strategic planners and developing a new management training program.

Once again, corporate restructuring would be characterized by simultaneous centralization and decentralization. While the distribution of investment funds (and other institutional support) would remain centralized, strategic planning for particular businesses would be thoroughly decentralized. This therefore meant a further shift within the firm toward financial control and market discipline. In place of a hierarchical bureaucracy in which planners would simply "tell [operational managers] what needed to be done, and they would do it," the company's organizational structure increasingly came to resemble a capital market, in which individual SBUs competed for investment.[85] If SBU managers behaved more like *owners* of individual firms, top executives became more like *investors*.

Yet SBUs were not independent businesses. They were protected, supported, and evaluated by centralized corporate structures. The corporation "incubated" these businesses, building their competitiveness over a relatively long time horizon while subjecting them to market discipline in a somewhat controlled manner within the context of the firm. By strategically allocating revenue among businesses, GE management flattened the business cycle, while "harvesting" revenue from mature businesses to support newer ventures. GE invested in these businesses more cheaply and in greater quantities than would have been the case if they were to independently raise capital on external financial markets. This "protection"

[83] Rothschild, *The Secret to GE's Success*, 163.

[84] Rothschild, *The Secret to GE's Success*.

[85] Rothschild, *The Secret to GE's Success*, 157; General Electric, "1972 Annual Report," 4.

for SBUs afforded by the corporate structure afforded GE a stability that, paradoxically, appealed to outside investors—which would become more important as growth slowed and GE became more reliant on external financing.

GE and the Emergence of Financial Hegemony

The relatively rapid evolution of corporate organization that was gaining steam by the 1970s was the result of a series of strategic responses to changing structural conditions rooted in the contradictions of managerial capitalism. This restructuring reflected the emerging structure of power within the capitalist class, especially the power of finance. Yet the new form of financial power was quite different from that which had characterized the finance capital period: it was far less centralized, less powerful relative to industrial firms, and its relationship to corporate governance more substantially mediated by institutions within which insiders retained considerable control. Similarly, industrial firms were much larger, more complex, and more powerful. This all placed a premium on insider knowledge, just as the lack of administrative and managerial capacity among industrial firms in the finance capital era had increased their dependence on the banks.

What was emerging was a form of *polyarchic financial hegemony*, in which constellations of competing financial institutions come together to exert broad influence and discipline on industrial corporations.[86] Financial hegemony was partly expressed through interlocking directorates possessed by financiers, but this hardly amounted to the webs of corporate control centered on individual investment banks that had existed during the finance capital era. Boards were themselves much less significant institutional spaces for organizing and expressing corporate control than they had been in the late nineteenth and early twentieth centuries, though they would become increasingly important over the 1970s as financial power

[86] William K. Carroll and Jean P. Sapinski, "Corporate Elite and Intercorporate Networks," in *The SAGE Handbook of Social Network Analysis*, ed. Peter J. Carrington and John Scott (London: Sage, 2011), 180–95; Scott, *Corporate Business and Capitalist Classes*, 139; Beth A. Mintz and Michael Schwartz, *The Power Structure of American Business* (Chicago: University of Chicago Press, 1987); Beth Mintz and Michael Schwartz, "Capital Flows and the Process of Financial Hegemony," *Theory and Society* 15, no. 1/2 (1986): 77–101; D. S. Glasberg and M. Schwartz, "Ownership and Control of Corporations," *Annual Review of Sociology* 9, no. 1 (1983): 311–32.

was consolidated. In one of his first moves in the job, in 1972 Jones began to implement a new Board of Directors committee structure, presented by the company as a concession to investors that would have the effect of "enabling your Directors to be more penetrating in their involvement in the business, as well as more informed and challenging in their appraisals of management's performance."[87]

However, corporate managerial structures were not merely subjected to greater external pressure, but also *changed from within* as institutional linkages to the external financial system deepened. While no major corporation had a CFO in 1963, beginning in the 1970s the trend began to sweep the business world, becoming all but ubiquitous by the 1990s—with diversified conglomerates in the lead, pointing to the significance of administrative decentralization as an institutional foundation for corporate financialization. This signaled "a fundamental redistribution of managerial roles, with greater relevance of financial considerations built into the executive structure and the decision-making process." "Financial" logics became increasingly paramount as CFOs "gained critical say in key strategic and operational decisions, from evaluating business unit performance, inventing new ways to leverage capital, managing acquisitions and divestitures, and fending off hostile takeover attempts, to serving as the company's primary ambassador to investors and financial analysts."[88]

This process was substantially accelerated by the 1971 abandonment of the Bretton Woods system of fixed exchange rates, based around pegging currencies to the value of the dollar, and the dollar to gold. The globally integrated financial system that emerged in its place created a need for extensive financial management capacities within the corporation to oversee flows of capital across internationally integrated networks of production and investment. The imperative to insure against the risks of unpredictable and potentially sudden currency value fluctuations in the context of floating exchange rates led to the rapid growth of derivatives markets, with these instruments emerging from obscurity over the 1970s to becoming "integral to corporate finance" in the 1980s.[89] Globalization

[87] General Electric, "1978 Annual Report," 5.

[88] Zorn, "Here a Chief, There a Chief," 347.

[89] Dick Bryan and Michael Rafferty, *Capitalism With Derivatives: A Political Economy of Financial Derivatives, Capital and Class* (Springer, 2005), 95; See also: Dennis Carlton, "Futures Markets: Their Purpose, Their History, Their Growth, Their Successes and

thus required industrial corporations to develop even more highly sophisticated financial capacities, and led them to become even more deeply embedded within the global financial system.

Most important for the return of financial power was the huge wave of concentration and centralization of equity in the hands of large financial institutions over the 1970s, fuelled especially by the massive pools of capital that emerged in the form of occupational pension funds.[90] Ironically, the proliferation of financialized pensions "reflected the strength of unions in collective bargaining in the 1960s," yet these victories for union power ended up contributing to the intensification of financial discipline on non-financial corporations and shifting the balance of class forces toward capital. The state, too, was essential to the tremendous growth of such funds: tax incentives for both corporations and workers played a significant role in the extension of pension plan coverage from a fifth of the private sector workforce in 1950 to almost half by 1970.[91] By the 1970s, pension funds had become the largest single holders of corporate stock, a process of concentration that would be complemented by the growth of personal pension accounts and mutual funds.[92] As a result, "institutional investors" came to either own directly, or indirectly manage, massive blocks of investment.

If the fragmentation of shareholdings had allowed internal managers to remain largely unchallenged by "outsiders" over the managerial era, the concentration of shareholdings by institutional investors reversed this. The sheer scale of these holdings prevented these investors from dumping shares of underperforming firms, as it would be impossible to sell such a large number of shares at once without depreciating their value. Such institutional investors therefore had to develop new means to coordinate with, and pressure, management. This was reflected in the growth

Failures," *Journal of Futures Markets* 4 (1984): 209–47; John Parsons, "Futures and Derivatives Markets" (Charles River Associates International, 1999), www.crai.com.

[90] Useem, *Investor Capitalism*.

[91] Panitch and Gindin, *The Making of Global Capitalism*, 121.

[92] Peter F. Drucker, *The Unseen Revolution: How Pension Fund Socialism Came to America* (New York, NY: Harper & Row, 1976), 1–2; Edward S. Herman, *Corporate Control, Corporate Power: A Twentieth Century Fund Study* (Cambridge, UK: Cambridge University Press, 1982), 138; David M. Kotz, *Bank Control of Large Corporations in the United States* (Berkeley, CA: University of California Press, 1978); Jeremy Rifkin and Randy Barber, *The North Will Rise Again* (Boston, MA: Beacon Press, 1978), 10, 234; Scott, *Corporate Business and Capitalist Classes*, 67.

of corporate "investor relations" functions overseen by the CFO, which contributed to the further financialization of the corporation. In addition to supplying data and making forecasts for investors, CFOs pushed forward the disciplines within the firm necessary to meet these expectations. This included ensuring that financiers "got their cut" in the form of interest, dividends, and asset valuations—shifting the distribution of profits across the capitalist class as a whole toward the financial sector, and culminating in what would later be called "shareholder value."

Tellingly, when Borch retired in 1972, he chose Jones, the company's first CFO, as his replacement. This was in part to appease Wall Street, which "was still not convinced the company was on the right track."[93] Jones' subsequent attentiveness to investors throughout his tenure was unprecedented. Though Cordiner had established the Office of Investor Relations in the 1950s, under Jones the office took on a new life, becoming a central nexus between the internal structure of the corporation and the financial sector. Investor Relations staff regularly interviewed Wall Street analysts to "determine what they were expecting" and then reviewed "all of the business strategies and their financial forecasts to determine if these would yield the results that were expected by Wall Street." Key to achieving this, the new management team believed, was continuing to push forward operational decentralization. Indeed, one of Jones' first policies was to require all SBUs to employ their own full-time strategic planners.[94]

Over the first half of the new decade, GE continued to struggle with "a deteriorating economy and the continued inflationary spiral [which] made it increasingly difficult to offset rapid cost increases."[95] Skyrocketing energy prices with the 1973 oil shock made matters significantly worse, changing the worries about inflationary pressures of earlier years into near-panic. At the same time, the emerging fiscal crisis of the state meant that an ever-growing portion of GDP was consumed by government expenditure. On top of the profit squeeze generated by declining productivity, wage militancy, international competition, and rising energy costs came also the increasing fiscal burden of supporting the New Deal state. This made it harder to form the necessary investment capital—and

[93] Rothschild, *The Secret to GE's Success*, 167.

[94] Rothschild, *The Secret to GE's Success*, 171–72.

[95] General Electric, "1974 Annual Report," 4.

further increased the firm's reliance on external finance. As GE reported in 1974:

> no thoughtful person can deny a sense of disquiet about the deep changes that are taking place in the world economy. Persistent inflation and the swift transfer of wealth from the industrialized nations to the oil-producing nations are causing great political and economic instability. Governments have promised more than their economic systems can produce. While demands have increased, the needs of producers have been ignored. Meanwhile the world's growing population presses hard against its available resources of energy, food and materials. Thus today there is an urgent need for problem-solving technology, fresh capital, organizational know-how and entrepreneurial commitment on a global scale.[96]

Nevertheless, the report continued, "in this context, we see General Electric as uniquely positioned both in terms of its long-range business prospects and as a force for human progress." Indeed, there was good reason to expect that the crisis presented GE with opportunities as well as costs. For one thing, the company produced the very labor-saving technologies that would be necessary to increase productivity and restore profits. Similarly, rising energy costs led to a renewed push to shift to nuclear power, as well as to undertake extensive research into alternative energies, both of which potentially represented significant opportunities for GE.

It was on this basis that Jones' management team "selected for special support a number of internally developed business ventures that have unusual long-term potential." These ventures were rooted in what were then seen as the "traditional strengths of the General Electric Company: sound accounting practices; a solid financial structure; a reputation for quality and service; a tradition of technological leadership; a worldwide range of operations; a strong outside Board; and a cadre of sophisticated managers at all levels of the organization." The key opportunities identified included nuclear power and energy, health care; land, sea, and air transportation; materials; computer services; and financial services.

It is clear from this assessment of the company's institutional strengths and strategic outlook that top executives understood financialized management as both a core operation and an important source of

[96] General Electric, "1974 Annual Report," 4.

competitive advantage. So too did management extol the penetration of market discipline throughout the organization, "a strategic planning system that allocates resources on a basis that favours businesses with high potential for earnings growth… and leads to the divestment of less promising operations."[97] In the context of the state spending cutbacks that GE itself, along with other major corporations, would insist were necessary to address the fiscal crisis, the growing force of competitive pressures at all levels of the organization increasingly led it to invest in financial services and industrial components—sectors that continued to grow faster than GDP.

That finance was growing faster, and capturing a larger share of profits, than industry reinforced the shift toward financialized strategies. As GE management put it, the "strategic allocation of GE interests and resources" was intended "to achieve growth that exceeds that of the U.S. economy as a whole."[98] The shifting balance of economic growth—with "declining profits for non-financial corporations" and finance capturing a larger share of the total—therefore further incentivized GE to invest in the financial sector.[99] By 1970, GECC had fully evolved into a business unit in its own right, with operations extending considerably beyond its initial ancillary role in supporting GE's industrial operations.

Unlike other business units, GECC was structured not as a corporate division, but a subsidiary company—even issuing its own annual reports.[100] As GE reported in 1972, GECC had "steadily expanded from its original base in GE consumer goods financing [to] become a broad-based, widely-diversified financial service business." By that time, GECC had nine divisions of its own to "serve a range of customers from heavy goods to the retail industry"—and the majority of the products it financed were manufactured by companies other than GE.[101] GECC earnings continued to grow through the 1970s, making up 6% of the company total by 1977—a far cry from the 50% comprised by its successor, GE Capital, at the end of the subsequent decade, but nevertheless significant enough for management to continually present GECC as one of the

[97] General Electric, "1974 Annual Report," 5.

[98] General Electric, "1977 Annual Report," 4.

[99] General Electric, "1975 Annual Report," 9.

[100] General Electric, "1970 Annual Report," 4.

[101] General Electric, "1972 Annual Report," 32.

company's core businesses and most important strategic growth areas.[102] At the end of the 1970s, GE was boasting that GECC was "an innovative leader in credit markets," and had "broadened its scope so that its earnings are better able to withstand the pressures of slower consumer markets and higher interest rates."[103]

That most companies responded to the slowdown by increasing investment to add manufacturing capacity and improve productivity worked to the benefit of GE, especially its fast-growing Industrial Components and Systems Division. Already by 1970 "the many interfaces between General Electric and industry [made] this category the largest sector of the Company's business."[104] Sales in this area increased by 21%—and earnings by 40%—in the year 1974 alone, comprising 29% of total corporate sales and 34% of total earnings. As such, it is not surprising that GE managers saw advocating for tax breaks on new investment and accelerated depreciation schedules as part of their "social responsibility to participate actively and forcefully in the evolving public debate over major economic and social issues of the day."[105] Indeed, this meant that "in the battle to bring inflation under control, General Electric technology provides one powerful weapon: innovations that increase industry's productivity and cost-efficiency in the manufacture of goods."[106]

Conversely, sales and earnings from military and space programs continued to decline—dropping to just 10% of total earnings by 1974, where they would hover for the remainder of the decade.[107] To compensate, the company expanded into "other government markets," including the departments of Health, Education, and Welfare; Housing and Urban Development; the Interior; the Environmental Protection Agency; and

[102] General Electric, "1977 Annual Report," 5.

[103] General Electric, "1978 Annual Report," 8.

[104] General Electric, "1970 Annual Report," 14.

[105] General Electric, "1972 Annual Report," 5.

[106] General Electric, "1974 Annual Report," 14–15.

[107] General Electric, "1972 Annual Report," 20; General Electric, "1974 Annual Report," 15; General Electric, "1975 Annual Report"; General Electric, "1976 Annual Report"; General Electric, "1977 Annual Report"; General Electric, "1978 Annual Report"; General Electric, "1979 Annual Report."

the National Oceanographic and Aviation Administration.[108] The long-term structural problem was clear: resolving the fiscal crisis of the state would mean state spending growing less quickly than GDP. Thus, if GE was looking to grow *faster* than GDP it would have to look elsewhere. The contradictions of this were manifest in the firm's political stance, which paired broad demands for cuts with an insistence on increasing investment through the industrial policy system that was more intimately coordinated with business.

Such a revitalized industrial policy was framed as being necessary to "reverse the decline in U.S. technological leadership."[109] As GE stated in its 1975 Annual Report, "the principal reason why many nations seek U.S. gas turbines, nuclear power systems and jet engines is simply that they are the world's best." Accordingly, "the future economic health of the U.S. depends on a vigorous research and development effort and the product leadership that flows from it." The report went on to cite a Department of Commerce study that found that "the United States is perhaps the only advanced industrial nation in the free world which has not undertaken national programs to stimulate technology development in the civilian sector." Furthermore, the 16% decline in state R&D spending over the previous decade had the effect of "substantially weakening the creative government/industry/university partnership of the 1950s and '60s." In order to reverse this, "the creative national teamwork that waned after putting men on the moon needs urgently to be rekindled and redirected toward strengthening the U.S. in productivity, innovation, and international competitiveness."[110]

This call was more than a little inspired by the success of the Japanese state's centralized industrial policy in generating competitive high-tech industries. State officials and business executives were initially mixed on whether to increase state support for US industry through a better funded and more centralized industrial policy system, or to pressure other states to reduce such support through multilateral negotiations aimed at eliminating what would later be referred to as "non-tariff barriers" to trade. As we shall see, supporters of a new industrial policy included some within the Department of Commerce who sought to reverse the long decline of

[108] General Electric, "1970 Annual Report," 19.

[109] General Electric, "1975 Annual Report," 17.

[110] General Electric, "1975 Annual Report," 18–20.

that agency's position within the hierarchy of state apparatuses, as well as the Export–Import Bank, which was responsible for providing export credit to foreign purchasers of large and expensive US exports, such as those produced by GE.

Despite these concerns, GE was still a leading spender on R&D, exceeding $890 million in 1974, 60% of which was financed by the state—a greater share than a decade before.[111] The following year, this grew to $938 million, almost two-thirds of which was state financed.[112] In 1977, at the same time GE announced that it had for the first time cracked $1 billion in after-tax earnings, it reported R&D expenditures of $1.16 billion.[113] Nevertheless, as military spending declined as a proportion of GDP, efforts were redoubled to better integrate state and corporate planning so as to more efficiently convert basic research into marketable commodities, and squeeze more economic value from the industrial policy system.[114] This took the form of a push within the company by the early 1980s to decentralize R&D functions such that they were more closely connected to product departments. But this came at the expense of the basic research, significantly removed from immediate market applicability, that had been a foundation of GE's technological dynamism since World War II.

International sales remained a bright spot for GE in the 1970s, as it continued delivering power generation systems across Western Europe, Latin America, and the Far East. By 1975, sales outside the US accounted for nearly a quarter of GE's earnings.[115] Europe remained GE's largest export market, though high growth rates in peripheral states meant that these increasingly became a priority. Beginning in the early 1970s, sales in the Middle East and North Africa grew at 50% per year.[116] This was because "developing countries… in various stages of building and modernizing their infrastructures… represent a good match for GE technologies."[117] GE provided the massive capital goods required, for

[111] General Electric, "1974 Annual Report," 22.

[112] General Electric, "1975 Annual Report," 20.

[113] General Electric, "1977 Annual Report," 4.

[114] General Electric, "1974 Annual Report," 18–20. d.

[115] General Electric, "1975 Annual Report," 18.

[116] General Electric, "1975 Annual Report," 18.

[117] General Electric, "1977 Annual Report," 20.

example, by Latin American states' "Import Substitution Industrialization" strategies, as well as all manner of core public infrastructure sought by developing states.[118]

Thus, GE built the physical infrastructures that integrated peripheral zones within the world economic system. Just as important, however, was its role in constructing the networks of international trade and investment that bound global capitalism together under American hegemony. The result was an international system comprised not merely of external relations between closed national economies, but rather united by flows of capital that penetrated different social formations from *within*, creating *internal* linkages among states. Ironically, in this way, American capital paved the way for the integration of peripheral states within the American empire *as a consequence* of the "national development strategies" that built up "national" capitalist classes. Foreign Direct Investment led American capital to become a class force in other social formations, contributing to the development of these bourgeoisies and assimilating them to international flows of trade and finance. These bourgeoisies themselves subsequently undertook to invest abroad, demanding greater integration with the world market and liberalization.

The economic stagnation in the US only pushed this process further, as capital internationalized in order to reduce costs and enter faster-growing markets—at least, that is, until the slowdown spread around the world. As "the U.S. economy reached the bottom of its most severe postwar recession" at the middle of the decade, "many other countries served by [GE] experienced equally severe downturns." In light of the intensifying "cost-price squeeze," GE was forced to further find ways to "cut back expenses rigorously" while striving to maintain its "level of activity in corporate research and development and our funding of promising new ventures."[119] Nevertheless, diversification, if not internationalization, helped the company achieve a modicum of stability during the recession—insulating GE from economic contraction as its overall sales and earnings reflected the cumulative result of investments in a variety of sectors.[120]

[118] General Electric, "1974 Annual Report," 21.

[119] General Electric, "1975 Annual Report," 4.

[120] General Electric, "1975 Annual Report," 4.

While this reinforced the company's financialization, as discussed above, the memory of the cash-flow problems that had so damaged the company's reputation on Wall Street in the late 1960s led GE to seek to "add a stable, predictable cash-flow generator to the GE portfolio."[121] The situation in the mid-1970s made coal seem like an ideal option. The emergence of OPEC as a geopolitical force following the 1973 Arab oil embargo appeared to leave the US politically vulnerable, and made "energy independence" a political hot-button issue. On this basis, GE pushed for the expansion of nuclear energy alongside "stepped-up research" into "advanced energy sources such as solar, geothermal steam and fusion." Meanwhile, the company argued that conservation efforts, which threatened to reduce energy consumption, should be downplayed, as these "cannot alone meet the energy demands" of the country.

Nuclear energy had finally become "marginally profitable," even as orders for new plants ground to a halt. Nevertheless, the victories of the environmental movement in expanding regulations left the future of the industry uncertain. Such public aversion to nuclear power appeared to make coal even more important to the future of energy-hungry US and global industry, and potentially more lucrative. It therefore made sense to acquire a strong market position in coal, uranium, natural gas, and oil. GE accomplished this through a merger with the mining giant Utah International—a merger worth $1.9 billion, the largest in the history of capitalism up until that time.[122] Jones believed that the acquisition would satisfy GE's strategic need for a stable cash-flow generator—a goal known firsthand to Utah CEO Edmund Littlefield, who was also a member of GE's Board of Directors.[123]

Despite Jones' focus on investor concerns and expectations, the announcement of the merger came as a complete surprise to both the financial sector and the government. Nevertheless, Wall Street came to agree "the deal would be a beauty" after they "got over their surprise." Similarly, antitrust officials were "miffed over the fact that neither firm bothered to clue them in before announcing the proposed merger."[124]

121 Rothschild, *The Secret to GE's Success*, 169.

122 General Electric, "1976 Annual Report," 17–18; Rothschild, *The Secret to GE's Success*, 169.

123 Rothschild, *The Secret to GE's Success*, 169.

124 "MERGERS: GE's Surprise Package," *Newsweek*, December 29, 1975.

Although at the time "the Justice Department [did] not look kindly on corporate giants acquiring other corporate giants," it approved the merger on the condition that GE set up "a separate company with a separate board to run Utah's uranium business." GE, of course, would "still reap the profits."[125] There could hardly have been a stronger indication that the crisis in state-capital relations, which had been so clearly signified by the Great Electrical Conspiracy, was a thing of the past.

As *Forbes* saw it, although the company had been "burned in computers and stymied in nuclear energy… Jones has opened great new prospect for GE." As a result, the magazine predicted, echoing the enthusiasm about the deal that had broken out on Wall Street, "ten, 20 years from now, they'll be talking about GE's historic corporate decision."[126] This would turn out to be correct—but not for the reasons the magazine expected. In fact, the deal would be another calamity for GE, from which it would take years to extricate itself. Rather than booming, Utah's coal business began to decline, failing to serve as the cash-generator Jones had hoped for. This mega-deal would be a key part of Jones' legacy, as "it was left to [Jones' successor, Jack] Welch to make the decision to divest Utah International."[127]

By the end of the 1970s, the world economy was again booming, and GE's extensive and diverse internationalization was paying off. Fully one-third of the company's 1978 revenues were derived from international sales.[128] The growing importance of these international operations for the company reinforced its interest in seeking stability and protection for foreign investment, and in supporting the American state's efforts to promote global economic liberalization. This proved to be more significant to GE and other major multinational corporations than the drive for domestic subsidies, which were increasingly defined in these very same multilateral trade agreements as non-tariff barriers to trade, and curtailed. This included subsidized Ex-Im Bank credit, of which GE was one of the largest beneficiaries. Yet by the end of the decade, the company was

[125] "GE-Utah International: More Than Just Another Merger," *Forbes*, January 15, 1977.

[126] "GE-Utah International: More Than Just Another Merger."

[127] General Electric, "1977 Annual Report," 4.

[128] General Electric, "1978 Annual Report."

supporting the free movement of investment and explicitly calling for the reduction of NTBs.

Through all these changes, the power of finance continued to grow, and investors were increasingly able to exert discipline on inside managers—including pushing for more substantial forms of manager accountability and "good governance." The subordination of Boards of Directors to insiders over the managerial period had been a reflection of the empowerment of industrial managers over investors. Now, with the rising power of the financial sector, Boards once again became more significant as institutional venues for expressing investor power, helping to assemble constellations of financial interests to influence the financing and governance of industrial assets. In its 1978 Annual Report, GE felt compelled to address pressures for Boards to take on a more expansive role:

> One issue that has been coming into increasing prominence directly concerns the relationships among share owners, their boards of directors and business managers. The shorthand term for this issue is 'corporate governance'...the focal point for this issue is whether sufficiently strong control mechanisms are in place to make sure that managers perform responsibly in the best interests of share owners, customers, employees and the other constituencies of business. ...the most substantive issue at present centers on the role and composition of corporate boards of directors. The critics claim that corporate boards, as presently constituted and organized, provide only a 'rubber stamp' function, automatically giving managers the approvals they need. ... This criticism does not seem to apply to General Electric. From the Company's beginnings, GE share owners have been represented by a Board made up predominantly of Directors from outside the Company. Your managers through the years can verify that the GE Board has been vigorous and highly independent in its vigilance on behalf of the interests of share owners and the public generally. ... Nevertheless, your Board has accepted corporate governance as a valid issue. Your Directors' early sensitivity has led to a structure of the General Electric Board that meets the objectives both of enlarging its role and of facilitating its work.[129]

The defensiveness in this statement is unmistakable. It is true that the GE Board had long been comprised almost entirely of outside directors.

[129] General Electric, "1978 Annual Report," 5.

This set it apart from others and was an important consequence of its diversification—maintaining links with suppliers, customers, and financiers across a wide range of economic sectors. It had also been an institutional foundation for GE's political centrality throughout the managerial period. Nevertheless, with the rise of finance, investors were making new demands on corporations to add outside directors and strengthen Boards. Like other industrial firms, GE—the preeminent managerial firm—was now feeling the pressure to pay still greater attention of shareholder interests. The stage was set for the "shareholder value" revolution of the 1980s, of which GE's Jack Welch would be the most prominent exponent.

CHAPTER 7

The Business Roundtable and the End of Managerialism

The decade-long "stagflation" crisis of the 1970s was characterized by the combination of inflation and economic stagnation. As productivity growth fell, union wage militancy squeezed profits, constraining investment and growth. In this context, the long looming "fiscal crisis of the state" became increasingly acute, as the taxation necessary to support the New Deal state, along with the mounting regulatory costs that had resulted from "new left" victories around the environment and labor rights, became increasingly burdensome. Policymakers and business sought to free up capital for investment by slashing taxes, cutting spending, and rolling back regulations. Similarly, the Nixon, Ford, and Carter administrations hoped that wage and price controls would allow them to "muddle through" as they worked out a strategy for disciplining labor and imposing wage restraint. But as the crisis dragged on, such a plan was not forthcoming from either the state or business.

As it became clear that a return to the "normal" that had existed through the postwar Golden Age was not on the cards, it was increasingly difficult to avoid the recognition that the only alternative was to provoke a recession that would raise unemployment and discipline labor—a painful prospect for business and state officials alike. This eventually came in the form of the 1979 "Volcker Shock," when Fed chair Paul Volcker hiked interest rates to unprecedented levels. As unemployment

© The Author(s), under exclusive license to Springer Nature Switzerland AG 2022

S. Maher, *Corporate Capitalism and the Integral State*, Marx, Engels, and Marxisms,
https://doi.org/10.1007/978-3-030-83772-3_7

climbed, and the economy registered negative growth as tens of thousands of firms went out of business, capital fell into line. This radical step marked the end of controls and the transition to "neoliberalism," animated above all by the conviction that only a return to liberalization could restore "business confidence" and economic growth—and that a dramatically empowered state economic apparatus would have to play a more active role in underwriting and supporting markets.

It was thus the crucible of class struggle, not state officials or corporate lobbyists seeking to impose Hayek's ideas, which led to neoliberal policies. Neither those within the state nor those managing corporations had anything like a ready-made plan to end the decade-long crisis. Indeed, "few executives accurately understood the degree of change they faced."[1] Nor did state officials in the early 1970s see how extensive, or how permanent, the restructuring would have to be. Rather, throughout the decade, state agencies and their business allies reluctantly worked to maintain a fraught consensus around wage and price controls. To accomplish this, the Treasury Department and the Federal Reserve helped organize the Business Roundtable (BR) in 1972. But the BR would also serve as a pivotal venue for developing a consensus among business and the state around a path out of crisis. Rather than lobbying the state for a specific agenda, the BR supported policy planning within the ascendent financial apparatus, working with state officials to *develop* policy and build political consensus.

Once again, GE was at the center of this process of integral state organization. CEO Fred Borch and his successor, Reginald Jones, were key leaders of the BR from its origins through its first decade. This was not without contradictions. Since the formation of the BAC, a small group of "corporate liberals" leading non-financial corporations embedded within the industrial policy system had been central to building class consensus, especially during times of crisis. This same group dominated the BR, though finance was now represented there as well. However, by the late 1970s, the BR sought—unsuccessfully—to defend non-financial managers from growing power of financiers, which was reinforced by the increasingly muscular Securities and Exchange Commission. The state's ability to organize an "unstable equilibrium of compromise" between these fractions was essential for the success of the Volcker Shock, as well as

[1] Waterhouse, *Lobbying America*, 78.

the establishment of financial hegemony over the subsequent neoliberal period.

The Pay Board and the Construction Users Anti-Inflation Roundtable

The reaction against the New Deal state emerged from within the state itself. Far from merely being electoral theater designed to give the Republicans a boost at the end of Eisenhower's term, the prosecution of the "Great Electrical Conspiracy" turned out to be just the beginning of a new wave of antitrust enforcement aimed at reinvigorating price competition. By 1968, the Department of Justice had put "the full weight of its institutional prestige, and of antitrust ideology, behind the public critique of the anti-competitive character" of New Deal regulations.[2]

But it was increasingly powerful and autonomous state regulatory agencies themselves that were "the most enthusiastic destroyers of the regulatory structure," responding both to the perceived inefficiencies of the regulatory system and growing concerns over the fiscal crisis of the state. The regulatory apparatus had grown massively as a result of the successful struggles of labor and the "new left" over the 1960s, including a "shop floor worker rebellion" that produced "a battery of legislative impositions on corporations in the areas of occupational health and safety and industrial pollution," as well as the consumer protection and environmental movements, all of which had "considerably burdened the regulatory agencies." In order to implement these programs, the number of federal regulatory personnel increased in 1970–1975 from under 10,000 to over 50,000.[3]

At the same time, the integral state was dramatically restructured and expanded. A growing number of corporations opened full-time public affairs offices in Washington, DC, known as "Washington Representatives." While 100 corporations had such offices in 1968, over 500 did a decade later. Only 175 firms had registered lobbyists in Washington in 1971; this rose to 2,445 by 1982. Similarly, the number of corporate Political Action Committees (PACs) increased from under

[2] Michael Moran, *The Politics of the Financial Services Revolution: The USA, UK and Japan* (New York: Palgrave Macmillan, 1991), 43.

[3] Panitch and Gindin, *The Making of Global Capitalism*, 141–42.

300 in 1976 to over 1,200 by the middle of 1980. The Chamber of Commerce, comprised primarily of smaller capitalists, doubled in membership between 1974 and 1980, while its budget tripled. The membership of the National Federation of Independent Business likewise doubled between 1970 and 1979. Meanwhile, the leaders of the National Association of Manufacturers (NAM) recognized that decades of anti-New Deal rejectionism had only marginalized the organization from the centers of power—and thus "how far the group had to go to... cultivate allies within government rather than simply screaming from outside the gates of power."[4]

Trade union militancy, rising regulatory costs, state spending, and taxation were all of great concern to business as growth slowed. Yet it is misleading to frame these factors as simply catalyzing an "organizational counteroffensive" autonomously initiated by business seeking to roll back the New Deal.[5] Rather, the growth of business associations unfolded as part of a dialectical process of state restructuring—and was even in many respects a *consequence* of the expansion of the state regulatory apparatus. As the range of firms and sectors impacted by state regulations increased, so did the need for state-corporate coordination. Not only were a greater number of firms now motivated to ensure their interests were heard by the legislators and regulators crafting the rules, but policymakers themselves depended upon this input to craft sound policy—and get it through Congress. Regulatory agencies also depended upon constant coordination with industry to implement their mandates. The need for increased coordination with business by an expanding regulatory system, along with pressures for more open and "transparent" government, was reflected in such measures as the Legislative Reorganization Act of 1970 and the Federal Advisory Committee Act of 1972. These acts encouraged the growth and formalization of business associations, redefining the legal modalities, and opening new institutional channels, for contact between corporations and the state, while generating an explosion of formal federal "advisory commissions."[6]

[4] Waterhouse, *Lobbying America*, 55–60.

[5] Drutman, *The Business of America Is Lobbying*; Waterhouse, *Lobbying America*; Mizruchi, *The Fracturing of the American Corporate Elite*; Phillips-Fein and Zelizer, *What's Good for Business*; Phillips-Fein, *Invisible Hands: The Businessmen's Crusade Against the New Deal*.

[6] Waterhouse, *Lobbying America*, 48.

After the BAC's split from Commerce in 1962, the most significant change in the integral state was the creation of the BR a decade later—which united "the CEOs of the country's largest corporations into a singular political powerhouse that would make an indelible imprint on the history of business and politics in the United States."[7] The BR was formed through a merger between three overlapping integral state organizations that had taken shape by the end of the 1960s: the Construction User's Anti-Inflation Roundtable (CUAIR), which had grown out of Boulware's "Wise Men" group; the Labour Law Study Committee (LLSC), originating in Cordiner's efforts on the BAC to coordinate a response to CIO-led labor union struggles; and the elite "March Group" of CEOs from the top firms, which had evolved out of Cordiner's exclusive "Links Club." After the formative efforts of Cordiner and Boulware, General Electric CEO Fred Borch, CFO Reginald Jones, and VP Virgil Day had been prominent within each of these organizational predecessors to the BR.

After he left the company in 1961, Boulware's apprentices Virgil Day and Jack Parker had been promoted as Vice Presidents to take his place. Day's extensive participation in Boulware's "Wise Men" meetings had helped him become one of the most well-connected executives in the country, known in corporate boardrooms and social clubs as well as in the halls of Washington, DC. Day formed the LLSC in 1965 in response to the threat of repeal of Taft-Hartley's "right-to-work" provisions, building on the organizing undertaken by Cordiner. The organization grew quickly from its origins as an informal lunch group to include approximately 60 member companies, represented by public affairs or labor-relations executives—effectively full-time participants in the public–private networks of power that comprised an important dimension of the integral state.

Day, who had long served as GE's representative in NLRB hearings and proceedings, was also a leading member of the CUAIR.[8] The CUAIR was another foundational institutional antecedent for the BR, incorporating medium and small capitalists at the local level. Chaired by Roger Blough, the former chair of US Steel, the CUAIR was founded

[7] Waterhouse, *Lobbying America*, 77.

[8] Evans, *The Education of Ronald Reagan*, 98, 136; Waterhouse, *Lobbying America*, 79–80, 86.

in 1969 to fight the first signs of the inflation crisis, which were then especially emerging in the construction sector. Construction contractors were weak and highly fragmented, and apparently at the mercy of the militant construction unions—leading wage increases in that sector to significantly outstrip the national average, and constituting an important engine of inflation across the economy as a whole. The CUAIR served as a means for large corporations to discipline construction contractors (and in turn their workers) by integrating them more tightly within production systems controlled by the big firms.

Just a few months after the CUAIR was launched, the 1970 Economic Stabilization Act (ESA) authorized the President to act to stabilize prices, rents, wages, salaries, interest rates, dividends, and other transfers. It created a Pay Board and a Price Commission to formulate nonbinding guidelines for wages and prices, respectively. With the passage of the ESA, the CUAIR effectively became a parastate institution as an appendage of the Pay Board, organizing business representation on that body.[9] The extent to which the Pay Board consolidated within the state apparatus the networks constituted through CUAIR is clear from the fact that Day himself would become the lead business representative on the panel.[10]

Part of Day's work as Chairman of the CUAIR Coordinating Committee was to spread the gospel of capitalist class cohesion, and to build the networks across business associations necessary to achieve it. The first issue of the CUAIR *Report*, five months after the passage of the ESA, summarized Day's call to action:

> Day contended that the nation can no longer afford to allow construction to continue 'on its reckless course,' adding that exhortation obviously has failed to rectify the situation and that bold action is needed aimed directly at improving the basic foundation of the industry. Focus of the effort, he said, must be on breaking the 'bottleneck of demand for labor.' ...[He] charged that the building trades unions – 'the personnel department of the industry' – are the principle culprits in the problem, chiefly through operation of the apprentice system.[11]

9 "Construction Users Anti-Inflation Roundtable Report," January 25, 1972.; "Construction Users Anti-Inflation Roundtable Report," January 28, 1972.

10 "Construction Users Anti-Inflation Roundtable Report," January 25, 1972.

11 "Construction Users Anti-Inflation Roundtable Report," December 7, 1970, 2.

The construction sector was a "giant in distress," and the ineffectiveness of the ESA in addressing the root of the problem was already becoming clear. As "existing medications have been too mild for all but the most patient of physicians," Day contended, "radical surgery" would be required to address union power in the building trades.

Yet the CUAIR refrained from explicitly calling for wage controls. In Congressional testimony in February 1971, for example, Blough emphasized that "skyrocketing wage settlements in construction [are] the most 'blameworthy' cause of the nation's inflationary problems and warn[ed] that unless the trend in construction is changed, 'the game is up for changing the trend in all wages.'" Yet he "quickly dismissed" a suggestion of a "wage-price control approach to the problem" as "unmanageable and undesirable under current conditions." Instead, Blough believed that the state could zero in on the "fountainhead of the wage problem" by increasing the supply of skilled workers available through new training programs, and ending the apprentice and hiring hall systems that were key mechanisms through which unions regulated the supply of construction labor. The attack on construction unions was cloaked in the language of increasing opportunities for "minority workers" who suffered from the "exclusionary practices" of the hiring hall and apprentice systems. Assistant Secretary of Labor Arthur A. Fletcher declared in a roundtable meeting that "the era of discriminatory union hiring practices has ended, to be followed by a 'great influx' of minority workers into the construction trades." As a result, "the institutional systems which have supported invidious racial discrimination in the construction industry are being destroyed."

The extent of the cooperation between the administration and the CUAIR was clear from Nixon's suspension of the Davis-Bacon Act, which required the government to pay the "prevailing wage" in a given region for construction contracts, immediately following Blough's testimony calling for this. As Blough told the same Roundtable meeting: "Washington is on your side."[12]

Nixon had come to office explicitly committed to curbing inflation, even if that meant bringing unemployment above 4%. He shared Fed chair William McChesney Martin's concerns about the "credibility gap over our capacity and willingness to maintain restraint." By hiking the

[12] "Construction Users Anti-Inflation Roundtable Report," February 17, 1971.

key funds rate to 9% at the beginning of 1970, the Fed had "seemed ready to do what in fact it would only do a decade later with the Volcker Shock": provoking a recession that would sharply increase unemployment and enforce wage restraint. Yet when this caused the first financial crisis in a decade—including the bankruptcy of Penn Central Transportation, the country's sixth largest corporation and largest bankruptcy to date—the Fed "quickly and drastically reversed direction." While the ability for companies like GE and IBM to offer relatively high interest rates on private bond markets made it easy for them to raise capital, such sources of funding could quickly dry up when the Fed raised rates. Consequently, incoming Fed chair Arthur Burns shifted from what he called "the policy of extreme restraint" to one designed to "get the large banks to furnish cash to corporations that were unable to sell their corporate bonds," as the federal funds rate was slashed by five full points over the 1970s.[13]

After the Fed's reversal, Burns "became the leading advocate" of a wage and price controls regime. Such a program also had the support of Paul Volcker at the Treasury Department, as well as his boss, Secretary John Connally. In mid-February, a joint memo from Housing and Urban Development Secretary George Romney, Secretary of Commerce Maurice Stans, Secretary of Transportation John Volpe, and Postmaster General Winton Blount warned Nixon that "wage settlements will continue to be excessive unless some action is taken in this area beyond that resulting from fiscal and monetary action."[14] These cabinet officials thereby recognized that more needed to be done to support business in pushing back against labor through some kind of direct corporatist arrangement, rather than the more indirect tools offered by traditional fiscal and monetary policy. However, implementing even limited economic controls remained controversial. Two days later, Council of Economic Advisors Chairman Paul McCracken argued that although there was "wide support for price and wage controls even in the business community," such a course was simply unacceptable. He preferred "to reassure the public of the soundness of the anti-inflation policy without embarking on a struggle with business and labor that cannot be won in a free economy."[15]

[13] Panitch and Gindin, *The Making of Global Capitalism*, 138–40.

[14] George Romney, "George Romney to President Nixon," February 14, 1970, Record Group 56, Entry Al 719, Box #3, National Archives College Park, MD.

[15] Paul McCracken, "Memorandum for the President," February 16, 1970, Record Group 56, Entry Al 719, Box #3, National Archives College Park, MD.

At the same time, inflationary pressures continued to strain the dollar's peg to gold, which was the cornerstone of the Bretton Woods monetary order. In June 1971, there was still a prevailing consensus within the administration around the need to avoid "the worst of outcomes – which would have been commitment to restriction of the domestic economy and widespread controls both at home and abroad."[16] The search for a way to avoid this involved developing a "plan for strengthening the leadership in the Treasury Department" within the state.[17] Accordingly, Connally requested "more top-level support" for Treasury from the White House Office of Management and Budget, as well as backing for "legislation to upgrade some of the top positions."[18] Treasury's growing prominence was registered in its leadership within the Quadriad, an interagency group that brought Connally together with the heads of the Fed (Arthur Burns), the Council of Economic Advisors (Paul McCracken), and the OMB.[19] Treasury was also at the center of integral state coordination, as Connally worked with the BC to establish a new Treasury "liaison council."[20] Nixon requested that Connally, Burns, McCracken, and Secretary of Commerce Maurice Stans be invited to all BC meetings.

On August 13, 1971, representatives from the Quadriad met secretly at Camp David. After fierce debate, Nixon sided with Connally in deciding to bring a final end to Bretton Woods, terminating the convertibility of the dollar into gold and instituting a 90-day mandatory freeze on price and wage increases. The President announced the decision on television two days later. Implemented by the Office of Emergency Preparedness, this would become known as "Phase I" of the wage and price controls program. By no means was this controls regime ever intended to be permanent. Rather, the hope was that either the 90-day freeze would be

[16] Paul McCracken, "International Monetary Reform," Memorandum for the President, June 2, 1971, Record Group 56, Entry Al 718, Box #8, National Archives College Park, MD.

[17] Charles Walker, "Charles Walker to George Shultz," July 9, 1971, Record Group 56, Entry Al 719, Box #2, National Archives College Park, MD.

[18] John Connally, "John Connally to George Shultz," June 15, 1971, Record Group 56, Entry Al 719, Box #2, National Archives College Park, MD.

[19] Panitch and Gindin, *The Making of Global Capitalism*, 124.

[20] John Burke, "John Burke to John Connally," February 19, 1971, Record Group 56, Entry Al 719, Box #1, National Archives College Park, MD.

sufficient, or at least that this would buy the administration enough time to figure out what to do next.

Even those who supported the program explicitly did so as a temporary resolution to the inflation problem—a "lesser evil" to runaway inflation. Some, including Connally, eventually reached the conclusion that controls would remain a feature of American economic life well into the future. But this was accepted with deep reluctance, on the understanding that it was an absolute last resort to deal with the irresolvable contradictions at the heart of the managerial order. The potential difficulty of rolling back controls was a constant feature of the discussion, as they would create new centers of power within the state, new demands for state economic management and intervention, and charges of politically motivated implementation. Though business support for temporary controls was initially strong, through the rest of the decade state managers had to work increasingly hard to maintain an ever more unhappy consensus for their continuation in the absence of any other clear way forward.

Gene Bradley, GE's Manager of International Government Relations and head of the International Management Association, wrote Chief of Staff John Ehrlichman just three days after the announcement: "I believe our new Institute… can help recruit corporate support on a broad front." The institute to which Bradley referred was the International Management and Development Institute, which was associated with Johns Hopkins and described itself as a "non-profit bridge between business and government." To begin the process of organizing corporate support for the new economic program, Bradley suggested "a special high-powered conference" involving "U.S. corporate chiefs in the whole thinking-planning process of the President's economic team."[21] Forwarding the offer to Connally, Ehrlichman noted that Bradley "has been helpful to the Administration in rallying support for the ABM, and other foreign policy."[22] GE, it seemed, was ready to play its traditional role in organizing a capitalist class consensus in support of state crisis management efforts, uncertain though the road ahead was.

Unsurprisingly, Connally took Bradley up on his offer as part of a broader effort to build corporate support for wage and price controls.

[21] Gene Bradley, "Gene Bradley to John J. Ehrlichman," August 17, 1971, Record Group 56, Entry A1 718, Box #8, National Archives College Park, MD.

[22] John Ehrlichman, "Memorandum for Secretary Connally," August 24, 1971, Record Group 56, Entry A1 718, Box #8, National Archives College Park, MD.

As the end of the initial 90-day freeze drew nearer, efforts to reassure business intensified while the administration worked out a plan for what would come next. Investment banker and presidential advisor Peter Peterson organized "a series of Blair House dinners," which would begin at the end of September and take place over the period of a year, "to meet with quite a large number of business leaders" and "explain the new economic policy." Connally, Stans, Shultz, McCracken, and Peterson all participated in these meetings.[23] As the end of the initial phase of controls drew nearer, the administration saw little choice but to continue with another round, given the persistence of inflationary pressures. What's more, the continuation of the program would come with precisely the institutional entrenchment of the regime within the state that skeptics had feared: "Phase II" of the program was implemented through a "convoluted system of councils, boards, and commissions designed to gradually liberalize prices and wages while still keeping inflation within a low target range of 2 to 3 percent."[24]

The March Club and the Business Roundtable

In January 1972, two months into the controls regime, the Chamber of Commerce convened its annual Association National Affairs conference in Washington, DC. Connally was the keynote speaker, and he fiercely scolded the assembled businessmen for their lukewarm response to Phase II:

> When you make up your minds that you can no longer… expect anybody to support unconscionable and unreasonable wage demands, and when you realize you can't continue to raise your prices in an unconscionable fashion, we will end controls… It could be next summer or next fall or maybe it will be four years from now – I don't know. It depends on you.[25]

Connally's harshness reflected the extent to which the program was already in serious trouble. Donald Rumsfeld, then serving as COLC

[23] Peter Flanigan, "Memorandum Secretary Connally, Secretary Stans, George Shultz, Paul McCracken, Peter Peterson," September 17, 1971, Record Group 56, Entry A1 719, Box #3, National Archives College Park, MD.

[24] Waterhouse, *Lobbying America*, 107.

[25] Waterhouse, *Lobbying America*, 108–9.

Director, was facing increasingly urgent demands from the Chairman of the Price Commission, Jackson Grayson, for "significantly greater resources." In a tersely worded memo, Grayson made no bones about the degree to which the monumental task of implementing the controls outstripped the Price Commission's capacities:

> (1) we are not capable at the present time of processing quarterly reports which we are due to receive from the 4500 Tier I and Tier II firms; (2) we are not capable of reviewing public utility requests; (3) we are not adequately reviewing retail and wholesale prenotifications; (4) we do not have yet [sic] received the bulk of the exception workload. Failure to act on these needs will further undermine the credibility of the program.[26]

Effectively carrying out controls would require a massive bureaucratic expansion. Yet this was the *opposite* of the emerging consensus within the state around fiscal austerity as an essential component of the fight against inflation—which went so far as to include substantial support within the administration for a government expenditure ceiling.[27]

If confidence in controls *within* the state was eroding, including among those responsible for implementing and overseeing them, business support followed closely behind. In June, an internal Chamber of Commerce committee recommended that the organization publicly renounce controls. However, the Board of Directors voted against the proposal, opting instead to continue tacit support for the program. The NAM, too, was paralyzed by internal divisions, with its own Ad Hoc Committee on Phase II unable to reach consensus. Nevertheless, the Executive Committee issued "a guarded vote of confidence to continue the controls."[28] Like those within the state, business was deeply divided, but saw little alternative to continuing the program. Such growing dissent fuelled concerns about the "credibility" of controls: if their efficacy or temporariness were in doubt, business could decide to publicly rebuke them or cease cooperating—leaving state officials with few cards to play.

[26] Jackson Grayson, "Memorandum for the Honorable Donald Rumsfeld, Director of the Cost of Living Council," February 3, 1972, Record Group 56, Entry A1 718, Box #8, National Archives College Park, MD.

[27] Herbert Stein, "Memorandum for the President's Files: 'Quadriad Meeting With the President, Camp David, December 8, 1972, 12:00 Noon,'" December 11, 1972, Record Group 56, Entry A1 718, Box #3, National Archives College Park, MD.

[28] Waterhouse, *Lobbying America*, 118.

These divisions spurred renewed efforts at organizing support for controls among business, in which GE executives played a substantial role. Since Cordiner's departure, his informal and exclusive "Links Group" had passed to the leadership of his successor, Fred Borch and Alcoa CEO John Harper. Over 1971, Borch and Harper met regularly in Washington and organized a series of "planning sessions with several of the most prominent and well-placed Washington Representatives, many of whom had begun forming ad hoc coalitions to combine their resources, staff, and strategies on specific legislative issues." Members of the executive branch and Congress participated in and encouraged these sessions. In early 1972, Connally and Burns met with Borch and Harper, and keenly urged them to develop this informal network into a more effective and unified organization of top executives that could work with those within the state.[29]

These objectives were partially accomplished at a meeting in New York on March 22, 1972, when the Links Group decided to formalize itself as the "March Club."[30] The group's declared purpose was "to streamline communication and strategy between lobbyists and chief executives," emphasizing the direct involvement of CEOs themselves and a structure based upon "clear top-down coordination." The problem was "not a shortage of business associations," but quite the contrary: "they believed that Washington had too many business lobbyists and that the cacophony of voices drowned out the central message."[31] As such, the March Club sought to consolidate disparate business associations and connect firms across sectors, thereby moving beyond the narrow interests typically expressed by lobbying groups. What was needed now was a vehicle for organizing a *class-wide consensus*.[32]

Like the BAC and later the CED, the March Group was not a vehicle for "lobbying" the government, and it strictly maintained a non-partisan orientation. The purpose of its efforts in organizing business was not to *advocate* for a particular policy perspective, but rather to help *develop* the policies necessary to resolve the crisis. It was in this way that the March

[29] Waterhouse, *Lobbying America*, 92.

[30] "March Group Washington Reps Memo," April 20, 1972. Quoted in: Waterhouse, *Lobbying America*, 92.

[31] Waterhouse, *Lobbying America*, 91.

[32] "March Groups Washington Reps Memo," April 20, 1972. Quoted in: Waterhouse, *Lobbying America*, 94.

Group set out to "fundamentally revolutionize the practice of corporate lobbying by involving CEOs in political strategy and coordinating the operations of Washington Representatives,"[33] thereby articulating a class-wide, rather than sectoral or firm-based, political vision. To do so, it formed subcommittees on particular policy areas: taxation, international trade, consumerism, and the environment. These subcommittees worked closely with state officials and members of Congress to write papers around which the organization then worked to build a consensus among CEOs.

Meanwhile, the role of the CUAIR in organizing capital, and integrating construction contractors more closely within networks dominated by large corporations, was on full display in May 1972 at the National Conference of User Groups it organized in Biloxi, Mississippi. The conference opened with a speech by Day, who set out the basic problem: "the unions really run the labor relations program as the wage setters, the trainers of craftsmen, the managers of benefits, and, regrettably, they have usurped most of the rights exercised by management in most other industries."[34] The weakness of the construction contractors in bargaining was having a hugely negative impact on large corporations, to whom these costs were passed on as "construction users." No company felt this so harshly as GE, with its continued losses from nuclear "turnkey" agreements. Construction contractors—the largest industry in the US—had "largely lost control of critical cost elements in his business to arbitrary outside influences." As a result, they were being asked to come together under the auspices of the CUAIR to find a way to "to eliminate or neutralize the heavy impact of restrictive work practices."[35] Government controls, it was emphasized, "attack only the symptoms" and "provide time, not relief" from inflationary pressures—and thus employers should not rest on their laurels.[36]

The Pay Board-CISC-CUAIR institutional nexus had by this time become integrated as a continuous extension of state power, the crux of the corporatist regime for managing the construction sector. The Pay Board provided "running lights for CISC" and was on its way to formally

[33] Waterhouse, *Lobbying America*, 92.

[34] "Construction Users Anti-Inflation Roundtable Report," June 1, 1972.

[35] "Construction Users Anti-Inflation Roundtable Report," May 2, 1972.

[36] "Construction Users Anti-Inflation Roundtable Report," June 1, 1972.

establishing a joint Pay Board-CISC committee. The CUAIR, for its part, had become entrenched as the key mechanism for integrating business with both the CISC and Pay Board. That Virgil Day was one of the main leaders of each, along with the LLSC, was significant in illustrating this interconnectedness.

On October 16, 1972, the leaders of CUAIR and LLSC—who were "nearly to a man" the same individuals who comprised the March Club—met once again at the Links Club in New York City, where they voted to merge the two organizations into the Business Roundtable for Responsible Labor-Management Relations (BR).[37] Despite this union of the CUAIR and the LLSC, the March Group remained a separate coordinating body. The merger was announced one month later, when "comprehensive statements on the structure and purpose of the new organization" were presented at a national conference in Houston and a subsequent meeting in Chicago.[38] Though Beverly Murphy, CEO of Campbell's Soup, was named the group's first chairman, this was likely done "to mollify LLSC members who still worried they would lose clout." The much more influential and well-connected Blough and Borch were designated as "co-chairs," which was formally considered "one notch down."

The BR was administered through an Executive Committee and a Policy Committee, and supported by committees for Construction (which was the former coordinating committee of the CUAIR, headed by Virgil Day), Economic Research, Government Relations, Legal, and Public Information. While Borch was on the Executive Committee as co-chair, Jones had a place on the powerful Policy Committee. GE's institutional centrality is further illustrated by the fact that Borch's two-year BR co-chairmanship, which came to an end with his retirement from GE, was followed by his 1969–1970 BC chairmanship. Moreover, when Jones succeeded Borch at GE, he also took over his position at the head of the BR—and remained a co-chair of that organization through the rest of its first decade, from 1974 to 1980.

It was Blough who inaugurated the new organization at the national conference in Houston, declaring, "we now have a bigger and better organization for a larger task, and more people to perform it." The new

[37] Waterhouse, *Lobbying America*, 87.

[38] "Business Roundtable Report," November 28, 1972.

organization was to be an organized class force that would fulfill Connally's demand that business push back against labor, such that controls could be lifted.[39] The BR accepted the premise that "while continuation of wage and price controls is a possibility, controls only get at the symptoms; accordingly, The Business Roundtable will continue to study and recommend needed structural changes to get at the root causes of inflation in the construction industry and the economy more generally."[40] In this, the BR was following in the footsteps of the CED and BAC: not lobbying, but developing a new political program, and then working to build a business consensus around it. Thus, the BR was emphatically "not a trade association, but one that will work with and through such associations for the attainment of mutual objectives."[41]

Business Organization and the Economic Policy Apparatus

The ascent of the economic apparatus within the state continued to be supported by the rapid development of new capacities around it. In December 1972, Nixon established another top-level economic policy council, chaired by Shultz. Burns described the Committee as a "consultative body… which would carry a weight in decisions on basic economic policies that would be fully comparable to that of the National Security Council in its sphere." The central problem to be managed was the tension between fighting inflation and maintaining full employment: as Burns put it, while "the nation needs greater assurance than it now has that our government is equipped to deal on a consistent basis with the threat of inflation," so too did it need "assurance that the government or one of its central organs will not become so engrossed in the long-run problem of creeping inflation that any immediate problem of recession is neglected."[42]

In November 1972, a group of BR members met with OMB Director Caspar Weinberger, CEA Chairman Herbert Stein, and Arthur Burns to

[39] "Business Roundtable Report," December 10, 1972.

[40] "Business Roundtable Report," November 28, 1972.

[41] "Business Roundtable Report," December 10, 1972.

[42] Arthur Burns, "Arthur Burns to George Schultz," December 5, 1972, Record Group 56, Entry A1 718, Box #3, National Archives College Park, MD.

develop a position on Phase II. Though the businessmen initially argued for a quick end to controls, the administration officials "persuaded the Roundtable CEOs that they were actively working on 'alternate plans to replace the present control program.'" As a result of this meeting, the BR would renew its patience with the controls—continuing to support even apparently ineffective state efforts to manage inflation in exchange for being granted a seat at the table in developing policy. Nor, for that matter, did the BR have any clear policy alternative to offer. This was an important "coming-of-age" moment for the BR, which came to see maintaining "a direct pathway to policymakers" as the crucial objective.[43]

A few weeks later, Weinberger received a BR "wage-price stabilization plan." Though insisting that "a suitable substitute for the present form of controls, designed to bring an end to formal controls without creating a high wage or price increase is highly desirable," the BR effectively assented to continuing the program. After the expiration of the enabling legislation on April 30, 1973, the BR suggested that new legislation "enacted prior to that date" should "provide the Executive with authority to establish wage and price anti-inflation criterion together with the minimum special staff required for administration, relying to the extent feasible on the cooperation of labor and management but with reserve enforcement powers."[44]

Nixon's announcement of Phase III of the program just weeks later, in January 1973, reflected the consensus around liberalization, and the optimistic conclusion within the administration that inflation had been broken. Phase III signaled the beginning of a transition away from controls, making them "even more palatable to business by jettisoning the Pay Board and Price Commission and implementing broad standards rather than rigid regulations."[45] BR Chairman W.B. Murphy sent a telegram to Shultz calling the action "a big step in the right direction." Murphy also agreed that "until the underlying causes of inflation are moderated, it is important to have a set of standby controls available,"

[43] Waterhouse, *Lobbying America*, 119.

[44] Caspar Weinberger, "Caspar Weinberger to George Shultz," December 8, 1972, Record Group 56, Entry Al 718, Box #5, National Archives College Park, MD.

[45] Waterhouse, *Lobbying America*, 119.

as well as for the "government to work to reduce the large deficits that have contributed to inflationary pressures."[46]

Despite the positive response from business to Phase III, with the removal of the enforcement apparatus business quickly raised prices to make up for reduced margins during the period of controls. Inflation reached 21% in the first three months of 1973, with core wage goods hit especially hard.[47] Consequently, in March, the administration was forced to reinstitute a freeze on prices of beef, pork, and lamb, along with a requirement that firms with greater than $250 million in sales submit prior notice of any price increases. With the earlier optimism dashed, and the enabling legislation set to expire in April, the administration's strategy was thrown into disarray. In a meeting on April 11, Connally soberly proclaimed that "some form of wage-price control must be accepted as part of modern life in the U.S."[48]

There was good reason to believe that it would be more difficult to impose new mandatory controls than it had been in August 1971. The abject failure to secure business compliance with voluntary controls, and the difficulties of implementing mandatory controls given the massive costs involved and inability to force corporations to invest at adequate levels, left the administration with few options—none of them good. If controls had to be reinitiated, it would be harder to convince business that these were merely temporary, increasing the likelihood that it would withhold investment, which would worsen the economic stagnation. Meanwhile, pressures from workers seeking to maintain consumption levels amidst falling real wages would be directed not at business, but at the state. Particularly worrisome was the extent to which the program was dangerously susceptible to pressure from Congress and labor, which meant that controls "could expand and even become a vehicle for keeping real wages high"—which of course no one wanted.[49] The paradox for state planners was that holding wages down required authoritarian practices, and thus institutions that were relatively insulated from the popular backlash that might ensue. The democratic institutions of the state left

[46] "Business Roundtable Report," January 31, 1973.

[47] Waterhouse, *Lobbying America*, 120.

[48] George Shultz, "Memorandum for the President," April 11, 1973, Record Group 56, Entry A1 718, Box #5, National Archives College Park, MD.

[49] Shultz, "Memorandum for the President," April 11, 1973.

it far too vulnerable to such a response; yet business seemed unable to push back against the unions in the absence of substantial and direct state coordination.

With tensions between the administration and Congress growing and inflation out of control, the work of organizing business into a class force took another substantial step forward. In May 1973, it was announced that the March Club would fold its task force committees—covering taxation, international trade, consumerism, and the environment—into the BR. Similarly, the chairmen of each task force would join the BR Policy Committee. The March Group would continue to play its vanguard role in organizing business, but as the BR took shape as a formal class-wide institution, there was simply less need to maintain a formal separation between the two. The merger was straightforward enough, since most of the individuals on the BR executive were also March Group members.

GE was a central institutional link that united both the BR and the March Group. Borch, for instance, who had just stepped down as the company's CEO, was one of two co-chairmen of both the BR and the March Group. Extending the formal relationship between the two organizations at this stage amounted to the BR taking on the other March Group co-chair, Alcoa Chairman John D. Harper—thus effectively building a broader institutional base for this elite vanguard group by augmenting the BR.[50] As the organization's internal newsletter put, the objective of the expanded BR was to "*rally support within the business community*" for the policy positions developed within its subcommittees.[51]

When Nixon implemented Phase IV controls in August 1973—which tightened enforcement on business but did not alter the wage standard—the boards of both NAM and the Chamber came out forcefully against it. NAM "declared war" on the Economic Stabilization Program. Its Board of Directors voted "overwhelmingly to steadfastly oppose the continuation of wage and price controls" and distributed a "fiery brochure" criticizing the program. By contrast, the BR's criticism was restrained, arguing that controls would "only aggravate dislocations which inevitably follow an extended period of interference with the operation of free

[50] "Business Roundtable Report," May 23, 1973; Waterhouse, *Lobbying America*, 94.

[51] "Roundtable and March Group in Affiliation Move," The Business Roundtable Report, May 23, 1973.

markets."[52] Yet neither the administration, nor its increasingly bold and numerous critics among business, in Congress, and the public at large, had any way out. As Nixon himself summarized the dilemma:

> Business is losing its appetite with the controls. So is labor. As Phase IV is pinching the economy, the public also appears to be learning that controls do not solve all our problems. It also appears that the Congress is becoming more unsure of how to live with the program, although equally unsure how to live without it.[53]

Despite the efforts of Day and his allies on the BR to build business support for controls, as gasoline prices skyrocketed, and grocery bills had become highly volatile with the lifting of Freeze II back in August, support among the public for Phase IV "decreased rapidly." The growing cantankerousness of NAM and the Chamber only added to the pressure.[54] Nevertheless, state officials persisted in trying to hold together a consensus among business, organizing a series of meetings between "top people in the administration" and "a dozen or so" corporate executives at a time at the White House, including GE's Jones, who had by then become CEO.[55] Secretary of Commerce Dent and Labor Secretary Peter Brennan also held a "series of dinners for an equal number of management and labor leaders for an informal discussion."[56]

It wasn't until February 1974 that prominent Roundtable executives began to come out for the "prompt termination" of controls, followed by the BR Policy Committee itself that April.[57] As state managers groped for

[52] Waterhouse, *Lobbying America*, 120.

[53] "Talking Points for the President, Cabinet Meeting 10/18/73," October 18, 1973, Record Group 56, Entry A1 718, Box #2, National Archives College Park, MD; "Business Roundtable Report," September 28, 1973; "Business Roundtable Report," October 29, 1973.

[54] Waterhouse, *Lobbying America*, 121.

[55] Peter Flanigan, "'Meetings with Business Leaders,' Memorandum for Secretaries Shultz, Schlesinger, Weinberger, Butz, Lynn, General Haig, Melvin Laird, Herbert Stein, Roy Ash, John Love, John Dunlop, William Casey, Paul Volcker," November 21, 1973, Record Group 489, Entry UD-WW, Box #4.

[56] Frederick Dent, "Frederick Dent to Richard Nixon," November 2, 1973, Record Group 56, Entry A1 718, Box #3, National Archives College Park, MD.

[57] "Business Roundtable Report," February 28, 1974; "Business Roundtable Report," April 1974.

a solution to the crisis without clear direction, and public opinion began to shift, business finally threatened to pressure Congress to bring controls to an end. Yet even then, the inauspicious end to Phase IV was far from being a simple matter of the state yielding to corporate lobbying pressure. Though much of business was clearly unhappy with the controls program by this point, so was just about everyone else. Indeed, the administration itself recognized the program was a failure—and prominent administration officials had concluded long before the shift in business opinion that controls should be wound down.

The chaos unleashed by the attempt to impose mandatory controls had made painfully clear just how very relative the state's autonomy in fact was. It simply could not compel corporations to invest without guaranteeing adequate profit levels, which could only be secured by reducing labor costs, or allowing a relative increase in prices (which amounted to the same thing). Moreover, as real wages began to fall, and profits (and prices) rose, the program ran into deep contradictions—not least in the form of popular pressures on the state's democratic institutions. In the face of growing dissatisfaction with the way controls had been implemented—and fears that the public would demand *more extensive* controls—even the administration itself had ceased defending them. It offered only a "tepid defense" of reauthorizing the program over the winter and spring of 1974, effectively allowing the Economic Stabilization Act to expire.

The Business Roundtable and the Fight for Deregulation

The end of controls potentially left the BR without a raison d'etre. However, at a seminar in Dearborn, Michigan, co-Chairman Roger Blough made the case that the organization remained relevant despite this—having undertaken "a broad but sensible mission" and being "equipped to deal with problems that individual corporations cannot handle alone." Among other work underway, "a complete program of labor-law revisions" had been developed, the intent of which, it was emphasized, was "not a punitive thrust organized against labor, but to safeguard a worker's right to decide whether or not to join a union"—that is, right-to-work. The organization was also commencing a fight against proposals for a Consumer Protection Agency, which appeared to foretell a dramatic expansion of the state's "public interest" functions, regardless of the effects on profits.

At the same time, Nixon advisor William J. Baroody spoke at a Washington luncheon session about the need to better integrate corporate power, as organized within the BR, with policymaking: "Our problem," he said, "has been hearing from business leaders only after we've made decisions adversely affecting business." The answer to this problem lay in an ongoing role for the BR as a corporate "advisory" group. Similarly, Virgil Day and the Construction Task Force advocated for a "'transition period' between the demise of controls and a return to unfettered bargaining," during which the BR would try to "accelerate formation of more wide area co-ordinated contractor bargaining units."[58] As had been the case with the original CUAIR, the "spillover effect on other industries" meant that this was a concern of all business, not merely one particular sector.[59]

For these reasons, at the subsequent semi-annual BR conference of Local User Groups in June 1974, "participants voted unanimously for continuing the national meetings." Blough was optimistic about the future, since "one major difference between now and the immediate pre-control years is the existence of The Business Roundtable." The BR thereby shifted from being a venue for organizing support for controls to managing the transition to the post-control environment—and working closely with the state in doing so. Just after the conference, Nixon invited top executives from 12 companies, including Jones, for a meeting at the White House "to discuss economic issues confronting the nation" with the president and his "chief economic advisors."[60] Indeed, the BR continued to work closely with the CEA through the rest of the Nixon administration, during which the fight against the Consumer Protection Agency and national health insurance consumed considerable time and energy, while the Economic Research Committee continued to gather information on "restrictive work practices" that impeded productivity

[58] "Business Roundtable Report," April 26, 1974.

[59] "Business Roundtable Report," April 26, 1974.

[60] "Business Roundtable Report," July 20, 1974.

growth.[61] So too did the organization support the passage of new campaign finance laws to increase "transparency."[62]

Yet it was the state that took the lead in developing a new program of restructuring to address the ongoing crisis. Gerald Ford came to office in August 1974 having declared fighting inflation to be his top domestic priority. To support and flesh out his agenda, he formed a Labor-Management committee, which included GE's Jones and fellow BR executive John Harper of Alcoa, along with several other BR members. That very month, three members of the BR Policy Committee appeared on an ABC program "Issues and Answers," and argued that truly ending inflation was not simply a matter of implementing controls for a limited period until the "normality" of the postwar order could be restored. Rather, attacking the crisis would demand much broader and deeper changes, which required workers to accept a new reality of belt-tightening, and the levelling off of the rising living standards that had characterized American capitalism since World War II.[63]

Once again, Jones would be a key figure in the effort to mobilize business in support for the state's agenda. His BR taxation committee "directed especially penetrating studies" into the capital formation problem, which served as vital props in the political theater of Congressional testimony. Testifying before the Subcommittee on Economic Growth of the Congressional Joint Economic Committee in August 1974, Jones argued that at the root of the crisis was underinvestment, which stemmed primarily from the inadequate profits that had resulted from reliance on state controls. The outcomes of this were shortages of goods, unemployment, and inflation. Rather than returning to controls, which would only make the problem worse, slashing corporate taxes would help restore profits, and thus investment and growth. The need to boost capital formation was made more urgent by the concern that other countries were investing a larger portion of GDP, allegedly contributing to US decline. The fundamental problem, therefore, was "a condition of underinvestment in this country whose consequences are catching up with us."[64]

61 "Business Roundtable Report," October 1974.

62 "Business Roundtable Report," July 20, 1974.

63 "Business Roundtable Report," August 31, 1974.

64 "Business Roundtable Report," August 31, 1974.

Coming to grips with this, Jones explained, would require a large-scale shift in both policy and psychology to recognize *investment*, rather than *consumption*, as the most important driver of growth and prosperity. "Since the great depression of the thirties, the United States has become an increasingly consumer-oriented economy," Jones said. This was reflected in the fact that "national policy has been directed primarily toward stimulating consumer demand, redistributing wealth, providing for social welfare, and increasing government services." Though these lofty goals were commendable, the economy could no longer support them. The crisis had made the structural limits to the postwar growth model clear. In referring to the 1930s as the pivotal point of departure, Jones indicated what was at stake: the undoing of the New Deal, and the model of class compromise that GE and its "corporate liberal" allies had been at the forefront of organizing.[65]

Six weeks after taking office, Ford rolled out a program of comprehensive regulatory reform under the slogan "Whip Inflation Now," and called on Congress to appoint a National Commission on Regulatory Reform. When Congress refused to act, Ford issued Executive Order 11821 in November mandating that all new regulations include an "inflation impact statement" that would be evaluated by the director of the OMB.[66] "Business leaders greeted Ford's policy with unmasked enthusiasm" as the executive order "fundamentally reframed policy debates over regulation."[67] Institutional change within the integral state rippled outward: within weeks, the BR's Policy Committee established a new task force on regulation, which would collaborate with state officials to identify areas to be targeted for deregulation. Task force Chairman Irving Shaprio reported that he expected "a reduction in all types of unnecessary government regulation, and we do not expect our work to be of short duration."[68]

At the same time, the BR also established two other committees, one on economic concentration and one on wage and price controls. The latter worked with the administration to fend off "growing pressure" from House Democrats to return to controls, while the former joined

[65] "Business Roundtable Report," August 31, 1974.

[66] Waterhouse, *Lobbying America*, 181.

[67] Waterhouse, *Lobbying America*, 182.

[68] "Business Roundtable Report," December 1974.

the taxation committee (chaired by Jones) to devise a longer-term restructuring.[69] In doing so, the BR drew on the extensive national network of Local User Groups it had painstakingly organized in the preceding years. Day continued to play a leading role in expanding and strengthening these Local User Groups, which met every year at a national conference. These included small and medium-sized businesses that would may not otherwise have had a substantial involvement in politics.[70] At the ninth national conference of Local Groups in May 1975, the organization sounded an appeal through these networks "to generate grass roots opposition to national economic planning."[71]

A primary objective of the BR in the post-Nixon era was increasing business coordination with Congress, efforts that were bolstered by post-Watergate legal changes increasing "openness" and "transparency" that served to further formalize and institutionalize such linkages. The BR's relationship with Congress was not simply about influencing elections, but also integrating corporate power with the policymaking process *between* elections. Far from being a matter of spontaneous advocacy, corporate power was systematically embedded within the institutional structure of Congress itself.[72] Thus, the BR emerged as an important mechanism for hashing out policy consensus among executive branch agencies, members of Congress, and business. BR subcommittees worked with policymakers in the administration and Congress to develop positions, and then the broader organization served to build a consensus around them. Despite the formal demise of the corporatist regime that had given birth to it, the BR continued to play a crucial mediating role *within* the state between different agencies and branches—and was thus *integral* to the internal functioning and organizational structure of state power.

In August 1976, BR Chairman Irving Shapiro, and co-chairmen John deButts and Reginald Jones, sent "personal letters" to every BR member containing "two guidelines" they believed were central to the organization's continued development. Most important was the recognition:

[69] "Business Roundtable Report," January 1975.

[70] "Business Roundtable Report," July 1975.

[71] "Business Roundtable Report," June 1975.

[72] "Business Roundtable Report," June 1975.

> that the adversarial relationship of business and government is exaggerated and counterproductive; that in most instances business and government seek the same ends; that the means to the end, not the end itself, is usually the principal concern; and the business and government must work together to find the best way to achieve agreed goals.

No one in the state pursued any other *end* than "making the system work"—which meant restoring profits, growth, and competitiveness. The only question was of the *means* through which this should be achieved. On this basis, business and the state should work together to devise solutions to common problems. The second "guideline" followed directly from this: "the Roundtable will receive better support for its views, and make a greater contribution to society, if it registers 'positive ideas and objectives,' and avoids the negative posture on important issues that critics of American capitalism often present as the stereotype stance of the business community."[73]

The crisis of the state-corporate relationship that had plagued the Kennedy years was now a distant memory. The BR represented an important step in overcoming this—not antagonistically seeking to *pressure* the state from outside, but fulfilling an *advisory* function. In this, it occupied a position not unlike that which the BAC had. Yet the BR was both more flexible and, ironically, more broadly interlinked with state power. Rather than being relegated to the Department of Commerce ghetto—which organized corporate power but also mediated its relationship with the rest of the state—the BR facilitated direct linkages with a range of state agencies and institutions.

Nothing indicated the broad accord around restoring capitalism to health than the struggle over the Humphrey-Hawkins full employment bill underway at that very moment. The bill called for guaranteed jobs for all, with the government acting as "employer of last resort." Yet even the bill's proponents had insisted that it was not a *challenge* to capitalism, but rather a *support* for it.[74] On these terms, it was easy for opponents of the bill—officials within the state economic apparatus as much as heads of corporations—to show how problematic it would in fact be. What was needed to sustainably reduce unemployment, they argued,

[73] "Business Roundtable Report," August 1976.

[74] Thomas Cate, *An Encyclopedia of Keynesian Economics, Second Edition* (Northampton, MA: Edward Elgar Publishing, 2013), 182–83.

was not a government guaranteed job for everyone, but to create the conditions whereby corporations could invest profitably. Guaranteeing a state job for all would only *increase* the tax burden on business, further squeezing investment—and, over the long run, result in a growing public sector workforce while the private sector continued to shrink alongside collapsing investment and growth. This raised the question of how these state employees would be paid if not increasing deficits, which would deal a knockout blow to the private sector.[75]

The BR's criticism of Humphrey-Hawkins was therefore a disagreement over the *means* to best serve the general welfare, maximize employment, and revive American capitalism. It was not a partisan argument, but a *reasonable* one—though premised on accepting that capitalism was immutable, and thus reflecting the lack of a movement capable of advancing a vision that pointed beyond it. Indeed, the BR's cooperative attitude toward the state persisted beyond the Republican Ford administration, extending to the new Democratic administration of Jimmy Carter as well. A position paper the BR issued just weeks after Carter's inauguration proclaimed that "cooperation is the most productive relationship that can exist between business and government leaders… Working together, each vigorously advancing its views and then making the decisions that lead to agreement and action – this is the road to effective national policies."[76]

This attitude was reciprocated in Vice President Walter Mondale's keynote address at the BR's fifth annual meeting in July 1977. In order to improve productivity, develop new sources of energy, and "maintain the crucial ability of America to play its rightful role in international affairs and in world markets," then "the recent lag in investment must be reversed" by bringing capital formation to a level comparable with that of the 1960s. Moreover, deregulation was an important aspect of doing so; as Mondale said, "regulatory programs which have failed to work properly have contributed to a decline in public respect for government." BR Chairman Shapiro echoed these sentiments, explaining that crucial to the BR was "the ability to act as a catalyst, to work cooperatively with other groups seeking similar goals, and to present government with reasoned alternatives and positive suggestions, rather than to engage

75 "Business Roundtable Report," August 1976.

76 "Business Roundtable Report," February 1977.

in mere opposition which contributes little to positive policymaking."[77] What was distinct about the BR was that it could assemble a class-wide consensus, working with other more narrow business groups as necessary, and articulate this *within* the policymaking process rather than against it. Regardless of which party won the election, the BR sought a permanent role as an advisory body *within the state*.

The Formation of the Neoliberal State in the Carter years

Throughout the Carter years, Jones played a pivotal role within the integral state, as indicated by the moniker "statesman of business" bestowed upon him by his fellow corporate elites.[78] Mondale concluded his comments at the BR conference with the announcement that Jones would serve on "a special group" in the White House—working with Robert Strauss, Carter's special advisor on inflation, to devise an anti-inflation program.[79] A few months later, in October, Jones was considered for the top job in the increasingly powerful OMB, which would soon take the lead in implementing Carter's extensive executive branch reorganization—and a position in which it was seen as essential to have someone who commanded the "confidence" of business.[80] Then, in November, Jones turned down the job of Chairman of the Federal Reserve—though he did serve on a special committee to identify and vet possible successors for Burns.[81] Finally, Jones served as Chairman of Carter's President's Export Council (PEC), working to organize a business consensus around a new post-Bretton Woods international trade regime. With this, he was *simultaneously* head of the Business Roundtable, Business Council, and PEC. The nearest historical precedent for such prominence was when GE's Charles Wilson simultaneously served as head of the WPB and ODM.

[77] "Business Roundtable Report," July 1977.

[78] Rothschild, *The Secret to GE's Success*, 183.

[79] "Business Roundtable Report," July 1977; Hobart Rowen, "Business Wary of Ending 'Double Tax,'" *The Washington Post*, July 13, 1977.

[80] Richard Steele et al., "Picking Up the Pieces," *Newsweek*, October 3, 1977.

[81] David Broder, "The Search for a New Federal Reserve Chairman: A Secretive, Significant Process," *The Washington Post*, December 30, 1977; Michael Ruby et al., "The Economy: New Look?," *Newsweek*, January 9, 1978.

The immediate task of Jones' BR taxation committee was to "prepare a comprehensive set of recommendations for submission to the Administration before President Carter announces his program of tax reform."[82] Unsurprisingly, the report stressed the cardinal point that "the United States must, as a national requirement, enlarge the share of its resources devoted to capital investment, in order to increase productivity and real wages, reduce inflation, provide jobs for a growing labor force, and meet such other needs as energy development, environment, housing, rebuilding of cities, and providing a tax base for social services."[83] The only way to achieve the social objectives of the New Deal state was by restoring economic growth—achieving which nonetheless required cutting taxes and rolling back that very New Deal state.

Weeks later, Carter asked for a meeting with Jones and Shapiro to discuss economic policy—in particular, how to "bring down unemployment, keep inflation from accelerating, and restore business and investor confidence." Jones and Shapiro responded by urging three key priorities. First, they cautioned, "the government must avoid overstimulating the economy in response to a slowing of growth that is unavoidable as the expansion matures." Second, they argued that the crucial lesson of the crisis of the postwar regime, and Nixon's disastrous attempt at wage and price controls, was that "the Government cannot successfully fine tune the economy." Therefore, "government economic policies should deal with fundamental problems and be as permanent as possible." Finally, they emphasized the importance of capital investment in sustaining growth, while asserting "major long-term investment projects are not being undertaken today because of uncertainties about the Government's economic policies… and the confusing and stifling array of environmental, safety, employment, and product regulations."[84]

In March, Carter proposed a tax package that included significant cuts for business. Jones testified before the House Ways & Means Committee that the BR "strongly supports President Carter's proposed permanent tax reductions for individuals and business, and believes Congress should approve them promptly."[85] Following this, the BR Economic Research

[82] "Business Roundtable Report," July 1977.

[83] "Business Roundtable Report," August 1977.

[84] "Business Roundtable Report," October 1977.

[85] "Business Roundtable Report," March 1978.

Committee issued a report on "Policies Necessary to Reduce the Rate of Inflation." Jones presented the report to the sixth annual BR meeting on June 12, where it was unanimously approved. A copy of the report was also sent to all members of Congress. It contained a "Roundtable pledge that its member companies will cooperate in efforts to reduce inflation," yet insisted that "effective price deceleration" depended upon "government policies that realistically minimize business costs." The report detailed four "pressure points for business" that needed attention, each of which corresponded with a BR task force: regulation, environment, employment, and taxation.[86]

Jones and other BR members then met with Robert Strauss, Carter's special advisor on inflation, on June 15. The meeting served as another expression of the consensus among the administration and business that seriously combatting inflation meant "a total approach involving all sectors of the economy must be taken." There was agreement that "the Federal Government must adopt responsible fiscal and monetary policies, with specific steps to cut Government spending; restore the stability of the dollar; and adopt sound regulatory policies that consider the cost implication of regulation." This would allow the private sector, for its part, to "use restraint in wage and price matters." This statement of consensus then served to support a campaign within the BR to secure business cooperation with the administration's program—in effect, a very weak and informal system of voluntary controls reliant on the "honor system."[87]

As the voluntary controls were rolled out, policymakers and advisors in the Carter administration continued grappling with how to address the underlying crisis. Central to this was Jack Watson, Carter's Special Assistant for Intergovernmental Affairs. Watson was in charge of "intergovernmental coordination," and later served as chief of staff in the last year of Carter's presidency. Not only had Watson led the 1976 Policy Planning Group that coordinated the transfer of power from Ford to Carter, he would also direct the transition from Carter to Reagan after the 1980 election. In July 1978, Watson and his deputy, Bruce Kirschenbaum, wrote a memo for the president laying out two major

[86] "Business Roundtable Report," June 1978.

[87] "Business Roundtable Report," July 1978; "Business Roundtable Report," September 1978.

"anti-inflation initiatives," both of which would entail a significant reorganization of state institutions, and would be implemented by concentrating power within OMB.

The first and most important component was deep budget cuts, from which even the most sacred expenditures should not be exempt:

> OMB budget reviews must concentrate generally on the large budget threats and/or costs such as public service employment levels, housing programs, highways, etc. Although these programs obviously have the highest potential return in reducing the deficit, they are also the very programs which are least susceptible to major reduction because of strong congressional and interest group pressure.[88]

The implication was that the needed restructuring was significantly more substantial than what had thus far been attempted, as successive administrations had avoided cutting popular New Deal programs, infrastructure spending, and public sector jobs. The consequences of this were sure to provoke opposition from Congress, service users, and public sector workers. Yet, Watson and Kirschenbaum held, such cuts were necessary to control inflation.

To contain the inevitable pushback against this, including from within state agencies themselves, Watson proposed creating incentives to encourage state agencies to identify and implement the necessary cuts. Watson's plan would effectively emulate the corporate decentralization that had taken on such enlarged dimensions in the 1970s. The strategy centered on the OMB distributing funds across executive branch agencies at reduced levels, and then leaving it up to individual agencies to identify cuts on their own. Cuts would be further incentivized by granting agencies a portion of the total savings to devote to their highest-priority programs. Thus, agencies would be faced with market-like discipline to make hard choices and identify a select group of high-priority programs to receive funding, while cutting others.[89] In this way, administrative decentralization could unleash pressure for whittling agencies down to core priorities.

[88] Jack Watson and Bruce Kirschenbaum, "Memorandum for the President Re: Anti-Inflation Initiatives," July 3, 1978, Record Group 429, Entry A1 1025, Box #13, National Archives College Park, MD.

[89] Watson and Kirschenbaum, "Memorandum for the President," July 3, 1978.

The second component of Watson's anti-inflation program was to press efforts for deregulation much more vigorously, and without waiting for Congressional action. "At present," Watson and Kirschenbaum wrote, "we have no aggressive Presidential effort to seek out major private sector 'de-regulation' possibilities which can be implemented administratively (or with minor legislation)." Such an initiative would obviously require extensive engagement with business to determine priority areas and maximize the "beneficial" effects of restructuring. Therefore, Watson argued, "we need a very focused action team which could consult with the private sector, agencies, constituent groups and others on 'ripe opportunities' for anti-inflation de-regulation, and which could follow through with implementation." That the BR was seen as perhaps the most important venue for such collaboration was indicated by Watson's suggestion to appoint Ira Millstein to head the program specifically because of his links to that organization.[90] The age of fiscal austerity, and the neoliberal rationalization of the New Deal-Great Society state bureaucracy, was underway.

The administration's planning effort culminated in Carter's official announcement of his anti-inflation program on October 24. Decrying the "familiar" policy options of either a "complicated scheme" of national wage and price controls or a "deliberate recession" that would "throw millions of people out of work" as both being "simplistic" and "too extreme," Carter proposed a new voluntary controls program he called "Phase II." He appointed Alfred E. Kahn as Chairman of the Council on Wage and Price Stability (COWPS), which had replaced the Nixon-era Cost of Living Council, and which would announce price targets for industry in addition to other anti-inflation measures.[91] Carter also created a new council in the White House to consolidate the deregulation effort.

The BR immediately issued a statement "applauding his efforts to reduce the Federal deficit, to put a tight rein on the growth of Federal spending, and to better coordinate regulation through the formation of a regulatory council." The BR also expressed support for Carter's tax bill, which made "a start – a modest start – on reducing the corporate income tax rate" as well as cutting capital gains taxes.[92] Nevertheless, as prices continued to rise, it seemed that business was unable, unwilling,

[90] Watson and Kirschenbaum, "Memorandum for the President," July 3, 1978.

[91] Jimmy Carter, "Anti-Inflation Program Speech," October 24, 1978.

[92] "Business Roundtable Report," October 1978.

or both to follow through on voluntary price controls. Though COWPS director Barry Bosworth (Kahn remained Chairman) threatened publicly on several occasions to impose mandatory controls, he was each time undermined by others in the administration.

As the voluntary controls program impotently sputtered along, COWPS officials began to advocate for setting up "an advisory commission for the voluntary control program." Such commissions, they observed, "can enlist the support of well known persons in the development or implementation of new programs, both to focus public attention in the area and to enhance political support." At the same time, they served a vital consensus-building function, as "a forum in which members can express diverse interests and points of view to educate the public, the agency, and each other about the potential impact of Council actions." This also meant such a commission could be a "sounding board to allow the government to explore informally the limitations of a proposed action before it becomes final." Perhaps most importantly, such advisory commissions "co-opt opposition to a particular program":

> If those to be regulated participate in developing the policy that will affect them, they feel an obligation to support the regulations which implement the policy. This 'legitimacy' is especially important in a program that relies on voluntary compliance.[93]

As we have seen, these functions had long been major objectives in establishing such advisory commissions. Yet it was doubtful, to say the least, that this would be sufficient to hold together Carter's voluntary controls program.

In fact, these dynamics were already on full display, as the administration had relied on the advice and counsel of the BR from the very start. Donald Seibert, Chairman of the J.C. Penney Company and of the BR Inflation Task Force, testified before the Senate Banking, Housing, and Urban Affairs Committee in February that COWPS "deserves to have its existence renewed by act of Congress." Seibert "commended the COWPS for its work in communicating the objectives of the Administration's anti-inflation program" and "restated the Roundtable's pledge of support for the anti-inflation effort." Seibert made clear that this support "has been

[93] Jane Campana, "Advisory Committees: Procedures–Pros and Cons," January 26, 1979, Record Group 429, Entry A1 1025, Box #1, National Archives College Park, MD.

earned, in part because President Carter perceives the wage and price standards 'as only one component of the anti-inflation effort. They should not be allowed to become the central focus of the program.'" Nevertheless, he was concerned "over reports that COWPS was considering the use of public funds to finance consumer monitoring of wage/price standards." This, he argued, would "cut at the heart of the cooperative spirit we believe the President was expecting from the various sectors of our society in fighting inflation."[94]

Even as state managers had the broader perspective necessary to formulate a project of restructuring, they were unwilling to use the coercive tools necessary to bring about the needed institutional changes. No doubt, the political will to endure the political and economic pain that would follow a recession was difficult to muster. Nor were those in the administration willing to construct the extensive apparatus that would be necessary to devise and enforce mandatory controls—in fact the consensus was moving in the opposite direction, toward cuts in taxation, spending, and regulations. Yet this was also a reminder of how very relative the state's autonomy in fact was. If the memory of the crisis that followed Nixon's abortive 1971 interest rate hike made the administration hesitant to follow such a course, the inability to force business to invest at adequate levels even if they did impose mandatory controls hardly made such an approach seem attractive. Yet in the absence of controls, competitive pressures led business to maximize profits however they could, including raising prices as far as the market would bear.

Four months later, Alfred Kahn, the administration's so-called anti-inflation czar, concluded that "the price statistics for the last six months indicate that the current voluntary standards have not been effective on the price side."[95] In response, the administration decided to once again call a meeting with major business leaders, including Jones, "to solicit increased participation of the business community in the anti-inflation program." The meeting began with a press photo-op and a boilerplate performative discussion that stuck to platitudes about the need for business and government to work together in fighting inflation. But after the press left, Carter's tone changed. He now made a direct plea for business

[94] "Business Roundtable Report," February 1979.

[95] Alfred Kahn, "Modifications in the Price Program," March 28, 1979, Record Group 429, Entry A1 1025, Box #13, National Archives College Park, MD.

cooperation and engaged in tough talk about what would happen should the voluntary program fail. Carter opened with the frank declaration that "where higher corporate profits reflect excessive price increases, they are unacceptable." Surging profits were publicly embarrassing for the administration, and made it "more difficult to secure the continuing willingness of labor to comply with the wage standard." Wages needed to be cut, but that would be much easier if prices, and profits, could be kept to reasonable levels.

Carter urged the assembled businessmen to help build broader support for his gentle approach to structural adjustment, while warning them of the consequences of failure:

> The alternatives to this current program are unpalatable to all of us – a recession or mandatory controls. I strongly oppose the use of mandatory controls, but in order to make <u>our alternative</u> work, I need your strong and explicit support. If this program is to survive and we are to turn the corner on inflation, I simply must have your commitment to devote your energies and your expertise and your influence. I promise you that it will be good for business – and the public – and history will thank you for it.[96]

Nevertheless, Bosworth's resignation three months later spelled doom for the voluntary controls program. That Carter had ruled out mandatory controls meant that the program would all but inevitably fall prey to the same structural pressures that made the capitalist state so necessary in the first place.

The very next day, March 30, 1979, Treasury Secretary Blumenthal sent a memo to the President on behalf of the Troika (now known as the Economic Policy Group, or EPG): "it is the unanimous opinion of your economic advisors that our anti-inflation program needs the strengthening of a somewhat more restrictive monetary policy." In addition, "your advisors also agree unanimously that action should be taken to limit the most liberal terms on consumer credit."[97] That same day, the President acted to further concentrate economic policymaking in the EPG, which

[96] Jimmy Carter, "Talking Points for the President – After the Press Leaves," March 29, 1979, Record Group 429, Entry A1 1025, Box #13, National Archives College Park, MD. Emphasis in text.

[97] W. Michael Blumenthal, "Memorandum for the President Re: Monetary Policy and Consumer Credit Creation," March 30, 1979, Record Group 429, Entry A1 1025, Box #14, National Archives College Park, MD.

was henceforth to be “the exclusive vehicle for coordinating the formulation, execution, and presentation of the Administration’s domestic and international economic policies.” This was partly a response to the confusion that resulted from apparently undisciplined and uncoordinated public statements by Kahn and Bosworth about the coming of a “depression,” or the looming imposition of mandatory controls. Now, the centralization of economic policymaking in the Treasury Department would be further formalized: the Secretary of the Treasury, “as Chairman of the EPG, is the Administration’s chief economic spokesman, and major statements on economic policy by Administration officials should, whenever possible, be reviewed and coordinated by the EPG Steering Group.”[98]

Shortly thereafter, Bosworth and other top COWPS officials sent a memo to the president declaring that the voluntary controls program was reaching the end of the road, but nevertheless pushing back against the EPG recommendation for monetary tightening:

> We do not believe that the currently preferred option of continuing existing economic policies… is viable. The pay/price standards will collapse unless the program can be dramatically rejuvenated. To attempt to do so by further tightening of fiscal/monetary policy, the other element of the anti-inflation program will result in an unacceptable level of unemployment.[99]

The only alternative COWPS could propose was stimulating investment through “tax incentives to encourage capital formation and… increasing funding for research and development.” Bosworth resigned a week later—for all intents and purposes the death knell of the COWPS program.

In June 1979, as COWPS officials were coming to dire conclusions about the future of the program, the annual BR meeting was being held. Chairman Thomas Murphy of GM was euphoric that “our counsel is

[98] Jimmy Carter, “Memorandum for the Heads of Executive Departments and Agencies, Re: The Economic Policy Group and the Coordination of Economic Policymaking,” March 30, 1979, Record Group 429, Entry A1 1025, Box #14, National Archives College Park, MD.; Alfred Kahn, “Long-Range Anti-Inflationary Policy,” May 17, 1979, Record Group 429, Entry A1 1025, Box #13, National Archives College Park, MD.

[99] Barry Bosworth and Robert Russell, “Barry Bosworth and Robert Russell to Michael Blumenthal, Stuart Eizenstat, Alfred Kahn, James McIntyre, Charles Shultze, Re: ‘Short-Term Inflation Policy Options,’” June 1, 1979, Record Group 429, Entry A1 1025, Box #13, National Archives College Park, MD.

valued" in the halls of Washington, because the BR was "emphasizing what is best for the nation as a whole, not just for business. There is rarely, if ever, a conflict between the two." As Murphy recognized, the BR's pragmatic orientation allowed it to participate in the process of devising policy solutions—rather than standing outside and denouncing the results of policymakers' efforts, as the NAM often seemed to do. Yet business could offer little help in resolving the central dilemma the administration faced between recession and failed voluntary controls. Jones, who was re-elected once again as co-chair, could only insist "inflation is made in Washington and has to be cured in Washington by means of restrained fiscal, monetary, and regulatory policy." The BR's position, as expressed by the inflation subcommittee, was practically identical to Bosworth's: ending inflation called for tax incentives for investment, R&D subsidies, and further deregulation.[100]

Even as the administration gradually abandoned any remaining illusions about the future of the anti-inflation program, the BR continued to explicitly support voluntary controls. The NAM, too, saw little alternative.[101] As BR chair Donald Seibert wrote to Kahn at the end of July in submitting the organization's "comments and recommendations" on the pay standards, despite its reservations the BR "supported the President's program because we believe that labor and business must cooperate with the Administration in the fight against inflation."[102] Kahn's reply, sent on the very day that Bosworth's resignation from the COWPS went into effect, politely stated that "we are also greatly appreciative of the understanding and cooperative attitude that The Business Roundtable has taken with respect to pay standards; I repeat my assurances that I don't like

[100] "Business Roundtable Report," June 1979; Council on Wage and Price Stability, "Memorandum from Deputies to Economic Policy Group Re: General Electric Proposal for Pay/Price Standards," July 16, 1979, Record Group 429, Entry A1 1025, Box #14, National Archives College Park, MD; Reginald Jones, "Reginald Jones to Alfred E. Kahn," July 12, 1979, Record Group 429, Entry A1 1025, Box #15, National Archives College Park, MD.

[101] Bradley Graham, "'Blockbuster' Inflation Plan Urged by GE Head," *The Washington Post*, April 26, 1979; Jerry Flint, "Why Shoot the Piano Player?," *Forbes*, July 9, 1979.

[102] "Business Roundtable Comments and Recommendations on the Voluntary Pay Standard," July 24, 1979, Record Group 429, Entry A1 1025, Box #15, National Archives College Park, MD.

them any more than you, but, like you, regard them as a necessity at this time."[103]

The same "cooperative attitude" could hardly be attributed to the NAM—though its more flagrant rejectionism did not mean that it had any more substantial conception for how to resolve the dilemma. On August 3, John Read, the Chair of the NAM task force on wage and price controls, sent NAM's "recommendations" for the voluntary program's second year. The tone—if not the ultimate position—of the letter was markedly different from that of the BR:

> We are deeply concerned over the Administration's statements and actions. There has been a definite drift during the past year away from an economic policy whose primary emphasis is on responsible monetary, budget, and regulatory restraint. The drift towards guidelines with all the characteristics of a mandatory program has been unmistakeable. ... Unless the Administration's policies are modified in the second year of the program to correct these problems, the future support of the NAM and its member companies for the program will be jeopardized.[104]

There was in fact a policy shift on the immediate horizon, but it was the precise opposite of what the NAM expected. Just three days after Read's letter, Carter appointed Paul Volcker to be Fed chair. Volcker was "singularly determined to save the dollar by squelching inflation permanently" and had been the most vocal supporter of sharply escalating interest rates as the only path to finally ending the decade-long crisis. After being approved by Congress on August 6, Volcker entered the Fed with a plan—and set to work almost immediately.

Under Volcker's stewardship, "a new and increasingly invariant ethos for monetary policy, designed above all to 'break inflationary expectations,' was in its formative stages."[105] What was required, in his words, was to "discipline ourselves" through "a policy of pushing interest rates

[103] Alfred Kahn, "Alfred Kahn to Donald Seibert," July 31, 1979, Record Group 429, Entry Al 1025, Box #15, National Archives College Park, MD.

[104] John C. Read, "NAM Recommendations for the Development of the Second Year Voluntary Wage/Price Standards," August 3, 1979, Record Group 429, Entry Al 1025, Box #15, National Archives College Park, MD.

[105] Panitch and Gindin, *The Making of Global Capitalism*, 167–68.

to such 'painfully high' levels... as would prove that beating inflation trumped all other policy goals."[106] The results of this policy were dramatic: a harsh economic "shock" followed by recession, rising unemployment, and intensified austerity. Yet the mood at the annual Business Council retreat in Hot Springs, Virginia, was jubilant. Irving Shapiro of du Pont gleefully proclaimed to reporters there that Volcker's move was "the most fundamental change in the management of the American economy that I've seen in 30 years." "The sooner we suffer the pain, the sooner we'll be through," he added.[107]

With interest rates climbing and inflation skyrocketing—six months after Volcker's appointment it climbed to 17%—Carter, the BR, and allies in Congress also went on the offensive on deregulation. In March, the BR had outlined a comprehensive regulatory reform program. The core of this was to follow the logic of Carter's earlier executive order and "eliminate the presumption of validity for agency action in interpreting or applying a regulatory statute." New regulations were not to be *presumed* legitimate, but would have to *justify* their existence. Moreover, they would have to do so in economic terms: "Regulatory agencies should be required to consider 'reasonable alternatives' to proposed rules and to justify the selection of more costly methods over those entailing lesser adverse economic effects."[108] While "providing safer, healthier working conditions for instance, and protecting the environment" may be laudable goals, they were only viable if they did not excessively impinge on profits, or go beyond what capitalism could support.[109] In issuing this program, Murphy commented that relations between business and the state "are better today than they were in the past," in large part because of the effort of the BR to "break down the adversary relationship that has been causing so much friction between our public and private sectors."[110]

[106] Panitch and Gindin, *The Making of Global Capitalism*, 163.

[107] Merrill Brown, "Why Are All These National Businessmen Smiling?," *The Washington Post*, October 15, 1979.

[108] "Business Roundtable Report," March 1980.

[109] "Business Roundtable Report," April 1980.

[110] "Business Roundtable Report," March 1980.

Finance, Industry, and Neoliberal Hegemony

Two months later, at the BR's annual conference in June 1980, Murphy, along with Jones and the rest of the organization's leadership, stepped aside. Jones had served in the leadership longer than any other executive. With his departure, for the first time no one from GE was on either the executive or policy committees. His replacement as CEO, Jack Welch, would not recapture the centrality to organizing class power that Jones, Borch, Cordiner, and Wilson had possessed—though he certainly "led by example," emerging as the paradigmatic model of neoliberal management for the next two decades. In his outgoing address to the conference, Murphy urged business to continue working "in a positive way, by continuing to strive for a less adversarial relationship toward those in government." "By following that course," Murphy said:

> The Roundtable will continue to move ever-closer to its originally-stated goal: to build a sound co-operative relationship among the various sectors of American society in which 'the national interest takes precedence over all others – over the purely political, over the purely business, over the militant coalition. The underlying conviction at the beginning of the Roundtable was – and remains today – that the furtherance of the national interest will benefit all the others, including our own.[111]

Murphy may be forgiven for confusing the national interest with the general interest of the capitalist system, but what was instructive about his comments was how clearly he identified the BR as an organ for articulating a class-wide political coalition. Not only did this mean expressing a broader view than other business groups, it also pertained to the *method* whereby these views were reached. Not unlike the CED and BAC, subcommittees worked collaboratively with state officials to develop policy positions, around which the organization then provided the means to build a broad business consensus.

Increasingly, this consensus had to incorporate finance, as well—whose meteoric rise economically had been reflected politically in Volcker's appointment, and would be solidified over the decade of recession and recovery that would follow. As had already been affected *economically* through the restructuring of the non-financial corporation, finance and

[111] "Business Roundtable Report," June 1980.

industry would establish a shared *political* consensus—around neoliberalism. This was by no means without contradictions. Indeed, the BR sought throughout the latter 1970s to protect "inside" managers of industrial firms from growing pressure by outside investors. This entailed a battle within the integral state over the specific form that interlocking state and corporate power would take. As the power of finance grew, it was further supported by corporate governance reforms pursued by the increasingly assertive Securities and Exchange Commission.

Such reforms aimed at empowering Boards of Directors and increasing the ability for shareholders to nominate and elect members; increasing required disclosures to shareholders; making it easier for investors to cooperate; increasing shareholder access to proxy ballots; and more. As such, the BR sought continuously—and almost entirely unsuccessfully—to limit the powers of the SEC and establish defenses from investor pressure. Even as the "deregulation" agenda gained steam within the state, rolling back regulations protecting the environment and labor, this apparently in no way pertained to those regulations which protected the rising power of investors, institutionalized in the ascent of the SEC as well as in the very governance structures of the industrial corporation. Curtailing these was the primary remit of the BR's Corporate Organization Policy Committee, which was engaged with the SEC continuously on corporate governance issues.

In his testimony at an October 1977s hearing on corporate governance, BR member and Federated Department Stores Chairman Ralph Lazarus commented that "there is a current strong move toward more active, independent boards."[112] The most important thing, reiterated by the BR throughout the late 1970s, was that "in view of the widespread and deep-seated changes presently under way, further changes in corporate governance should continue to be voluntary, not legislated."[113] In January 1978, the BR Policy Committee approved "a definitive statement" on "The Role and Composition of the Board of Directors of the Large Publicly-Owned Corporation" in which the BR endorsed

[112] "Business Roundtable Report," October 1977.

[113] "Business Roundtable Report," September 1978; "Business Roundtable Report," October 1978; "Business Roundtable Report," December 1978; "Business Roundtable Report," August 1979; "Business Roundtable Report," December 1979; "Business Roundtable Report," August 1977.

"the strong tendency" for corporations "to move toward a majority of 'outsiders' on their boards of directors."

As we have seen, this had been true of GE for some time, and had allowed its board to serve as an important venue for organizing and reproducing the capital relations across sectors that were necessary to manage its highly diversified operations. The centrality this afforded the company had been an important foundation for the political role GE managers had played throughout the managerial period. Now, more firms were following suit, which was being held up by the BR as evidence of the responsiveness of industrial managers to investor calls for "good governance" and "transparency." However, the report also concluded "that greater participation by shareholders in the management of corporations is impractical."[114]

It was thus not insignificant that, for the first time since the organization's founding, the 1980 conference included a discussion of "financial market prospects," led by Bank of America President A. W. Clausen—who had previously been considered by Carter for Treasury Secretary.[115] Though "financial markets have been reflecting a turbulence that is almost without precedence," he said, "the recent trends in monetary policy have provided the most encouragement." Despite the positive consequences of Volcker's policy, Clausen felt that, "the expansion of the Federal Reserve's arsenal of powers… is substantial and leaves one a little uneasy." Clausen was prepared to accept this, however, as it had been accompanied by measures to "stimulate competition among financial institutions," which was "a beneficial objective." What business needed now was "visible confirmation by the Federal Government that it is reducing its proportionate role in the economy" which meant "that in the budget process, spending restraint is preferable to raising revenue." Moreover, "if tax cuts are made, supply-side incentives to retool our capital base must take precedence over stimulation of consumer demand."[116] The neoliberal paradigm—and the class coalition that would support it—was thus distilled within the BR by June 1980.

Though Clausen was optimistic about Volcker's monetary tightening nearly a year into his tenure at the Fed, he concluded that "only

114 "Business Roundtable Report," January 1978.

115 Steele et al., "Picking Up the Pieces."

116 "Business Roundtable Report," June 1980.

time will answer the crucial question whether our government at long last has embarked on a steadfast program of non-inflationary monetary discipline." Given the consequences, it could not be ruled out that the draconian policy would be reversed. Yet Volcker stayed the course, earning him—and the Fed—the respect of business in the US and elsewhere, successfully ending the long inflation crisis and protecting the international role of the dollar. At the end of Carter's presidency, the federal funds rate was at 19.1%, where it remained six months into Reagan's tenure. Unemployment climbed to 11% by the fall of 1982, the highest level since the Great Depression. It was only then, after three years, "that Volcker let it be understood that the 'shock' was finally over: the Fed's 'policy objective' had at last changed to monetary 'easing.'"[117] Even when growth finally resumed in 1983, inflation hovered around 3%, where it remained for the rest of the century.

The policy shift signaled by the Volcker Shock was possible because "by the end of the 1970s most industrial sectors of capital had come to accept the need to give priority to fighting inflation and defeating labour, and agreed the strengthening of financial capital this would involve was in their own interest."[118] Yet this consensus among capitalists by no means emerged spontaneously or automatically. The rise of finance was reflected in conflicts around the restructuring of the institutions of capitalist class power—the state and the corporation—which reverberated throughout the integral state. The neoliberal consensus that ultimately emerged was supported by the fact that, despite their attempts to limit investor discipline, industrial managers relied increasingly upon global finance, both to circulate value through ever-more internationalized production chains and as an outlet for investment.

Moreover, the financialized restructuring of the big conglomerates tended to transform top executives of industrial firms into financiers—thereby promoting a commonality of interests with investors. While this created the possibility for an alliance between finance and the largest corporations around free trade and other elements of neoliberal restructuring, it also opened vast new contradictions—economically, in the form of increased volatility and the growth of the financial sector, but also in the political backlash to "deindustrialization" and intensified conflict

[117] Panitch and Gindin, *The Making of Global Capitalism*, 168.

[118] Panitch and Gindin, *The Making of Global Capitalism*, 163.

between big corporations and smaller business. The latter would require considerable effort, not least on the part of Jones as head of the President's Export Council, to build a consensus around neoliberal free trade that would incorporate big business, small business, and labor. It is to these efforts to build consensus around neoliberal free trade, and the internationalization of the state, that we now turn.

CHAPTER 8

From Capital Controls to Free Trade: The Making of the Internationalized Neoliberal State

As we saw, after World War II the American state took on unprecedented responsibility for constructing and managing a new international order. This required implementing new rules to govern world trade, based on reciprocal obligations among states to reduce tariff barriers. However, American capitalists were by no means automatically supportive of liberalization, nor of the state taking on a wide range of expensive international responsibilities, to say nothing of rebuilding their major industrial rivals in Europe. Business consent for, and participation in, the construction of a new imperial state to facilitate the making of global capitalism had to be actively organized by the state. Particularly contentious was securing and entrenching the autonomy of the trade policy apparatus, responsible for negotiating and implementing reductions in trade barriers.

Faced with the choice between either gaining the opportunity to appeal for limited trade protections on a "special case" basis, or nothing at all, skeptical businesses had ultimately seen little alternative to backing continued liberalization, and the agencies that drove this process forward. Nevertheless, conflicts around trade had again flared up when the unprecedented tariff reductions of the Kennedy Round trade talks exacerbated the crisis of the state-capital relationship of the 1960s. The economic crisis of the 1970s further destabilized this consensus. Growing international competition increased pressure on businesses also facing

© The Author(s), under exclusive license to Springer Nature Switzerland AG 2022

S. Maher, *Corporate Capitalism and the Integral State*, Marx, Engels, and Marxisms,
https://doi.org/10.1007/978-3-030-83772-3_8

wage pressure from below, further squeezing profits and intensifying frustrations with liberalization. Protectionist pressures grew, as business felt it had not been adequately consulted in the Kennedy Round.

The end of the Bretton Woods system of capital controls and fixed exchange rates in 1971 meant that the international trade regime had to be fundamentally redesigned. The elimination of wage and price controls at home would be accompanied by the elimination of controls internationally, first and foremost among the core capitalist countries. Such controls would be replaced by global financial integration to support the free movement of investment, paving the way for a transition from the "soft integration" of lower tariffs and more trade to the "hard integration" of cross-border corporate production. Once again, it was state agencies, especially the ascendant Treasury Department, and the Office of the Special Trade Representative (STR), which took the lead in policy planning. Meanwhile, the Commerce Department worked to overcome distrust among business by organizing an advisory architecture of unprecedented scope, through which capitalists from every sector of the American economy systematically offered input into what would become the most significant round of trade negotiations since World War II.

GE was deeply involved in these efforts from the beginning, working closely with Commerce officials to lay crucial foundations for the advisory system. It was the only company to have executives nominated to represent multiple economic sectors on the Policy Advisory Committee, and it also participated on the Technical Advisory Committees. In 1979, President Carter appointed Reginald Jones chair of the President's Export Council (PEC), organized by the Department of Commerce and ostensibly the top trade advisory body to the president. Though it did not become a vehicle for a new state-led export promotion strategy, as some in Commerce had hoped, the PEC nevertheless helped institutionalize the advisory system and solidify the free trade consensus among big multinationals, while working to extend this to smaller, nationally focused businesses.

For Commerce, this was an opportunity to boost its long-flagging position within the hierarchy of state apparatuses by proving its usefulness to the administration and business alike. In fact, the advisory system was essential for gathering the huge volume of information necessary for conducting trade negotiations, for legitimizing the process and its outcome among business, and for implementing the agreements after they had been signed and ratified. The importance of state autonomy for the articulation of the general interests of capital was highlighted by the fact that responsibility for trade *policy* was located within the more independent STR, while Commerce took on *implementation* of these policies. This institutional separation between Commerce and STR was intended to *insulate* policy from pressure from capitalists or Congress. Commerce mediated the relationship between business and the trade policy apparatus, distilling and generalizing the input it received in the process.

The new trade negotiations would go considerably beyond prior rounds—not merely reducing tariffs and promoting trade, but shifting relations of power within the state and restructuring its institutions to secure the new regime in coordination with other states. The *internationalization of the state* would serve to entrench and constitutionalize the new order. This was not least noticeable in the case of Commerce, with its long history of protectionism and close ties to capital, as it was restructured to enforce the new regime. The ad hoc trade advisory system developed by Commerce around the trade negotiations would be consolidated into a permanent integral state mechanism, which would support permanent new multilateral trade policy venues. In this regard, the PEC would play an important role in integrating business with the new International Trade Administration (ITA)—which became the most important among Commerce's disparate programs, and the chief state mechanism facilitating the implementation and enforcement of the new order.

The End of Bretton Woods and the Renewal of State-Business Trade Collaboration

In May 1979, just weeks before the first meeting of the PEC, Jones delivered a major address at the National Journal Conference on International Trade and Investment Policy.[1] The speech revealed much about why Jones had been chosen to head that organization. He possessed a sophisticated grasp of state autonomy and the dynamics of integral state organizing as a result of his role on the Business Roundtable, as well as of the evolving global economy as a result of GE's place at the leading

[1] Reginald Jones, "Expanding Exports: What Can Government and Industry Do? Address to the National Journal Conference on International Trade and Investment Policy, Washington, D.C.," May 10, 1979, Record Group 151, Entry UD-05 W 5, Box #3, National Archives College Park, MD.

edge of developing the new forms of internationalization that would characterize the post-Bretton Woods world.

Like other businessmen, Jones believed that the balance-of-payments deficit that had been such a focus of policymakers since the 1960s put pressure on the dollar and therefore contributed to the inflation crisis, problems with job creation, and ultimately loss of tax revenue. Yet he emphasized that "the point I want to make to our friends in government is that individual companies do not take on the risks and opportunities of the export trade in order to change national trade statistics. They do it when they think it will help them make more money." Export promotion could not rely on merely persuading businessmen to take the initiative as a matter of national pride, nor for the larger benefit of the system as a whole. Rather, this had to be based in the recognition that corporations act strictly in the interests of their own bottom lines.

In illustrating this, Jones outlined GE's success in moving from a "national strategy to a world strategy" in the 1970s. One reason foreign operations and affiliates were important, Jones claimed, was that they "pull through" exports from the US continuously "just because <u>they are there</u>, as a part of the local business community." Thus "when we establish or expand a foreign affiliate, the result is almost always a sharp increase in export sales to that country out of production from our U.S. facilities." However, framing this merely in terms of "exports" obscured the extent to which this was about constructing internationalized production chains, and locating particular stages wherever it was cheapest, rather than simply exporting finished products from the US to other markets. It wasn't merely a matter of boosting exports, but restructuring production itself. With globalized production, "trade" was increasingly a matter of large corporations moving value and goods within cross-border networks they controlled. Indeed, Jones reported that in the eight years since the company had adopted its "world strategy," its exports went from $600 million to $3 billion. "It is against the background of this profitable experience," Jones concluded, "that we urge other companies in the United States to go after the export business." While "it is more risky, more complex, and more difficult to sustain than domestic business… we have found it is well worth the effort."

The complexities and difficulties entailed by cross-border integration meant that business needed to work with the state to develop the policies, practices, and frameworks necessary to support such internationalization. For Jones, "the first and fundamental requirement is a government policy to improve the productivity and competitiveness of American industry"—starting with a "committed effort" by the state "to reduce the regulatory burden that stifles innovation, and reform the tax structure to encourage business investment in productivity improvement." This included reducing the "array of environmental reviews, human rights maneuverers, antitrust limitations, and arbitrary export controls" imposed by the state on American business, unlike its competitors. As we have seen, this was broadly consistent with the program that emerged over the 1970s within the BR. The second policy change was the need for "a determined effort to knock down the artificial barriers to U.S. products abroad." The response to perceived inequities in "free trade" Jones pointed to was not to increase protections around the US market, but to pressure others to reduce their own barriers.

This perspective was central to the neoliberal trade regime seeded by the state over the course of the 1970s. Though it had long been marginal to policymaking, the Department of Commerce had been able to maintain a significant role within the state by virtue of its place as home of the BAC. The severing of the BAC from Commerce in 1961 further marginalized the department, in addition to signifying a deep crisis in the relationship between capital and the state. While this would not be substantially resolved until a decade later, the new BC quickly moved to develop closer relations with the ascendant Treasury Department. International trade negotiations were already a major focus of the meetings of the new Treasury Liaison Council through the 1960s, which were often joined by the STR. The balance-of-payments problem was a regular topic of discussion, possible resolutions to which included "fiscal incentives to promote export growth,"[2] as well as "the reduction of tariff and non-tariff barriers to trade."[3] These linkages grew over the 1970s as an extensive array of policy planning capacities was built around Treasury, supported by the Business Roundtable.

Four months before the president declared the end of Bretton Woods, top officials at Treasury were counseling that although "controls should

[2] Treasury Department, "Summary of Meeting of the Treasury Consultative Committee of the Business Council," April 18, 1967, Record Group 56, Entry Al 736, Box #5, National Archives College Park, MD.

[3] Treasury Department, "Summary of Meeting of the Treasury Consultative Committee of the Business Council with Treasury Officials," December 1, 1965, Record Group 56, Entry Al 736, Box #5.

be removed as soon as the U.S. balance of payments position permits, we believe that it would be a serious mistake to remove them at the present time," which "would be interpreted abroad as 'malign neglect' of our responsibilities," as Volcker put it. Therefore, "beyond any effort on our part to explain the 'ineffectiveness' of the controls, action could not only trigger loss of confidence in the dollar and a major international financial crisis, but, in the eyes of much of the world, cast us in the role of initiating villain."[4] The need to dismantle capital controls only gradually would mean that the state "muddled through another international monetary crisis" in the words of CEA chair Paul McCracken. Although he concluded that "we can congratulate ourselves that we have so far escaped the worst of outcomes – which would have been a commitment to restrictions on the domestic economy and widespread controls both at home and abroad," nevertheless "we cannot be sure of having escaped entirely or permanently."[5]

What was for sure was that "muddling through" was not an adequate basis for managing global capitalism. As McCracken saw, "allowing a 'crisis' to develop and then floating outside the rules of the system, is too uncertain and risky to be repeated." Given that "a system that combined rigidly fixed exchange rates with free trade and capital movements appears to be unworkable," he concluded, "there seem to be two alternatives – either more extensive use of direct controls to support a system of fixed exchange rates or an internationally-agreed upon system of greater flexibility." Volcker, along with the State Department, favored the latter. However, not only foreign countries facing "excessive" dollar inflows with the removal of controls, but also even "our own businessmen and bankers appear to be generally opposed to wider use of floating rates." Policymakers therefore had to take the lead in bringing business on board with the move toward floating exchange rates. The first step would be to "convene the Council on International Economic Policy to reassert our position in favor of an updating of IMF rules," while also "reaffirming our attachment to the basic principles of the Bretton Woods system."[6] This would effectively buy time to develop a more detailed plan for reforming

[4] Paul Volcker, "Paul Volcker to Peter Peterson," April 1, 1971, Record Group 56, Entry A1 718, Box #5, National Archives College Park, MD.

[5] McCracken, "International Monetary Reform," Memorandum for the President, June 2, 1971, Record Group 56, Entry A1 718, Box #8.

[6] McCracken, "International Monetary Reform," June 2, 1971.

the international trade system—which also entailed expanding the policy planning capacities around the Treasury Department, complementing the efforts we observed in Chapter 7.

A month after the President announced the formal end to Bretton Woods, Burns advised the President to publicly express that "we have in mind much more than patching up the old monetary system with a new set of exchange priorities." Rather, "we want a new crisis-free monetary system that will serve the needs of all countries in an increasingly interdependent world."[7] An important feature of the new order would be an increased role for central banks. Accordingly, Peterson had informed Connally prior to the formal announcement of the end of Bretton Woods that Burns was pushing for "the Chairman of the Federal Reserve Board being more actively represented in the world's international monetary institutions." Specifically, he wanted to "take the spot now occupied by State."[8] The State Department, however, did not take kindly to this encroachment. Upon hearing of the request, Acting Secretary John Irwin called Volcker "urgently requesting that State be involved in any decision-making in the international monetary arena."[9] Nevertheless, discussions over the next year within the Treasury Department and STR envisioned a primary role for those two agencies, with the State Department clearly in a secondary position.

Early discussions of restructuring within STR, Commerce, and Treasury took place around Harald Malmgren's *International Economic Peacekeeping in Phase II*. Malmgren was a senior Nixon advisor and long-time veteran of STR, as well as an advisor to the OECD, who would subsequently be made Deputy Trade Representative in 1972. He was also a leading figure in developing neoclassical "institutional economics" and the Austrian School theory of the firm, influenced by the ideas of economists such as Ludwig von Mises, Oskar Lange, and

[7] Arthur F. Burns, "Memorandum For President," September 21, 1971, Record Group 56, Entry Al 718, Box #8, National Archives College Park, MD.

[8] Peter Peterson, "Peter Peterson to John Connally," August 10, 1971, Record Group 56, Entry Al 718, Box #7, National Archives College Park, MD.

[9] Paul Volcker, "Note For Secretary Connally," August 13, 1971, Record Group 56, Entry Al 718, Box #7, National Archives College Park, MD.

Friedrich von Hayek.[10] *Economic Peacekeeping* was enormously influential, and at the time the most substantial treatment of the issues to be addressed in the new round of trade negotiations. Perhaps more importantly, it sketched out the considerable institutional reorganization of nation states that would be necessary to implement the new global trade regime—effectively amounting to an extensive reorganization of the trade apparatus.

Malmgren's crucial argument was that "the United States should have a grand overall economic strategy in which both domestic and international interests are closely harmonized." Such an approach, he concluded, "can only be achieved at the White House level under the direction of a Presidential appointee who has line authority over the various Executive Branch agencies."[11] This could take the form of a Council on International Economic Policy (CIEP), which would "coordinate policy, bridge domestic political and economic interests, police implementation and organize voting in Congress… so that the full weight of the White House can be brought to bear on international economic issues in relation to Congress." Treasury's leadership role should be joined by a more robust STR, so that "Treasury would implement policy and conduct negotiations regarding monetary matters, and the President's Special Trade Representative would take care of all trade matters, and the State Department 'most other matters'." The autonomy that such capacities would afford this apparatus, Malmgren realized, would be further bolstered by the multilateral framework these agencies would help to institutionalize, which was explicitly intended to contain protectionist forces. As summarized by STR, "the existence of international rules, institutions, and procedures for regulating international commerce also serve to restrain, if not to frustrate, the tendency for legislatures to yield to the pressures of special interest groups who want protections from some forms of foreign competition."[12] The subsequent restructuring of the trade apparatus would in fact proceed along precisely these lines, beginning with

[10] Nicolai Foss, "Austrian Insights and the Theory of the Firm," in *Advances in Austrian Economics*, vol. 4, 1997.

[11] Bill Bray, "Comments on 'International Economic Peacekeeping in Phase II' by Harald B. Malmgren," March 10, 1972, Record Group 56, Entry A1 718, Box #8, National Archives College Park, MD.

[12] Bray, "Comments on 'International Peacekeeping in Phase II'."

the establishment of the CIEP shortly thereafter, chaired by Treasury Secretary Shultz.[13]

A few months later, Assistant STR for Industry and Labor Theodore Gates posed the problems facing state officials seeking to organize business for a new round of trade talks before a group of businessmen. Nixon's announcement of the end of Bretton Woods almost exactly one year previously had "clearly and sharply brought an end to one era and the beginning of a new one." The challenges of ushering in this new era were considerable, especially given that "the remaining problems" of world trade to be worked out through multilateral negotiations "are usually the more sensitive and the more difficult to solve for they are the ones with deep roots in domestic economic, political, social, or security considerations in each country." These issues "go beyond the scope of trade matters, narrowly defined, and stem from or are related to policies and practices hithertofore [sic] not involved in international negotiations." As a result, the forthcoming negotiations would "bear little resemblance to their predecessors."[14]

In order for the state to be able to address such matters, it would need to devise extensive new mechanisms for systematically coordinating with corporations. Yet large segments of business remained intensely distrustful as a result of what they saw as a lack of meaningful consultation during the prior Kennedy Round. New promises had to be made to assuage the anger of those who felt their interests had been disregarded, particularly as the costs of liberalization hit home in the form of intensified competition, breeding a rise in protectionist sentiment. Gates acknowledged that "many of the efforts [in Industry-Government collaboration] in the Kennedy Round were frankly experimental – on both sides. Most of them had few antecedents and the participants little experience in such collaborations. They had to be built up from scratch." Thus "the results,

[13] U.S. Congress, Senate, Committee on Finance, *Executive Branch Organization for International Economic Policy*, 93rd Congress, 2d session, February 18, 1974, S. Rep. S362-5, pp. 1–3.

[14] Theodore Gates, "Address by Theodore R. Gates, Assistant Special Representative for Industry and Labor before 164th Meeting of the American Chemical Society, New York, N.Y.," August 28, 1972, Record Group 489, Entry UD-WW 18, Box #4, National Archives College Park, MD.

inevitably, were mixed." Nevertheless, Gates argued that the consultative mechanisms constructed during the Kennedy Round should not be discarded, but rather built upon.

"Obviously," Gates said, "the overall results were far better from the point of view of our total, national interest, than had such efforts not been made." This was because "government agencies simply do not have all of the information required even for a negotiation as limited as was the Kennedy Round, nor are there in existence government experts with the technical, managerial, and all the other insights which are absolutely necessary to make all of the right decisions."[15] Nor were there many in the business world "with the scarce combination of thorough knowledge of a U.S. industry and virtually limitless knowledge of foreign interests, negotiating details, and international rules, as well as, of course, with limitless time to devote to liaison with government."[16] There was also a fundamental "problem for which there may probably be no acceptable solution, under any circumstances": As Gates saw it, "only King Solomon faced more difficult decisions" than those faced by the state in articulating a "national interest" on the basis of myriad particular interests. Thus "it is not fair to allege that government-industry or other liaison efforts have failed because the advice of specific interest was, in the end, not always accepted."[17]

Most important in building on the Kennedy Round experience was the need to "formalize and make permanent a more effective government-industry liaison in trade matters, and for the long run, not just for a particular negotiation." This "new, cooperative structure" should be "supplemented by two additional groups." One should be a "Presidentially-appointed, public-advisory body of distinguished citizens who would be called upon for advice and council, not as spokesmen for their particular interests, but for the national interest as they collectively judged it." The other would be a "much larger" technical advisory group "nominated

[15] Theodore Gates, "Address by Theodore R. Gates, Assistant Special Representative for Industry and Labor before 164th Meeting of the American Chemical Society, New York, N.Y.," August 28, 1972, Record Group 489, Entry UD-WW 18, Box #4, National Archives College Park, MD.

[16] Gates, "Address before 16th Meeting of the American Chemical Society," August 28, 1972.

[17] Gates "Address before 16th Meeting of the American Chemical Society," August 28, 1972.

and supported by the specific interests concerned." This would constitute "a broad and informed mechanism for insuring (sic) that all the diverse interests within the American economy and within complex industries are covered and understood."

As an alternative to an "overly cumbersome three-tier approach," Gates proposed "a single industry council on trade and related economic matters… This broad, senior body, perhaps along the lines of the Business Council, would be charged with developing the supporting network of qualified advisors, of insuring (sic) that all issues were adequately studied by industry and that experts were made available whenever necessary, and of attempting the initial reconciliation of any divergent interests."[18] Gates thereby envisioned a permanent trade policy system which would integrate business within the policymaking process and provide the necessary technical advice to trade negotiators, while reciprocally educating and building consensus among business itself. Though Gates framed this as an alternative to the tiered advisory structure, the broad corporate "advisory" body that was actually created in the form of the President's Export Council (PEC) was a *supplement* to such a system. Organized within the Department of Commerce in a way that did indeed resemble the BAC, the PEC was ostensibly the top trade advisory body to the President.

The advisory commission structure that would be organized by Commerce would strive to integrate the broadest possible base of corporate power within a policymaking processes that would be centralized under an expanded STR. The structure of this advisory apparatus was intended to encourage the assimilation of the myriad *particular* interests within a *general* interest by creating layers of institutional mediation: from the particular sectoral industrial interests of the technical groups, to the broader interest of the policy group, and finally to the state. Further mediations existed within the state itself, as the Commerce Department intervened between STR and the advisory commission. At the same time, this structure would help extend the political consensus worked out at the top between the state and the largest, most diversified, and most internationalized firms downward to smaller firms.

That the corporate executives in the political advisory group were "general" managers was also important for this two-way dynamic. As we saw in the case of GE, these general managers sought to approximate

[18] Gates "Address before 16th Meeting of the American Chemical Society," August 28, 1972.

abstract *capital-in-general*—taking on investment functions, as operational tasks were relegated to divisional managers. The tiered advisory structure therefore reflected the structure of the multinational corporation itself, with those at the top possessing a broader and more general perspective, while those embedded more closely in specific concrete operations, with narrower perspectives, were subordinate. Building an advisory system whereby these particular interests would be mediated by the broader political group would, it was hoped, facilitate the emergence of a perspective approximating the general interest of capital, and institutionalize the free trade consensus, while also supplying policymakers with the technical information necessary to formulate a negotiating position.

Relative Autonomy and the National Interest

As another international crisis of capitalism unfolded, the fact that the current treaty framework lacked any significant coverage of so-called Non-Tariff Barriers (NTBs) increasingly became a concern of those preparing for negotiations. NTBs consisted of "export and domestic subsidies, product standards, and government procurement practices." There was a ban on export subsidies for "non-primary products," but this contained "no definition of what measures constitute an export subsidy." Nor was there any provision within the GATT rules for dealing with subsidized exports. There were thus few tools to restrain the dynamic of competitive subsidization, which intensified with the crisis. Addressing this required the "international harmonization and certification of product standards" and "codes of conduct," such that national regulatory incongruences could not even inadvertently generate monopolistic privileges. This was of particular concern in light of "European plans to conclude regional standards and certification agreements on an exclusive basis."[19] Thus the elimination of NTBs entailed the deeper penetration of the transnational trade regime into institutions and policy areas generally thought to be the remit of national governments. This, in turn, entailed a considerable extension of the US empire in generalizing standards across nation states—which would be facilitated by *permanently* institutionalizing the international venues within which trade policy was made.

[19] Department of Commerce, "Industry Consultations Background Information," September 23, 1974, Record Group 489, Entry UD-WW 18, Box #4, National Archives College Park, MD.

Nor was the problem merely coming from abroad. Along with the wage pressures from below, US manufacturers increasingly felt the pinch of export competition from foreign rivals, particularly Germany and Japan. Business had succeeded in pressing Congress in 1971 to mandate that the Export–Import Bank provide financing to help American manufacturers compete with subsidized foreign firms. Established during the New Deal, the Ex-Im Bank was a state financial institution that provided subsidized financing for US exports—of which GE was a major beneficiary. In the 1960s, it had mitigated the negative effects of the overvalued dollar that resulted from the Bretton Woods system on capital goods exports. Despite the advent of floating exchange rates, demands on the bank from business intensified in the 1970s: in addition to competing with subsidies extended by other states and dealing with the skyrocketing price of oil, business saw the bank as essential to counteract the interest rate hikes the Fed implemented in 1969–70 to fight inflation. As a consequence of the increased costs to the bank that resulted from rate hikes, during the 1970s the bank lent funds below its cost of capital.[20]

At the same time, leading state agencies sought to restrain such practices—both at home and abroad—by branding them NTBs within the multilateral trade framework. Even as the role of the Ex-Im Bank was extended, the state required it to participate in OECD negotiations aimed at limiting these very practices. Multilateral trade negotiations therefore helped the American state secure the autonomy necessary not only to extend liberalization abroad, but also to discipline *its own* capitalist class.

As the pressures of economic crisis and foreign competition mounted, leading state officials recognized the need to act quickly to forestall protectionist forces that were becoming emboldened within Congress. Peter Flanigan, an investment banker and top economic adviser to Nixon, pushed for new legislation to be passed as quickly as possible "to sustain the impetus of the international economic reform process launched by the President" a year and half prior when he declared a formal end to Bretton Woods. Getting the process moving as soon as possible would have the effect of "at worst containing in a negotiating forum the politically damaging impact of competitive trade disputes" while working "to offer Congress a constructive Administration alternative to the extreme

[20] William H. Becker and William M. McClenahan Jr, *The Market, the State, and the Export–Import Bank of the United States, 1934–2000,* (Cambridge, UK: Cambridge University Press, 2003), 161–95.

protectionism" of the Burke-Harte bill then under consideration. This would "maximize our chances of breaking down existing tariffs and non-tariff obstacles" as well as "to neutralize new discriminatory tariffs before they are fully in effect in Europe."[21]

The trade bill Flanigan and others sought would concentrate unprecedented power in the trade apparatus. It granted the President "unlimited authority to raise or lower tariffs" and called upon Congress "to delegate a great deal of authority to the President ranging well beyond the tariff area," on top of cutting trade "adjustment assistance" for struggling firms. Similarly, the president would be empowered to negotiate arrangements "beyond principal trading partners," including Eastern bloc countries, which had not been covered by prior trade legislation. Moreover, for the first time, these powers would encompass "authority to negotiate on international investment rules and business practices," among other non-tariff issues.[22]

Treasury continued to lead the charge. As Shultz wrote, "the actions we have taken, important as they are, don't solve all of our international economic problems, and we must resist any temptations to consider them so. We must press ahead on fundamental reform of the international monetary and trading system, and we must proceed promptly with necessary legislation for negotiations on tariff and non-tariff barriers."[23] The focus was especially on deepening integration with the core capitalist countries of Europe, which were assumed to have a shared position around "increased market access opportunities" on the global periphery in that these regions should "treat the exports of all developed countries equally."[24] As the department concluded, "the U.S. national interest would be served by an international economic system" which "facilitated international trade and capital flows among nations," and which "involved a minimum of governmental restraints and subsidies on international economic transactions and a maximum of market-directed U.S. and world

[21] Peter Flanigan, "Memorandum for George Shultz," January 3, 1973, Record Group 56, Entry Al 718, Box #6, National Archives College Park, MD.

[22] Flanigan, "Memorandum for George Shultz," January 3, 1973.

[23] George Schultz, "Department of Treasury Status Report on the Monetary and Trade Situation," February 16, 1973, Record Group 56, Entry Al 718, Box #2, National Archives College Park, MD.

[24] Treasury Department, "U.S.-European Relations: Economic Objectives," Record Group 56, Entry Al 718, Box #6, National Archives College Park, MD.

trade and investment." Crucially, this should be a system that "preserved the habit of cooperation which has become established in international economic affairs."[25]

Meanwhile, efforts to organize a business advisory mechanism to support negotiations got underway in earnest. Commerce Secretary Peter Peterson, as well as STR William Eberle and Peter Flanigan, began "encouraging" representatives from different business associations to meet and gather "detailed" information on NTBs by product line and country. This information would then "be channelled into a broad industry study on NTB's (sic) for submission to the US negotiating team."[26] In November 1972, Commerce convened a large meeting of representatives from a range of business associations, including General Electric's Vice President for Corporate Public Relations, Douglas Moore, as well as officials from STR and Treasury. The meeting resulted in the formation of an "Inter-Association Trade Council," which integrated these different business associations into a broader, informal class-wide group.[27]

The Council was formalized the following April as the "Inter-Industry Advisory Council for Trade Negotiations" (IIAC-TN): "a high-level, autonomous group made up of one corporate spokesman from a broad range of industry groups which have interests in trade negotiation planning." The organization "would be sponsored by a coordinating group of trade associations, with industry representatives on the Council chosen and supported by the staffs and technical working groups of the respective trade associations." Far from seeking to impose a political position on the state through lobbying, the whole endeavor was based on the understanding that "the challenge to industry and government which comprehensive negotiations themselves pose can hardly be underestimated or even perhaps fully comprehended at this point." Indeed, it was recognized that "these negotiations will shape a new world trading

[25] Treasury Department, "U.S. Objectives for Trade Negotiations and Monetary Reform," Record Group 56, Entry A1 718, Box #6, National Archives College Park, MD.

[26] "Trade Association Group Considers New Action on Trade Negotiations," *Commerce Today*, November 27, 1972.

[27] "Inter-Association Non-Tariff Barrier Trade Negotiation Project, Coordination Meeting, Attendees," November 10, 1972, Record Group 489, Entry UD-WW 18, Box #4, National Archives College Park, MD.

system in at least certain areas." Meeting dates and agendas would be discussed and coordinated with "key Administration officials" based on their current needs, and would often take place in government facilities so as to "maximize discussions and briefings with officials." Regular dinners with "prominent government officials" would further increase such contact, as would special working sessions organized on an ad hoc basis.[28]

Commerce and STR worked with the IIAC-TN, as well as individual business associations, to develop an advisory mechanism that would include an unprecedented range of businesses and sectors.[29] In May, Secretary of Commerce Dent and STR Eberle laid out in a memo to Treasury Secretary Shultz a plan for a joint Commerce and STR mechanism that would overcome the "shortcomings" of the system developed during the Kennedy Round. This would take advantage of "Commerce's close working relationship with industry" while supplementing "the small STR staff" with Commerce personnel.[30] Equally important as improved *technical* support for negotiations was greater attention to the system's *political* function: the need to legitimate the process by allowing businessmen to feel that they had the opportunity to offer substantial input. Indeed, Dent and Eberle observed, "the fact that industry felt that it was not brought into the picture soon enough and was given little opportunity for real input [during the Kennedy Round] underscores the need for a different procedure to support the Administration trade policy objectives."[31]

Dent and Eberle formulated a three-stage program of industry consultations to begin the following month. These were effectively a means for state officials to educate corporate elites about international trade

[28] "Proposal for an Inter-Industry Advisory Council for Trade Negotiations, Submitted for Consideration to Inter-Asoscation Presidents' Meeting," April 24, 1973, Record Group 489, Entry UD-WW 18, Box #4, National Archives College Park, MD.

[29] Arch Booth, "Arch Booth to Frederick Dent," May 29, 1973, Record Group 489, Entry UD-WW 18, Box #4, National Archives College Park, MD; "Background Paper: Position of the U.S. Chamber of Commerce," June 1973, Record Group 489, Entry UD-WW 18, Box #4, National Archives College Park, MD.

[30] Frederick Dent and William Eberle, "Memorandum for George P. Shultz From Frederick B. Dent and WIlliam D. Eberle, 'Industry Consultations in Support of Multilateral Trade Negotiations,'" May 21, 1973, Record Group 56, Entry A1 718, Box #3, National Archives College Park, MD.

[31] Dent and Eberle, "Memorandum for George P. Shultz," May 21, 1973.

policy, and to shape their interests and perspectives. In the first stage, STR and Commerce would make "policy presentations" to "key business leaders." The second stage would then consist of "an expanded set of technical level discussions," whose "principal purpose" would be to "obtain from industry economists, marketing experts, managers of international operations, etc. views on what U.S. negotiating objectives should be in various product sectors." Third would come the establishment of "formal standing industry advisory groups," which would build on, and largely incorporate, the IIAC-TN. As Dent and Eberle saw it, these advisory groups would "be established at two levels: a high level industry group to provide overall policy advice… and technical groups or task forces to conduct detailed studies to determine precise U.S. negotiating interests at the product level."[32]

NAM, on the other hand, preferred for the IIAC-TN itself to serve as the advisory mechanism for the trade negotiations. However, "from the U.S. Government point of view" there were "basic problems" with this proposal, both of which illustrate the importance of a relatively autonomous state in managing the trade-offs and compromises entailed by the articulation of the *general* interest of capital. The most important concern was around "the protection and adequate presentation of minority views in any proposals or positions adopted by such a Council and the apparent monopoly position envisioned for the Council in the Government-industry consultative process." The question was not whether business associations should be involved in the process, but rather whether any *individual* association that was not directly overseen and organized by the state could claim a *monopoly* on representing business.[33]

Thus, "any Inter-Industry Advisory Council or similar group might be a participant in whatever consultative mechanism is ultimately created but would not constitute industry's sole representation." The important thing was that, "given the Government's broad responsibility to the U.S. business community, adequate access must be accorded to all segments

[32] Dent and Eberle, "Memorandum for George P. Shultz," May 21, 1973.

[33] "Background Paper: NAM Proposal for an Inter-Industry Advisory Council for Trade Negotiations," June 1973, Record Group 489, Entry UD-WW 18, Box #4, National Archives College Park, MD.

of industry."[34] Only on this basis could the state ensure adequate representation across sectors, firms, and regions; only on this basis could the state ensure that it was acquiring information that was not tainted by informal hierarchies and networks that might shape the "general" perspectives generated by more autonomous business organizations; and only on this basis could the state ensure that a truly broad-based consensus could be constructed around policy, rather than simply a cluster of particular interests.

As stage II of the consultations got underway, policymakers asked business "to evaluate the content of these meetings and assess the current situation regarding industry/government trade negotiation consultations." NAM produced a report underlining the frustration among business that the meetings were insufficiently collaborative, with business expected to simply accept the positions of state officials "essentially as given."[35] To address this, the NAM report requested an expanded role for trade associations. Although "acting as the channel in most cases for industry nominations, the Commerce proposal does not provide any specific linkage or coordinating role" for trade associations "for data collection, transmission of advice and preliminary consensus development." While admitting that "trade associations would be of uneven ability as representatives," NAM believed "it is hard to imagine effective consultative mechanism run by government without a strong supportive role played by trade associations."[36]

The challenge mounted by NAM primarily pertained to the degree of autonomy claimed by the trade apparatus, demanding that it be more beholden to the specific interests of particular capitalists. As we have seen, the autonomy of the trade apparatus was protected in part by the mediation of business input through the Commerce Department—which would *generalize* from the perspectives of many corporations in *representing* a broader business view to STR. Thus the NAM report criticized the way that the advisory structure "interposes additional filtering screens between

[34] "Background Paper: NAM Proposal for an Inter-Industry Advisory Council for Trade Negotiations," June 1973.

[35] Nicholas Hollis, "Improved Industry/Government Trade Negotiation Planning: What Are the Next Steps?," July 2, 1973, Record Group 489, Entry UD-WW 18, Box #4, National Archives College Park, MD.

[36] Hollis, "Improved Industry/Government Trade Negotiation Planning," July 2, 1973.

non-governmental parties and negotiators." Even worse were the "recent attempts of CIEP to incorporate STR into its highly politicized and unreviewable White House operation." The underlying problem, the report held, was the "fallacious 'umbrella' view of industry" upon which the advisory structure was based:

> There is no single industry viewpoint, which reduces consensus points to common denominators. ...U.S. industry cannot assume so single-minded an advisory role – and it is unlikely that the negotiators would accord 'industry' such an advisory role even if such consensus was possible.[37]

This amounted to a claim that *there was no general interest of capital.* There were only myriad *particular* interests, which should therefore have a direct say in determining policy governing their sectors. In suggesting that there was a "common denominator" to which these particular capitalist interests could be "reduced," the state was in fact substituting *its own* distinct interest for that of capital. The NAM report thus failed to perceive (or at least pretended to) the state's *active* role in shaping and articulating the general interest. Business was incapable of developing positions in relation to trade negotiations without the support of the state, as executives lacked the necessary knowledge of rules and protocols, the positions of other trading partners, and the like. It was up to the state to negotiate trade agreements and to impose the trade-offs among firms they entailed. That the state did not simply *transmit* a pre-existing "general interest," but rather had to actively *articulate* this, is precisely what made its role so difficult.

While NAM set up a "Trade Negotiators Coordinator Program" on the periphery of the formal advisory structure "to complement and supplement this government mechanism, primarily as a disseminator of information,"[38] the IIAC-TN also continued to meet independently to enhance business coordination. Yet neither had much influence on the preparations for the talks. Indeed, they were barely informed about the process, as indicated by communiqués sent from Tokyo by Nick Hollis of

[37] Hollis, "Improved Industry/Government Trade Negotiation Planning," July 2, 1973.

[38] "NAM-Trade Negotiations Corporate Coordinator Program," August 27, 1973, Record Group 489, Entry UD-WW 18, Box #4, National Archives College Park, MD.

the NAM. Despite the fact that "preparatory meetings between government officials [had] been underway for several years, particularly on the problem of non-tariff barriers," which would "set the parameters on the subjects to be negotiated and the objectives to be sought," little input had been formally solicited from business. As a result, Hollis feared, "industry could find itself on the outside looking in" during the critical preparatory meetings "on the structure of the negotiations themselves."[39]

Hollis understood that while "the Kennedy Round… produced the most far-reaching series of tariff cuts in history," the "scope of talks" in the Tokyo Round "promises to be much more wide-ranging." This was partly because "the method of negotiating tariffs was changed from tedious item-by-item duty schedule adjustments to across-the-board linear ad valorem cuts, with exceptions only allowed in circumstances of significant national economic or security importance." In addition to tackling NTBs, the new round would also develop a framework for "trade safeguards" that would limit states' ability to resort to even short-term protections for industry—"the first systematic attempt to wrestle with these issues." At issue for the state was therefore the need to discipline capitalists in the US, just as much as its trading partners. Furthermore, the entanglement of the trade apparatus in multilateral governance increased its capacity to do so: as Hollis warned in no uncertain terms, "look closely at how 'reciprocity' is defined" as this "could allow the negotiators a great deal of flexibility in putting together deals."[40]

The Integral State Trade Apparatus

As preliminary talks continued, the Commerce Department raced to complete two overlapping initiatives: forming the stage III advisory mechanism and organizing the new President's Export Council (PEC). Like business, Commerce identified a "primary goal" of the advisory process as being "to avoid the shortcomings of previous efforts." But for Commerce, these shortcomings pertained to a failure *on the part of business*. While in the Kennedy Round, "the U.S. negotiators received a plethora of information regarding where U.S. concessions should not

[39] Nicholas Hollis, "GATT Ministerial Meetings in Tokyo – The Opening Curtain for Multilateral Trade Negotiations and Industry's Responsibilities," September 5, 1973, Record Group 489, Entry UD-WW 18, Box #4, National Archives College Park, MD.

[40] Hollis, "GATT Ministerial Meetings in Tokyo," September 5, 1973.

be made," they received a "dearth of guidance concerning those concessions [from other states] which would provide maximum U.S. export benefits."[41] For this reason, it was necessary "to emphasize the focus on exports and stress to industry participants in our consultations the necessity for providing U.S. negotiators with detailed guidance regarding those U.S. product areas whose exports would benefit most from a reduction or removal of specific foreign trade barriers."[42] Nor should the PEC simply become a venue for expressing complaints about the costs of liberalization. Rather, "U.S. industries suffering from substantial import competition will have two other channels for directing their advice to the negotiators, i.e., the Tariff Commission and the Trade Information Committee hearings."[43] Crucially, however, even if this failed to contain such criticism, it need "not necessarily conflict with our emphasis on export orientation," as such sentiments could be redirected toward "those foreign concessions we should seek."[44]

On October 11, 1973, as the oil crisis dramatically intensified pressures around the world to increase export subsidies while renewing fears about the risks of liberalization, the administration held a massive "President's Conference on Export Expansion" organized by the Commerce Department. At the conference, the administration simultaneously launched both the PEC and a President's Interagency Committee on Export Expansion led by Commerce and chaired by Dent.[45] In attendance were 175 leaders "of the Nation's leading corporations,"[46] including Reginald Jones; featured speakers were William Rogers, Peter Flanigan, George

41 Louis Murphy, "Stage III Program - Industry-Government Consultations in Support of Multilateral Trade Negotiations," September 29, 1973, Record Group 489, Entry UD-WW 18, Box #4, National Archives College Park, MD.

42 "Revised Program for Stage III Industry-Government Consultations in Support of Multilateral Trade Negotiations," November 14, 1973, Record Group 489, Entry UD-WW 18, Box #4, National Archives College Park, MD.

43 Murphy, "Stage III Program - Industry-Government Consultations in Support of Multilateral Trade Negotiations," September 29, 1973.

44 "Revised Program for Stage III Industry-Government Consultations in Support of Multilateral Trade Negotiations," November 14, 1973.

45 Bruce Kehrli, "Bruce Kehrli to Ken Dam," July 10, 1973, Record Group 56, Entry A1 718, Box #4, National Archives College Park, MD.

46 Hawley and Huebner, "Suggested Remarks: Export Expansion Conference," October 10, 1973, Record Group 56, Entry A1 718, Box #4, National Archives College Park, MD. (Emphasis in text).

Shultz, and President Nixon.[47] As Nixon said at the conference, he sought to "enlist the efforts of the assembled business leaders in meeting this export goal and balance of payments objectives." The most important aspect of this was pressing forward with liberalization: "we are entering a new economic era – one of growing economic interdependence and shared economic leadership. If we are to thrive in this new era, then we must be active and eager participants in the adventures of international trade."[48] Despite the large number of invitees to the conference, the PEC would include just 22 members, appointed by the President. Its work was to be supported by 22 Regional Export Councils, each of which would be "led by a chairman and vice chairman who are also members of the PEC and who are appointed by it to their regional posts." These "regional units" would then nominate chairmen for 43 District Export Councils. This would facilitate the organization of a coalition among smaller regional companies and big multinational firms, within a structure dominated by the latter.

Even as the PEC was being established, the focus of international economic policy was shifting toward increasing the mobility of investment, rather than merely boosting trade or securing monetary stability. As Flanigan put it in a memo to Treasury Secretary Shultz, "it has been recognized for some time now that international investment and investment related matters should receive attention independently of trade and monetary matters… But we have barely scratched the surface." As such, a new interagency group should be established to "meet on a regular and continuing basis so that a U.S. position on investment issues… would evolve as circumstances changed and we learned more about the economic, social and political effects of international investment." The Interagency Investment Working Group, as it was called, would be housed within the CIEP and consist of Treasury, State, Commerce, CEA, OMB, and the Fed, with support as needed from the SEC and Ex-Im Bank.

[47] Frederick Dent, "Frederick Dent to George Shultz," August 22, 1973, Record Group 56, Entry A1 718, Box #4, National Archives College Park, MD; "President's Conference on Export Expansion, White House Conference Attendance List," October 11, 1973, Record Group 151, Entry UD-05 W 5, Box #1, National Archives College Park, MD.

[48] Hawley and Huebner, "Suggested Remarks: Export Expansion Conference," October 10, 1973.

Flanigan's "initial list of subjects for discussion" comprised many of the central issues of the neoliberal globalization that would unfold over the following decade and beyond, focusing on the connection between American policies and institutional structures, on the one hand, and global flows of investment governed by the giant multinational corporations, on the other—and zeroing in especially on the financial sector:

1. The multinational corporation and the economic and political problems stemming from the internationalization of production in a world of nation states.
2. Restrictions, explicit or implicit, on foreign investment by host countries.
3. Incentives, explicit or implicit, to inward foreign direct investment.
4. Internal economic policies and their effect on international production and investment decisions.
5. The impact of U.S. and foreign environmental policies on international investment.
6. Security industry laws and regulations and their effect on international investment.
7. Banking industry laws and regulations and their effect on international investment.[49]

As would be the case again at the end of the decade, the PEC appeared to sweeten the deal of liberalization for manufacturers by holding out the promise of state-supported export expansion. For its part, the Commerce Department saw in the PEC an opportunity to improve its position within the hierarchy of state apparatuses, reprising the integral state role it had lost with the departure of the BAC. However, leading policymakers would gradually realize over the rest of the decade that exports of financial services, and imports of capital, were just as good as other commodities in their impact on the balance of payments. The post-Bretton Woods trade regime would be as much focused on facilitating the free global movement of capital as it would be about increasing "trade" of raw materials and finished products.

[49] Peter Flanigan, "Memorandum for George Shultz," December 1973, Record Group 56, Entry A1 718, Box #5, National Archives College Park, MD.

The new pattern would be based on the construction of internationally integrated production chains, rather than redundant processes carried out by subsidiaries within distinct economic zones cordoned off by tariff walls. Imports and exports would now represent not exchanges of final products, but stages within global corporate production networks passing through different national territories. This allowed for greater efficiency by integrating global systems and dismantling redundant processes, locating production in those economic zones where they could be completed most cheaply—thus exerting competitive pressure on wages as well as on environmental and labor regulations, both within the US and elsewhere. Though this would depend on the integration of global finance, and thus the empowerment of financial capital, large industrial MNCs also supported it as essential to their own restructuring—a consensus that was underpinned by the extent to which these firms had already evolved into "systems of investment."

Concurrently, Commerce began setting up the stage III advisory system to support "the most comprehensive and complex" negotiations in US history: "an unprecedented, multi-year undertaking on a U.S. industry-wide basis." This entailed tremendous demands on department resources and personnel, including "participation in the various meetings of all advisory committees, preparation of requisite documentation, coordination of interagency review, maintenance of a close and continuous industry liaison, etc.," all of which "will require majority, if not full time, attention on the part of the Commerce officials concerned."[50] This was the grunt work of organizing the integral state in an increasingly complex, globalizing economy. The task was made more difficult by the "hangover of suspicion by industry of government… from the Kennedy Round days." To enhance the legitimacy of the undertaking, Eberle proposed to Shultz that the government could "improve our credibility" with business by employing McKinsey & Company to review the "information that industry and agriculture should be preparing for us and vice versa."[51]

Nevertheless, Commerce found that "the proposal to undertake comprehensive industry-government consultations… was well received." Perhaps surprisingly in light of business complaints about inadequate

[50] Murphy, "Stage III Program - Industry-Government Consultations in Support of Multilateral Trade Negotiations," September 29, 1973.

[51] William Eberle, "William Eberle to George Shultz," October 9, 1973, Record Group 56, Entry A1 718, Box #5, National Archives College Park, MD.

access to the process, Commerce officials "still [had] not received nominations and/or views on the organizational structure from a majority of the 600 industry participants in the Stage I and II briefings" two months after the fact. The department therefore had to "move ahead with stage III planning and implementation" on the basis of those responses they had received.[52] There was simply no time to lose—as Commerce officials Tilton Dobbin and Henry Turner wrote in November 1973: "The urgent need for industry consultations is underscored by the fact that government officials simply do not have all the information needed—or the expertise to get it—to successfully conduct a major multilateral trade negotiation. Accordingly it is imperative that industry advice be obtained on a massive and unprecedented scale."[53]

The system would be divided into two tiers: the Policy Advisory Committee (PAC) and Technical Advisory Committees (TACs). The PAC, appointed by the Secretary of Commerce and the STR, would comprise twenty "key U.S. industry and business leaders having sufficient standing and perspective to function as advisors regarding overall U.S. industry objectives, rather than solely as spokesmen for their own sector."[54] The PAC would thus integrate the particular interests expressed through the TACs within a class-wide perspective. It would provide general policy advice "as may be requested" by Commerce and STR, meeting "at irregular intervals at the call of the Secretary of Commerce and the Special Representative for Trade Negotiations."[55] Notably, GE was the only firm to have executives nominated to represent multiple sectors on the PAC, with four executives nominated for three different sector groups, including Fred Borch and Jack Parker. Other PAC members were from the steel, tire, and materials industries, as well

[52] "Revised Program for Stage III Industry-Government Consultations in Support of Multilateral Trade Negotiations," November 14, 1973.

[53] Tilton Dobbin and Henry Turner, "Operational Handbook for Stage III, Industry-Government Consultations in Support of Multilateral Trade Negotiations, for Review At Your Meeting with Ambassador Eberle," November 29, 1973, Record Group 489, Entry UD-WW 18, Box #4, National Archives College Park, MD.

[54] "Revised Program for Stage III Industry-Government Consultations in Support of Multilateral Trade Negotiations," November 14, 1973.

[55] Frederick Dent and William Eberle, "Memorandum for George P. Shultz, Joint STR/Commerce Industry-Government Consultations in Support of Multilateral Trade Negotiations," December 7, 1973, Record Group 489, Entry UD-WW 18, Box #4, National Archives College Park, MD.

as high-tech manufacturers including Hewlett-Packard, Motorola, and Boeing.[56]

The TACs, meanwhile, were comprised of "all major firms and trade associations," as well as "a representative sampling of medium and small firms" which the department felt "should be given the opportunity to participate." Each TAC had an average membership of 25–30—totaling 600 people, each of whom needed to be granted security clearance. Despite this large number of business representatives, Commerce predicted that "our need to limit the total number of TACs for reasons of USG resources and manageability is likely to give rise to objections from a few specific industry sub-sectors wishing for more narrowly-constructed groups."[57] Each TAC would also include a coordinator from both Commerce and STR, a legal advisor from one of these departments or the DOJ, Commerce commodity specialists, international economists from the White House Office of Trade Policy, members of the US trade delegation, Government Liaison Officers with extensive responsibilities, and various other specialists.[58] On this basis, TACs were intended to be vehicles for supplying negotiators with the necessary information to develop strategic positions at the negotiations, including product lines with the greatest export potential, barriers inhibiting US exports, areas where foreign concessions should be opposed, U.S. product lines best able to absorb concessions, and the limits to be placed on such U.S. concessions.[59]

This was the organizational infrastructure for determining the general interest of capital, which would fully be articulated only after these inputs were processed through the contradictory institutional ensemble that was the overall state complex. It would allow policymakers to solicit the necessary *technical* information from a wide range of businesses, while working

[56] Dent and Eberle, "Memorandum for George P. Shultz, Joint STR/Commerce Industry-Government Consultations in Support of Multilateral Trade Negotiations," December 7, 1973.

[57] "Revised Program for Stage III Industry-Government Consultations in Support of Multilateral Trade Negotiations," November 14, 1973.

[58] "Stage III Technical Advisory Committees: Organization, Responsibilities, Membership," October 26, 1973, Record Group 489, Entry UD-WW 18, Box #4, National Archives College Park, MD.

[59] "Revised Program for Stage III Industry-Government Consultations in Support of Multilateral Trade Negotiations," November 14, 1973.

with the largest multinationals to build a *political* consensus. This formation of this consensus was by no means automatic, and deep concerns about the outcomes of liberalization, as well as the ability for the state to implement it in a way that broadly benefitted *American* capitalists, persisted. In the face of protectionist pressures from business, Congress, and even within the executive, the trade policy apparatus pressed on with liberalization. This was supported by the institutionalization of important aspects of policymaking in multilateral venues, where decisions would be coordinated with other states, thereby pre-empting opposition. As STR Eberle wrote, it was important "to get negotiations moving not only to liberalize trade barriers, but also to provide an ongoing process that would place new problems into the broader perspective of world economic interdependence."[60]

Constructing the stage III mechanism rapidly became "a major Department of Commerce program," and as of January 1974 was "fast reaching the scale of a full-fledged operation." There were also encouraging signs that Commerce was succeeding in assuaging the doubts left over from the Kennedy Round that had been expressed so powerfully by NAM and IIAC-TN. As Assistant Commerce Secretary Tilton Dobbin reported, "Industry now seems convinced of Commerce's and the Administration's good faith and resolve to work for a meaningful consultation mechanism."[61] Nevertheless, STR Eberle doubted that Commerce "could effectively carry out its primary role in this joint undertaking" and continued to suggest that McKinsey be brought in to support these efforts. Dent, who would go on to become STR months later, maintained "that Commerce would be able to carry out the program without such outside resources."[62]

That smaller businesses still harbored doubts were clear from the conclusions of the Chamber of Commerce "Task Force on Government Industry Liaison." It was obvious to the Chamber that the point of the advisory commission structure was to build a policy consensus among the largest firms and then work to extend this consensus downward. Thus

[60] William Eberle, "'Suggested Talking Points for Rome,' W.D. Eberle to George Shultz," January 9, 1974.

[61] Tilton Dobbin, "Additional Resources Needed for Industry Consultations Program," January 15, 1974, Record Group 489, Entry UD-WW 18, Box #4, National Archives College Park, MD.

[62] Dobbin, "Additional Resources Needed," January 15, 1974.

the Task Force felt "that Commerce and STR intend that the 26 technical advisory committees be nothing more than glorified data groups," and insisted that "advice from the 26 technical committees should not be filtered through the Industry Policy Advisory Committee but should go directly to top U.S. government negotiation officials."[63] However, given the tremendous resources necessary to organize a consensus even among the largest firms, whether it would have been feasible to directly work with a much greater number of smaller firms was doubtful. It was far easier, as in the case of the New Deal, WWII mobilization, and beyond, to work with a smaller number of large corporations. The range of sectors with which such firms maintained relations allowed them to function as important foundations for extending any policy consensus. But, as we have seen, this was not the whole story: policymakers had also carefully structured the process so as to limit unwanted business pressure. The advisory mechanism was not about subjecting the objectives of trade talks to the broadest possible range of business input, but rather building a consensus around a basic orientation that was already largely fixed, while gathering technical information.

In addition to its prominent role on the PAC, GE was a major participant within the ITACs/ISACs. Wayne Rush, manager of GE's Communications Systems Division, eagerly convened "closed meetings" of ISAC 22 (dealing with communications equipment) outside trade association conferences. Since private actors led these meetings—albeit in coordination with state agencies—they were not subject to the publicity requirements of government advisory committees. While their resemblance to the price-fixing meetings discussed in Chapter 3 should have been enough to raise eyebrows, when Rush communicated about them to Commerce officials they expressed nothing but encouragement. At the same time, Rush was clearly aware of the limits of the ISACs' ability to generate a consensus without state coordination, relaying to Commerce officials his perception that "the chances of industry members correctly foreseeing the specific items our negotiators will be asked to consider are rather low."[64]

[63] "Report of Task Force on Government Industry Liaison," U.S. Chamber of Commerce, February 27, 1974, National Archives College Park, MD.

[64] Wayne Rush, "Wayne Rush to Mario Molinari," January 29, 1975, Record Group 489, Entry UD-WW 18, Box #3, National Archives College Park, MD.

The Tokyo Round was particularly complex because it involved the internationalization of the state to a new extent. This included effectively institutionalizing *permanent* trade negotiations, which would take the form of a series of multilateral forums whose horizons were not limited to a particular "round" of trade talks or specific agreement. Indeed, "the negotiations beginning in Geneva will seek common solutions to international trade problems on a continuing basis"—meaning that "these negotiations should not end on a fixed date as have prior negotiations." Rather, the establishment of the venue was *itself* part of the objective. As the Department of Commerce suggested, "there might be considered for the GATT something along the lines of the [IMF's] Committee of Twenty and Deputies groups," which "would provide a higher level body to discuss trade problems."[65] This would take the form of the G7, later expanded into the G20 and beyond, a core feature of the US-managed international system throughout the neoliberal period. Trade talks were not merely about tariff reductions; they were about building an entirely new international institutional architecture. Moreover, this was not a matter of constructing multilateral institutions which would constrain or discipline states from without, but rather restructuring nation states *themselves*—and thus integral state linkages with corporations. This would be supported by the Commerce advisory system, which would ultimately be formalized in the Trade Act of 1974, and would remain a similarly lasting feature of the US integral state.

By the time the Trade Act was passed at the end of the year, the advisory mechanism was already well on its way to being organized. It was Commerce, not corporate lobbyists, which "took the lead in planning and supporting the program from its inception," including "work[ing] closely with both Congressional committees during their drafting and mark-up efforts." Yet the final version of the legislation explicitly subordinated Commerce to STR, while heaping even more logistical responsibilities onto the former.[66] STR wasted no time in making sure that Commerce respected its enhanced power over the process, informing the department

[65] Department of Commerce, "Industry Consultations Background Information," September 23, 1974.

[66] "Program and Policy Implications of the Trade Act of 1974 for the Department of Commerce," January 15, 1975, Record Group 489, Entry UD-WW 18, Box #4, National Archives College Park, MD.

shortly after the legislation passed that "the revised IPAC/ISAC Charters should delete mention of the Secretary of Commerce in this context."[67]

Meanwhile, as the department's internal report noted with a hint of bitterness, "Commerce will continue to be responsible for furnishing the vast majority of administrative, staff, and informational support for the advisory committees." The department recognized that "if Commerce is to remain a truly joint partner with STR in the Program and maintain its effectiveness in U.S. MTN policy formulation," it would have to cultivate a business constituency that could support this role.[68] The result of being downgraded within the advisory system was thus for Commerce to seek to become an even more committed advocate for business interests within the state. And yet, this is the very thing that had led to its isolation, with policy entrusted to more autonomous agencies. The paradox confronting Commerce was that without cultivating its business constituency, the integral state function that had long been its raison d'être would be weakened; yet the lack of autonomy from business this entailed actually led to the further diminishment of the department's policymaking role.

Undersecretary L.J. Murphy would take the lead within the Commerce Department in developing a plan for the longer-term institutionalization of the advisory mechanism. Failing to promptly initiate planning for the next phase, Murphy believed, would generate "'requests' for time-consuming meetings" that "would put our limited [Office of Trade Policy] staff in the unfortunate position of informing/placating the committees' membership at the expense of the Program's substantive work preparations and actual MTN activities." The most important task in avoiding this was "to convince the IPAC members – within the near future – that we have a consistent, viable work program for them."[69]

GE remained a crucial partner in this. A few months before the ITAC/ISAR process came to a formal close, GE's Manager for International Trade Policy Development, Peter Levin, wrote to Forest Abbuhl, Director of the Industry Consultations Policy Staff in the Department of Commerce, to express his desire for a seamless continuation of the

[67] "Program and Policy Implications of the Trade Act of 1974 for the Department of Commerce," January 15, 1975.

[68] "Program and Policy Implications of the Trade Act of 1974 for the Department of Commerce," January 15, 1975.

[69] L. J. Murphy, "ICTN Proposal," Handwritten Notes, March 13, 1975, Record Group 489, Entry UD-WW 18, Box #4, National Archives College Park, MD.

relationship. Even the very job titles of the correspondents indicated the extent of the expansion, and the permanence, of integral state organs both within state and corporate bureaucracies. As Levin wrote, "clearly, there is much in the national interest that can result from the MTN with a working together of Commerce and STR on the one side and industry on the other." Crucially, he continued, "looking beyond the negotiations themselves, such involvement by industry will do much to gain acceptance in the U.S. for the MTN's ultimate results."[70]

The Department of Commerce and the President's Export Council

If integral state linkages were essential for the success of the trade negotiations themselves, so too were they important for the *implementation* of these agreements after they were signed. This required that enforcement mechanisms be constructed not merely *between*, but *within* nation states—internationalizing components of the state regulatory apparatus and its manifold linkages with corporate power. If Commerce had been focused on politically organizing corporations, and representing their views within the state complex, now the department would constitute a primary point of contact between US corporations and the new global trade regime. The consolidation of the trade advisory system into a lasting integral state mechanism was a vital foundation of this, supporting the permanent institutionalization of multilateral trade policy venues. Similarly, if business sought redress from the impacts of liberalization, it was to the Department of Commerce that it would turn. In these ways, over the late 1970s Commerce was reorganized as a component of a transnational neoliberal governance structure.

This reorganization of state power required support among corporations, not to mention an extensive program to educate capitalists about the new governance procedures, and their supposed benefits. This was spearheaded by the Department of Commerce, particularly through the reformation of the PEC. Commerce also sought to promote through the PEC a state-led export strategy supported by Ex-Im Bank credit and other subsidies. This would both fix the balance-of-payments problem

[70] Peter Levin, "Peter Levin to Forest Abbuhl," April 20, 1976, Record Group 489, Entry UD-WW 18, Box #3, National Archives College Park, MD.

and help resolve the "stagflation" crisis, which continued to drag on with no clear resolution in sight. However, while Commerce sought to use the PEC to build momentum behind such an industrial policy, more prominent state agencies were working to constrain these very practices by branding them NTBs. By the time the PEC was launched in 1979, it would not be discounted credit to subsidize exports and boost growth, but rather sky-high interest rates in the form of the Volcker Shock and subsequent recession that would be on the agenda for the most prominent policymakers.

In August 1977, Assistant Secretary of Commerce for Domestic and International Business Frank Weil wrote a memorandum to Secretary Juanita Kreps laying out "a plan for the restructuring of the Domestic and International Business Administration [DIBA]." This was necessary because "DIBA is no longer properly structured to deal with a world economy that has changed greatly in recent years, nor is it well structured to provide maximum service to the business community." If executed correctly, he believed the restructuring could serve to "strengthen the Department's role in interagency councils in the formulation of both domestic and international economic policy, to revitalize export expansion efforts through export awareness of trade promotion, and to foster positive relationships between business, the public, and government."[71]

This would be achieved by reorganizing the DIBA into the International Trade Administration (ITA), which would become the new center of the Commerce Department. Developing the reorganization plan had "been a complex and, on occasion frustrating, experience." Years of decline had been exacerbated by "the damaging history of management turnover (laced on occasion with plain incompetence) that plagued this part of the Department for some years."[72] Nevertheless, within a year, the restructuring had "proceeded with a degree of effectiveness unknown over the Department's 65-year history," as Commerce was converted "from the loose conglomeration of seemingly unrelated entities of the

[71] Frank Weil, "Memorandum for Secretary Juanita Kreps, Restructuring of the Domestic and International Business Administration," August 11, 1977, Record Group 40, Entry A1 177, Box #5, National Archives College Park, MD.

[72] "Assistant Secretary for Domestic and International Business to Secretary of Commerce," October 1, 1977, Record Group 40, Entry A1 177, Box #5, National Archives College Park, MD.

past into a cohesive organization capable of meeting the challenge of today's problems."[73]

This reorganization sought not to increase the autonomy of the Commerce Department from business, but rather to *use* its closeness to particular firms as an asset in supporting internationalization. As Weil saw, the "unique resource" Commerce possessed was its "longstanding relationship with the private sector." Though it "is not, and should not be an unqualified representative of business and industry within the Federal Government," Weil wrote, "that is one of its roles." Crucially, "no other organization plays or could play" this role, which "includes a longstanding tradition of exchange of information… and a series of literally thousands of continuing Commerce-industry contacts from the testing of new materials to the provision of overseas market advice to a small firm." This offered Commerce the opportunity to cultivate support among business by advocating for its interests *within* the new trade regime, supporting the international competitiveness of American firms through whatever state supports were available. While denouncing the "self-defeating, inflationary, 'border protection' schemes" of the past, Commerce now saw its role as developing "our trade position by enhancing our exports and making our own products more competitive with foreign ones in the domestic market."[74]

This was reflected in discussions within Commerce of developing a new industrial strategy that it would coordinate, framed as a response to the competitive threat from state-supported, export-oriented Japanese and German firms. Rather than broadly stabilizing GDP growth through macroeconomic demand management in Keynesian fashion, some within Commerce sought to develop an industrial policy that would target specific domestic sectors, firms, or technologies for state support. Deputy Secretary Sidney Harman laid out such a plan in a 1978 memo, in which he advocated moving beyond what he saw as the existing "approach to industrial policy… characterized by a priority emphasis on macroeconomic tools to maintain broadly-based health in the U.S. economy"—in other words, the Keynesian model, which had been "bolstered in the early

[73] "The Department of Commerce," 1978/1979 (?), Record Group 40, Entry A1 177, Box #5, National Archives College Park, MD.

[74] "The Department of Commerce," 1978/1979 (?), Record Group 40, Entry A1 177, Box #5, National Archives College Park, MD.

1960's (sic) with the Kennedy Administration's success in using tax cuts and other measures to stimulate growth."

According to Harman, "a number of recent trends," especially the "rise of international competition" and the "reduction in international trade barriers," had "increased the vulnerability of particular U.S. industries to more rapid and deeper incursions into their markets by foreign producers." This was substantially the result of "an unmistakeable trend" then "underway in developed and undeveloped nations alike, toward more involvement by national governments in industrial production and trade." Remaining the dominant global power would therefore require a "fresh approach to the development of U.S. policies with respect to individual industries." Nevertheless, he believed that a "direct leap into a comprehensive and effective industrial policy apparatus... would involve fundamental and probably unacceptable changes in Governmental and private sector practices and philosophy." Instead, Harman proposed that such an apparatus should "build on existing resources and institutions to forge in a deliberate, but incremental, way a revitalized government/private sector partnership."[75]

The response from Commerce officials to Harman's "concept paper" was largely positive. "You may have in this little paper," Frank Weil exclaimed, "the beginnings of one of the most important initiatives this Department will undertake."[76] Weil even went so far as to extol the "healthy influence on the international economic environment" such a policy would have—despite the fact that it ran directly counter to efforts to restrain precisely such competitive hiking of NTBs insofar as, rather than *emulate* the German and Japanese model, STR and Treasury sought to dismantle it through international negotiations.

Similarly, Deputy Under Secretary Lawrence Houston cited the development of atomic energy as a model of the kind of "long-term, massive government intervention consisting of the research, technological, trade,

[75] Sidney Harman, "Concept Paper: An Industrial Policy in the United States," June 27, 1978, Record Group 40, Entry A1 177, Box #5, National Archives College Park, MD.

[76] Frank Weil, "Memorandum for Sidney Harman," June 29, 1978, Record Group 40, Entry A1 177, Box #5, National Archives College Park, MD.

regulatory, technical assistance and financing programs" that were necessary to achieve the objectives Harman laid out.[77] The key question was how the "national interest" would come to be defined: Obviously, every manufacturing firm would seek state support, and not all of them could or should be supported. It was unclear how such decisions could be made in a coordinated and centralized fashion, other than through the current model of corporations "spinning off" technologies developed for military purposes based on market-disciplined investment decisions. Robert Hall, Assistant Secretary for Economic Development, was one of the few within the department who understood this: "…the U.S. has always had an industrial policy – explicit or implicit. Indeed we were one of the world's leaders in developing an 'industrial policy' albeit one centered in the private sector but with much government support and acquiescence. The roots of this 'laissez-faire' model with the government role hidden are quite strong." As a result, he strongly urged caution in pursuing a project that would alter these well-developed and highly functional institutional relationships between corporations and the state.[78]

Particularly concerning for Commerce in considering a new industrial strategy was the "erosion of the Department's central constituency, the American business community," which was seen as vital to "the integrity of the Department." These worries were expressed in another paper circulated in the summer of 1978 lamenting "that American business considers the Department irrelevant to several of its most important problems." This was especially apparent in the fact that, over "the past ten years, no business organization has testified for or against the Commerce budget." This was a consequence of "the weak leadership afforded the Department of Commerce in previous administrations," but it was also the result of the fact that Commerce had "long ignored the necessity of systematically

[77] Lawrence Houston, "Lawrence O. Houston to Sidney Harman," June 28, 1978, Record Group 40, Entry Al 177, Box #5, National Archives College Park, MD.

[78] Robert T. Hall, "Memorandum for Under Secretary Harman," June 30, 1979, Record Group 40, Entry Al 177, Box #5, National Archives College Park, MD. The level of confusion that sometimes characterized the discussion was striking. General Counsel C. L. Haslam replied, "I do not have a clear concept of what an industrial policy is or how it is supposed to work," though he "would be interested in learning more about the industrial policies of other countries which, I am sure, must vary widely." C.L. Haslam, "Memorandum for the Undersecretary Re: Concept Paper Regarding An Industrial Policy," June 29, 1978, Record Group 40, Entry Al 177, Box #5, National Archives College Park, MD.

developing goals and policies necessary to compete among the Nations of the world and to meet the employment and income needs of substantial numbers of our own people." Rebuilding support among business meant developing and advocating for policies that business found beneficial in a very immediate economic sense. To begin remedying this, the paper held, "the Department needs first to recognize that our current communication with American business is not adequate to the needs of the Administration or the concept of a viable and continuing Department of Commerce."[79]

Commerce Department Director of Communications Ernest Lotito saw the paper as tackling "what many consider to be the Department's Number 1 problem: how it is perceived by the constituency which it was presumably created to serve." "To the business community," Lotito wrote, "the [ITA] is the Department of Commerce… [it] is the only government agency solely concerned with representing the interests of the Nation's domestic and international business enterprises." Therefore, "any effort to beef up the Department's image in the business community must rest on a solid base of performance by the ITA." However, the department "over the past two decades has opted increasingly for concentrating its resources on export expansion"—which is "a concern of only a relatively small segment of the American business community." Rebuilding business support should therefore include an effort to bring a broader group, including smaller businesses, into the department's export promotion and trade activities.[80]

By the end of 1978, the matter of trade apparatus reorganization was coming to a head. As Harman wrote Secretary Kreps, "the Commerce Department is institutionally weak because it often seems less than the sum of its parts. It suffers from a split personality. It houses major program elements which have different and, sometimes, fundamentally contradictory missions." To resolve this, he argued that the Department should be reorganized as "a Cabinet Department of Trade and

[79] "The Business Constituency," July 1978, Record Group 40, Entry A1 177, Box #5, National Archives College Park, MD.

[80] Ernest Lotito, "Ernest Lotito to Lawrence Houston, Re: The Buisiness Constituency," July 11, 1978, Record Group 40, Entry A1 177, Box #1, National Archives College Park, MD; "Memorandum of Understanding Between the Industry and Trade Administration and the Economic Development Administration," August 4, 1978, Record Group 40, Entry A1 177, Box #1, National Archives College Park, MD.

Economic Development," focused around implementing free trade agreements and advancing deregulation. If the Department became an "institutional exponent of the Administration's commitment to economic growth through more competition and less reliance on government," it would be "much more credible in and outside government."[81]

This meant fundamentally moving away from programs Harman referred to as "redistributive," or those that pertained to economic distribution and development across specific geographical regions or economic sectors, and toward those he called "expansive," that is, which aim to promote growth and competitiveness. On this basis, Commerce should redouble its efforts to "increase the opportunity for greater cooperation between big and small business to the benefit of the total economy." Indeed, Commerce was already organizing consultations with smaller business groups, including Chambers of Commerce, to feel out the response from these sectors for such an orientation. If this agenda could be achieved, policy planners in the department hoped, "DOC's stature as a coherent commercial trade and investment entity would rise."[82]

An opening for the new Commerce strategy appeared in April 1978, when, as "inflation and dollar problems brought into sharp focus the fact that U.S. export performance was a severe national problem," Carter asked Commerce Secretary Juanita Kreps to "convene a task force to work towards a national export policy." Three months later, he announced a "first phase" of this policy with the "reconstitution" of the PEC.[83] But it wasn't until May 1979 that the new PEC was established under the auspices of the Commerce Department, and Jones appointed its chairman. The new Council would not just represent big business, but rather "the economy as a whole," with smaller businesses included through regional "District Export Councils" (DECs). The PEC

[81] Sidney Harman, "A Perspective on Reorganization: Expansion, Redistribution and Institutional Credibility," December 8, 1978, Record Group 40, Entry A1 177, Box #5, National Archives College Park, MD.

[82] C. Robert Kemp, "C. Robert Kemp to Jerry Jasinowski, Elisa A. Porter, Lucy Falcone Re: Reorganization Option," January 4, 1979, Record Group 40, Entry A1 177, Box #1, National Archives College Park, MD.

[83] Department of Commerce, "Charter of President's Export Council," May 18, 1979, Record Group 151, Entry UD-05 W, Box #2, National Archives College Park, MD.

would include 28 non-government members (two from labor, two governors, and the rest businessmen, lawyers, and academics), seven cabinet members, three Senators, and House members.[84]

As Bob Barrie reported from GE's Washington office, Carter's Executive Order represented "the culmination of a long effort" by GE personnel and Commerce officials "to get the President's Export Council into being."[85] In the lead-up to the first meeting, Barrie met with Frank Weil, Peter Gould, and "others in the Commerce Department to discuss in general terms an agenda for the first meeting." It was agreed that the Council should address the "ways in which the private sector can intensify its efforts to obtain additional exports and a review of government policies that either inhibit exports at the moment or ways in which the government can positively promote exports by altered policies."[86] Meanwhile, White House staffers requested Carter "drop by" the first PEC meeting, to which the press were invited, in hopes that they could "contribute to building support for the MTN by giving visibility to the PEC and its efforts." Indeed, presenting the "expansion of export opportunities" as one of the "major benefits to the United States from the MTN" was recognized as important for increasing business support for the trade agreement. The PEC would be useful in this regard, as its members "are recognized leaders in the business community and friends of the Administration." Thus an appearance by Carter at the meeting "would be an important public sign of the support you are receiving from the business community, and your personal participation in efforts to improve the economy."[87]

As Jones would later conclude, "the real work of the Council takes place in the Subcommittee meetings," while the EC undertook broad

[84] "President's Export Council Inaugural Meeting – Agenda and Minutes," May 24, 1979, Record Group 151, Entry UD-05 W, Box #2, National Archives College Park, MD.

[85] Bob Barrie, "Bob Barrie to P.S. Peter Re: President's Export Council," April 26, 1979, Record Group 151, Entry UD-05 W 5, Box #3, National Archives College Park, MD.

[86] Barrie, "Bob Barrie to P.S. Peter," April 26, 1979.

[87] "Tim Kraft and Arnie Miller to President Carter Re: Announcement of President's Export Council," April 24, 1979, Collection: Office of Staff Secretary, Series: Presidential Files; Folder: [4/25/79 - Not Submitted] [CF, O/A 548]; Container 114, Carter Library.

political coordination.[88] GE personnel worked in the PEC's six subcommittees—which, not coincidentally, corresponded with the ITA's six bureaus. GE's William Durka was on the Export Administration Subcommittee, concerned with reducing US export controls on advanced and potentially sensitive technologies. Jones was on the Subcommittee on GATT and the Multilateral Trade Agreements, which "work[ed] with the Office of the Special Trade Representative, the Department of Commerce, and other government agencies to identify the specific export opportunities resulting for U.S. exporters from the Tokyo-Round trade agreements." This subcommittee would also "consider remaining foreign trade barriers and… the steps that should be taken by the U.S. to bring about an elimination or reduction" of them. Jones served as well on the Export Promotion Subcommittee, responsible for working with the DECs to bring smaller businesses into the process. The Export Expansion subcommittee, meanwhile, evaluated "disincentives to exports"—especially "regulations pertaining to environmental effects in foreign countries"—and supported enlarging the Ex-Im Bank. The final two subcommittees focused on trade with Soviet-bloc countries and agricultural exports, respectively.[89]

At the first PEC meeting, Commerce's Frank Weil, who would serve as the PEC's Executive Director, offered a "description of the purpose of the Council and the Commerce Department role." The central problem to be confronted was that "the US is losing its export position vis-à-vis Germany and Japan, and that Japan is about to overtake the U.S. in exports of manufactures." Therefore, "the most important issue we have to address," Weil said, is "what are those long term steps this country must take to begin to regain our market share." Weil believed the PEC should begin by dealing with legislation then before Congress that pertained to controls on high-tech exports, the multilateral trade agreement enabling legislation, and "the reorganization of the Executive Branch relative to trade." There was unanimous agreement with Deputy STR Alan Wolff that the MTN was "an extraordinary set of international agreements"—including "codes of conduct in all areas the U.S.

[88] Reginald Jones, "Reginald Jones to Philip Klutznick," March 13, 1980, Record Group 151, Entry UD-05 W 5, Box #3, National Archives College Park, MD.

[89] Department of Commerce, "President's Export Council: Membership, Commerce Department Support, Executive Committee, Subcommittees," June 11, 1979, Record Group 151, Entry UD-05 W 5, Box #3, National Archives College Park, MD.

had considered there were unfair practices" and additional bilateral agreements with 42 countries. The task now was to "aggressively move to take advantage of our rights in these agreements," since "the foreign barriers removed are of no value to us unless we sell."

It is noteworthy that Commerce framed the question of trade in explicitly *nationalist* terms: insofar as increased liberalization promoted US export growth, and manufacturing employment in the US, not just big business but also smaller capitalists and labor had an interest in pursuing such a policy. This framing obscured the more significant differences between these groups, which would become increasingly clear with time. For the time being, the PEC displayed its enthusiasm by passing a resolution at its first meeting expressing "strong support" for the multilateral agreement, which it described as "a tremendous accomplishment."[90] Congress overwhelmingly passed the trade legislation soon thereafter. Importantly, even though members of Congress attended PEC meetings (and were PEC members), it did not directly engage in "lobbying," though individual firms of course did.[91] However, the PEC was nevertheless embedded within the very structure of Congressional policymaking: In PEC meetings, legislation was discussed; the positions of different actors within the state bureaucracy, members of Congress, and business clarified; and consensus was formed.

As the PEC got up and running, Commerce and OMB worked through proposals for restructuring the trade apparatus, weighing the pros and cons of allocating increased responsibility to STR, Commerce, State, or creating an altogether new cabinet-level agency that would combine dispersed trade functions and replace the Commerce Department. The administration was hesitant to grant Commerce more power, as it "may be viewed as having constituency bias," while STR was "perceived to be impartial." Indeed, "Commerce's industry constituency may make it suspect to trade liberals, agriculture, and certain labor interests." On the other hand, STR was "an independent White House agency" and

[90] "President's Export Council Inaugural Meeting – Agenda and Minutes," May 24, 1979.

[91] While Commerce lawyers concluded that "the PEC would be acting outside its charter by promoting its views or recommendations regarding pending or future legislation," on the other hand, "there is no prohibition against individual PEC members promoting their own views." Sally Lord Ellis, "Sally Lord Ellis to Peter Gould, Re: President's Export Council," November 21, 1979, Record Group 151, Entry UD-05 W 5, Box #3, National Archives College Park, MD.

"would be least identified with any foreign or domestic constituency." If still greater autonomy was necessary, the State Department could be made the lead agency for trade activities. However, while it "would not be perceived as having close relationships with or responsiveness to the private investment community," it might by the same token be seen as insufficiently "responsive to domestic interests."[92]

As this suggests, the institutional balance between Commerce, STR, and State—which the PEC played a role in shaping and reproducing—reflected the contradictions of the project of making global capitalism: between pressures on the state to respond to the specific interests of particular domestic capitalists, on the one hand, and its responsibility for managing the global system, on the other. Once again, domestic protectionist pressures would contribute to the concentration of power within a more autonomous trade apparatus—secured partly through the institutional balance between Commerce and STR—yet this autonomy would remain strictly relative, dependent on its legitimation among leading sectors of business.

It was not overly ambitious to conclude in June 1979 that "Commerce is a Department on the ascendancy with new capacity for the addition of enlarged responsibilities." Commerce, it was emphasized, "is the logical base for consolidated trade and investment functions," and could "easily be restructured to absorb new trade functions and to demonstrate a new U.S. emphasis on trade and investment."[93] While some argued that "there should not be extensive consolidation of trade functions in Commerce because Commerce is said to be a weak department and because Commerce would handle trade matters with a protectionist bias," Kreps insisted that "even if one were to accept the outmoded notion that business is the Department's 'constituency,' that 'constituency' is itself divided on issues of trade."[94]

Of course, as we have seen, this is *precisely* how policy planers in Commerce conceived of the relationship with business. Partly because of

[92] Homer Moyer, "Homer Moyer to John White Re: P.R.P. Paper on Trade Reorganization," April 17, 1979, Record Group 40, Entry A1 177, Box #1, National Archives College Park, MD.

[93] Department of Commerce, "International Trade and Investment," June 1979, Record Group 40, Entry A1 177, Box #1, National Archives College Park, MD.

[94] Juanita Kreps, "Report to the President," April 27, 1979, Record Group 40, Entry A1 177, Box #1, National Archives College Park, MD.

this, the administration had decided to locate *implementation* functions within Commerce, and *policy* functions within the more autonomous STR. This would allow Commerce to capitalize on its close relationships with particular firms in supporting the MTN, positioning itself as fighting for their interests within the transnational venues created by the treaty framework. Thus OMB described the "main element" of the reorganization as being "to give the Special Trade Representative clear-cut authority in trade policy as chief negotiator, policy coordinator, decision-maker, and dispute-resolver short of the President." Meanwhile what would now be called the Department of Trade and Commerce would take on the "operational functions of trade policy including responsibility for countervailing duty and anti-dumping cases"—investigating allegations of treaty violations and bringing complaints to the proper channels, as spelled out in the agreements. To this end, it would receive a substantial upgrade of its analytical and research capacities, and would also take on import relief functions from Treasury as well as State Department commercial officers in major trading nations. Meanwhile, a new Interagency Trade Policy Committee would "assume coordinating responsibility for import relief policy, energy trade issues, East–West trade policy, international investment policy, and international commodity negotiations."[95] While signaling the growing importance of investment issues, this further constrained the use of import relief by subjecting it to interagency discipline—thereby restricting Commerce's authority in this area.

Kreps presented this to the PEC as a step toward the more substantial concentration of power within Commerce—which, she promised, would afford industry "a clearer voice on behalf of trade concerns in the councils of Government."[96] Opponents on the PEC nevertheless advocated for still greater consolidation within Commerce, and clearer strides toward an export-driven industrial strategy. To this end, Senator Adlai Stevenson III presented to the PEC "his own proposal" to consolidate STR, the Department of Commerce, and the ITPC into a

[95] "Summary of the Minutes, President's Export Council Executive Committee," July 19, 1979, Record Group 151, Entry UD-05 W, Box #2, National Archives College Park, MD.

[96] Assistant Secretary for Industry and Trade, "Briefing Memorandum for the Secretary of Commerce on President's Export Council Executive Committee Meeting, Thursday, July 19, 8:30 AM," Record Group 151, Entry UD-05W, Box #2, National Archives College Park, MD.

Department of Commerce, Trade, and Technology. This, he held, would "enable the U.S. to negotiate and implement trade regulations with one strong voice."[97] Stevenson thus imagined a thorough reorganization of the industrial and trade policy apparatus along the lines discussed in the Harman memo, which Kreps had also advocated for within the administration—precisely the neo-protectionist perspective that officials in Treasury and STR were so concerned to marginalize.

Though it contradicted Commerce's hopes, as well as those of neo-protectionist-minded business, GE's Reginald Jones supported the administration's plan on the grounds that "a separate department for international trade didn't seem feasible." While praising the decisions to move commercial attaches from State to Commerce and transfer responsibility for countervailing duties from Treasury to Commerce, Jones explicitly backed "strengthening the policy-making function of STR." He then turned to urging the MTN subcommittee he chaired "to work with the Executive Branch to develop specific proposals for vital, meaningful and early implementation of the MTN agreements." To assuage fears of the autonomy this would establish for the trade apparatus, he reassured the council that the private sector advisory committees used during the trade negotiations would "continue to provide advice to STR, which will have more resources to take advantage of this advice."[98]

To extend this consensus through the rest of the PEC, STR and Commerce officials gave presentations for the subcommittees and the general membership selling the reorganization plan.[99] The MTN had secured "significant reductions in world tariffs, improvements in the framework of the GATT system, a new international discipline over the use of nontariff measures." It was now "the responsibility of the Commerce Department to oversee the operational side of the implementation and monitoring of these agreements, as well as the investigation and resolution of problems associated with foreign country application of

[97] "Summary of the Minutes, President's Export Council Executive Committee," July 19, 1979.

[98] "Meeting Minutes, President's Export Council Subcommittee on GATT and the MTN," September 17, 1979, Record Group 151, Entry UD-05 W, Box #2, National Archives College Park, MD.

[99] "Summary of the Minutes, President's Export Council Meeting," September 20, 1979, Record Group 151, Entry UD-05 W, Box #2, National Archives College Park, MD.

these agreements," wherever they may occur. One of the most immediate tasks before the department now was "a major effort to inform and educate U.S. business on specific aspects of the MTN." This would include organizing conferences and seminars to "ensure that specific trade opportunities under the MTN are communicated to U.S. firms," as well as the establishment of "a trade complaint center, where firms will receive advice as to the resources and remedies available to them."

In a letter to Carter, Jones relayed the PEC's support for this "monitoring and enforcement partnership," in which Commerce would "investigate subsidy complaints and determine injury before imposing countervailing duties."[100] Commerce would become an integral state mechanism for disciplining capital by channeling opposition into a push for further liberalization, while working to assist US business in pursuing opportunities abroad. It would thus sustain the free trade consensus by safeguarding the interests of American business *within* the new trade regime. At least for the time being, this appeared to have overcome business doubts from the Kennedy Round and successfully legitimated the trade agreement: As Jones reported, PEC "consultations have indicated a strong desire on the part of the private sector for the government to continue actively and vigorously to pursue other trade agreements."[101]

If the PEC involved building integral state networks between large corporations and state institutions, it also entailed constructing linkages with smaller capitalists, local business associations, state governments, and municipalities. This occurred primarily through the organization of "District Export Councils" by the Commerce Department and the Export Promotion Subcommittee, of which Jones was a member. Ideally, DECs would serve as "a vehicle for educating the district's legislators and business community of the importance, benefits, and requirements of increased exports" while gathering "export policy and legislative recommendations."[102] Chairing the Export Promotion subcommittee

[100] Reginald Jones, "Reginald Jones to Jimmy Carter," December 10, 1979, Record Group 151, Entry UD-05 W 5, Box #3, National Archives College Park, MD.

[101] "Summary of the Minutes, President's Export Council Executive Committee," December 6, 1979, Record Group 151, Entry UD-05W, Box #2, National Archives College Park, MD.

[102] "Summary of the Minutes, President's Export Council Executive Committee," December 6, 1979.

was Herta Seidman, Assistant Secretary of Commerce for Trade.[103] As Seidman explained, Commerce Department Field Offices "should become the focal point for export promotion activities, and their efforts should be closely coordinated with District Export Councils, Chambers of Commerce, local labor organizations, industry associations, etc." She suggested "a system similar to the National Alliance of Business should be used to reinforce the Commerce District Office efforts, with personnel loaned by private companies." Importantly, this effort had to be organized and led by Commerce Department field offices, as these "are the only organizations that have national capability in exporting and can provide the infrastructure to coordinate work with other organizations."[104]

The Commerce Department and Export Promotion Subcommittee thereby sought to create "a nationwide export multiplier group which would effectively support federal export programs." This nationwide group should "combine the efforts of the private sector with the efforts of government"—both to better organize government programs to "advise and assist the exporter," as well as to "centralize and strengthen the efforts of private industry and of private industry councils, trade associations, committees, and the like." This would then be a means to "foster export consciousness among viable and well established small and middle-size companies and close the gap between the support available and the people who need it."[105] Such entreaties to smaller businesses were made more enticing through proposals to establish trading companies whereby "small and medium sized firms could 'pool their resources' to 'overcome problems associated with export commencement'."[106] Jones even endorsed a proposal for MNCs to become "big brothers" to smaller exporters by

[103] "President's Export Council, Export Promotion Subcommittee, Meeting Notes," November 26, 1979, Record Group 151, Entry UD-05 W, Box #2, National Archives College Park, MD.

[104] "Summary of the Minutes, President's Export Council Meeting," September 20, 1979, Record Group 151, Entry UD-05W, Box #2, National Archives College Park, MD.

[105] "President's Export Council, Export Promotion Subcommittee, Meeting Notes," Record Group 151, Entry UD-05W, Box #2, National Archives College Park, MD.

[106] "Summary of the Minutes, President's Export Council Meeting," September 20, 1979.

setting up trading companies to "guide" them for a year, while owning part or all of these firms.[107]

Thus large corporations were enlisted to sell "free trade" to smaller capitalists partly on the grounds that, even if they were unable to construct international production processes, these agreements also opened vast new *export* opportunities for them as well. The PEC, in this regard, seemed to promise these capitalists that they would receive support from the state and larger firms to increase their exports—including through integration as suppliers or contractors within global processes controlled by the giant MNCs. Deals made in the US with these firms could therefore have global implications. That this was not without contradictions is indicated by the difficulties in raising the question of antitrust reform at the PEC, which big business believed was necessary to compete globally.

Though Jones proclaimed that "anything that tends to split the business community between large and small is not in the interest of the business community," by the end of the year the DECs had been marginalized from the PEC—causing "a certain amount of frustration" among smaller capitalists.[108] Commerce worked to bridge between large and small business, "seeking ways to enhance the relationship between the PEC and DECs," but this proved difficult. Seidman supported expanding the DECs, as well as increasing their profile by convening regional and national meetings. She also encouraged Jones to invite regional DEC representatives to participate in EC meetings.[109] However, Jones insisted he was only "willing to continue to receive written recommendations from the DECs."[110] Similarly, Tom Crowley, Jones' assistant, informed

[107] "Summary of the Minutes, President's Export Council Executive Committee," December 6, 1979. To achieve this, Senator Stevenson introduced a bill into the Senate that "proposes certain legal, financial, and tax benefits" for such export companies. See: "Summary of the Minutes, President's Export Council Meeting."

[108] J. Raymond DePaulo, "Summary of Area Meetings of District Export Council Officers," September 8, 1980, Record Group 151, Entry UD-05 W 5, Box #4, National Archives College Park, MD.

[109] "Report of the Export Promotion Subcommittee to the Executive Committee of the President's Export Council," June 17, 1980, Record Group 151, Entry UD-05 W 5, Box #4, National Archives College Park, MD.

[110] Department of Commerce, International Trade Administration, "Subcommittee on Export Promotion, President's Export Council / District Export Council Cooperation," September 1980, Record Group 151, Entry UD-05 W 5, Box #4, National Archives

Commerce that "Reg Jones is not particularly happy about these DEC meetings," and that "the GE people are satisfied with the PEC/DEC relationship as it is and are not interested in creating a more formal or broader relationship"—though this was not discussed openly.[111] The Export Promotion Subcommittee withered soon thereafter. In July, Commerce recommended shutting it down, with Haimes indicating that it "did not have any more substantive issues to discuss and that another meeting of the subcommittee was probably not necessary."[112]

Corporate Power and the Internationalized Neoliberal State

The fissure between large firms and smaller capitalists pointed to the fundamental limits of the PEC's ability to overcome the contradictions entailed by the restructuring of global capitalism at the dawn of the neoliberal era. These limits were also a result of the configuration of state power—which the BR played an integral role in shaping and supporting. Even as the ostensible point of the PEC was to extend support for the multilateral treaty framework through state export promotion, that very framework simultaneously curtailed the space in which it could do so. Commerce could advocate for US businesses within these confines, but it couldn't challenge them. Commerce's role in representing the views of its "business constituency" took place on the basis of, and had to conform to, institutional scaffolding developed in other agencies.

Whether Commerce or the leading members of the PEC initially realized it or not, export promotion was to a huge extent a false promise, if for no other reason than that the tools necessary to really implement such an approach were being negotiated away before they could even be constructed. As the MTN Subcommittee itself reported, "there is

College Park, MD; Herta Lande Seidman, "Herta Landa Seidman to Reginald Jones," July 31, 1980, Record Group 151, Entry UD-05 W 5, Box #4, National Archives College Park, MD.

111 Wendy Haimes, "Wendy Haimes to Peter Gould," July 30, 1980, Record Group 151, Entry UD-05 W 5, Box #4, National Archives College Park, MD.

112 One Commerce attendee at the June 12 meeting even reported that "the subcommittee had a difficult time filling its agenda". Wendy Haimes to Peter Gould, July 30, 1980, Record Group 151, Entry UD-05W 5, Box #4, National Archives College Park, MD.

concern that the MTN may have locked the U.S. into a position where we are limited in subsidy actions while leaving our negotiating partners free to continue their subsidy practices." While the latter could be addressed through vigorous monitoring and enforcement by Commerce, this would also come at the expense of the ability for the American state to support its own firms through such means. As would increasingly become apparent, given the nature of the multilateral agreements, not to mention the political consensus that had been developed within the state around the ascendant Treasury Department (with the support of the BR), the primary remaining strategy for export promotion was "a logically developed tax program."[113]

Furthermore, it became increasingly clear that MNCs were not primarily concerned with *exports*, but *investment*. Of course, individual firms would be more than happy to avail themselves of any subsidies or support that was on offer. But increasingly, exports were relevant inasmuch as they represented stages within internationalized networks of production. As Jones advised Commerce, the new Foreign Commercial Service should not seek to directly increase sales of US manufactured products abroad, but rather to facilitate corporate internationalization by gathering expertise in each local context "in the areas of licensing, financing, insurance, patents and trademarks, co-production, and/or investment."[114] It would thus serve to facilitate the *internal integration* of American capital *within* other social formations and to facilitate the internationalization of American standards, practices, and institutional forms. This was similarly reflected in the EC's support for expanding the Overseas Private Investment Corporation (OPIC), which "served to assist capital formation in friendly [developing] countries through programs ensuring investment activities in such countries by American firms."

Though the EC "note[d] the concern of Council members representing the labor sector regarding the 'question of 'runaway investment,' …the great majority of our members have indicated, OPIC plays an

[113] "Summary of the Minutes, President's Export Council Executive Committee," July 19, 1979.

[114] Reginald Jones, "Reginald Jones to Robert Herzstein," July 1, 1980, Record Group 151, Entry UD-05 W 5, Box #4, National Archives College Park, MD.

important role which should be better recognized both within government and the private sector."[115] Labor may have had an interest in boosting employment through exports, but it had no stake in exporting jobs. Just as it became clear over the 1970s that the corporatist model would prove unable to resolve the "stagflation" crisis at home, so too would it fail to build such a class compromise around trade policy. Neoliberal internationalization would contribute to resolving the crisis through a direct attack on the power of the trade unions, which realized too late the consequences of the new global integration.

Insofar as MNCs remained embedded within the industrial policy system, they continued to face the contradiction, as they had since the 1950s, between supporting low taxes and fiscal restraint, on the one hand, and the desire for an expansive industrial policy on the other. This contradiction, needless to say, was not felt by financial firms. While the rise of finance had been associated with that of the Treasury Department, Commerce's push for a state-led export promotion strategy was in direct conflict with both the policy program associated with this state apparatus and the power of the financial sector that supported it. Not only would implementing a Commerce-coordinated export-oriented industrial policy require confronting the power of the Treasury and the DOD within the state complex, but also the very structure of global integration itself.

As industrial firms like GE were internationalized, their interests aligned more closely with those of the financial sector—and any willingness they might have had in pursuing such a massive reorganization of industrial policy faded, particularly insofar as this would contribute to inflationary pressures, destabilize the international role of the dollar in a world of floating exchange rates, or higher taxes. If Commerce officials like Harman had envisioned the PEC as a step in an incremental process of building a centralized apparatus for an export promotion industrial strategy, time was not on their side. Instead, this impulse was increasingly the remit of smaller firms, which GE and others were happy to integrate with their global operations, but did not feel the need to subsidize, especially inasmuch as this challenged the "free trade" consensus. The free global mobility of investment, rather than a state-coordinated

[115] "Meeting on June 17, 1980 of Executive Committee of the President's Export Council," June 17, 1980, Record Group 151, Entry UD-05 W 5, Box #4, National Archives College Park, MD.

export strategy, increasingly emerged as the true substance of "export promotion."

Though the PEC would continue, GE would be absent from the leadership in its next iteration. The restructuring of the integral state to account for the evolving structure of capitalist accumulation would continue to provoke contestation around the weight of different voices within the "general interest" articulated by the state. Nevertheless, given that integral state organization remained crucial for crafting policy and securing legitimacy, Commerce would continue to have a role in organizing (and reorganizing) capital. To do so, it had to work with Congress to make "significant changes" to the advisory system. The 1979 Trade Agreements Act provided for "functional (issue-oriented) committees" to supplement the sectoral ones that were the basis of the existing system. This reflected the growing clarity around the core problems to be addressed by the emerging neoliberal paradigm. Yet despite the overall consensus between MNCs and the financial sector on trade issues, the restructuring of the ISACs was not without contradictions: When Commerce "broached" the issue in ISAC meetings, only "a few" thought this was a good idea. Those opposing the plan primarily did so on the grounds that "an individual voice will be diluted by being submerged into a larger group."[116]

Contestation within the "unstable equilibrium of compromise" around trade persisted not only among business, but also within the state itself—conflicts that were themselves shaped in important ways by the mobilization of corporate power. As Commerce prepared for the continuation of the PEC, regardless of who won the election in November, it was concerned that Jones might suggest changes that could jeopardize Commerce's role. Most alarming was the possibility that he would propose that "the PEC no longer reports to the President through the Secretary of Commerce." As an internal Commerce memo stated, Jones' "staff has informed us that he is considering the merits of having the administrative responsibilities for the Council moved to the Office of the Vice President, and possibly having the Vice President serve as Council Chairman." Jones felt that "this would ensure that the Council receives more attention in the White House." Commerce, on the other hand,

[116] Assistant Secretary for Industry and Trade, "Restructuring of Industry Consultations Program for Trade Policy," November 1979, Record Group 489, Entry UD-WW 18, Box #4, National Archives College Park, MD.

wanted to protect its function "as an advocate for exporters' needs within the Executive Branch."[117]

Both the continuities as well as the changes within capitalism and the integral state as the neoliberal consensus matured were on clear display when, five years later, Commerce again began to work with the advisory system to build momentum for another trade round. Ed Pratt, chairman of Pfizer, now headed the Advisory Committee on Trade Negotiations. In addition to reducing NTBs, the issues that would dominate the negotiations now included codifying intellectual property rights, and advancing a sweeping new agreement on financial services. In 1985, Pratt authored "a report summarizing the views of the Industry, Services, Investment, Defense, and Labor Policy Advisory Committees," as well as those of "a number of business groups, including the Business Roundtable and the NAM." This, Commerce concluded, represented "a significant sampling of private sector opinion which will be important in developing our business and legislative strategies on the new round." The report's findings were revealing:

> While the views of the various advisory groups diverged widely, the business community on balance gave 'moderate support' to the idea of a new round. Their support was conditioned, however, on parallel efforts, both domestic and foreign, to address the causes of America's trade problems. This includes efforts to address the budget deficit and to coordinate monetary and fiscal policies with our trade policy. The business community sees us entering a new round from a position of weakness, given the overvalued dollar and the deficit, and fears that we may give away more than we get. Strongest support comes from those in the private sector most interested in expanding GATT into new areas like services, investment, and intellectual property.[118]

[117] Department of Commerce, International Trade Administration, "Subcommittee on Export Promotion, Continuation of the PEC," September 1980, Record Group 151, Entry UD-05 W 5, Box #4, National Archives College Park, MD. Moreover, after the underlined phrase "for your information only," the memo added, "we are concerned that, if the responsibility for administrative and staff support for the Council were to be transferred to the Executive Office, the Vice President might not wish to undertake operational responsibility for the Council, and oversight of the PEC would effectively be given to [STR]."

[118] Timothy J Hauser, "Information Memorandum for Under Secretary for International Trade," 1985, Record Group 151, Entry UD-05 W 5, Box #4, National Archives College Park, MD.

The new high-tech and pharmaceutical companies, whose key assets were their portfolio of (state subsidized) intellectual property, as well as the financial sector, now sat at the center of the liberalization consensus. Traditional industrial firms, on the other hand, were hesitant around a new trade round without state subsidization—especially given the effect of a now-strong dollar in making exports more expensive, while sucking up cheap imports. What was crucial about the new coalition around trade by the mid-1980s was the recognition by those leading it that manufactured goods were only part of the story of economic globalization: "exports" of services, including financial services, were just as significant to America's position in the world market.

It is therefore hardly surprising that, as the report noted, financial firms key supporters of another round of trade liberalization. Thus "the Industry Policy Advisory Committee, noting that the U.S. manufacturing sector is 'carrying the major burden of the imbalance in U.S. international accounts,'" observed that this sector "was the least enthusiastic about a new round"; conversely, "the investment advisors, noting the lack of progress on investment issues… strongly urged a 'rolling negotiation format'." Services advisors "prefer[ed] an umbrella agreement, which would provide a 'constitution' of general services trade principles, along with specific sectoral agreements." This new constitution "would include the principles of transparency, balance of concessions, conditional MFN, and national treatment [of foreign capital]."

This was not just a "constitution" of a single state; rather, it was an international agreement, to be adopted and enforced by states around the world as a core component of their own juridical orders. No distinctions were to be made between foreign investment and domestic capital. That this regime, superintended by the American state, was afforded "constitutional" status meant that it would not be open to challenge by national governments or legislatures that might seek to enforce specific labor, environmental, or consumer safeguards—nor protections for specific domestic firms. The internationalization of the state, the empowerment of the trade and economic apparatus, and financial hegemony were mutually reinforcing, core features of the neoliberal integral state.

Though labor "argued for encouraging more domestic investment rather than developing new rules internationally" aimed at securing the free flow of capital, whatever possibility there may have been to craft an industrial policy aimed at promoting firms that were nationally, as opposed to internationally, oriented, or which would limit the globalization of production had already been left behind. Not only were remaining barriers to the free movement of capital steadily dropped, but the latitude to implement even limited palliatives to particular domestic firms to compensate for the effects of new competitive pressures had also been sharply constrained. This did not entail *reducing* the power of the state, but rather reorganizing and reintegrating state and corporate power to facilitate globalized governance of markets, finance, and production.

By the 1980s, the end of the class compromise model that had prevailed throughout the managerial period, and the rise of globally integrated financial markets, was plain enough—and labor had neither the power nor vision to alter this trajectory. The era of neoliberal globalization was well in train.

CHAPTER 9

General Electric, Financialization, and the Neoliberal Integral State

The analysis of General Electric and the integral state presented here ends just as the neoliberal era begins. And yet, this study may help to answer the question of *where neoliberalism came from,* and to understand why the dominant explanations within both the critical and mainstream literature are, in general, unsatisfactory. Getting past the limits of existing explanations for political and economic change required developing an alternative conception of the structure of political order in the United States, in particular clarifying the mechanisms that organize class power through periods of both instability and relative stability. Indeed, some of the primary problems with current explanations are rooted in their erroneous assumptions about the nature of state and corporate power, which do not fully capture the historical dynamics at play in the organization of class power. Understanding the origins of neoliberalism involves explaining the corporate political mobilization that occurred in the 1970s, which the dominant neo-pluralist framework, as we have seen, is ill-suited to do. In tracing historically how particular firms develop institutional relationships with the state, this study opened a window on the organization of integral state structures through which wider class coalitions were built in favor of policy agendas and business support was mobilized.

As we saw, GE played a pivotal and, in some ways, unique role in organizing corporate power within the hegemonic apparatus during the decade of the 1970s, when the neoliberal era was seeded. This did not

© The Author(s), under exclusive license to Springer Nature Switzerland AG 2022
S. Maher, *Corporate Capitalism and the Integral State*, Marx, Engels, and Marxisms,
https://doi.org/10.1007/978-3-030-83772-3_9

amount to imposing a pre-given body of Hayekian ideas. On the contrary, it was a process of holding together a coalition of large corporations in favor of continued international economic liberalization, and a program of restructuring at home, devised within leading state agencies amidst economic crisis and deep uncertainty about the nature, scope, and permanence of the necessary institutional changes. Neither business nor state officials had a sense of just how impossible it would be to return to postwar "normalcy" as the crisis of the 1970s got underway. And even as this became increasingly clear over the decade, the precise nature of what would follow remained unclear. Even the content of international liberalization became murky as the crisis unfolded, and Bretton Woods collapsed. It took the entire decade for a new regime to be worked out, and further extensive coordination between the state and corporations for it to be implemented. Rather than business seeking to lobby for a fixed program, state officials and a core group of firms closely linked to the state constructed institutional mechanisms to collaboratively develop policies that would permit the full and final lifting of wage and price controls at home, and capital and currency controls internationally, which were essential preconditions for the emergence of neoliberalism.

In this new era, while General Electric's CEO Jack Welch would attain widespread fame in the business world as the foremost spokesman for "shareholder value," GE's pivotal role within the integral state for nearly a half-century appeared to fade away. Shifts in industrial policy, and the new configuration of capitalist class power, also saw GE become less central to the industrial policy system, as military spending resumed its long decline as a proportion of GDP after a bump in the Reagan years. It could hardly be counted among the cutting-edge high-tech firms that emerged from the new industrial policy structure, which included pharmaceutical and biotechnology companies as well as a new group of computer-related firms such as Apple and Microsoft. Nor was it at the center of the research into semiconductor technology that the federal government undertook in the 1980s. Shifts in the structure of the industrial policy system—which were hardly dysfunctional for American capitalism—and financial discipline may have contributed to GE's move away from these activities. Similarly, over the 1980s, the Business Roundtable seemed to be a far less prominent force within the executive branch than it had been during the 1970s. The iteration of the Roundtable that had developed over the 1970s was tied to the power of the group of firms around GE, their linkages to particular state agencies, and a specific form of class hegemony. It is left to future research to determine whether another firm, or cluster of firms, came to take on this function in the subsequent period.

Political and Economic Origins of Neoliberalism

Very broadly speaking, there are basically two sorts of explanations for the rise of neoliberalism: *political* and *economic*. For their part, political explanations primarily tend to emphasize either the role of *lobbying* or *ideology*—though many contain a mixture of the two. Ideological explanations see neoliberalism as the result of the influence of a more or less coherent body of ideas rooted in the work of Friedrich von Hayek, Milton Friedman, and other such thinkers on key state officials.[1] At the most extreme, this is depicted as the project of a "neoliberal thought collective" that imposed these ideas upon the state at a moment of crisis, when a prior, "Keynesian" paradigm was crumbling.[2] Policy is thus primarily seen as the outcome of a particular dominant paradigm enshrined in state institutions. While ideological explanations may also argue that lobbying played an important part in the ascent of neoliberal ideology within the state, explanations that *primarily* focus on lobbying, on the other hand, need not necessarily claim that lobbying organizations were working from a coherent ideological paradigm in undertaking political advocacy on behalf of business.[3] Indeed, accounts which foreground the causal force of lobbying pressure on the state may not consider at all the process whereby the ideas for which political interest groups advocate are developed. Instead, they may argue that policy is the result of "organized combat," in which not specific *paradigms*, but the relatively fixed and self-evident *interests* of business are pitted against others in a

[1] David Harvey, *A Brief History of Neoliberalism* (Oxford, UK: Oxford University Press, 2007); Naomi Klein, *The Shock Doctrine: The Rise of Disaster Capitalism* (New York: Alfred A. Knopf, 2007); Philip Mirowski, *The Road from Mont Pèlerin: The Making of the Neoliberal Thought Collective*, Second Edition (Cambridge, MA: Harvard University Press, 2015); Dani Rodrik, *Straight Talk on Trade: Ideas for a Sane World Economy* (Princeton, NJ: Princeton University Press, 2017); Joseph E. Stiglitz, *People, Power, and Profits: Progressive Capitalism for an Age of Discontent* (New York: W. W. Norton & Company, 2019).

[2] Mirowski, *The Road from Mont Pèlerin.*

[3] Waterhouse, *Lobbying America*; Drutman, *The Business of America Is Lobbying*; Phillips-Fein, *Invisible Hands*; Phillips-Fein and Zelizer, *What's Good for Business*; Hacker and Pierson, *Winner-Take-All Politics.*

contest of organizational strength.[4] Thus, lobbying explanations tend to see neoliberal restructuring as a more or less incremental process whereby business won out over other interests, especially labor, environmentalists, and consumer rights groups.

As should be clear from the preceding analysis, both of these forms of political explanation are inadequate. Conceiving of neoliberalism as the outcome of business lobbying fails to account for the dynamic and systematic role of state agencies in working to organize class power and resolve the crisis of the 1970s. Moreover, in ignoring the process of developing the ideas that would underpin neoliberal hegemony, they obscure the collaborative, integral state relationship between the most prominent state agencies and business associations. This was not a matter of business *advocating* for fixed interests, but rather state agencies and business associations working together to *develop* policies to discipline labor and break inflation. Similarly, the argument that a coherent body of neoliberal ideas gained sway over state officials was not borne out by a survey of the archival record of the most active and prominent state agencies. On the contrary, there was immense uncertainty among state agencies and business alike about the nature, scope, and permanence of the necessary restructuring. For an entire decade, Nixon, Ford, and Carter fumbled with controls, buying time in hopes that eventually a solution would present itself, or that growth and normalcy would be restored. It was only gradually that an alternative emerged over the Carter years—*before* Reagan was elected. Far from approaching the state with a resolution it had already worked out, business consistently followed the lead of state officials. Neoliberal restructuring was not a matter of importing a fixed ideology wholesale into state institutions. Rather, these policies emerged from the crucible of class struggle, formulated and implemented by a state bureaucracy working to resolve an unprecedented crisis. As the capacities of the most prominent state agencies were expanded, new integral state institutions were developed to collaborate with and build consensus among business.

Economic explanations, on the other hand, focus on "financialization" as the essence of neoliberalism.[5] Though these accounts may see

[4] Hacker and Pierson, *Winner-Take-All Politics*. See, especially, Chapter 5.

[5] William Lazonick, "Profits Without Prosperity," *Harvard Business Review*, September 1, 2014; William Lazonick, "The Financialization of the U.S. Corporation: What Has Been Lost, and How It Can Be Regained," *Seattle University Law Review* 36, no. 2

a role for politics in advancing a regulatory regime that reinforces financial power, the emphasis is on finance as a corrosive and parasitic force on the "real" industrial economy. Such accounts frequently emphasize the increasing "short-termism" in corporate strategy that has supposedly resulted from financial pressure, which has led firms to restructure in ways that are dysfunctional to long-term economic health and stability. This has been epitomized in the doctrine of "shareholder value," according to which firms identify the maintenance of a high share price as the fundamental goal of corporate strategy. To achieve this, management has undertaken a range of short-sighted strategies, including diverting investment funds to engage in stock buybacks—whereby a firm repurchases its own stock—to drive up the price of shares. Thus, rather than investing capital in the development and renewal of the "productive" base and the "good jobs" that come with it, managers have used corporate resources to simply line the pockets of wealthy and powerful investors. As these managers are themselves compensated with stock options, they have a direct incentive to undertake such damaging misuse of funds, since they can reap windfall gains by exercising options after inflating the share price. Furthermore, in these accounts, "financialization" also involves industrial firms themselves becoming financial institutions, diverting investment from traditional "productive" activities. In this way, this model depicts financialization as akin to the "hollowing out" of production, as financial services have come to replace "real" commodities. The implication is that finance can be separated from industry, and in fact *must be* if pre-neoliberal prosperity is to be restored.

Understanding the ascendancy of finance as part of the restructuring of the integral state leads to very different conclusions than those prevalent

(March 10, 2013): 857; William Lazonick and Mary O'Sullivan, *Corporate Governance and Sustainable Prosperity* (Springer, 2001); Greta R. Krippner, *Capitalizing on Crisis* (Cambridge, MA: Harvard University Press, 2011); Michael Hudson, *Killing the Host: How Financial Parasites and Debt Bondage Destroy the Global Economy* (New York: Perseus Books Group, 2015); Michael Hudson, *The Bubble and Beyond: Fictitious Capital, Debt Deflation and the Global Crisis* (Islet, 2014).

in these economic accounts.[6] Rather than asking whether the empowerment of finance is economically efficient from the point of view of capital accumulation, contextualizing this as a shift within the integral state means situating it as part of an emergent pattern of institutional power and class rule. We therefore identify the institutional shifts empowering finance as an aspect of a specifically neoliberal form of capitalist hegemony. This includes changes in the command-and-control structures of individual corporations themselves, as well as in the functional integration of particular firms within the overall structure of accumulation, and finally shifts in state organization that reproduce this new phase of political hegemony. The empowerment of finance has been crucial to reproducing this configuration of class power, including through disciplining surplus extraction and competitiveness, facilitating internationalization, and circulating and valorizing capital.[7] The theory of the integral state thus leads us to examine financialization in terms of the consolidation of a particular structure of class power traversing the institutions of corporate governance, civil society, and the state.

If these represent some important foundations for a study of the neoliberal integral state, the analysis presented here already points to some of the problems with the economic accounts of the rise of neoliberalism described above. Much of this contemporary thinking on financialization underplays the extent to which corporations are *inherently* financial entities. As a consequence of the capitalist tendency to separate ownership and possession of productive assets, different forms of "financialization" are present from the very beginning of the emergence of corporate organization. There is a huge range of possible mediations between ownership and possession, but all involve the formation of specific mechanisms for

[6] In fact, there is scant reason to believe that the rise of finance has been fundamentally accompanied by a growing 'short-termism' on the part of non-financial corporations. See: "Corporate Short-Termism Is a Frustratingly Slippery Idea," *The Economist*, February 16, 2017; Jesse Fried, "Trump and Warren Offer the Wrong Diagnosis of Short-Termism," *Financial Times*, August 27, 2018; Charles Nathan and Kal Goldberg, "The Short-Termism Thesis: Dogma vs. Reality," Harvard Law School Forum on Corporate Governance and Financial Regulation, March 18, 2019, https://corpgov.law.harvard.edu/2019/03/18/the-short-termism-thesis-dogma-vs-reality; Lizanne Thomas, "Stop Panicking About Corporate Short-Termism," *Harvard Business Review*, June 28, 2019; Stephen Maher, "The Truth About Finance," *Jacobin*, January 5, 2016.

[7] As reviewed in detail in: Greg Albo, "Contesting the 'New Capitalism,'" in *Varieties of Capitalism, Varieties of Approaches*, ed. David Coates (New York, NY: Palgrave Macmillan, 2005).

interacting with financial markets, mobilizing capital, allocating investment, and managing assets. As we have seen, these institutions crystallize hierarchies and are structured by state regulations. In the American case, the creation of the modern corporation took place in tandem with the development of the financial system, as the vast concentrations of capital controlled by banks afforded them the capacity to merge isolated enterprises into larger corporations they controlled. In keeping with the classical "finance capital" pattern, banks organized these larger firms into networks connected through "interlocking directorates" through which the banks exerted control. However, as non-financial corporations became more autonomous from banks by World War I, they internalized a range of financial functions—forming the foundation for the distinctly American model of corporate organization. This model was consecrated through New Deal regulations, which formally separated banks from the governance of industrial corporations. In the neoliberal period, investors have again become more active in the governance of industrial corporations.

Furthermore, as we saw in the case of GE, the growth of financial functions within the firm has deep historical and institutional roots. GE's embeddedness within the industrial policy system led to the tremendous expansion of its engineering capacities, generating a range of new technologies and new product lines. Whereas a functionally departmentalized structure (divided into units concerned with corporate sales, legal, accounting, engineering, etc.) was adequate for a firm oriented around a single business, as the range of businesses increased GE adapted by implementing a multidivisional structure, beginning with Cordiner's 1951 "Great Reorganization." This was a process of simultaneous *centralization* and *decentralization*: on the one hand, the decentralized organization of production and operational management into autonomous divisions, and on the other, the centralization of investment functions in the hands of top executives. *Operational* functions related to particular businesses were devolved to lower-level divisional managers, while top management increasingly concentrated on *investment* functions. By the 1950s, top executives were known as "general managers," seeking to approximate capital *in general* as bearers of abstract money-capital. Unable to master the particularities of each different business within highly complex multi-process firms, these general managers depended on the corporate financial unit to apply quantitative metrics to qualitatively distinct processes of production. This culminated in the firm's restructuring as a "system of investment," whereby its operations were managed as a portfolio of assets. This was implemented through the restructuring of corporate planning as an internal capital market. Individual business units were encouraged to act as independent firms, developing their own business plans, and competing for a finite sum of investment funds distributed by top management.

Administrative decentralization, the empowerment of the corporate financial unit, and the conversion of top general managers into money-capitalists were thus three dimensions of the same institutional process. Far from being "parasitic" on GE's "productive" businesses, this amounted to restructuring the governance of these assets so as to enhance market discipline, increase efficiency, and thin the bureaucracy. Financial functions and practices were not "added on" to the company's industrial operations, but were core to its basic operations. These operations were then commodified as "financial services" through the General Electric Credit Corporation (GECC). Already by the 1960s, GECC sold a range of financial services, including credit, insurance, mutual funds, and investment advice—taking advantage of the competitive-edge New Deal regulations afforded it as a "non-financial" corporation, which allowed it to sell products that formally "financial" firms could not. As industrial profits fell with the winding down of the postwar boom, GECC expanded in inverse proportion. This was partly about "padding" industrial profits and boosting consumer demand by adding a range of ancillary services, financing packages, and the like. But, as we saw, it also went much further. By the end of the 1960s, GE management bragged that GECC was a diversified financial institution, and that the majority of its financing business pertained to non-GE products. GECC developed its own divisional structure, and as of 1970 was issuing its own Annual Reports. Corporate planners over the 1970s further facilitated the commodification of these financial capacities by creating markets for such services within the firm, making internal business units purchase internal management and financial services from their own operating budgets. Just as financial operations were core corporate functions, which evolved as an intrinsic part of the restructuring of industrial assets, it is hard to find an intrinsic basis for separating these "financial" businesses from other operations in the firm's "portfolio."

These processes of centralization–decentralization, and the empowerment of the corporate financial unit, were also linked with the broader rise of the financial sector. While the comfortable margins of the managerial period had allowed the firm to finance its activities internally, when the boom crashed into stagnation and crisis over the 1970s, the firm became more dependent upon external finance–which thereby gained greater leverage over corporate "insiders." At the same time, a wave of concentration and centralization of equity holdings, driven especially by the expansion of worker's pension plans, meant that vast blocs of corporate stock were either managed or owned directly by "institutional investors." Together, these trends reversed the relative powerlessness of investors that had characterized the managerial period. The increasing involvement of more powerful external financiers in corporate governance was supported by the return to prominence of Boards of Directors as venues for organizing and expressing corporate control, bolstered by new regulations issued by an increasingly assertive SEC. Investors also pushed for the further empowerment of the corporate financial unit, transforming the relatively minor role of treasurer into a powerful Chief Financial Officer (CFO), the right-hand of the CEO; all this ensured that "financial" concerns would carry much more substantial weight in corporate strategy and governance. Beginning in the mid-1960s, this trend swept the corporate world, with CFOs becoming ubiquitous by the 1990s. Crucially, the CFO is a major institutional link between the external financial system and internal processes of corporate restructuring. As the primary site of "investor relations" functions and an increasingly powerful voice in corporate governance, CFOs both managed investor expectations and simultaneously played a major role in shaping corporate strategy so as to ensure these expectations were met.

This was what Claude Serfati has referred to as the reorganization of the corporation as a "financial group"—not an apparatus organized to govern specific concrete production processes, but rather a group of investors who manage a pool of capital and seek to build a portfolio of investments.[8] Nevertheless, it must be pointed out that industrial corporations, unlike banks, directly control productive assets that produce commodities and generate technologies. This therefore remains a different structure from a group of fund managers. However, this restructuring, whereby GE management came to think more in terms of accumulating capital in general rather than in one given sector, did constitute an important part of the material basis for the coalition between

[8] Claude Serfati, "The New Configuration of the Capitalist Class," in *Socialist Register 2014: Registering Class*, ed. Leo Panitch and Greg Albo (London, UK: Merlin Press, 2013).

finance and industry that supported neoliberal restructuring. As we saw, though GE was an industrial firm, through its role on the Business Roundtable, the President's Export Council, and other integral state bodies, it was crucial for bringing industry into the neoliberal consensus. This consensus in some ways challenged the interests of smaller, less diversified, more nationally focused—and less financialized—manufacturing companies. Yet, it was not *finance* per se that harmed smaller, nationally based firms, but the intensification of *competition* that came with globalization. Firms that were excessively tied to one geographical zone or economic sector, and unable to restructure globally or become mobile across sectors, would increasingly face pressure from those firms which could—a process that was *facilitated* by global finance. Those that could not internationalize would either be increasingly squeezed, or become integrated within the international networks of larger firms as suppliers or contractors.

Though the BR had sought as early as the 1970s to push back against SEC regulations that would further empower Boards of Directors to discipline and monitor internal management, these efforts would largely fail as the meteoric rise of finance proceeded apace. Managers of non-financial firms would seek to appease investors by conceding to boards composed of larger numbers of "outside directors," including executives from other firms and financiers. GE, for its part, had long maintained a Board comprised primarily of outsiders, but it nevertheless pointed to this as evidence that it was complying with investor demands for greater accountability, transparency, and "good governance." Yet this was only the beginning. With the financial deregulation of the 1980s, and greater concentration and centralization within the financial sector, the pressures on industrial corporations to maximize returns increased, not least so as to ensure that financiers "got their cut" in the form of dividend payments and asset valuations. The growing power of outside investors could not have been clearer than in the emergence of the "corporate raiders" in the early part of the new decade, who mobilized investors to fire ineffective managers, or to force underperforming firms to restructure—or else simply dismembering them. While managers lobbied the federal government to protect them from this, the Reagan administration was unsympathetic to these calls, which would have entailed challenging the financial intuitions that were at the center of the new global system. Even as these conflicts began to cool, financial institutions holding large blocs of equity found they could no longer simply follow the "Wall Street rule" and sell shares of troubled or underperforming companies. This illiquidity meant that more direct involvement in corporate governance became necessary to exert pressure on management to boost performance and improve "shareholder value."[9]

As we have seen, this increased power of financiers cannot simply be reduced to an effect of financial "deregulation," since financial power within corporate governance was enforced through *extending* state regulations. Rather, this was an institutional contestation within the integral state, as managers sought to secure a regulatory structure that would constrain external financial discipline and allow them to maintain their preeminent position in controlling corporate assets—even as they continued to rely on finance to restructure their global operations. Managers' efforts to defend themselves through anti-takeover laws at the state level, where they had more leverage, as well as by implementing golden parachutes and poison pills within the firm itself, were equally ineffective—particularly as investors could insist that firms either opt out of regulations, or incorporate in states without them. Shifts in SEC regulations continued to facilitate investor power, such as a 1992 change that allowed groups of investors to discuss a possible takeover, without public notice, of a company in which they hold large blocs of shares.[10] As the conflict between owners and managers cooled with the crystallization of the new power relations, executives gradually routinized and expanded contact with investors. Similarly, investors began to pursue less destructive ways to exert power, undertaking a wave of proxy fights over the 1990s to extend "shareholder democracy." GE, which had been the paradigmatic managerial firm, did not participate in the defensive behavior of other industrial companies. Rather, as early as 1981—immediately after he became CEO—Jack Welch emerged as the foremost champion of the doctrine "shareholder value." With this, GE had come full-circle: from paragon of managerialism to aggressive champion of the shareholder value that symbolized the return of investor power.

[9] Scott, *Corporate Business and Capitalist Classes*; Useem, *Investor Capitalism*; Michael Useem, *Executive Defense: Shareholder Power and Corporate Reorganization* (Cambridge, MA: Harvard University Press, 1993); Waterhouse, *Lobbying America*.

[10] Useem, *Investor Capitalism*, 35.

Jack Welch and "Shareholder Value"

As he prepared to retire at the end of the 1970s, Reginald Jones "was much praised at business school forums," and GE was regarded as "one of the strongest in America." Its triple-A bond rating, $2.2 billion in cash and marketable securities, and 19.5 percent return on equity "attested to GE's position as a pillar of financial integrity." It had never had an unprofitable year, had paid a divided annually since 1900, and had "virtually no debt." GE was "American's most admired company" and Jones "was the most admired CEO."[11] Nevertheless, "Wall Street had found his company decidedly unelectric." This was reflected in the firm's share price: "an investor who in 1971 had bought $1,000 worth of GE stock would have seen the value of his investment cut in half in constant dollars, and even including GE's generous dividends, the shareholder wouldn't have beaten inflation."[12] Moreover, though GE revenues had doubled over the war years, and doubled again in the decade after the war, they had *merely* doubled between 1958 and 1981. This generated further pressure to cut costs by thinning the bureaucracy, which, as we have seen, had not been checked sufficiently by successive rounds of decentralization. By the end of Jones' tenure in 1981, nine layers of management "separated him from the lowly foot solider in the factory." GE was "a suffocatingly ossified place," governed by a maze of "rules, procedures, and hierarchies that dictated everything":

> Employees were assigned to one of twenty-eight civil service style levels of rank, which determined office size even down to a standardized number of ceiling tiles. Subordinates fawned over their bosses, spoke only when spoken to, kept their ties knotted and their shirtsleeves clean, and, above all, followed orders, whether they made sense or not.[13]

Though the reorganization of the firm's operations into strategic business units helped to rationalize planning by organizing it around the competitive distribution of investment across the firm's "portfolio" of operations, this structure created its own inefficiencies. Extensive administration was necessary to organize market relations among business units: executing

[11] O'Boyle, *At Any Cost*, 49.

[12] O'Boyle, *At Any Cost*, 68.

[13] O'Boyle, *At Any Cost*, 53.

transactions, applying standards and performance metrics, and conducting surveillance and oversight. Downloading responsibility for strategic planning also meant imposing new demands for developing business plans on divisional managers, as well as organizing and administering a range of venues, apparatuses, and processes through which these plans could be defended and approved by central planners. Meetings for reviewing and defending strategic plans proliferated, and central corporate planners ended up spending an "inordinate amount of time and effort reviewing plans and forcing the business units to allocate time defending the plans rather than running the business."[14] In short, despite all efforts, decentralization had resulted not in *less* bureaucracy, but rather had evolved a *different kind* of administrative apparatus: one that was organized around a financialized logic, but which nevertheless used just as much managerial manpower. In the emerging era of neoliberal financialization, not stability, but *growth*, and especially a rising share price, were the most important indicators of corporate success. If such growth could not be secured through industrial operations, other divisions would receive investment funds per GE's strategic planning model and centralized–decentralized structure.

Jones devoted a huge amount of time and energy identifying a successor, beginning the search less than two years into his tenure as CEO. That Jones considered CFO Al Way disqualified by virtue of his lack of operating experience indicates the as-yet incomplete nature of the separation of investment and operating functions within the company. Yet, at the same time, Jones' methods pointed to the evolution of general managers into abstract money-capitalists. Beginning in 1977, Jones appointed his shortlisted candidates as "senior executives," giving each responsibility for a multibillion-dollar portfolio of businesses. As if to prove the importance of being able to operate as an abstract investor, without needing to rely on concrete knowledge of a particular business, Jones specifically made "each man responsible for a business he was unfamiliar with." At the end of the experiment, and after conducting a series of "airplane interviews" with the candidates over 1978, Jones "came away convinced that Welch was the only leader tough enough to bring about the changes he believed were necessary – a levelling of the GE bureaucracy." Welch would execute this and more over his unprecedented two

[14] William E. Rothschild, *The Secret to GE's Success* (New York: McGraw Hill Professional, 2007), 171.

decades as top executive. "Take a look around you," he reportedly told "a roomful of alarmed corporate planners" soon after becoming CEO, "because you won't be seeing each other anymore." Not long thereafter, "all but a dozen of the two hundred positions in corporate planning were eliminated."[15] This was accompanied by the ruthless imposition of "lean production," whereby the workforce was cut to the bone—earning Welch the nickname "Neutron Jack" after the bomb that kills humans, but leaves buildings intact. This "downsizing" of the workforce—carried out not as a last-ditch effort to save a failing company, but rather during good economic times to enhance margins and meet earnings targets—was draconian: just three years into his reign, Welch had eliminated 37,000 of 404,000 employees; in his first five years, he eliminated 130,000 jobs, generating savings of approximately $6.5 billion.[16]

Shocking though this may have been for workers and managers alike, it was aggressive moves such as these that would turn Welch into a celebrity CEO in business circles. Despite the increasingly tough capital market, and more competitive product markets, Welch "finally won the universal acclaim of Wall Street."[17] Just as Cordiner symbolized the managerial phase of capitalist development, no one encapsulated the new neoliberal "shareholder value" ethos more than Welch. Welch's restructuring clearly signaled that the managerial era, in which companies endlessly grew by adding divisions, units, and bureaucracy, was over. Welch paired aggressive cost cutting with extensive investments in financial services, successfully boosting the share price to unprecedented heights and appearing to position the firm at the forefront of a new corporate revolution. Nevertheless, while Welch may have become an icon in the business world as GE's stock price climbed, he did not possess anything like the integral state clout that Jones had. Indeed, Welch largely refrained from politics, though he served as chair of the Business Council from 1991 to 1992. Even as the 1970s crisis faded into history, GE seemed determined not to return to the bloated bureaucratization that had plagued it throughout the managerial period. Management pushed hard a new emphasis on "lean production," intensified competitiveness, and enhanced margins, which brought a new discipline to the organization. GE's financialized restructuring since the

[15] O'Boyle, *At Any Cost*, 64–5, 68.

[16] O'Boyle, *At Any Cost*, 71, 91.

[17] O'Boyle, *At Any Cost*, 141.

1950s, and its "portfolio" management model, allowed it to exit sectors that had lower growth potential while entering new sectors and markets. Rather than specializing in producing specific products and technologies, the firm was increasingly oriented toward buying and selling businesses, restructuring and selling off those that it deemed a drag on long-term performance.

While the shifting composition of GE's "portfolio" reflected the changing American economy, it also pointed to the company's increasing distance from the industrial policy system. In his first years on the job, Welch made extensive investments in high-tech R&D alongside a range of acquisitions seeking to position the company at the cutting edge of the emerging consumer electronics market as well as industrial automation. However, the lack of success with which these projects met led to a change in tack.[18] This became especially apparent after the 1987 purchase of RCA, which had itself evolved into a multidivisional conglomerate. Though some hoped this—the largest takeover in history at that time outside of the oil sector—would form the basis for a stronger consumer electronics business, GE broke the company up and sold off its assets separately, retaining only NBC by the time Welch retired in 2001.[19] Then, in 1992, Welch sold GE's aerospace division to Martin Marietta for $3 billion.[20] Welch also decentralized R&D, so that this was funded not by central corporate planning, but rather individual business divisions. In seven years, R&D staff was reduced by 30%. "We are not interested in incubating new businesses," Welch explained.[21] Instead of "incubating new businesses" (though as we have seen, these were in fact spun off from the industrial policy system), the company's decentralized structure increasingly resembled a private equity firm: buying, restructuring, and selling assets. GE became a perpetual motion machine, relying on its triple-A bond rating and cash from its industrial operations

[18] Peter Petre and Rosalind Klein Berlin, "How GE Bobbled the Factory of the Future," *Fortune*, November 11, 1985.

[19] L.J. Davis, "Did RCA Have To Be Sold?" *The New York Times Magazine*, September 20, 1987; O'Boyle, *At Any Cost*, 212.

[20] Anita Womak, "Martin Marietta Announces Purchase of GE's Aerospace Division," *AP*, November 23, 1992.

[21] Jeff Madrick, *Age of Greed: The Triumph of Finance and the Decline of America, 1970 to the Present* (New York: Vintage Books, 2012), 199.

to support continuously undertaking large-scale acquisitions and divestment of business units.[22] At the same time, Welch bought off financial pressure by undertaking stock buybacks, including announcing the largest to that time in November 1989.[23] And GECC—renamed GE Capital—was radically expanded, from $11 billion to $70 billion in assets between 1981 and 1991. By the time Welch retired in 2001, GE Capital would comprise fully 40% of GE profits, as the economy hurtled toward another catastrophic crisis.

In 1999, as his twenty-year tenure as CEO was nearing its end—the longest in GE history—*Fortune* magazine named Welch "manager of the century."[24] Yet, Welch's successor, Jeff Immelt, would spend a good portion of his own years in the leadership spot—from 2001 to 2017—trying to undo what Welch had done. Though he initially built up GE Capital still further, expanding its debt and moving aggressively into commercial real estate, after the 2008 crisis appeared to leave GE dangerously vulnerable to financial volatility, he reconsidered this strategy. Indeed, by 2007, GE Capital had come to account for 55% of the company's profits.[25] As the stock price crashed, a timely investment—some would say "bailout"—from Warren Buffet's Berkshire Hathaway in October 2008 kept the company afloat.[26] If this wasn't enough, pressure to exit financial services markets intensified after the new Financial Services Oversight Committee, created as part of the Dodd-Frank financial reform legislation, threatened to regulate GE as a Systemically Important Financial Institution.[27] This would have included more stringent reporting requirements, stress tests, and other regulatory measures.

[22] Froud et. al. refer to this as GE's "undisclosed business model." See: Julie Froud et al., "General Electric: The Conditions of Success," CRESC Working Paper Series (Manchester, UK: Centre for Research on Socio-Cultural Change, The University of Manchester, September 2005).

[23] Steven Mufson, "GE Announces Five-Year, $10 Billion Stock Buyback," *Washington Post*, November 18, 1989.

[24] Geoffrey Colvin, "The Ultimate Manager," *Fortune*, November 22, 1999.

[25] Geoff Colvin, "What the Hell Happened at GE?" *Fortune*, May 24, 2018.

[26] Steve Lohr, "Buffett's Bet on G.E.: Almost as Good as a Bailout," *New York Times*, October 1, 2008; Matt Egan, "Inside the Dismantling of GE," *CNN Money*, June 13, 2018.

[27] Ted Mann and Ryan Tracy, "GE Capital Sheds 'Systemically Important' Label," *Wall Street Journal*, June 29, 2016.

Instead, the company agreed to break up and sell off GE Capital, which Immelt had largely completed by 2016, one year before he would hastily and prematurely resign. Even as Immelt worked to get GE out of financial services and lending, his resignation indicated the extent to which financial power had been rebuilt—and even strengthened—coming out of the 2008 crisis.[28] Observers widely attributed Immelt's early retirement to pressure from a few activist investors, especially Nelson Peltz, whose Trian Fund Management had been publicly exerting pressure on GE's management to improve performance. "Looking almost teary-eyed" in a videoconference announcing his retirement, Immelt admitted, "I always knew my name wasn't over the door. You owned the company." Indeed, Wall Street found his performance widely disappointing: shares fell 31% during his tenure, making GE the Dow's worst performer.[29]

Retrospective assessments of Welch's tenure as CEO have differed significantly from those that prevailed over the 1980s and 1990s. Even Welch himself famously declared in 2009 that shareholder value is "the dumbest idea in the world."[30] However, the difficulty Immelt had with "returning" to what he saw as the company's "core" business areas pointed to the extent to which deeper structural shifts, rather than just particular "bad" choices Welch had made, underpinned the changes at GE. Though he attempted to expand into high-tech manufacturing by turning to "Industrial Revolution 2.0" technologies and products, such as 3-D printing and especially the "Industrial Internet of Things," these ventures appeared not to have the purchase the company had initially hoped they would.[31] In the wake of the 2008 crisis, Immelt had been determined to restructure—but exactly how to do this, and whether it

[28] Stephen Maher, "GE's Switch," *Jacobin,* July 31, 2017. That Trian subsequently fought for and won a seat on GE's Board further indicated the extent of investor power, as well as the growing importance of Boards of Directors. See: Ed Crooks and Lindsay Fortado, "Activist investor Trian wins seat on GE Board," *Financial Times*, October 9, 2017.

[29] Christopher Helman, "Unloved Immelt Out At General Electric; Shares Surge," *Forbes*, June 12, 2017.

[30] Francesco Guerrera, "Welch condemns share price focus," *Financial Times*, 12 March 2009.

[31] Steve Lohr, "G.E. to Spin Off Its Digital Business," *New York Times*, December 13, 2018; Ron Miller, "GE's Digital Future Looking Murkier with Move to Spin Off Industrial IoT biz," *TechCrunch*, December 14, 2018; Ron Miller, "In Spite of Digital Transformation, 2017 Did Not Yield the Desired Financial Results for GE," *TechCrunch*,

could be successful, remained unclear by the time of his departure. In fact, the crisis at the company only worsened after Immelt left, making it even clearer just how difficult a "back to basics" strategy would be to execute. His successor, John Flannery, had spent thirty years in GE's finance division—having served as the head of the corporate restructuring unit, where he played a large role in the company's mergers and acquisitions strategy, before moving to become chief of GE's private equity group.[32] This suggested that although the firm may have by then largely gotten out of financial services, Welch's assessment that the firm's core strengths lay in its financial and management capacities was perhaps closer to the mark than Immelt's post-2008 view. This was reinforced by Flannery's sale of the healthcare division, which had long been framed as a core business.[33] Nevertheless, amidst further revelations of financial problems, and technical issues with GE's new line of gas-powered turbines, Flannery's failure to move quickly enough for investors led to his stepping down after less than two years in the top spot—far and away the shortest of any top GE executive in history.[34]

Replacing him was the so-called turnaround artist Larry Culp, the first outsider ever to occupy GE's top executive position. This was a dramatic move indeed for a company that had been known throughout the postwar period, as we saw, as the pinnacle of managerial prowess. It was quite a reversal from the Cordiner years, when other firms sought out those trained at GE's Crotonville facility. As GE's stock lost 45% of its value in one year, Culp initiated a flurry of deals that many believed amounted to continuing the "slow-motion breakup" of the conglomerate that had begun with Immelt's exit.[35] Culp had previously been credited

December 10, 2017; Ed Crooks, "General Electric: Post-Industrial Revolution," *Financial Times*, January 12, 2016.

[32] Roger Yu, "Who is John Flannery, GE's next CEO?" *USA Today*, June 12, 2017; John Gapper, "Flannery's General Electric May Not Hold Together Long," *Financial Times*, November 15, 2017.

[33] Alwyn Scott, "GE Breakup Leaves it with Best and Worst Performers," *Reuters*, June 26, 2018.

[34] Michael Sheetz, "Why GE Removed John Flannery as CEO After Little More than a Year," *CNBC*, October 1, 2018; "GE Power CEO Reveals Problem with New Turbine Model, Shares drop," *Reuters*, 20 September 2018.

[35] Brooke Sutherland, "GE Gives Investors a Breakup. That's Something," *Bloomberg*, June 26, 2018; Matt Egan, "Inside the Dismantling of GE," *CNN Money*, June 13,

with turning around the Danaher Corporation, a much smaller conglomerate, through a decentralized restructuring whereby the company was run as "a collection of independent businesses orbiting a small central staff." This was not unlike the vision that Flannery had advanced for GE—though the difference was that Culp was, for the moment at least, trusted by increasingly active outside investors like Peltz.

Not long after he took the CEO position, amidst intense speculation about the future of the company as questions emerged about GE accounting practices, including an SEC investigation and allegations of "Enronesque fraud,"[36] Culp gathered the top GE executives for a summit in New York to insist "he wasn't going to dismantle their company." He projected a slide showing "two organizational extremes": on one side was a continuation of GE's model of centralization–decentralization, while at the other extreme was "Berkshire Hathaway's Warren Buffett sitting with just a handful of staff" managing independent businesses.[37] Culp claimed to prefer the former option—but whether this would be possible remained to be seen.

2018; Michael Sheetz, "CEO Culp Likely to Break Up and Sell Pieces of the Struggling Power Business, RBC says," *CNBC*, March 27, 2019.

[36] Matt Egan, "GE is under SEC Investigation," *CNN Business*, January 24, 2018; Dominic Rushe, "General Electric Shares Tank Following Accusation of 'Bigger Fraud than Enron'," *The Guardian*, 15, August 2019. Nevertheless, there was good reason to doubt the accusations of fraud launched against GE by "whistleblower" Harry Markopolos. See for instance: Shawn Tully, "How the Man Who Nailed Madoff Got GE Wrong," *Fortune*, October 3, 2019.

[37] Thomas Gryta, "Larry Culp's GE Plan: a Fix, Not a Reinvention," *Wall Street Journal*, October 7, 2019; Al Root, "GE CEO Larry Culp Talks Progress, Debt, and Restructuring," *Barron's*, September 13, 2019; Rick Clough, "Larry Culp's GE Turnaround Plan Is Starting to Take Hold," *Bloomberg*, October 30, 2019.

Bibliography

Manuscript and Archival Sources

Business Roundtable Archives, Washington, DC

General Electric Annual Reports, 1920–1980.

Jimmy Carter Presidential Library, Atlanta Georgia

- White House Central Files.
- Office of Staff Secretary Papers.

U.S. National Archives, College Park, Maryland.

- Department of Commerce records.
- Department of Justice records.
- Department of State records.
- Department of the Treasury records.
- Executive Office of the President records.
  - Office of the United States Trade Representative records.
  - Office of Management and Budget records.
  - Council on Wage and Price Control records.
- Office of Production Management records.
- Office of Defense Mobilization records.
- President's Export Council records.
- U.S Information Agency records.
- U.S. Foreign Assistance Agencies records.
- War Production Board records.

United States Senate Committee on Finance. "Review of Findings of the President's Commission on Industrial Competitiveness." Pub. L. No. S. HRG. 99-75 (1985).

© The Editor(s) (if applicable) and The Author(s), under exclusive license to Springer Nature Switzerland AG 2022

S. Maher, *Corporate Capitalism and the Integral State*, Marx, Engels, and Marxisms,
https://doi.org/10.1007/978-3-030-83772-3

United States Senate Committee on Finance. "Executive Branch Organization for International Economic Policy," 93rd Congress, 2d session, February 18, 1974, S. Rep. S362-5.

Periodicals

Associated Press.
The Atlantic.
Barron's.
Bloomberg.
Commerce Today.
CNBC.
CNN.
Financial Times.
Forbes.
Fortune.
The Guardian.
Jacobin.
NBC.
New York Times.
New York Times Magazine.
Newsweek.
Reuters.
TechCrunch.
Wall Street Journal.
Washington Post.

Books and Articles

Aglietta, Michel. *A Theory of Capitalist Regulation: The US Experience*. New York: Verso, 2000.

Albo, Greg. "Contesting the 'New Capitalism.'" In *Varieties of Capitalism, Varieties of Approaches*, edited by David Coates. New York, NY: Palgrave Macmillan, 2005.

Allen, James. *Atomic Imperialism*. New York: International Publishers, 1952.

Archer, Margaret. *Realist Social Theory: The Morphogenetic Approach*. Cambridge, UK: Cambridge University Press, 1995.

Arrighi, Giovanni. *The Long Twentieth Century: Money, Power, and the Origins of Our Times*. New York: Verso, 1994.

Baran, Paul A., and Paul M. Sweezy. *Monopoly Capital: An Essay on the American Economic and Social Order*. New York: Monthly Review Press, 1966.

Barkan, Joshua. *Corporate Sovereignty: Law and Government Under Capitalism.* Minneapolis, MN: University of Minnesota Press, 2013.

Barnhill, John. "Great Electrical Equipment Conspiracy." In *Encyclopedia of White-Collar & Corporate Crime*, edited by Lawrence Salinger, 1: 377–78. Thousand Oaks, CA: Sage, 2005.

Barrow, Clyde W. *Critical Theories of the State: Marxist, Neomarxist, Postmarxist.* Madison, WI: University of Wisconsin Press, 1993.

Bartlett, Christopher A., Francis J. Aguilar, and Kenton W. Elderkin. "General Electric: Reg Jones and Jack Welch." Harvard Business School, June 1991.

Becker, William H., and William M. McClenahan Jr. *The Market, the State, and the Export-Import Bank of the United States, 1934–2000*. Cambridge, UK: Cambridge University Press, 2003.

Berle, Adolf A., and Gardiner C. Means. *The Modern Corporation and Private Property.* New York: Macmillan Co., 1933.

Berle, Adolf A. *Power Without Property: A New Development in American Political Economy*. Boston: Harcourt, Brace, 1959.

Berry, John. "The Hot Battle Over Labor Law Reform." *Forbes*, September 1, 1977.

Bhaskar, Roy. *A Realist Theory of Science.* Second Edition. Brighton, UK: Harvester Press, 1978.

Bilder, Richard B. "The Office of the Legal Adviser: The State Department Lawyer and Foreign Affairs." *American Journal of International Law* 56 (1962): 633–84.

Block, Fred L., and Matthew R. Keller. *State of Innovation: The U.S. Government's Role in Technology Development*. Oxfordshire, UK: Routledge, 2015.

Boulware, Lemuel R. *The Truth About Boulwarism: Trying to Do Right Voluntarily*. Bureau of National Affairs, 1969.

Brenner, Robert. "The Social Bases of Economic Development." In *Analytical Marxism*, edited by John Roemer. Cambridge, UK: Cambridge University Press, 1986.

Brenner, Robert, and Mark Glick. "The Regulation Approach: Theory and History." *New Left Review* I, no. 188 (August 1991): 45–119.

Brinkley, Alan. *The End of Reform: New Deal Liberalism in Recession and War.* New York: Knopf Doubleday Publishing Group, 2011.

Bryan, Dick, and Michael Rafferty. *Capitalism With Derivatives: A Political Economy of Financial Derivatives, Capital and Class*. Springer, 2005.

Buchanan, Norman S. "The Origin and Development of the Public Utility Holding Company." *Journal of Political Economy* 44, no. 1 (1936): 31–53.

Bukharin, Nikolai. *Imperialism and World Economy.* New York: Monthly Review Press, 1917.

Burnham, James. *The Managerial Revolution*. Penguin Books, 1962.

Cambone, Stephen A. *A New Structure for National Security Policy Planning*. Washington, DC: Center for Strategic and International Studies, 1998.

Cammack, Paul. "Bringing the State Back In?" *British Journal of Political Science* 19, no. 2 (1989): 261–90.

Carlton, Dennis. "Futures Markets: Their Purpose, Their History, Their Growth, Their Successes and Failures." *Journal of Futures Markets* 4 (1984): 209–47.

Carroll, William K. *The Making of a Transnational Capitalist Class: Corporate Power in the 21st Century*. London: Zed Books, 2010.

———. "Whither the Transnational Capitalist Class?" In *Socialist Register 2014: Registering Class*, edited by Leo Panitch, Greg Albo, and Vivek Chibber. London: Merlin Press, 2013.

Carroll, William K., and Jean P. Sapinski. "Corporate Elite and Intercorporate Networks." In *The SAGE Handbook of Social Network Analysis*, edited by Peter J. Carrington and John Scott, 180–95. London: SAGE Publications, 2011.

Case, Josephine Young, and Everett Needham Case. *Owen D. Young and American Enterprise: A Biography*. Boston: David R. Godine Publisher, 1982.

Castells, Manuel. *The Rise of the Network Society: The Information Age: Economy, Society, and Culture*. Second Edition. Hoboken, NJ: Wiley, 2009.

Cate, Thomas. *An Encyclopedia of Keynesian Economics*. Second Edition. Northampton, MA: Edward Elgar Publishing, 2013.

Caves, Richard. *Multinational Enterprise and Economic Analysis*. Third Edition. Cambridge, UK: Cambridge University Press, 2007.

Chandler Jr., Alfred D. *The Visible Hand: The Managerial Revolution in American Business*. Cambridge, MA: Belknap Press, 1977.

———. *Scale and Scope: The Dynamics of Industrial Capitalism*. Cambridge, MA: Harvard University Press, 1994.

———. *Strategy and Structure: Chapters in the History of the American Industrial Enterprise*. Cambridge, MA: MIT Press, 2000.

Chandler, Alfred D., Jr., and Takashi Hikino. *Big Business and the Wealth of Nations*. Cambridge, UK: Cambridge University Press, 1997.

Chernow, Ron. *House of Morgan: An American Banking Dynasty and the Rise of Modern Finance*. Boston: Atlantic Press, 1990.

Chibber, Vivek. "What Is Living and What Is Dead in the Marxist Theory of History." *Historical Materialism* 19, no. 2 (2011): 60–91.

Clarke, Lee. "The Origins of Nuclear Power: A Case of Institutional Conflict." *Social Problems* 32, no. 5 (June 1985): 474–87.

Clifton, James A. "Competition and the Evolution of the Capitalist Mode of Production." *Cambridge Journal of Economics* 1, no. 2 (June 1, 1977): 137–51.

Collier, Andrew. *Critical Realism: An Introduction to Roy Bhaskar's Philosophy*. New York, NY: Verso, 1994.

Collins, Robert M. "Positive Business Responses to the New Deal: The Roots of the Committee for Economic Development, 1933–1942." *The Business History Review* 52, no. 3 (1978): 369–91.

———. *The Business Response to Keynes, 1929–1964*. New York: Columbia University Press, 1981.

Committee for Economic Development. "An American Program of European Economic Cooperation: A Statement on National Policy by CED". Washington, DC: The Committee for Economic Development, February 1948.

———. "Working Paper: Business Leadership and Sustainable Capitalism: Can Corporate Leaders Help Put America and American Business Back on Track?" Washington, DC: The Committee for Economic Development, May 28, 2013.

Cordiner, Ralph J. *New Frontiers for Professional Managers*. New York: McGraw-Hill, 1956.

Cox, Robert. "Global Perestroika." In *Socialist Register 1992: New World Order?*, edited by Ralph Miliband and Leo Panitch. London: Merlin, 1991.

———. *Production, Power, and World Order: Social Forces in the Making of History*. Columbia University Press, 1987.

Creaven, Sean. *Marxism and Realism: A Materialistic Application of Realism in the Social Sciences*. New York, NY: Routledge, 2000.

Crump, Jeffrey. "The Spatial Distribution of Military Spending in the United States 1941–1985." *Growth and Change*, Summer 1989.

Cuff, Robert. "From the Controlled Materials Plan to the Defense Materials System, 1942–1953." *Military Affairs* 51, no. 1 (January 1987): 1–6.

Dahl, Robert. *After the Revolution?* New Haven: Yale University Press, 1970.

———. *Dilemmas of Pluralist Democracy: Autonomy Vs. Control*. New Haven: Yale University Press, 1982.

———. *Pluralist Democracy in the United States: Conflict and Consent*. Chicago: Rand McNally, 1967.

———. *Polyarchy: Participation and Opposition*. New Haven: Yale University Press, 1971.

———. *Who Governs?: Democracy and Power in an American City*. New Haven: Yale University Press, 1961.

Dahl, Robert, and Charles Lindblom. *Politics, Economics, and Welfare: Planning and Politico-Economic Systems*. Chicago: University of Chicago Press, 1976.

Davis, Christopher. "9/11 Commission Recommendations: Joint Committee on Atomic Energy—A Model for Congressional Oversight?" CRS Report for Congress. Congressional Research Service, August 20, 2004.

Drucker, Peter. *Concept of the Corporation*. Routledge, 2008.

———. *The Unseen Revolution: How Pension Fund Socialism Came to America*. New York, NY: Harper and Row, 1976.

Drutman, Lee. *The Business of America Is Lobbying: How Corporations Became Politicized and Politics Became More Corporate*. Oxford, UK: Oxford University Press, 2015.

Engels, Friedrich. "Letter to Joseph Bloch, September 21–22, 1890." In *The Marx-Engels Reader*, ed. Robert Tucker, Second Edition, 1978: 762–63.

Evans, Thomas W. *The Education of Ronald Reagan: The General Electric Years and the Untold Story of His Conversion to Conservatism*. New York: Columbia University Press, 2007.

Fligstein, Neil. *The Transformation of Corporate Control*. Cambridge, MA: Harvard University Press, 1993.

Foley, C. Fritz, and Michael Lemm. "The Role of the Chief Financial Officer." Harvard Business School Technical Note, June 2016.

Foss, Nicolai. "Austrian Insights and the Theory of the Firm." In *Advances in Austrian Economics*, Vol. 4, 1997.

Friedman, Tami. "Exploiting the North-South Differential: Corporate Power, Southern Politics, and the Decline of Organized Labor after World War II." *Journal of American History* 95, no. 2 (September 2008): 323–48.

Froud, Julie, Sukhdev Johal, Adam Leaver, and Karel Williams. "General Electric: The Conditions of Success." CRESC Working Paper Series. Manchester, UK: Centre for Research on Socio-Cultural Change, The University of Manchester, September 2005.

Gable, Richard W. "Birth of an Employers' Association." *Business History Review* 33 (January 1, 1959): 535–45.

Galbraith, John Kenneth. *The Affluent Society*. Boston: Houghton Mifflin, 1978.

———. *The Galbraith Reader*. New York: Palgrave Macmillan, 1977.

———. *The New Industrial State*. Princeton, NJ: Princeton University Press, 2015.

Glasberg, D. S, and M Schwartz. "Ownership and Control of Corporations." *Annual Review of Sociology* 9, no. 1 (1983): 311–32.

Gramsci, Antonio. *Selections from the Prison Notebooks*, edited by Quintin Hoare and Geoffrey Nowell-Smith. New York: International Publishers, 1973.

Green, Harold, and Allen Rosenthal. *The Joint Committee on Atomic Energy: A Study in the Fusion of Government Power*. Washington, DC: The National Law Center, George Washington University, 1961.

Greenwood, Ronald G. *Managerial Decentralization: A Study of the General Electric Philosophy*. Hive Publishing Company, 1982.

Hacker, Jacob S., and Paul Pierson. *Winner-Take-All Politics: How Washington Made the Rich Richer–and Turned Its Back on the Middle Class*. Simon and Schuster, 2010.

———. "Winner-Take-All Politics: Public Policy, Political Organization, and the Precipitous Rise of Top Incomes in the United States:" *Politics & Society*, May 24, 2010.

Hall, Peter, and Rosemary Taylor. "Political Science and the Three New Institutionalisms." *Political Studies* 44, no. 5 (December 1996): 936–57.

Harvey, David. *A Brief History of Neoliberalism*. Oxford, UK: Oxford University Press, 2007.

———. *The Limits to Capital*. New York: Verso, 2006.

Hausman, William J., Peter Hertner, and Mira Wilkins. *Global Electrification: Multinational Enterprise and International Finance in the History of Light and Power, 1878–2007*. Cambridge, UK: Cambridge University Press, 2008.

Henwood, Doug. "Trump and the New Billionaire Class." In *Socialist Register 2019: A World Turned Upside Down?*, edited by Leo Panitch and Greg Albo. London: Merlin Press, 2018.

———. *Wall Street: How It Works and for Whom*. New York: Verso, 1998.

Herman, Arthur. *Freedom's Forge: How Business Produced Victory in World War II*. New York: Random House, 2012.

Herman, Edward S. *Corporate Control, Corporate Power: A Twentieth Century Fund Study*. Cambridge, UK: Cambridge University Press, 1982.

Heskett, James. "Succession at GE: What's Next?" Harvard Business School. Working Knowledge: Business Research for Business Leaders, November 6, 2000.

Hewlett, Richard, and Oscar Anderson. *A History of the United States Atomic Energy Commission, Volume I: The New World (1939–1946)*. University Park, PA: Pennsylvania State University Press, 1962.

Hewlett, Richard, and Francis Duncan. *A History of the United States Atomic Energy Commission, Volume II: Atomic Shield (1947–1952)*. University Park, PA: Pennsylvania State University Press, 1972.

Hewlett, Richard, and Jack Holl. *Atoms for Peace and War: Eisenhower and the Atomic Energy Commission 1953–1961*. Berkeley, CA: University of California Press, 1989.

Hilferding, Rudolf. *Finance Capital: A Study in the Latest Phase of Capitalist Development*. Routledge, 2006.

Hindery, Leo. *It Takes a CEO: It's Time to Lead with Integrity*. New York: Simon and Schuster, 2005.

Hudson, Michael. *Killing the Host: How Financial Parasites and Debt Bondage Destroy the Global Economy*. New York: Perseus Books Group, 2015.

———. *The Bubble and Beyond: Fictitious Capital, Debt Deflation and the Global Crisis*. Islet, 2014.

Hughes, Thomas. *Networks of Power: Electrification in Western Society, 1880–1930*. Baltimore, MD: Johns Hopkins University Press, 1983.

Hunter, Floyd. *Community Power Structure: A Study of Decision Makers*. Chapel Hill, NC: University of North Carolina Press, 1953.

Hyman, Louis. "Rethinking the Postwar Corporation." In Kim Phillips-Fein and Julian E. Zelizer, *What's Good for Business: Business and American Politics Since World War II*. Oxford, UK: Oxford University Press, 2012.

Immergut, Ellen. "The Theoretical Core of the New Institutionalism." *Politics & Society* 26, no. 1 (March 1998): 5–34.

Ingham, Geoffrey. *Capitalism: With a New Postscript on the Financial Crisis and Its Aftermath*. Hoboken, NJ: Wiley, 2013.

Jasper, Herbert. "The Oversight Role of the Joint Committee on Atomic Energy." CRS Memorandum. Congressional Research Service, 1975.

Jessop, Bob. "Regulation and Politics: The Integral Economy and the Integral State." In *Hegemonie Und Staat*, edited by Alex Demirović, H Krebs, and Thomas Sablowski. Münster: Westfälisches Dampfboot Verlag, 1992.

———. "Regulation Theories in Retrospect and Prospect." *Economy and Society* 19, no. 2 (1990): 153–216.

———. *State Theory: Putting the Capitalist State in Its Place*. Pennsylvania State University Press, 1990.

———. "Survey Article: The Regulation Approach." *Journal of Political Philosophy* 5 (December 16, 2002): 287–326.

———. "The Strategic Selectivity of the State: Reflections on a Theme of Poulantzas." *Journal of the Hellenic Diaspora* 25, no. 1–2 (1999): 1–37.

Kaufman, Burton. "Mideast Multinational Oil, U.S. Foreign Policy, and Antitrust: The 1950s." *The Journal of American History* 63, no. 4 (March 1977): 937–59.

Kauper, Thomas. "The Report of the Attorney General's National Committee to Study the Antitrust Laws: A Retrospective." *Michigan Law Review* 100, no. 7 (June 2002): 1867–99.

Klein, Naomi. *The Shock Doctrine: The Rise of Disaster Capitalism*. New York: Alfred A. Knopf, 2007.

Konings, Martijn. *The Development of American Finance*. Cambridge, UK: Cambridge University Press, 2011.

Kotz, David. "Social Structure of Accumulation Theory, Marxist Theory, and System Transformation." *Review of Radical Political Economics* 49, no. 4 (December 1, 2017): 534–42.

———. *Bank Control of Large Corporations in the United States*. Berkeley, CA: University of California Press, 1978.

———. *The Rise and Fall of Neoliberal Capitalism*. Cambridge, MA: Harvard University Press, 2015.

Kotz, David, Terrence McDonough, and Michael Reich, eds. *Social Structures of Accumulation: The Political Economy of Growth and Crisis*. Cambridge, UK: Cambridge University Press, 1994.

Krippner, Greta R. *Capitalizing on Crisis*. Cambridge, MA: Harvard University Press, 2011.

Laskin, Alexander. "Investor Relations as a Public Relations Function: A State of the Profession in the United States." *Journal of Public Relations Research* 26 (2014): 200–214.

Lazonick, William. "Profits Without Prosperity." *Harvard Business Review*, September 1, 2014.

———. "The Financialization of the U.S. Corporation: What Has Been Lost, and How It Can Be Regained." *Seattle University Law Review* 36, no. 2 (March 10, 2013): 857.

Lazonick, William, and Mary O'Sullivan. *Corporate Governance and Sustainable Prosperity*. Springer, 2001.

Lenin, Vladimir. "Imperialism: The Highest Stage of Capitalism." In *Essential Works of Lenin*, 177–270. New York: Bantam Books, 1987.

———. "The State and Revolution." In *Essential Works of Lenin*. New York: Bantam Books, 1987.

Lichtenstein, Nelson. *State of the Union: A Century of American Labor*. Revised and Expanded Edition. Princeton, NJ: Princeton University Press, 2002.

Lindblom, Charles. "Another State of Mind." *The American Political Science Review* 76, no. 1 (1982): 9–21.

———. *Politics and Markets: The World's Political Economic Systems*. New York: Basic Books, 1977.

Linowitz, Sol. "Antitrust Laws: A Damper on American Foreign Trade." *American Bar Association Journal* 44, no. 9 (September 1958): 853–56.

Lo, Clarence Y. H. "Theories of the State and Business Opposition to Increased Military Spending." *Social Problems* 29, no. 4 (April 1982): 424–38.

Loth, David. *Swope of G. E.: The Story of Gerard Swope and General Electric in American Business*. New York: Simon and Schuster, 1958.

Madrick, Jeff. *Age of Greed: The Triumph of Finance and the Decline of America, 1970 to the Present*. New York: Vintage Books, 2012.

Magdoff, Harry. *The Age of Imperialism: The Economics of US Foreign Policy*. New York: Monthly Review Press, 1969.

Maher, Stephen. "Escaping Structuralism's Legacy: The Renewal of Theory and History in Historical Materialism." *Science & Society* 80, no. 3 (June 14, 2016): 291–318.

———. "The Capitalist State, Corporate Political Mobilization, and the Origins of Neoliberalism." *Critical Sociology*, August 4, 2016.

Maher, Stephen, and Scott M. Aquanno. "Conceptualizing Neoliberalism: Foundations for an Institutional Marxist Theory of Capitalism." *New Political Science* 40, no. 1 (January 2, 2018): 33–50.

Manley, John F. "Neo-Pluralism: A Class Analysis of Pluralism I and Pluralism II." *The American Political Science Review* 77, no. 2 (1983): 368–83.

Marx, Karl. "Critique of the Gotha Program." In, *The Marx-Engels Reader*, edited by Robert Tucker. Second Edition 1978 [1875].

———. "The Eighteenth Brumaire of Louis Bonaparte." In *The Marx-Engels Reader*, edited by Robert Tucker. Second Edition, 594–617, 1978.

Matles, James J., and James Higgins. *Them and Us: Struggles of a Rank-and-File Union*. Englewood Cliffs, NJ: Prentice Hall, 1974.

Mazzucato, Mariana. *The Entrepreneurial State: Debunking Public Vs. Private Sector Myths*. New York: Anthem Press, 2013.

McGuire, Patrick, Mark Granovetter, and Michael Schwartz. "Thomas Edison and the Social Construction of the Early Electricity Industry in America." In *Explorations in Economic Sociology*, edited by Richard Swedberg. New York: Russell Sage Foundation, 1993.

McKenna, Christopher D. "The Origins of Modern Management Consulting." *Business and Economic History* 24, no. 1 (1995): 51–58.

McQuaid, Kim. "Competition, Cartellization and the Corporate Ethic: General Electric's Leadership During the New Deal Era, 1933–40." *The American Journal of Economics and Sociology* 36, no. 4 (1977): 417–28.

———. *Uneasy Partners: Big Business in American Politics 1945–1990*. Baltimore, MD: Johns Hopkins University Press, 1994.

———. "Young, Swope and General Electric's 'New Capitalism': A Study in Corporate Liberalism, 1920–33." *The American Journal of Economics and Sociology* 36, no. 3 (1977): 323–34.

Melman, Seymour. *Pentagon Capitalism: The Political Economy of War*. New York: McGraw-Hill, 1970.

Miliband, Ralph. *Class Power and State Power*. New York: Verso, 1983.

———. *The State in Capitalist Society*. London: Merlin Press, 2009.

Mills, C. Wright. *The Power Elite*. Oxford, UK: Oxford University Press, 1956.

Mintz, Beth, and Michael Schwartz. *The Power Structure of American Business*. Chicago: University of Chicago Press, 1987.

———. "Capital Flows and the Process of Financial Hegemony." *Theory and Society* 15, no. 1/2 (1986): 77–101.

Mirowski, Philip. *The Road from Mont Pèlerin: The Making of the Neoliberal Thought Collective*. Second Edition. Cambridge, MA: Harvard University Press, 2015.

Mirrlees, Tanner. *Hearts and Mines: The US Empire's Culture Industry*. Toronto: University of British Columbia Press, 2016.

Mizruchi, Mark. *The Structure of Corporate Political Action: Interfirm Relations and Their Consequences*. Cambridge, MA: Harvard University Press, 1992.

———. *The Fracturing of the American Corporate Elite*. Cambridge, MA: Harvard University Press, 2013.

Moran, Michael. *The Politics of the Financial Services Revolution: The USA, UK and Japan*. New York: Palgrave Macmillan, 1991.

Northrup, Herbert Roof. *Boulwarism: The Labor Relations Policies of the General Electric Company*. Bureau of Industrial Relations, 1964.

O'Boyle, Thomas F. *At Any Cost: Jack Welch, General Electric, and the Pursuit of Profit*. New York: Knopf Doubleday Publishing Group, 1999.

O'Connor, James. *The Corporations and the State*. New York: Harper and Row, 1974.

———. *The Fiscal Crisis of the State*. New York: St. Martin's Press, 1973.

Offe, Claus, and Helmut Wiesenthal. "Two Logics of Collective Action: Theoretical Notes on Social Class and Organizational Form." *Political Power and Social Theory* 1 (January 1, 1980): 67–115.

Panitch, Leo. "Elites, Classes and Power in Canada." In *Essential Readings in Canadian Government and Politics*, edited by Peter H. Russell, Francois Rocher, Debra Thompson, and Linda A. White. Toronto: Edmond Montgomery Publishing, 2010.

———. "Globalisation and the State." In *Socialist Register 1994: Between Globalism and Nationalism*, edited by Ralph Miliband and Leo Panitch. London: Merlin Press, 1993.

———. "The Impoverishment of State Theory." *Socialism and Democracy* 13, no. 2 (July 1, 1999): 19–35.

———. "Trade Unions and the Capitalist State." *New Left Review* 1, no. 125 (February 1981).

Panitch, Leo, and Sam Gindin. "Marxist Theory and Strategy: Getting Somewhere Better." *Historical Materialism* 23, no. 2 (2015): 3–22.

———. *The Making of Global Capitalism: The Political Economy of American Empire*. New York: Verso, 2012.

Parker, Richard. *John Kenneth Galbraith: His Life, His Politics, His Economics*. New York: Farrar, Straus and Giroux, 2015.

Parsons, John. "Futures and Derivatives Markets." Charles River Associates International, 1999. www.crai.com.

Paxton, Robert. *A Case Study of Management Planning and Control at General Electric Company: Based on Reports by Robert Paxton: Presented at the Annual National Conference, Controllers Institute, October 11, 1954*. Controllers Institute of America, 1961.

Phillips, Kevin. *The New Republican Majority*. Princeton, NJ: Princeton University Press, 2014.

Phillips-Fein, Kim. "'If Business and the Country Will Be Run Right:' The Business Challenge to the Liberal Consensus, 1945–1964." *International Labor and Working-Class History* 72 (Fall 2007): 192–215.

———. *Invisible Hands: The Businessmen's Crusade Against the New Deal*. New York: W. W. Norton, 2009.

Phillips-Fein, Kim, and Julian E. Zelizer. *What's Good for Business: Business and American Politics Since World War II*. Oxford, UK: Oxford University Press, 2012.

Pierpaoli, Paul G. "Truman's Other War: The Battle for the American Home-front, 1950–1953." *Organization of American Historians Magazine of History* (Spring 2000).

Post, Charles. *The American Road to Capitalism: Studies in Class-Structure, Economic Development and Political Conflict, 1620–1877*. Chicago: Haymarket Books, 2012.

Poulantzas, Nicos. *Classes in Contemporary Capitalism*. London: NLB, 1975.

———. *Political Power and Social Classes*. London: NLB, 1975.

———. *State, Power, Socialism*. New York: Verso, 2000.

———. *The Poulantzas Reader: Marxism, Law, and the State*. New York: Verso, 2008.

Reich, Leonard S. "Lighting the Path to Profit: GE's Control of the Electric Lamp Industry, 1892–1941." *The Business History Review* 66, no. 2 (1992): 305–34.

Rifkin, Jeremy, and Randy Barber. *The North Will Rise Again*. Boston, MA: Beacon Press, 1978.

Robinson, William I. *A Theory of Global Capitalism: Production, Class, and State in a Transnational World*. Baltimore, MD: Johns Hopkins University Press, 2004.

Rodrik, Dani. *Straight Talk on Trade: Ideas for a Sane World Economy*. Princeton, NJ: Princeton University Press, 2017.

Rosenberg, Justin. "Globalization Theory: A Post-Mortem." *International Politics* 42 (2005).

Rothschild, William E. *The Secret to GE's Success*. New York: McGraw Hill Professional, 2007.

Roy, William G. *Socializing Capital: The Rise of the Large Industrial Corporation in America*. Princeton, NJ: Princeton University Press, 1999.

Ruggie, John Gerard. *Winning the Peace: America and World Order in the New Era*. New York: Columbia University Press, 1996.

Sartre, Jean-Paul. *Search for a Method*. New York: Vintage Books, 1968.

Sayer, Andrew. *Realism and Social Science*. London, UK: Sage, 2000.

Scanlan, Alfred L. "The Defense Production Act of 1950." *Rutgers Law Review* 5, no. 8 (1951): 518–29.

Schacht, Wendy H. "The Bayh-Dole Act: Selected Issues in Patent Policy and the Commercialization of Technology." Congressional Research Service Report 7-5700, 3 December 2012.

Schattschneider, E. E. *The Semisovereign People: A Realist's View of Democracy in America*. New York: Holt, Rinehart and Winston, 1960.

Schriftgiesser, Karl. *Business Comes of Age*. Harper & Brothers, 1960.

Schulman, Bruce J. *From Cotton Belt to Sunbelt: Federal Policy, Economic Development, and the Transformation of the South, 1938–1980*. Oxford, UK: Oxford University Press, 1991.

Scott, John. *Corporate Business and Capitalist Classes*. Oxford, UK: Oxford University Press, 1997.

Serfati, Claude. "The New Configuration of the Capitalist Class." In *Socialist Register 2014: Registering Class*, edited by Leo Panitch and Greg Albo. London: Merlin, 2013.

Shaikh, Anwar. *Capitalism: Competition, Conflict, Crises*. Oxford, UK: Oxford University Press, 2016.

Shenk, Gerald. *"Work or Fight!": Race, Gender, and the Draft in World War One*. Springer, 2005.

Shermer, Elizabeth Tandy. *Sunbelt Capitalism: Phoenix and the Transformation of American Politics*. Philadelphia: University of Pennsylvania Press, 2013.

———. "Take Government out of Business by Putting Business into Government: Local Boosters, National CEOs, Experts, and the Politics of Midcentury Capital Mobility." In *What's Good For Business: Business and American Politics since World War II*, edited by Kim Phillips-Fein and Julian E. Zelizer. Oxford, UK: Oxford University Press, 2012.

Shoup, Laurence H., and William Minter. *Imperial Brain Trust: The Council on Foreign Relations and United States Foreign Policy*. New York: Authors Choice Press, 2004.

Simon, Miguel Cantillo. "The Rise and Fall of Bank Control in the United States: 1890–1939." *American Economic Review*, no. 88 (1998): 1077–1093.

Sklair, Leslie. *Capitalism and Development*. London: Routledge, 1994.

———. *Sociology of the Global System*. London: Harvester, 1991.

Sklar, Martin J. *The Corporate Reconstruction of American Capitalism, 1890–1916: The Market, the Law, and Politics*. Cambridge, UK: Cambridge University Press, 1988.

Skocpol, Theda. *Bringing the State Back In*. Cambridge, UK: Cambridge University Press, 1985.

Skowronek, Stephen. *Building a New American State: The Expansion of National Administrative Capacities, 1877–1920*. Cambridge, UK: Cambridge University Press, 1982.

Stiglitz, Joseph E. *People, Power, and Profits: Progressive Capitalism for an Age of Discontent*. New York: W. W. Norton and Company, 2019.

Sultan, Ralph G. M. *Pricing in the Electrical Oligopoly*. Cambridge, MA: Harvard University Press, 1974.

Teschke, Benno, and Hannes Lacher. "The Changing 'Logics' of Capitalist Competition." *Cambridge Review of International Affairs* 20, no. 4 (2007): 565–80.

Thelen, Kathleen. "Historical Institutionalism in Comparative Politics." *Annual Review of Political Science* 2 (June 1999): 369–404.

Thompson, E. P. *The Making of the English Working Class*. Penguin UK, 2002.

United States Civilian Production Administration. *Industrial Mobilization for War.* Washington, DC: Government Printing Office, 1947.

Useem, Michael. "Corporations and the Corporate Elite." *Annual Review of Sociology* 6 (1980): 41–77.

———. *Executive Defense: Shareholder Power and Corporate Reorganization.* Cambridge, MA: Harvard University Press, 1993.

———. *Investor Capitalism: How Money Managers Are Changing the Face of Corporate America.* New York: Basic Books, 1999.

Waddell, Brian. *Toward the National Security State: Civil-Military Relations During World War II.* Westport, CT: Praeger Security International, 2008.

Wala, Michael. "Selling the Marshall Plan at Home: The Committee for the Marshall Plan to Aid European Recovery." *Diplomatic History* 10, no. 3 (July 1986): 247–65.

Waterhouse, Benjamin C. *Lobbying America: The Politics of Business from Nixon to NAFTA.* Princeton, NJ: Princeton University Press, 2014.

Weber, Max. *Economy and Society: An Outline of Interpretive Sociology.* Berkeley, CA: University of California Press, 1978.

———. *The Theory of Social and Economic Organization*, translated by A. M Henderson and Talcott Parsons. Oxford, UK: Oxford University Press, 1947.

Werking, Richard Hume. "Bureaucrats, Businessmen, and Foreign Trade: The Origins of the United States Chamber of Commerce." *The Business History Review* 52, no. 3 (1978): 321–41.

White, Katherine. "Preserving the Patent Process to Incentivize Innovation in the Global Economy." *Journal of Science and Technology Law* (March 18, 2006).

Whitham, Charlie. "The Committee for Economic Development, Foreign Trade and the Rise of American Corporate Liberalism, 1942–8."*Journal of Contemporary History* 48, no. 4 (October 2013): 853–54.

Wilkins, Mira. *The Maturing of Multinational Enterprise.* Cambridge, MA: Harvard University Press, 1975.

Wood, Ellen Meiksins. "Rational Choice Marxism: Is the Game Worth the Candle?" In *Rational Choice Marxism*, edited by Terrell Carver and Paul Thomas, 79–135. London: Palgrave Macmillan, 1995.

Zeitlin, Maurice. *The Large Corporation and Contemporary Classes.* New Brunswick, NJ: Rutgers University Press, 1989.

Zorn, Dirk. "Here a Chief, There a Chief: The Rise of the CFO in the American Firm." *American Sociological Review* 69, no. 3 (June 1, 2004): 345–64.

Index

© The Editor(s) (if applicable) and The Author(s), under exclusive license to Springer Nature Switzerland AG 2022

S. Maher, *Corporate Capitalism and the Integral State*, Marx, Engels, and Marxisms,
https://doi.org/10.1007/978-3-030-83772-3

C

D

E

F

G

H

I

GPSR Compliance
The European Union's (EU) General Product Safety Regulation (GPSR) is a set of rules that requires consumer products to be safe and our obligations to ensure this.

If you have any concerns about our products, you can contact us on

ProductSafety@springernature.com

In case Publisher is established outside the EU, the EU authorized representative is:

Springer Nature Customer Service Center GmbH
Europaplatz 3
69115 Heidelberg, Germany

www.ingramcontent.com/pod-product-compliance
Lightning Source LLC
Chambersburg PA
CBHW072042020726
47387CB00048B/901
9783030837716